The lives of the
KINGS & QUEENS
OF ENGLAND

The lives of the KINGS & QUEENS OF ENGLAND

edited by Antonia Fraser

Heraldic consultant : J. P. Brooke-Little
Richmond Herald of Arms

Weidenfeld and Nicolson
London

Copyright © Weidenfeld and Nicolson 1975, 1993
First published in 1975 by
George Weidenfeld and Nicolson Limited,
Orion House, 5 Upper St Martin's Lane,
London WC2H 9EA

First published in paperback in 1993 by
George Weidenfeld and Nicolson Ltd

ISBN 0 297 83238 7

British Library Cataloguing in Publication Data
A catalogue record for this book is available
from the British Library

House editor Celia Clear
House art editor Tim Higgins
Layout by Juanita Grout for
George Weidenfeld and Nicolson Ltd

Filmset by Keyspool Limited, Golborne, Lancs.
Printed in Italy

CONTENTS

INTRODUCTION   by ANTONIA FRASER   page 9

COATS OF ARMS   by J. P. BROOKE-LITTLE
Richmond Herald of Arms   19

LIST OF COATS OF ARMS   21

1 THE NORMANS   by JOHN GILLINGHAM

William I   1066-87   26
William II   1087-1100   30
Henry I   1100-35   35
Stephen   1135-54   39

2 THE ANGEVINS   by JOHN GILLINGHAM

Henry II   1154-89   46
Richard I   1189-99   55
John   1199-1216   63

3 THE PLANTAGENETS   by PETER EARLE

Henry III   1216-72   72
Edward I   1272-1307   79
Edward II   1307-27   88
Edward III   1327-77   98
Richard II   1377-99   108

4 THE HOUSE OF LANCASTER

by ANTHONY CHEETHAM

Henry IV   1399-1413   118
Henry V   1413-22   125
Henry VI   1422-71   133

5 THE HOUSE OF YORK

by ANTHONY CHEETHAM

Edward IV   1461-83   149
Richard III   1483-5   155

6 THE TUDORS

by NEVILLE WILLIAMS

Henry VII   1485-1509   168
Henry VIII   1509-47   177
Edward VI   1547-53   189
Mary I   1553-8   195
Elizabeth I   1558-1603   202

7 THE STUARTS

by MAURICE ASHLEY

James I   1603-25   216
Charles I   1625-49   221
Charles II   1660-85   232
James II   1685-88   238
William III   1688-1702
   and Mary II   1688-94   245
Anne   1702-14   252

8 THE HOUSE OF HANOVER

by JOHN CLARKE

George I   1714-27   262
George II   1727-60   269
George III   1760-1820   276
George IV   1820-30   285
William IV   1830-37   292

by JASPER RIDLEY

Victoria   1837-1901   296

9 THE HOUSE OF SAXE-COBURG-GOTHA

by Jasper Ridley

Edward VII   1901-10   314

10 THE HOUSE OF WINDSOR

by Richard Luckett

George V   1910-36   326
Edward VIII   1936   336
George VI   1936-52   341
Elizabeth II   1952-   348

INDEX   354

GENEALOGICAL TABLES

The Normans and Angevins   24-5
The Plantagenets   70-1
The Houses of Lancaster
    and York   142-3
The Tudors and Stuarts   214-5
The House of Hanover   260-1
The Houses of Saxe-Coburg-Gotha
    and Windsor   322-3

Acknowledgments

Photographs and illustrations are supplied by, or reproduced by kind permission of the following. The pictures on pages 166–7, 180, 203, 219, 222–3, 229, *237*, 238, 271, 278, 279, 283, 286, 290, 295, *297*, 298, *300*, 304, 315, 318–19, 328–9, 337, 349 are reproduced by gracious permission of Her Majesty the Queen. Ashmolean Museum, Oxford 174; His Grace the Duke of Atholl 217; Bibliothèque Nationale 58–9, *92*, 94 top, 103; Bodleian Library, Oxford 99, 174; Bomann-Museum, Celle 263; Brighton Pavilion 288, 289; British Library 34, 36, 40, 42, 43, 44–5, 47, 50–1, *61*, *64*, 76, 80, 84, 86, 90, 94 btm, 95, *104*, 111, 112, 115, 116–17, 119, 121, 123, 131, 132, 134, 136, *148*, 150, 151, 163, 175, 192–3, 199, 210, 212–13, 218, 227, 230, 233, 234, 239, 243, 257, 264, 267, 269, 275, 280, 294, 302, 306; His Grace the Duke of Buccleuch and Queensberry *160*; Burgerbibliothek Berne 56; Master and Fellows of Christ Church, Oxford *89*; Master and Fellows of Corpus Christi College, Cambridge 72–3, 75; College of Arms 154, 178; Mrs M. E. Dent-Brocklehurst 204; Department of the Environment 258; Major Gerald Flint Shipman 309; Glasgow Art Gallery and Museum (Burrell Collection) 33; Guildhall, King's Lynn 67; Guildhall Library and Art Gallery 321, 335; Robert Harding 31; Illustrated London News 307; Imperial War Museum 347; Keystone Press 85, 351, 352–3, 339, 345, 348; Lambeth Palace Library (Courtesy of His Grace the Archbishop of Canterbury) 144, 147; Edward Leigh 153; Louvre (photo Bulloz) *228*; Master and Fellows of Magdalen College, Oxford 172; Mansell Collection 244, 247, 320; National Army Museum 254; National Galleries of Scotland 293; National Gallery 109; National Gallery of Art, Washington 191; National Monuments Record 37, 82, 176; National Portrait Gallery 125, 158, 186, 195, *200*, 253; Phaidon Press 22–3, 27; Phoebus Picture Library 196; Photo Boudot-Lamotte 38; Pitkin Pictorial Ltd 97; Popperfoto 324–5, 332, 340, 342; Private Collection 248; Public Record Office 29; Radio Times Hulton Picture Library 250–1, 310–11, 317, 337, 346; Rijksmuseum, Amsterdam 246; Master and Fellows of St John's College, Cambridge 169; Society of Antiquaries 137, 141; Victoria and Albert Museum 268, 284; Dean and Chapter of Westminster 63, 139; Dean and Canons of Windsor 164; Simon Wingfield-Digby Esq. 208–9; Dean and Chapter of Worcester Cathedral 62.

Numbers in italics refer to colour illustrations.

Picture research by Andra Nelki.
Genealogical tables devised by Cynthia Finch Garner and drawn by Design Practitioners Limited.
Calligraphic titles by Freda Harmer.

INTRODUCTION
by Antonia Fraser

IN ONE SENSE a volume of the lives of the kings and queens of England needs no introduction. The popularity of biography among the reading public is a byword of contemporary publishing. Royal biography, if anything, leads the field. It is not difficult to see why this should be so. Most people learn history early on in terms of the reigns – if not the lives – of the sovereigns, for the simple reason that otherwise history to the young can seem all too open-ended. The reigns of the monarchs provide natural frameworks for this vast apparently amorphous mass of material. At the same time there is the perennial appetite for a story provided by the lives. And on one level the biographies of the kings and queens are certainly stories, the stories of great, or at least prominent men and women. Once again, history told in the form of stories (the German language actually equates the two words in *Geschichte*) is most palatable to us in childhood . . . the death of Prince Henry in the White Ship and the King who never smiled again, the rescue of King Richard with the aid of the minstrel Blondel, a girl Queen who vowed 'I will be good', such tales have a habit of lingering in our imagination. H. A. L. Fisher once said that history is 'one damn thing after another': in the seemingly endless chronicle of events in English history, the reigns of individual kings and queens provide a convenient memorable pattern.

It is then the theory of history via biography of royal personages which needs defending, not the practice of it: its perennial popularity will certainly ensure the practice.

An early sample of the popular taste is provided by the success, from the 1840s onwards, of the *Lives of the Queens of England* by

Agnes Strickland. The series received instantaneous acclaim and ran through many editions. The Lives of the Tudor Princesses, The Stuart Princesses, and Lives of the Queens of Scotland followed, with equal public support, even if one reverse should be recorded, when, led on by her enthusiasm, Agnes Strickland embarked on the *Lives of the Bachelor Kings of England*, only to find that there was a singular dearth of authentically unmarried sovereigns. Yet the lessons of Agnes Strickland's work can still be learned today. She combined sympathy for her subjects with meticulous scholarship and research, praised by such authorities of the time as the historian Guizot. And her zeal for research was particularly commendable in an age when State papers were largely uncalendared; moreover when the State Paper Room was finally opened, women were at first not admitted, reversal of this decision only being secured by prolonged protests on Miss Strickland's part. It was the measure of her fame that when, as an old lady, Agnes Strickland went down to Oxford, she was acclaimed by the undergraduates with the merry cry: 'The Queens! The Queens! Three cheers for the Queens!'

Of course it is true that the professional historians of the nineteenth century were also often best-sellers, and incidentally very often chose biography as their mode of telling history. In any case they wrote, in general, the kind of wide and sweeping books which both carried away the public and were easily assimilated by them. In contrast, the modern view of history, like the truth, is rarely so pure and certainly never simple; it might be summed up as implying that things are frequently more complicated, more fragmented than has been thought heretofore. Fernand Braudel, for example, the leading living exponent of the mighty modern French school of history, observed in his own great work on the Mediterranean: 'Thus confronted by man, I am always tempted to see him as enclosed in a destiny which he scarcely made, in a landscape which shows before and behind me the infinite perspectives of the *longue durée*.' Inevitably, in expounding such views, the professional historians today write in more obscure terms, less easily assimilated by the non-professional public. Yet this very public is increasingly highly educated in a basic way, a development which might be dated from the nineteen-forties; increasingly it is fed with facts, brought up to expect information, not only via books, but also other media. The very word beloved of television, the 'documentary', presupposes the existence of and the use of documents, even if there is none to be seen, and what there might be have not necessarily been used. An educated and voracious public fed by these tendencies, unable to read the work of professional historians with great ease, turns to biography to fill the gap and satisfy its appetite.

Popular demand, however explicable, is not of course in itself a justification. It still needs to be demonstrated for the purposes of this volume how far the history of England can actually be usefully told through the lives of its sovereigns. In sheer sweep, our history can certainly be told in this mode (as that of the United States might be told in terms of Presidents but for a far shorter span) with the sole exception of the eleven year interlude of the Commonwealth and Protectorate. Even that interregnum is in effect covered by the life of King Charles II, who although not officially restored until 1660, was after all hailed by legitimists immediately after his father's death. This sweep is in itself a remarkable progression. But how far is this segmentation historically justified? How far indeed are we justified in studying individual lives of monarchs as a method of under-standing our history? Which last question is rooted in the further question as to how far, if at all, the individual lives of monarchs have actually affected the course of events. These are the legitimate enquiries which the protagonists of biography have to answer, if they are to justify the theory as well as the practice.

Let us take the last question first: it will be obvious to all but the most dedicated supporters of the Marxist theory of history that the personalities and peculiar characteristics of various sovereigns played at least some part in the shaping of events. For this view, the present volume certainly provides ample evidence. It is not only the more obvious examples which spring to mind, although it is easy to cite such: the innate weaknesses of King Charles I undoubtedly affected the course of the Civil War period, just as the coincidental inability of George I to speak English or understand England unarguably allowed ministerial politics to develop freely during his reign. The highly moral family life of Queen Victoria gave its character to an entire British age, which not for nothing bore her name. It is inconceivable that the English Reformation would have taken precisely the form it did had not the personality of Henry VIII been shaped as it was. England in the age of Elizabeth would surely not have developed as it did, under the aegis of a different sovereign, as for example under her cousin Mary Queen of Scots, a woman of totally conflicting nature to say nothing of religion. It hardly needs pointing out along these lines that the religion of England changed with the death of Edward VI, and again with the death of Mary Tudor.

But there are subtler points, if we look deeper into our chronicles.

Did the amiability of Stephen, compared with the arrogance of
Matilda, affect their respective fortunes? How much did the likes and
dislikes of Queen Anne, which at first sight had a strong effect on the
changing fortunes of the newborn political parties, actually do so?
The madness of King George III has been much stressed, yet it is
possible that his personal integrity during the long years of his sane
rule contributed to the preservation of the English throne in an age
of European revolution. The personality of King George VI might
not at first thought appear one of the most striking in our long line of
monarchs. Yet his particular combination of courage and devotion
to his people, albeit quietly expressed, enabled the House of Windsor
to survive in the Abdication what was surely the greatest crisis of the
monarchy since the flight of James II. Once again, in the nineteen
thirties, monarchy was under general examination in an age of
changing values, and the dutifulness of George VI, continued into
wartime, was a factor which cannot be ignored in its survival.

In this volume appear the biographies – albeit told briefly – of
each of the men and women who have inherited, or who have seized
possession of, the crown of England since 1066, the most famous
date in English history. It was then, with the Battle of Hastings, that
England came under the sway of Norman kings; and, because of the
early establishment of the hereditary principle, the crown has since
that time remained within a succession of ruling families who have
changed only when there was no undisputed heir or when there was
a violent usurpation. Such changes of dynasty have marked important epochs in English history, and in this book we have followed the
course of each from the Normans to the present-day House of
Windsor.

More than nine hundred years of monarchy present widely different problems of scope and perspective for the historian. For
medieval times records are relatively few and the personalities of the
sovereigns, in a period when their actions were decisive in shaping
the course of events, remain on the whole shadowy and insubstan-
tial. In later times there is a wealth of material and we know far
more about the characters of the monarchs; but their roles become
more difficult to interpret as the scope of government widened and
the crown's role within it changed. In this book we have not
attempted to impose any artificial uniformity or pattern of approach;
rather, we have invited individual historians to write their own
interpretations of the lives of the sovereigns in their own specialist
field of interest. What emerges is, I trust, a book which is not only
a biographical guide to England's kings and queens but also a

contribution to the understanding of the overall development of English history.

Such a volume inevitably calls into question the interesting subject of hereditary kingship. It is a topic on which time's revolutions have brought about some striking changes in general thinking. The death of Charles I caused a *frisson* of horror in Europe, and understandably so, since the execution of an anointed king threatened in theory every crowned head. And from the time of the French Revolution onwards, despite the restoration of the English hereditary principle under Charles II, it might be said to have been heavily under fire. In this attack, the history of the United States under elected Presidents certainly made a notable contribution. After the American Declaration of Independence, England was often seen as being weighed down by a hereditary monarchy and a hereditary royal family of princes and princesses. Recently, however, as Americans tend to create their own 'royal families' out of the families of their Presidents, and as European Presidents come and go, not always with the ceremonial grace of the hereditary British royal family, it is notable that there has been some rethinking on the subject: if the desire for ceremony is inherent in human nature, then at least our royal family is trained for the job. In the eighteenth century Gibbon had some wise words to say on the subject: 'Of the various forms of government which have prevailed in the world, an hereditary monarchy seems to present the fairest scope for ridicule. Is it possible to relate without an indignant smile, that, on the father's decease, the property of a nation, like that of a drove of oxen, descends to his infant son, as yet unknown to mankind and to himself; and that the bravest warriors and the wisest statesmen, relinquishing their natural right to empire, approach the royal cradle with bended knees and protestations of inviolable fidelity. . . .' Nevertheless 'The superior prerogative of birth, when it has obtained the sanction of time and popular opinion, is the plainest and least invidious of all distinctions amongst mankind . . . To the firm establishment of this idea we owe the peaceful succession and mild administration of European monarchies'. These words, if not totally apposite to the present situation, would at least find more echoes today than in time gone by.

The strengths and weaknesses of the hereditary principle are fully demonstrated in the pages which follow. One observes how it has in fact, *pace* Gibbon, not infrequently been breached, when the incumbent was not up to the task before him, for one reason or another: like animals, the herd have tended to drive out their leader when they considered him too weak to tame them or hold them in check.

Edward II is rightly described here as 'a standing indictment of hereditary monarchy', just as his father, the mighty Edward I, with his extreme toughness in any situation which demanded it, could be claimed as a justification for it. But one would have to admit that Edward III, that unlikely son of his *fainéant* father, was another witness for the defence, so that at least the wretched Edward II propagated the right type of species to rule, if he could not rule himself. Of Henry VI, it is rightly observed that 'if the man was a saint, the King was a political simpleton'. James II, Richard III, and in a manner of speaking Edward VIII, for different reasons could not hold their position. Henry VII, a strong man but without any particularly strong hereditary claim, and like George I, living in an age when there were others whose purely hereditary claims were preferable, survived through strength to found a dynasty. Charles II provides an interesting example of the ambivalence at the heart of the question: as a monarch he undoubtedly fortified the succession politically, and yet by failing to provide a legitimate heir, condemned the country on his death to the care of his unsatisfactory brother, a king who was almost bound to undermine by his personality all his elder brother had achieved.

How much of this is, historically speaking, distortion? Obviously no one is suggesting that history should be studied entirely through the lives of kings and queens. One ignores social history at one's peril; economic history is a rich field in itself, if full of unsuspected quagmires, and few would go as far as Emerson in postulating that 'there is no history, only biography'. In a certain sense, all written history is a form of distortion, and biography is merely imposing one of a number of possible patterns. Yet it does have a particular use, not only in its own right, but also as the groundwork for more generalised studies. After all, the most brilliant generalisations can properly only be made on the basis of biographical studies of much detail: Emerson's point is a valid one, taken from the angle that the most sweeping statement can only be historically valid if the accumulated biographies of the people concerned support the theory. The relative influence of each monarch, the personal involvement of Henry VIII in the Reformation, the interplay of his desires and his statecraft, all this must be taken into account before any kind of remarkable generalisation about the trends of the age is brought to birth.

The value of biography is surely just this specificity. In his *Poetics*, Aristotle contrasted the function of the poet and the historian – 'The true difference is that one relates what has happened, the other what may happen . . . poetry tends to express the universal, history the particular.' One might adapt Aristotle's distinction nowadays to the relative functions of the historian and the biographer. There are obvious traps lying in wait for those historians who aim to propound a general theory of history, particularly if it leads them into predictions which are not fulfilled or a highly stylised series of abstractions. It is just this sort of trap which is avoided by the specific nature of biography. Aristotle, distinguishing once again between poetry and history, wrote that 'the poet should prefer probable impossibilities to improbable possibilities'. The biographer interests himself or herself in improbable actualities.

It still has to be considered whether such reigning men and women as lie within the confines of the present study are being inflated beyond their deserts, simply on grounds of their royal birth. In a recent article, *Fiction in History*, A. J. P. Taylor took the medieval historian Bruce Macfarlane to task for describing Henry v as 'the greatest man that ever ruled England'. He questioned not only whether the famous warrior king was great compared to Churchill, let alone Cromwell, before going on to state more categorically: 'I doubt whether he was much improvement on Ramsay Macdonald. Looking around the crowned heads who have bestrewn the European stage over the centuries, I cannot see any other than Frederick the Great as a man of more than common abilities, and even his abilities were on the thin side. Of course many kings conducted the affairs of state in a reasonably competent way just as the wealthy man who inherits a great industrial undertaking makes a tolerable chairman of the board. But we cannot be content with that. We manufacture heroes simply because they occupy great position. . . .' This of course is an extreme statement of the view. I am convinced that the present volume demonstrates not only that with kings and queens – as with family firms – there were heroes as well as anti-heroes, and of course mediocrities as well, but also that these individuals, whatever their precise nature, did have a profound effect on our history.

Of course, had these biographies all been written by Carlyle, who considered that the history of the world was but the history of great men, we should have been presented with a gallery of heroes. Lytton Strachey would have endowed us no doubt, if not with anti-heroes, at least with heroes or heroines whose whole bodies, to say nothing of their feet, were made of clay. But it is to be hoped that we live in a cooler age when neither extreme of attitude is necessary. In contrast, it cannot be denied that in the nineteenth century, heroism was an important putative element in any chosen biographical subject. A. J. Cockshut has pointed out in his study of nineteenth-century biography, *Truth to Life*, that throughout the period there was 'a persistent attempt to establish heroism' and even if it were not successful, 'the assumption remained that the fundamental reason for writing a man's life was that he was admirable.' It is easy to understand how George Eliot was brought to the opinion that biographies were the disease of English literature. It was exactly this assumption which Lytton Strachey intended to extinguish with the cold water of his lively criticism, or as he put it himself, to replace the two thick hagiographical volumes in which reputations were so often interred.

It is pleasant to record that in our own day we seem to have benefited from the corrective influence of Lytton Strachey in terms of style and presentation, without inheriting, it is to be hoped, his somewhat wayward treatment of historical truth. What are the other elements which go to make up excellence? Another important element might seem to be sympathy, such as the Stricklands possessed – and yet on second glance that is not necessarily so, and as this volume shows, it is possible to sum up some unsympathetic monarchs with equal verve. If sympathy were always an essential, or for that matter self-identification, then it would be impossible to write about Henry VIII, in terms of the latter, without six wives, an arduous assignment for any practising historian, or in terms of the former, to attempt an analysis of William II in the first place.

No, the real essential virtue of biography, if it is to succeed as an art, is surely that of balance. There are two aspects to this quality of balance. In the first place, there is the vital assessment of the evidence, or as Professor Elton put it, in *The Practice of History*: 'there is a single question which the researcher must ask himself in assessing his evidence: how and why did this come into existence?' and he goes on to divide the evidence into two categories, 'that produced specifically for the historian's attention, and that produced for some other purpose.' It is, concretely put, the distinction between chronicles, memoirs, notes of self-justification and letters intended for publication on the one hand, and state papers and law reports on the other. Secondly – and this is always crucial with regard to sovereigns – there is the proper balancing of the subject in relation to the age in which he lived, in order that the reproaches of A. J. P. Taylor can be anticipated and avoided.

It seems to me that even in a brief biography the point of view of the monarch concerned should be given, along with his political setting. And then there are other standards by which a reign should be judged, other than those of pure politics. Henry III, Richard II and George IV might all be cited as examples of monarchs under whose auspices the arts flourished in our country, and civilisation itself was enhanced, even if they were not politically successful. Kings and queens should never be allowed to degenerate into mere hierarchical figures, otherwise this segmentation by reigns will tend to fall into the category of artificial divisions. Should the biographer take it upon him or herself to judge the subject? There is always an inherent danger in moral judgments, made about another age, whose moral standards were undoubtedly, for better or for worse, so very different from our own. Nor do these standards stand still after a hundred years or so: there is always the potentiality of further change, which will leave the historians' over-strident moral condemnation stranded and out of fashion even with his own time. The homosexuality of James I provides a case in point. It used to be much condemned by biographers' whose disapproval sometimes extended to every aspect of the King's career. A blanket condemnation, based on tastes outside the normal family life, was clearly too extreme. The attitude of our own day to these matters is certainly permissive, in the sense that it attempts to be based on understanding how such developments should come about. Yet it would be quite wrong for any biographer writing now to ignore the widespread damage done to King James's career by the political – as opposed to sexual – status of his male favourites. This was the phenomenon which preoccupied King James's own contemporaries.

There is one respect in which the biographer of royal personages should find it an easier task to maintain balance than those who delineate the more lowly born. For such, the period of childhood is often a very difficult field to till, since the words 'obscure origins' only too often mean exactly what they say. Before 1500, kings and queens are in the fortunate but small class of those about whom we know at least something of their dates and the details of their personal appearance. In the same way, the enormous problem that other biographers face of how to keep their subject in the centre of the *book*, at a moment when he was not in the centre of the stage in his own time, is in some measure solved for the royal biographer. Monarchs tended to be central, at any rate for large periods of their lives, giving their biographers a natural advantage.

There is another asset at their command. It has always appeared to me very much the duty of the biographer to discuss, analyse and if necessary dismiss the myths which gather about the subject. Sovereigns, because they represent their people, gather more myths than those rolling stones, their subjects. Biography does not consist totally in the selection of the facts. Nor should these myths be dismissed out of hand, even if demonstrably untrue, since the legends with which a people surrounds its ruler can tell us much about the age, the nature of monarchy at the time, and finally the man himself. Analysing these myths in *The Undergrowth of History*, Robert Birley wrote that such apocryphal stories generally survive because they encapsulate a true facet of an historical period, however false the facts on which they are based. Thus the story of Alfred and the cakes expresses the extreme destitution of the monarchy at that date, just as the story of Elizabeth, Raleigh and the cloak illustrates the chivalrous hold on her subjects' imagination which the Virgin Queen had been careful to cultivate as a measure of government.

Is there some further merit to the reading of biography other than the pleasure it gives, and the information it provides? Perhaps there are lessons to be learnt, as Machiavelli thought the ancient Romans could teach his age of the Renaissance via *The Discourses* and Gibbon too believed something could be learnt from ancient Rome. I myself am constantly struck by the insights to be derived from the perusal of history – the reign of William I for example is an apposite study in an age which has seen Britain's entry into the Common Market. The ultimate effects of the Conquest, whether good or bad, are still discussed (as no doubt entry into the Common Market will remain a topic for controversy); but at least the ruthless suppression of the previous English ruling class, with its subsequent loss of culture and richness, at the hands of the Normans, must be seen to be bad, however highly continental involvement is rated. So that from the reign of William I one lesson at least can be learned that integration should never mean the exclusion for the future of the native culture.

There are many other obvious parallels according to individual taste, from the position of Queen Elizabeth I as a woman in a world previously dominated by men and holding her own most successfully – in an age when that topic too has risen to the fore – to the loss of America in the reign of George III, when our present Queen also has presided over the disintegration of an Empire; the debatable character of Richard III provides at least an example of a career in which much administrative good work was fatally vitiated by one alleged evil deed. There will be favourite parallels, as there will be favourite monarchs – there always have been. One might quote Pieter Geyl, the great historian of *Napoleon – For and Against* who said that history is an argument without an end. In the course of this argument, the biography of kings and queens has an honourable place, and can be said perhaps to be a study without an end, and an enjoyable one.

COATS OF ARMS

by J. P. Brooke-Little
Richmond Herald of Arms

ONE OF THE FASCINATIONS of royal heraldry is the way in which the development of the royal arms reflects the story of the kings and queens who bore them. Territorial claims and acquisitions, conquests and sometimes changes of dynasty have been mirrored in the arms of the sovereigns. To call heraldry 'the shorthand of history' is perhaps an extravagant claim but it certainly adds another and colourful dimension to the study of history.

Looked at from another angle, a knowledge of royal heraldry enables the student of history to identify and so date innumerable artefacts for, understandably, representations of the royal arms are manifold. To a great extent arms are used wherever they can beautify or identify. As no one boasts greater possessions nor wider patronage than the Crown, so the mark, that is the arms, of the Crown is to be found everywhere, from on a mouldering thirteenth-century tomb to a jar of the Queen's favourite marmalade.

I have always maintained that heraldry was originally a haphazard way of decorating shields and flags, which was moulded into an ordered form of personal symbolism by the ceremonial officers of the Crown, the heralds. Hence the study of coats of arms came to be called heraldry; the principal business of the heralds.

We know, from the evidence of tombs and seals, that the early Norman kings and nobles used decorated shields but, from the same evidence, we also know that these were not used consistently and do not appear to have been inherited. Yet, by the beginning of the thirteenth century, a system of hereditary symbolism, obeying definite canons of design, was everywhere in use by the nobility. Not only that but the nobles jealously guarded both their right to use certain devices and the right of the whole noble caste to be distinguished from lesser men by the bearing of arms. Obviously order could not have emerged from chaos so swiftly if the process had not been accelerated by someone and it is my contention that it was the heralds who did this. After all, it was very much in their interests to do so, for they marshalled the feudal host and the great tournaments and so needed to know who was who. A well-designed coat of arms freely displayed on the coat armour (the coat worn over the mail; hence the term coat of arms for that which was shown on it), shield, flag and horse trappings made it easy to recognise a man from a distance. The advent of heraldry must have made the job of the medieval herald much less arduous. All he had to do was to remember who bore what arms; this he did by making rolls and books of arms, many of which are still extant.

As I have suggested, an important aspect of heraldry is its hereditary character. A coat of arms is inherited, in much the same way as a surname, by the legitimate descendants of the person to whom the arms were first assigned or allowed. Another characteristic of heraldry is that no two people shall bear the same coat. How is this apparent contradiction resolved? By the use of brisures for cadency or, in layman's terms, the adding by junior members of a family of small marks, such as a star or crescent, to the arms of the head. In medieval times, when it was necessary to recognise these distinctive marks from afar, they were more dramatic and could involve a change of colour or of a fairly major feature in a coat, but when heraldry left the battlefield for the book plate the need for such changes disappeared and more modest distinctions were used. Today the rule that junior members of a family must add an appropriate mask of difference to their arms is often more honoured in the breach than the observance, except in the royal family.

Royal heraldry differs from ordinary, familial heraldry in that the arms of the monarch are not personal arms but arms of dominion or sovereignty. If it were otherwise the Queen would bear a most complicated shield containing the various coats borne by her paternal family of Saxe-Coburg-Gotha and the Prince of Wales would bear his father's not his mother's arms. The sovereign bears arms to represent his possessions and his children bear them likewise but with such differences as shall be assigned to them. According to heraldic law a woman bears her father's arms on a lozenge (a diamond shape) without helmet crest or mantling until she marries, when she bears her husband's arms in conjunction with her own. In royal heraldry this is not the case. The sovereign is always regarded as masculine and never bears arms conjoined in any way with those of his or her wife or husband. If the sovereign is a woman then her children will be assigned her royal arms and will not, as in familial heraldry, automatically inherit their father's arms at birth.

In the pages accompanying the coats of arms I shall trace how, when and why the royal arms have, from time to time, been altered to symbolise the dominions over which the English kings have reigned or, in one noted case, have hoped to reign.

LIST OF COATS OF ARMS

1	Some Attributed Arms of Pre-Norman Kings	*page* 49
2	The Arms of The Norman Kings	53
3	The Arms of Edward III and Richard II	101
4	The Royal Arms In The Fifteenth Century	157
5	The Arms of Henry VII and Henry VIII	185
6	The Arms of Philip and Elizabeth I	197
7	The Arms of The Stuarts	225
8	The Royal Arms 1707–1837	240
9	The Royal Arms	312

I THE NORMANS

William (carrying a mace) leads his nobles into battle, from the Bayeux Tapestry.
This famous tapestry, 231 feet long and 19 inches wide, tells the complete story of
the Norman Conquest in over seventy scenes. It was probably commissioned by
William's half-brother Odo, bishop of Bayeux.

1066~1154

THE NORMANS AND ANGEVINS

Judith of Brittany m. Richard II Duke of Normandy d. 1026

Richard III Duke of Normandy d. 1028

Robert the Devil Duke of Normandy d. 1035 ∞ (1)Herleva(2) m. Herluin Viscount of Conteville

Matilda of Flanders d. 1083 m. WILLIAM I the Conqueror c. 1025-87

Robert Count of Mortain

Odo Bishop of Bayeux Earl of Kent d. 1097

Robert III Curthose Duke of Normandy c. 1054-1134 m. Sybil of Conversano

Richard c. 1054-75

Cecily d. 1127

WILLIAM II Rufus 1057-1100

Agatha

HENRY I 1068-1135 (1) m. Edith (Matilda) 1079-1118 (2)m. Adelaide of Louvain d.1151

William III Count of Flanders 1101-28

(1)

William Athling d.1120 m. Matilda of Anjou

Richard (illeg.) d.1120

Robert of Gloucester (illeg) d. 1147

Henry V m. Emperor 1086-1125 (1)Matilda(2) m. Geoffrey 1102-67 Plantagenet Count of Anjou d.1150

(1)

HENRY II 1133-89 m. (2) Eleanor of Aquitaine 1122-1202

Geoffrey VI of Anjou 1134-57

William Count of Poiton 1136-64

William 1153-6

Henry, the Young King 1155-83 m. Margaret of France d.1198

Matilda 1156-89 m. Henry Duke of Saxony d.1195

RICHARD I Coeur de Lion 1157-99 m. Berengaria of Navarre 1163-1230

Geoffrey 1158-86 m. Constance of Brittany d.1201

Eleanor 1161-1214 m. Alfonso King of Castile d.1214

Arthur 1187-1203

Richard I the Fearless m. Gunnor of Denmark
Count of Normandy
d.996

Elgifu of   m. (1)CNUT(2)   m. (2)Emma(1)   m. (2)ETHELRED II, the Unready(1) m.Elfreda
Northampton   d.1035   of Normandy   d.1016   (Elgifu)

Godwin
Earl of Wessex

HAROLD I   Swein   HARTHACNUT
d.1040   King of   d.1042
    Norway
    d.1036

Edmund
Ironside
d.1016

EDWARD the Confessor m. Edith   HAROLD II   Edward Athling
c.1005-66   d.1075   c.1022-66   d.1057

Malcolm III   m. St. Margaret   Edgar
King of Scots   d. 1093   Athling
d.1093

Adela   Edgar   Alexander I   David I   Mary
d.1137   King of Scots   King of Scots   King of Scots   m. Eustace III
m. Stephen Henry   c.1074-1106   1077-1124   c.1080-1153   Count of
   Count of Blois   Boulogne
   d.1102

Theobald   Henry   STEPHEN   m. Matilda of Boulogne
Count of Blois   Bishop of Winchester   c.1096-1154   d.1151
d.1151

Eustace   William
c.1130-52   c.1135-59

Joan   JOHN
1165-99   Lackland
(1)m.William II   1167-1216
    of Sicily   (1)m.Isabelle de Clare (div.)
    d.1189   d.1217
(2)m.Raymond VI   (2)m.Isabelle of Angoulême
    Count of
    Toulouse
    d.1222

HENRY III   Richard   Joan   Isabelle   Eleanor
1207-72   of Cornwall   1210-38   1214-41   1215-75
         King of the Romans
         1209-72

WILLIAM I

r. 1066–87

WILLIAM WAS BORN at about the time that his father, Robert, became Duke of Normandy (1028). William's mother was Herleva, daughter of a wealthy citizen of Falaise. Not long after William was born she was given in marriage to one of Duke Robert's followers and by him she had two more sons: Robert, who became Count of Mortain, and Odo, who was made Bishop of Bayeux in 1049 when he was not yet twenty years old. William therefore was illegitimate and most contemporary writers refer to him as William the Bastard. But he was his father's only son and shortly before Duke Robert went on a pilgrimage to Jerusalem (1034), he persuaded the Norman barons to recognise William as his heir. On the way home Robert died in Asia Minor and so, in 1035, young William found himself Duke of Normandy.

In practice this meant that for the next ten years Normandy was without a ruler and a great deal of disorder went unchecked. William was lucky to survive these years. Several of his cousins would have preferred to see him out of the way. He had some narrow escapes, but survive he did – largely thanks to the support of his mother's kinsmen. William's boyhood was spent among scenes of violence and intrigue. As a result he learned that not many men could be trusted, and those few in whom he did place his trust were mostly the friends he made in childhood.

In the mid-1040s William began to govern for himself. He was almost continuously at war, either against Norman rebels or neighbouring princes, or both. He became a hard and ruthless campaigner – though flatterers liked to say that he was the best knight in the world. His most powerful neighbours were King Henry of France, Count Geoffrey of Anjou and Count Baldwin of Flanders. Between 1052 and 1060 two of these, France and Anjou, were hostile to Normandy so it was well for William that he could count on the friendship of Flanders. He had asked Count Baldwin for the hand of his daughter Matilda, but in 1049 the Pope forbade the marriage, presumably on the grounds that William and Matilda were too closely related. Despite this William went ahead; the Flemish alliance was more important than papal disapproval. William and Matilda must have been an odd-looking couple. The evidence of the bones found in their graves suggests that he was about five foot ten inches tall and she about four foot two inches. But by all accounts it was a successful marriage. She bore at least nine children (four of them sons) and most contemporaries believed that William was never unfaithful to her.

In 1060 both King Henry and Count Geoffrey died. The heir to France was a small boy and in Anjou there was all the trouble of a disputed succession. The consequent weakness of his neighbours left the way clear for William to conquer the county of Maine in 1063 and then turn his eyes on England.

Although William was only a distant cousin of Edward the Confessor, in 1051, perhaps to win Norman support in a quarrel with his powerful father-in-law, Earl Godwin, Edward dangled before William the prospect of succeeding to the English throne. Edward himself was childless and since monarchs were not yet chosen in strict order of heredity, there were several candidates for the succession. Among these was Harold, son of Earl Godwin and brother of Edward's wife Edith. By 1066 Edward was reconciled with the Godwin family, and on his deathbed he nominated Harold, the chief magnate of the kingdom, as his heir.

UBI HAROLD:SACRAMENTVM:FECIT:~ HIC HAROLD:DVX
VVILLELMO DVCI:~

Harold swears allegiance to Duke William in the castle of Bayeux; one hand is upon an altar and the other on a chest of sacred relics.

William felt cheated and prepared at once for an invasion of England. He insisted that Edward had promised him the throne and that on a visit to Normandy in 1064, Harold had sworn an oath to support his accession; he claimed that Harold was thus both usurper and perjurer and so won papal approval for his expedition. In the careful preparations for invasion William showed himself at his best. It was an enterprise far beyond the resources of his duchy and so he recruited soldiers from all over northern France and Flanders. The prospect of laying hands on the wealth of England, its land and its silver, attracted thousands to his banner. Throughout the spring and summer of 1066 ships were built and military supplies assembled. But however meticulous his preparations, William cannot have expected anything like the rapid and overwhelming success he in fact achieved. It must have seemed likely that he

was facing many years of hard campaigning against an enemy whose wealth and military resources were greater than his own. But an extraordinary series of lucky chances brought things to a swift and dramatic conclusion.

By August 1066 William's expeditionary force was ready. If he had sailed when he wanted to he would have found Harold and an English fleet waiting to receive him. If he had managed to defeat the English he would then have had to face another contender for the throne, Harold Hardrada, the King of Norway and a famous Viking warrior. But, as it happened, throughout August and most of September the wind was against William. Merely to hold his waiting army together was, in these circumstances, a great achievement, yet while he impatiently kicked his heels some of his greatest problems were being solved for him. In September Harold Hardrada, accompanied by one of his

27

wives and several of his children, reached the Tyne and then defeated the northern levies in a pitched battle near York. As soon as he heard of the Viking landing Harold Godwinsson marched north and routed Hardrada and his allies at Stamford Bridge on 25 September 1066. Two days later the wind in the Channel changed direction. William set sail and was able to make an unopposed landing at Pevensey. During the next two weeks his soldiers fortified their beachhead and pillaged the area. But what then? Would William dare march far inland, losing contact with his fleet and the line of communication with Normandy. Fortunately the problem was solved by Harold who came rushing back from the north and allowed William to challenge him to battle. If Harold had held aloof it is hard to see what William could have done, but Harold was confident of his military prowess and, as a new king with an uncertain title, he wished to see the matter settled once and for all. Thus on 14 October 1066 the two armies met at Hastings.

After a long and desperately hard struggle William's skilful handling of a combined force of archers and cavalry enabled him to break down the English shield wall. The fact that Harold and his brothers died fighting meant that after Hastings there was no leader capable of organising further resistance. The English earls and bishops hesitated, took a few indecisive steps and then decided to submit. On Christmas Day 1066 William was crowned in Westminster Abbey. In February 1067 he returned to Normandy leaving his half-brother Odo of Bayeux, now Earl of Kent, in charge. Apart from the destruction of the Godwinsson dynasty he left the English scene much as he had found it. All this, however, was to change as a result of the events of the next four years. All over England revolts broke out. They were unplanned and unco-ordinated. Some of the leaders, like Hereward the Wake, passed into legend, but none of them was capable of more than local action. Thus William was able to

deal with one minor uprising after another and by 1071 he had subdued the whole country. The turbulent north had been devastated. Several hundred castles had been built and within their walls the outnumbered Normans could sleep safely. William punished rebels by confiscating their estates and giving them to Normans. Thus the native English aristocracy was wiped out. Within the areas covered by the Domesday Book only two English landowners of any note survived the Norman flood.

The English church suffered the same fate as the English nobility. At William's request papal legates deposed five English bishops in 1070. They were replaced by men from the continent. Outstanding among them was Lanfranc, the new Archbishop of Canterbury. From now on whenever a bishop or an abbot died the same policy was pursued. By 1096 there was not a single bishopric or important abbey in English hands. The traditional learning and liturgy of the English church was treated with contempt by men educated in the schools of Europe. Probably no other conquest in European history ever had such disastrous consequences for the defeated ruling class. This had not been intended, for William was a conservative by temperament; but he was also ruthless and when events pushed him to destroy then he destroyed thoroughly. His own prestige and power were, of course, tremendously enhanced. He was able to bestow huge gifts of land upon his followers without impoverishing himself. As for England, that was now ruled by a French-speaking aristocracy and although the broad outline of the social structure remained unchanged, there was an entirely new and alien ruling class; the language barrier only served to widen the gulf between it and the peasantry.

After 1071 William's hold on England was fairly secure and he came to regard it chiefly as

RIGHT A page from the survey of Wiltshire in the Domesday Book, compiled under William's instructions to assess the wealth of the kingdom.

In Burgo MALMESBERIE habet rex .xx.vi. masuras hospitatas. 7 xx.v. masuras in qb3 se dom. que n reddut geld pluiq3 uasta tra. Una quaq3 haru masuraru redd .x. den de gablo. hoc e simul .xl.iii. sot. 7 vi. den. sequitur redditu.

De feudo epi barocsis. e ibi dimidia masura uasta. que nulli redd.

Abb malmesbie he .iii. mas 7 dimid. 7 fors burg .ix. colcez q geldas cu burgsib3. Abb Glastingbiens he .ii. masur.

Eduuard .iii. masur. Radulf de mortin .i. 7 dimid. Durand de Gloucec .i. 7 dim. Wills de ow .i. Hunfrid de insula .i. Ostn Eisard .i. Alured de Merleberge. dimid mas uasta. Costrid similr Iouin .i. qrta parte uni mas. Drogo fr ponz. dimid. Vxor Edric .i. Rog de berchelai .i. mas de firma regis. 7 Ernulf .i. simile de firma regis. qua in caut accep. hec due nulli sequitu reddut.

Rex he una uasta masuram de tra qua Azor tenuit.

HIC ANNOTANTUR TENENTES TRAS IN WILTESCIRE.

I. REX WILLELMUS.

- .II. Eps Wintoniensis.
- .III. Eps Sariberiensis.
- .IIII. Eps Baiocensis.
- .V. Eps Constantiensis.
- .VI. Eps Lisiacensis.
- .VII. Abbatia Glastingberiens.
- .VIII. Abbatia Malmesberiens.
- .IX. Abbatia Westmonasterii.
- .X. Abbatia Wintoniensis.
- .XI. Abbatia Crenburnens.
- .XII. Abbatia Scefesberiens.
- .XIII. Abbatia Witauniens.
- .XIIII. Abbatia Wintoniensis.
- .XV. Abbatia Romesiensis.
- .XVI. Abbatia Ambresberiens.
- .XVII. Ecta Beccensis.
- .XVIII. Radulf pbr de Wiltune.
- .XIX. Canonici Lisiacenses.
- .XX. Comes Mortoniens.
- .XXI. Comes Rogerius.
- .XXII. Comes Hugo.
- .XXIII. Comes Albericus.
- .XXIIII. Wills Eduuard de Sarisbere.
- .XXV. Ernulf de Hesding.
- .XXVI. Aluredus de Merleberge.
- .XXVII. Hunfridus de Insula.
- .XXVIII. Milo crispin.
- .XXIX. Isleberius de Breteuile.
- .XXX. Durand de Gloucestre.
- .XXXI. Walterius Gifard.
- .XXXII. Wills de ow.
- .XXXIII. Wills de braiose.
- .XXXIIII. Wills de Molin.
- .XXXV. Wills de falaise.
- .XXXVI. Alcanus de Dowai.
- .XXXVII. Walscan uenator.
- .XXXVIII. Willm filius Widonis.
- .XXXIX. Henricus de fereres.
- .XL. Ricard filius Gisleb.
- .XLI. Radulf de Mortemer.
- .XLII. Robertus fili Giroldi.
- .XLIII. Oserus fili Rolf.
- .XLIIII. Ogerius de Curcelle.
- .XLV. Rogerius de berchelai.
- .XLVI. Ernard panceuolt.
- .XLVII. Berenger Gifard.
- .XLVIII. Osbernus Gifard.
- .XLIX. Rogo filius ponz.
- .L. Hugo lasne.
- .LI. Hugo filius baldrici.
- .LII. Hunfrid camerarius.
- .LIII. Gunfrid maldurch.
- .LIIII. Aluredus de Ispania.
- .LV. Aiulfus uicecomes.
- .LVI. Igellus medicus.
- .LVII. Osbernus pbr.
- .LVIII. Ricard puingiant.
- .LIX. Obtus marescal.
- .LX. Robertus flauus.
- .LXI. Ricardus Sturmid.
- .LXII. Ainald canud.
- .LXIII. Aci de Moretania.
- .LXIIII. Gozelin Riuere.
- .LXV. Godescal.
- .LXVI. Herman 7 alii seruients regis.
- .LXVII. Hugo 7 alii taini regis.
- .LXVIII. Henricus 7 alii ministri regis.

Rex habet de burgo Wiltuniensi .L. lib. 7 do heuricus recepit ad custod. reddeb .xx.vi. libras.

De Wiltescire he rex .xx. lib de caprario. 7 xx. solid de numario. 7 feno .c. solid. 7 v. oras.

De dimid molino ap SARISBERIE he rex .xx. solid ad pensum.

De tcio denario SARISBERIE he rex .vi. lib. De tcio denario Merleberg. iiii. lib. de tcio denar enchelesie .iii. lib. 7 vi. de tcio denario bade. .xl. lib. De tcio denario MALMESBERIE. vi. lib.

De Crecco .xx. lib ad pondus. 7 reddit .c. 7 iii. lib.

Alfredus de .ii. parab burg Malmesberie. redd .vi. lib. 7 ...

... predc ipsi burgi T.R.E. 7 in hac firma e qdam placita hundredi de licentione Suelesberg rex pannec. De moneta redd ipsi burg .c. solid.

... burgo habuit Regisdus uni agr ipse. in q sunt .iiii. masure. 7 alie uaste. uni molin redd .x. solid. hoc totu redd .c. solid. T.R.E.

... p ire in expeditione t ira t mari. habeb de hoc burgo aut .xx. solid ad pascendos suos burecar. Aut unu homine ducel seu p honore .v. hidaru.

R. TERRA REGIS.

Rex tenet CALNE. Rex.E. tenuit 7 nung geld dauit. ido nescit quot hide sint ibi. Tra e .xx.x. car. In dnio sunt .vii. car. 7 viii. serui. Ibi .xxx.vii. uilli 7 xx.ix. bord. 7 xx. cotba. hntes .xxi. car. 7 d. v. burgenses. 7 v. molini reddut. iiii. lib. 7 xi. sot. 7 vi. den. 7 i. ac pa. 7 pastura .ii. leu lg. 7 una leu lat. de Silua redd firma uni noctis. cu omib3.

Huic co eccłam ten Nigel de rege. cu .i. hida ip3 eccłie. Tra e .v. car. In dnio st .ii. 7 vi. serui. Ibi .vii. uilli .ii. bord. 7 ix. cotez. Ibi .ii. molin de .xx. sot. 7 xx.v. burgses. redd .xx. sot. Silua .ii. q'e lg. 7 una q'e .xxiii. ac lat. Pastura .iii. q'e lg. 7 ii. q'e lat. Tot uat .vi. lib.

Aluredus de hispania ten .v. hid. cue q' Nigel cotinuit. h ira testimonio scire pannuit ad eccłam T.R.E.

Rex ten BEDUINE Rex.E. tenuit. Nung geld dauit. nec h ira fuit. 7 q' io. xx. car una mttr. In dnio sut .iiii. car. 7 xii. serui. Ibi .ix. uilli .7 xi. cotez. 7 xvii. coliba. Ibi .vii. molini redd .c. sot. Due silue hntes .ii. leu lg. 7 una leu lat. Ibi .i. ac pa. 7 xii. q'e pasture lg. 7 vi. q'e lat. Io uic co pan .xx.v. burgenses.

Io uilla redd firma uni noctis cu omib3 cuedinib3. In hoc co sunt T.R.E. luci hnt dimid leu lg. 7 tm q'e lat. 7 ep't in dnio regis. Mos ten eu Henric de ferrers.

Rex ten AMBLESBERIE Rex.E. tenuit. Nung geld dauit. nec hidata fuit. Tra e .xl. car. In dnio sunt .xx. car. 7 lv. serui. 7 u. coliba. Ibi q'e .xx. 7 v. uilli 7 l. vi. bord hntes .xxiiii. car. Ibi .viii. molini. redd .iii. lib. 7 x. sot. 7 lxx. den. Pastura .iiii. leu lg. 7 ii. lor lat. Silua .vi. leu lg. 7 ii. leu lat.

Hoc co cu appendic suis redd firma uni noc...

In hoc co numerant ire .iii. tainoz quiisuis ...hid deb Watt com in Lomlesbie p municatione Boue.. De huic co tra .ii. hid deb rex.E. in sua infirmitate abbatie Witauniensi. q nunc aurt habuerat. postea ... u eat tenuit. 7 Wills com ea a qintone Suindone 7 cheurel que etiam tainlande. q ira de insula de Wch. que panc. ad firma de Amblesbie.

Rex ten COSANESIE.E. Rex.E. tenuit. Non geld daui. nec hidata fuit. Tra e .xi. car. In dnio st .vi. car. 7 xiii. serui. 7 xi. porcarii. Ibi .xx. uilli. 7 viii. cotez. 7 vii. coliba. cu .xx.vi. car. Ibi .ii. molini de .xx. lib. 7 q' .xx. ac pa. pastura .i. leu lg. 7 dmd leu lat. Silua .ii. leu lg. 7 ii. lat. Ibi .xxx. burgses.

Hoc co redd firma uni nocal cu omib3 cuerudinib3 suis.

Rex ten CHEPEHA. Rex.E. tenuit. Non geld daui. nec hidata fuit. Tra e .c. car. In dnio sunt .xxvi. car. xxviii. serui. Ibi .xl. vii. uilli 7 xt. e. bord. 7 xx. porcarii snt oms hntes. lx. vi. car. Ibi .xii. molini de Vii. lib. 7 fra. Silua .iiii. leu in lg. 7 lat pasture .ii. leu lg. 7 i. leu lat. hoc co cu append suis redd firma uni nocal cu omib3 cuerudimb3. uat .c. xi. lib ad numeru.

Huic co eccłam cu .ii. hid ten Osbn eps a T.R.E. Una ecct hit p stalande atq p gran ecct. Tot uat .i. v. lib.

Huic co pan una tra qua rex.E. dedaut Uluet uenator suo. 7 ep't de dnio suo. h infirma regis e m punc hid habet Tra e .i. car. 7 ipsi ibi st. 7 iii. serui. 7 vii. uilli 7 iiii. coceti cu .i. car. pastura .iii. q'e lg. 7 una q'e lat. Vat .ii. lib.

In firma huic e dimid v ire que fuit uastat inde Edricus tenet T.R.E.

a source of revenue. The extensive royal estates and the sophisticated English financial machinery brought in huge sums. The Welsh and the Scots gave him little trouble; Scandinavian rulers continued to look greedily towards England but the ever-present threat of another Viking invasion never quite materialised. From 1071 to 1084 most of William's attention was taken up by war and diplomacy on the continent. Normandy was his homeland and far more vulnerable to sudden attack than was his island kingdom. Moreover the King of France and the Counts of Anjou and Flanders were alarmed by William's newly acquired power and took every opportunity to diminish it. Their best opportunities were provided by William's eldest son Robert (born 1054). Recognised as the heir to Normandy as long ago as 1066 he had never been permitted to enjoy either money or power and from 1078 onwards he became involved in a series of intrigues, a tool in the hands of William's enemies. In one skirmish William was actually wounded by his son.

Then in 1085 William returned to England with a huge army of mercenaries ready to counter the invasion planned by King Swein of Denmark. The administrative effort involved in catering for this army seems to have persuaded William that he ought to have more precise information about the distribution of wealth among his barons. So in 1086 commissioners were sent from shire to shire and the results of their inquiries are now enshrined in the Domesday Book. It listed the major landholders in each county and provided William with a remarkably full description of their sources of revenue. But although the book has been of great value to historians, it seems unlikely that William was able to make much use of it. Before the end of the year he had been recalled to Normandy. Once again he found himself campaigning against the King of France and, as usual, the war was concentrated in the Vexin, a disputed territory lying between Rouen and Paris. In July 1087 William launched a surprise attack on Mantes and took it, but during the sack of the town he received the injury from which, on 9 September, he died. His body was carried to the church of St Stephen at Caen for burial. Unfortunately during the last few years he had grown very fat. King Philip of France used to say that he looked like a pregnant woman. When the attendants tried to force his body into the stone sarcophagus it burst and filled the church with a foul smell. It was an unpleasant ending, but unlike many kings he had unquestionably lived more successfully than he died. Few kings can have enjoyed so much luck as William the Bastard, but few took such full advantage of their good fortune as William the Conqueror, founder of a new royal dynasty.

WILLIAM II

r. 1087–1100

WILLIAM, THE THIRD SON of William of Normandy and Matilda, was born about 1057. Almost nothing is known of his youth, but it is at least clear that the time he spent in the household of Archbishop Lanfranc made little impression upon him. He was deeply attached to his father and while Robert rebelled, William never wavered in his loyalty. When the second son, Richard, died in a hunting accident in the New Forest it seemed possible that William might take Robert's place as chief heir. William, moreover, was at the bedside of the dying King

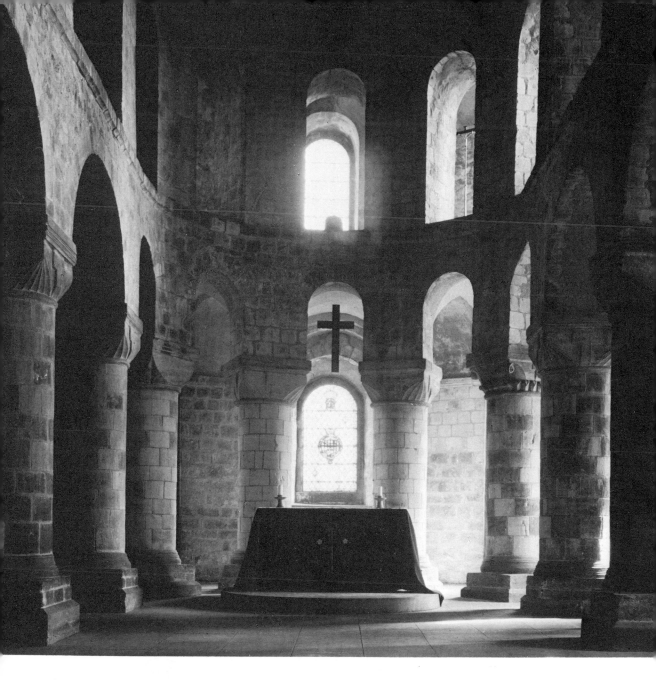

The Norman chapel in the White Tower of the Tower of London, built in the last two decades of the eleventh century by a Norman monk, Gandulf. Much of the stone used was brought over from Caen.

to hear his last wishes while Robert remained at the court of his father's enemy, Philip of France. But the custom which gave the ancestral lands, the patrimony, to the first-born son proved too strong. Robert succeeded to Normandy. To William, however, the old King gave his newly conquered land, England. Lanfranc, following the instructions of the old King's will, crowned William at Westminster on 26 September 1087. Like his father, William was inclined to stoutness. He had fair hair, piercing eyes, a red face (thus his nickname

Rufus) and a tendency to stutter when excited.

The division of the Conqueror's lands created political difficulties. Many Norman lords held estates on both sides of the Channel. Their dilemma was summed up by the greatest of them, the new King's uncle, Odo of Bayeux. 'How can we give proper service to two mutually hostile and distant lords? If we serve Duke Robert well we shall offend his brother William, and he will deprive us of our revenues and honours in England. On the other hand if we obey King William, Duke Robert will deprive us of our patrimonies in Normandy.' By 1088 it was already plain that some barons, inspired by Odo, would prefer to have Robert as their lord on both sides of the sea. But Robert failed to appear in England, William acted firmly and the revolt soon collapsed. Now it was the younger brother's turn. In 1089 he laid claim to Normandy. With English silver he was able to buy support in Normandy. Gradually Robert's position became more and more difficult until in 1096 he was glad to join the crusade preached by Pope Urban II. In order to equip himself and his retinue for the long march he pawned Normandy to William for 10,000 marks.

The new Duke's main task was to recover Maine and the Vexin, lost during Robert's slack rule. By 1099 he had successfully accomplished this. In England meanwhile he had, in 1095, suppressed a rebellion led by Robert Mowbray, Earl of Northumberland. In Wales and Scotland the Normans were on the march again. On every front William's combination of diplomacy, bribery and war proved effective; an archbishop of Lyons referred to him as 'the victorious King of the English'.

Yet for all his success as a generous leader of soldiers William's reputation has remained consistently low. Unfortunately for him the history of the time was written almost entirely by monks and they did not like him; nor did he respect them. On one occasion when a monk came to him to report a dream in which he had

foreseen William's death, the King dismissed him mockingly – 'he is a monk and so, of course, he dreams for money'. After the death of Lanfranc in 1089 Rufus seemed to throw off all restraints. Serious-minded churchmen, accustomed to the conventional piety and sober discretion of his father's court, were appalled by the gaiety and licentiousness which prevailed under his son. Since neither mistresses nor illegitimate children are ever mentioned in connexion with William it is possible that he was a homosexual. He never married. He was sceptical of the claims of religion and treated the church purely as a rich corporation which needed taxing. He was never in a hurry to appoint bishops and abbots, for during vacancies he could help himself to the church's revenues. In carrying out these profitable policies Rufus relied on the ingenious aid of the quick-witted and worldly clerk, Ranulf Flambard, whom he eventually made Bishop of Durham.

Above all, William's reputation has suffered because in 1093 when he thought he was dying he appointed a saint as Archbishop of Canterbury (after having kept the see vacant for four years). What made this appointment so disastrous from William's point of view was the fact that it occurred at a time when a European movement for church reform was creating an atmosphere in which saints were only too likely to become political radicals. The new archbishop was Anselm, a scholar monk who had previously been Abbot of Bec. As a Norman abbot Anselm had already sworn to obey Urban II; but in England neither Urban II nor his rival Clement III were recognised as pope. William, following in his father's footsteps, preferred to remain uncommitted and he was angry when Anselm took it for granted that Urban was the rightful pope. In 1095 the King called a council at Rockingham in order to settle this and other matters which were in dispute between him and Anselm. But to the consternation of all, Anselm appealed to Rome, claiming that as Archbishop of Canterbury he

Norman soldiers depicted on a fragment known as the Temple Pyx, discovered during excavations of the Temple Church. The soldiers are three inches high and are thought to represent the sleeping soldiers at the tomb of Christ. The shields and helmets are very like those shown on the Bayeux tapestry (see pages 22–3).

The mysterious death of William Rufus, killed by an arrow while hunting in the New Forest in the summer of 1100. Many twelfth-century writers regarded his death as divine retribution for the savage manner in which William I had made the New Forest a royal hunting preserve.

could not be judged in a secular court. This was too much for Rufus who now determined to rid himself of the Archbishop. He would even recognise Urban if the Pope, in his turn, would depose Anselm. A papal legate was sent to England and Urban was publicly proclaimed as the canonical Pope; but this achieved, the legate would make no move against Anselm. Dismayed by the failure of his plot William continued to harass the Archbishop and he never showed any sympathy for his attempts to reform the church. Eventually Anselm could bear it no longer. In 1097 he sailed from Dover, leaving the Canterbury estates to be taken into the King's hands.

Besides helping to blacken William's reputation, the quarrel with Anselm is a significant indication of the growing importance of the papacy. For centuries no-one had taken much notice of the bishops of Rome but now, as a result of the eleventh-century Gregorian reform movement (named after its most zealous advocate, Pope Gregory VII), they began to wield an influence which not even Rufus could entirely ignore. In the short run, however, William II had gained from the quarrel. In 1100

he enjoyed the revenues of three bishoprics and twelve abbeys. Nor was there as yet any sign that the conflict had tarnished men's belief in the potency of royal magic. Even Eadmer, the Canterbury monk who wrote the *Life of Anselm*, noted that 'the wind and the sea seemed to obey him. Whenever he wished to cross from England to Normandy or back again every storm – and sometimes the storm was raging wildly – was stilled so that his crossings were always attended by a wonderful calm.' Indeed, Eadmer went on, 'in war and in the acquisition of territory he enjoyed such success that you would think the whole world smiling upon him'.

But on 2 August 1100, at the height of his success and full of plans for further conquests, William was struck down by an arrow while hunting in the New Forest. It may have been an accident, or he may have been murdered. His body was carried to Winchester and interred in the cathedral directly below the main tower. In the following year the tower collapsed – though, as one monk wrote, 'it might have collapsed anyway, even if he had not been buried there'.

HENRY I

r. 1100–35

HENRY, THE FOURTH SON of William and Matilda, was born in England in 1068. He was better educated than his brothers and felt at ease in the company of learned men. From this time onwards the kings of England were normally able to read. From his dying father he received no land, but was given instead £5000 in silver – an enormous sum. At once he left the old King's bedside and hurried to the Treasury to supervise the weighing out of the money.

When his elder brothers, Robert of Normandy and William of England, quarrelled, he flitted from side to side, always seeking his own advantage and eventually making himself thoroughly distrusted by both. In 1091 they were temporarily reconciled and marched together against Henry. They made a treaty whereby they agreed that if either died without leaving a legitimate son he would be succeeded by the other. This was to disinherit Henry.

When Robert went on crusade Henry's hopes naturally rose. Should the childless William die now, he was the man on the spot and the obvious heir. But by the summer of 1100 everyone knew that Robert was on his way home, accompanied by a rich and beautiful wife and basking in the prestige due to a man who had fought his way into Jerusalem. Henry's chance seemed to be slipping away from him. Perhaps it was just coincidence that William died when he did and where he did – for Henry too was hunting in the New Forest on 2 August 1100. As soon as he knew that his brother was dead Henry moved fast; it was as though he had been prepared for this to happen. He rode to Winchester and took possession of the Treasury. Then he went straight on to Westminster where he was crowned on 5 August. On the same day he issued his coronation charter, renouncing the oppressive practices of his brother and promising good government.

The reverse of a silver penny of the reign of Henry I, showing the cross marked on all coins for clipping into half or quarter pieces.

A few weeks later Robert arrived back in Normandy. Henry had to prepare to meet the inevitable invasion. His policy was to buy support by granting favours and making wide-ranging concessions along the lines laid down in the coronation charter. 'If they ask for it give them York or even London' was the advice given to Henry by his shrewdest counsellor Count Robert of Meulan. By inviting Anselm to return to England he hoped to win over both the English church and the papacy; by marrying (in November 1100) Edith, sister of King Edgar of Scotland, he was ensuring that he would not be attacked in the north while he had his hands full in the south. He secured the alliance of France and Flanders, neither of whom wanted to see England and Normandy united under one all-too-powerful ruler. Thus when Robert landed at Portsmouth in July 1101 he found he could make little headway. With Anselm as the intermediary a treaty was arranged. Henry was to keep England and pay his brother an annual pension of £2000.

But not for one moment did Henry trust those who had hoped to protect their Norman estates by aiding Duke Robert in 1101. Above all he distrusted the rich and brutal Earl of Shrewsbury, Robert of Bellême, and he systematically set about the task of breaking him. This he accomplished in 1102. He captured Robert's chief strongholds in the Welsh marches and then banished him. But Robert, like others in his position, found in his Norman properties a safe base from which he could hope to organise the recovery of his English lands. By perpetuating the division of the Conqueror's lands the treaty of 1101 had ensured the continuance of political instability. So the pattern of the previous reign was repeated as Henry gradually manoeuvred himself into a commanding position in Normandy. In 1106 the issue was decided by the battle of Tinchebrai. The knights in Henry's vanguard dismounted in order to beat off the charge of Duke Robert's cavalry. Robert himself was captured in the

The effigy of Robert Curthose, Duke of Normandy, in Gloucester Cathedral.

moral and spiritual life of the clergy; in order to do so they believed that it was necessary to free the church from secular control. The most hated symbol of this control was lay investiture, a ceremony in which a new abbot or bishop received the ring and staff of office from the hands of the secular prince who had appointed him. Although the first papal decree against lay investiture had been issued as long ago as 1059 and many more prohibitions had been published since, no-one in England seems to have been aware of their existence until Anselm returned in the autumn of 1100. While in exile he had attended papal councils at Bari (1098) and Rome (1099). There he learned of the papal attitude to lay investiture. Thus although he himself had been invested by Rufus in 1093 he now refused either to do homage to Henry or to consecrate those prelates whom Henry had invested. This placed the King in a difficult position. Bishops and abbots were great landowners and key figures in central and local administration; he needed their assistance and had to be sure of their loyalty. On the other hand, unlike Rufus, he was unwilling to provoke a quarrel, so for years he found it more convenient to postpone the problem rather than try to solve it. Henry's delaying tactics were intolerable to Anselm and in 1103 he once again took the path into exile.

But then, in 1105, at a critical moment in Henry's Normandy campaign, the Pope threatened to excommunicate him so the King hastened to come to terms. Agreement was reached in 1106 and ratified at a council in London in 1107. Henry renounced lay investiture, but prelates were to continue to do homage for their fiefs. In practice the King's wishes continued to be the decisive factor in the making of bishops. To some extent it can be said that Henry gave up the form but preserved the reality of control. When Anselm died in 1109 he kept the see of Canterbury vacant for five years. Yet he had lost something and he knew it. In the fierce war of propaganda which ac-

battle and spent the last twenty-eight years of his life as his brother's prisoner. Other great barons who fell into Henry's hands, including Robert of Bellême, were also condemned to life imprisonment.

Although in the first years of his reign Henry was preoccupied with Norman affairs, he was not as free to concentrate on them as he would have liked. Traditional royal rights over the church were threatened by the new ideas associated with the Gregorian reform movement. The reformers did not only wish to purify the

37

An enamel of Geoffrey Plantagenet, Duke of Anjou, from his tomb in Le Mans Cathedral. He was the second husband of Henry I's daughter Matilda and their son Henry II was the founder of the Plantagenet dynasty.

companied the 'Investiture Contest' the Gregorians had insisted that the King was a layman, nothing more, and as such he was inferior to all priests, for priests were concerned with the soul and the king only with the body. The church could no longer tolerate the old idea that anointed kings were sacred deputies of God. In giving up lay investiture Henry was acknowledging the merely secular nature of his office. It was an important moment in the history of kingship. And yet it is precisely at this time that we first come across the claim that kings possessed a healing magic. It was said that if a person suffering from scrofula were touched by a king, the disease – known as the 'king's evil' – would at once be cleared up. Whatever learned churchmen might say, in popular thought there was still something miraculous in kingship.

Once Normandy had been conquered and a compromise solution found to the investiture dispute, Henry's main concern was to hold on to what he had. Few kings ever did this more tenaciously or effectively. He was a hard man who knew how to keep men loyal; he may not have won their hearts but they looked forward to the rewards he had to offer and they certainly feared his wrath. In 1090 he had pushed a man off the top of Rouen Castle for betraying the oath of allegiance which he had sworn to Duke Robert. With this example before them men took seriously the oaths which they swore to King Henry. The most famous of the King's servants was Roger of Salisbury, the archetypal bureaucrat, competent and discreet. Under his direction there are clear signs of the development of the English civil service, notably the rise of the court of the exchequer.

Normandy, of course, was the most vulnerable part of his empire and after 1106 Henry spent more than half the remainder of his reign there facing the traditional enemies of the Norman dukes. The year 1118, as described by the Anglo-Saxon Chronicle, was typical. 'King Henry spent the whole of this year in Normandy on account of the war with the King of France, Count of Anjou and Count of Flanders. ... England paid dearly for all this in numerous taxes from which there was no relief all year.' By 1119 all seemed well. Henry, who never risked battle until he had already won the diplomatic war which preceded it, beat King Louis VI of France in the battle of Brémule. Angevin friendship had been secured by the marriage of his only legitimate son, William, to the daughter of the Count of Anjou. But the whole carefully-contrived edifice came tumbling down when William was drowned in the wreck of the White Ship (November 1120).

From then on the succession problem dominated the politics of the reign. Less than three months after William's death Henry married Adelaide of Louvain (his first wife, Edith, had died in 1118), but the hoped-for heir was never born. So although Henry acknowledged more than twenty bastards he was survived by only one legitimate child, his daughter Matilda. When her husband, the Emperor Henry V of Germany, died in 1125 Henry recalled her to his court and made the barons swear to accept

her as their ruler in the event of his dying without a male heir. Somewhat against her will Matilda was then in 1128 married to a sixteen-year-old boy, Geoffrey of Anjou, for Henry was determined to continue the Angevin alliance. But the prospect of being ruled by an Angevin did not please the Norman barons and Geoffrey was well aware of this fact. Thus he asked to be given custody of some key Norman castles while Henry was still alive and able to help. But the old King refused to give up any of his power. The result, in summer 1135, was war. In these melancholy circumstances Henry died, supposedly of a surfeit of lampreys, in December 1135.

Although he ruled for thirty-five years few English kings are as little known as Henry I. Careful, sober, harsh and methodical he chose his servants from men of a similar stamp. When compared with Rufus and Ranulf Flambard, Henry I and Roger of Salisbury are drab and colourless characters. But from 1102 until the end of his reign there was no revolt in England. A king who could keep the peace for over thirty years was a master of the art of government.

STEPHEN

r. 1135-54

STEPHEN WAS A YOUNGER SON of Stephen, Count of Blois and Champagne, and of Adela, daughter of William the Conqueror. He was born about 1096, some half-dozen years earlier than his cousin and rival for the crown, Henry I's daughter, Matilda. Stephen's mother was a formidable woman. When her husband returned early from the First Crusade she sent him away again. As a result he was killed in the Holy Land in 1102 and responsibility for seeing that young Stephen was properly looked after

fell upon his uncle the King of England. King Henry provided for him on a grand scale. He granted him estates on both sides of the Channel and by 1130 Stephen was the richest man in his uncle's empire. Henry I also looked after Stephen's younger brother, Henry of Blois, making him both Abbot of Glastonbury and Bishop of Winchester, and thus the wealthiest churchman in England. By his generosity Henry made sure that Stephen's elder brother, Count Theobald of Blois, did not join the anti-

Norman coalition organised by France and Anjou. In 1125 Stephen married Matilda, the heiress to the county of Boulogne. Her loyalty and energy were to be a great help to Stephen in later years and meanwhile the acquisition of her territories, which included the port of Wissant, meant that Stephen was profitably placed to dominate cross-Channel trade.

Inevitably Henry I's death in 1135 was followed by a dispute over the succession. There were very few Anglo-Norman lords who wished to be ruled by his daughter and her Angevin husband. One group of Norman barons wanted to elect Count Theobald of Blois but their deliberations were cut short by the news that Theobald's younger brother Stephen had already been crowned (22 December 1135). Advised by Henry of Blois and acting with great decisiveness Stephen had crossed the Channel and taken control of England. Count Theobald at once dropped his claim to the crown, but he still hoped to become Duke of Normandy. The Norman lords, however, were not prepared to face again the problem of divided loyalties; to Theobald's disappointment they transferred their allegiance to Stephen.

For two years Stephen had little trouble, but in 1138 Geoffrey of Anjou invaded Normandy, King David of Scotland (Matilda's uncle) invaded the north, and Robert of Gloucester (Matilda's half-brother) raised the standard of rebellion in the west country. Initially Stephen was able to weather the storm, but he then made three fatal mistakes. In December 1138 he offended Henry of Blois by not making him Archbishop of Canterbury. In the summer of 1139 he arrested three influential 'civil-service' bishops, including the great Roger of Salisbury, and thus enabled Henry of Blois to claim that ecclesiastical liberties had been infringed. In the autumn, when Matilda fell into his hands, he

allowed her to go free when the ruthless, if un-chivalrous, thing to do was to keep her in prison. From now on there were always two rival courts in England, though Stephen was generally in a better position than the Empress who rarely held more than a few west-country shires. Their relative strengths are indicated by the number of surviving charters: 720 issued by Stephen, only 88 by Matilda. But at one stage Matilda had a clear-cut chance of victory. In February 1141 Stephen rashly accepted battle at Lincoln and fought on bravely when he might have escaped. As a result he was captured and put in prison in Bristol. Henry of Blois, now acting as papal legate, openly went over to the Empress's side and in the summer she was able to enter London. But she spurned the peace terms worked out by the legate and offended the Londoners with her high-handed and tactless behaviour. When Stephen's queen, Matilda of Boulogne, advanced towards the city the Londoners took up arms and drove the Empress out. Thus the planned coronation at Westminster never took place. Matilda never became queen of England. A few months later Robert of Gloucester was captured and since he was the mainstay of her party Matilda had to agree to an exchange of prisoners: Stephen for Robert. Her chance of winning the crown was lost and the status quo in England was restored.

In 1142 Robert left England on a mission to Geoffrey of Anjou. But Matilda's husband had his hands full in Normandy and Anjou and refused to disperse his forces still further. Taking full advantage of Robert's absence Stephen moved rapidly and after a skilful diversionary move laid siege to Oxford Castle where Matilda was in residence. This time he was determined not to let her go and pressed the siege relentlessly. But once again the Empress escaped. One December night she was lowered by rope from the castle walls, and with just four

LEFT The Norman kings of England represented as patrons of the Church – each is holding a model of a church he founded. Left to right, top row: William I and William Rufus. Bottom row: Henry I and Stephen.

companions – all of them wrapped in white cloaks, for there was snow on the ground – she crossed the frozen river on foot, passed through the King's pickets and made her way to safety. After the violent see-saw of fortunes in 1141-2, the civil war settled down into a kind of routine. Stephen's habit of arresting without warning men who were supposed to be his supporters tended to lose him friends, but neither side could make much headway at a time when the art of war revolved around castles and the defenders generally held the advantage. In October 1147 Robert of Gloucester died. Disheartened, the Empress left England early in 1148, never to return. Next year the struggle was taken up by Matilda's son Henry fitzEmpress, but the sixteen-year-old youth simply did not have the resources to alter the balance of power, and while he remained in England, in danger of being captured, he put the whole Angevin cause in jeopardy. It was better that he should return to Normandy and consolidate his position there.

If Stephen ever felt confident that he was going to win the civil war then a glance at Normandy should have made him realise that he would not. The Normans had been thrown into confusion by the news of Stephen's capture at Lincoln and Geoffrey of Anjou had at once taken advantage of the situation. By the time of Stephen's release he had clearly gained the upper hand and few Normans were prepared to fight a losing war on behalf of a king who took so little interest in them – only once in his entire reign, in 1137, did he even visit Normandy. In 1144, Rouen fell and Geoffrey was solemnly proclaimed duke. From now on those English barons who also held land in Normandy had good cause not to offend the Empress and her son. The result was a stalemate which Stephen was unable to break.

In the last years of his reign Stephen's chief ambition was to secure the throne for his elder son, Eustace. He planned to have him crowned king in his own life-time and for this he required the co-operation of the Archbishop of Canterbury, Theobald. But since 1148 the Archbishop had shown that he had a mind of his own, and although he was prepared to recognise Stephen as king he would do nothing which would tend to prolong the civil war. So, with papal backing, he refused to grant Stephen's request.

In January 1153 Henry fitzEmpress returned to England. He was now a great man: lord of Normandy and Anjou and, in the right of his

The story of Stephen's reign is reflected in the variety of coins issued.

TOP LEFT A silver penny from the reign of King Stephen shows the King holding a sceptre.

TOP RIGHT A silver penny depicting Eustace, the elder son of Stephen who was appointed Governor of York and permitted to strike coins there.

LEFT Stephen with his wife on a coin issued when his wife had effected Stephen's release by capturing Robert of Gloucester and exchanging him for the King.

RIGHT Robert of Gloucester, an illegitimate son of Henry I, who was the chief commander of Matilda's forces.

BOTTOM A silver penny of Matilda.

A fifteenth-century picture of Matilda in the history of England written by the monks of St Albans.

son and heir. William was to inherit all Stephen's baronial lands. This, in essence, was a repeat of the peace terms proposed by Henry of Blois in 1141. Matilda's intransigence then had cost the country another twelve years of civil war. Now, at last, Stephen could rule unchallenged and at peace, but he was a tired man and he did not live long to enjoy it. On 25 October 1154 he died and was buried by the side of his wife and elder son in the monastery they had founded at Faversham.

It is clear that Stephen must take some responsibility for the troubles of his reign. It is true that he was faced by a disputed succession, but then so were William I, William II and Henry I. Stephen was a much more attractive character than any of these kings, but he lacked their masterfulness. Without it he was unable to dominate either his court or his kingdom. Yet he was no fool and occasionally he made the mistake of trying to be too clever. But it was hard not to like Stephen. Even a chronicler who wrote under the patronage of Robert of Gloucester had to concede that 'by his good nature and by the way he jested and enjoyed himself even in the company of his inferiors, Stephen earned an affection that can hardly be imagined'. He was a competent commander and a gallant knight – too brave perhaps for his own good. Basically he was a kind and amiable man whose friends would not abandon him when he was in trouble.

Above all, of course, he owed much to the courage of his wife in the critical months after the battle of Lincoln. In sharp contrast, Matilda's marriage to Geoffrey of Anjou was an unhappy one, and in 1141 her tactlessness and arrogance provided an object lesson in how to lose friends. Thus Stephen was unlikely to lose the war, but lacked the qualities which were needed to win it. Yet he never lost heart, remaining cheerful and buoyant until the day when the sudden death of his son Eustace made the whole nineteen years seem pointless. Then he resigned himself to the inevitable.

wife Eleanor, ruler of Aquitaine. By now it was generally accepted that peace would come only if Henry was recognised as Stephen's heir. The baronial class as a whole was never in favour of long-drawn-out hostilities; their landed estates were too vulnerable to the ravages of war. The problem was to make Stephen see it in the same light. The task was made unexpectedly simple when Eustace died in August 1153. Stephen's second son, William, had never expected to be king and so the way was opened for a negotiated peace. By the Treaty of Westminster it was agreed that Stephen should hold the kingdom for his life and that he should adopt Henry as his

43

2 THE ANGEVINS

The great seal of Henry II.

1154–1216

HENRY II

r. 1154-89

HENRY WAS BORN at Le Mans on 4 March 1133. He was the first of three sons born to Matilda, daughter of Henry I, by her second husband Count Geoffrey of Anjou. He first came to England in 1142 in order to show the world that there was more to the Angevin cause than his mother's haughty behaviour. Having successfully carried out his first foray into the world of politics, the nine-year-old Henry returned to the greater security of his father's dominions. By the time he was fourteen he was eager to try his luck again and in 1147 he arrived in England with a small band of mercenaries. But he soon ran out of money. Both his mother and Robert of Gloucester disapproved of this escapade and refused to help. So with the impudence of youth he applied to the man against whom he was fighting and with characteristic generosity Stephen sent him enough money to pay off his mercenaries and go home. Two years later Henry was back. First he went north to be knighted by his great-uncle, King David of Scotland. But their military plans went awry and Henry only just managed to avoid being captured in one of the ambushes laid for him. Yet his early life was not all adventure. His education was in the hands of famous scholars and he grew up with a love of reading and a taste for intellectual discussion.

Soon he was lord of Normandy (from January 1150) and Anjou (at his father's death in September 1151). In May 1152 he married Eleanor of Aquitaine, the greatest heiress in Western Europe, just eight weeks after her marriage to King Louis VII of France had been annulled, ostensibly on grounds of consanguinity but in reality because in fourteen years of marriage she had failed to bear him a son. Henry and Eleanor had better luck. In the first six years of their marriage she had five children,

four of them boys: William, who died very young, Henry, Richard and Geoffrey. Altogether they had eight children, the last of whom, John, was born in 1167. Eleanor was a remarkable woman, surrounded all her life by an aura of romance and scandalous rumour. A German poet wrote:

> Were the world all mine
> From the sea to the Rhine
> I'd give all away
> If the English Queen
> Would be mine for a day.

Nonetheless after 1167 she and Henry drifted apart and towards the end of the reign she spent the greater part of each year in prison while he enjoyed a succession of mistresses.

In January 1153 Henry surprised Stephen by crossing the Channel in midwinter. By this time the English magnates were weary of war and convinced that peace would come only if Stephen recognised the justice of the Angevin claim. Under pressure from their supporters the two leaders made a series of truces which were turned into a permanent peace when the death of his son Eustace persuaded Stephen to give up the struggle. By the Treaty of Westminster (Christmas 1153) he was allowed to keep the kingdom on condition that he adopt Henry as his son and heir. Thus when Stephen died in October 1154 Henry took over without difficulty; it was the first undisputed succession to the throne since the Conquest. Henry was now the greatest prince in Western Europe, lord of an empire which stretched from the Scottish border to the Pyrenees. But it is important to remember that although England provided him with great wealth as well as a royal title, the heart of the empire lay elsewhere, in Anjou, the land of his fathers.

Henry II quarrelling with Becket in the presence of his soldiers.

In England his first task was to destroy those baronial castles which had been built without royal licence and make good the losses suffered during Stephen's reign. By 1158 these two aims had been achieved. In addition the English King's overlordship of Scotland and Wales had been restored. But it was naturally his continental dominions which took up most of his attention. They were always more vulnerable than the island kingdom and more interesting too, since socially and culturally England was a bit of a backwater compared with France. Henry spent twenty-one of the thirty-four years of his reign on the continent. He began by re-asserting his overlordship of Brittany. Then in 1159 he launched a major campaign against Toulouse, a county which Henry claimed was rightfully a part of his wife's inheritance. But outside the walls of Toulouse Henry suffered his first real setback. King Louis hurried to support his brother-in-law the Count of Toulouse and rather than attack his overlord Henry de-

cided to withdraw. It did not take him long to get his own back. In 1158 he had betrothed his eldest surviving son Henry to Margaret, Louis VII's daughter by his second wife. Her dowry was to be the Vexin castles so long in dispute between France and Normandy but since she was only six months old at the time of the betrothal Louis naturally did not expect to see the Vexin in Henry's hands for many years to come. In 1159, however, there was a disputed election to the papacy and as the price for agreeing to accept Alexander III as the rightful pope, Henry persuaded Alexander's legates to marry the two children in November 1160. Louis VII was furious but there was nothing he could do about it.

A few months later Archbishop Theobald of Canterbury died. The see was kept vacant for more than a year and then, in June 1162, Thomas Becket was consecrated as his successor. In the eyes of respectable churchmen Becket, who had been chancellor since 1155,

(continues on page 54)

1 Some attributed Arms of Pre-Norman Kings

THE FIRST ENGLISH KING to bear truly heraldic arms was Richard I. This means that those who came before him, although they may have used various devices, cannot be regarded as having borne coat armour.

However, the ingenious heralds of the middle ages amused themselves by designing arms for the pre-armorial monarchs. As early as the mid-thirteenth century Matthew Paris illustrated his *Historia Anglorum* with arms both real and attributed. Not surprisingly, different heralds often made different attributions, so that one king may have had several coats attributed to him at various times and by various armorists, not necessarily professional heralds. The shields illustrated here are perhaps more frequently used than many, as they are taken from a comprehensive roll of attributed arms contained in an early-seventeenth-century manuscript (L14) in the library of the College of Arms.

The first row of shields shows those assigned to Arthur, who probably flourished at the beginning of the sixth century, Alfred, King of Wessex (died *c.* 899) and his grandson Athelstan (died 940).

The first shield in the second row is that of Athelstan's half brother Edmund 'The Elder', who was murdered in 946. The next is that of Edmund's brother Edred (died 955), and the last is that of his son Edwy 'The Fair', who succeeded his uncle and died in 959.

The third row contains the arms attributed to both Edgar 'The Peaceful' (Edwy's brother), who died in 975, and to his eldest son Edward 'The Martyr', who was murdered at Corfe Castle in 978. The shield in the middle is that of Ethelred 'The Unready', the martyr's half-brother, who was deposed in 1013 and died three years later. Edmund Ironside's is the last shield. He was Ethelred's son and died in 1016.

The throne was usurped by Cnut (died 1035) whose second wife Emma was Ethelred's widow and a great-aunt of William the Conqueror. His arms are the first in the bottom row. The centre shield is that of St Edward 'The Confessor' and the third is that of Harold II. Both kings died in 1066.

The arms attributed to St Edward were used by King Richard II out of devotion to the saint and have become universally accepted. The coat is based on the reverse of a penny minted in Edward's reign.

RP

The crowning of the Young King, Henry II's eldest
son, by Archbishop Roger of York in 1170, from *Vie de
St Thomas* written in England in the mid-thirteenth century.
To the right Henry is shown serving his son at table.

2 The Arms of the Norman Kings

THE FIRST FIVE POST-CONQUEST KINGS witnessed the birth of
heraldry and there is evidence to suggest that they favoured the
use of a lion as a symbol.

The coat of two gold lions *passant guardant* on a red shield is
frequently attributed to the early Norman kings, although
Matthew Paris backdates the coat of three lions and makes it do
for all the Norman kings including Stephen. Others attribute a
quite different coat to Stephen, presumably because he was not of
the House of Normandy, although Henry II, the first Angevin
king, is accorded the lions. Stephen's arms are illustrated beside
those of the Normans and consist of a gold sagittary on red.
This coat is given in College of Arms manuscript L14 but a coat
consisting of three sagittaries firing over their shoulders is also
frequently used and is mentioned in a treatise on heraldry written
by Nicholas Upton *c.* 1400.

Henry II's queen, Eleanor of Aquitaine, lived until 1204 and the
reverse of her seal, cut after her husband's death, shows a shield
bearing the three lions. This coat later appears on the second great
seal of Richard I and thereafter is universally recognised as the
royal arms of England and was used by succeeding monarchs until,
in about 1340, Edward III styled himself King of France and
assumed the royal arms of France, quartering them with the
English arms.

The beasts in the arms of England are frequently referred to as
leopards. This is not because they were ever shown as or regarded
as leopards but because the early heralds described a lion when
rampant (rearing up aggressively) as a *lion*, but when walking
along, whether looking to his front or looking out of the shield, as
a *leopard*, really a contraction for leopard-like lion. Later, to avoid
confusion, this term was dropped in favour of *passant*. Later still
refinements in the blazon of a lion *passant* were adopted, the simple
term *passant* being used simply for a lion looking ahead. When he
looked out of the shield, like a lion of England, he became
passant guardant and when he was shown looking over his shoulder
he was *passant reguardant*.

did not deserve to be archbishop. He was too worldly and too much the King's friend. Wounded in his self-esteem Becket set out to prove, to an astonished world, that he was the best of all possible archbishops. Right from the start he went out of his way to oppose the King who, chiefly out of friendship, had made him an archbishop. Inevitably it was not long before Henry began to react like a man betrayed. In the mid-twelfth century church-state relations bristled with problems which could be, and normally were, shelved by men of goodwill but which could provide a field-day for men who were determined to quarrel. Henry chose the question of criminous clerks as the issue on which to settle accounts with his Archbishop. Like many laymen Henry resented the way in which clerks who committed felonies could escape capital punishment by claiming trial in an ecclesiastical court. At a council held at Westminster in October 1163 Henry demanded that criminous clerks should be unfrocked by the church and handed over to the lay courts for punishment. In opposing this Becket carried his episcopal colleagues with him in defence of the privileges of their order, but when Pope Alexander III asked him to adopt a more conciliatory line he indicated his willingness to do so. In order to press home his advantage Henry summoned a council to Clarendon (January 1164). He presented the bishops with a clear statement of the King's customary rights over the church – the Constitutions of Clarendon – and required from them a promise to observe these customs in good faith. Taken by surprise Becket argued for two days and then gave in. But no sooner had the rest of the bishops followed his example than Becket repented of his weakness. Thoroughly exasperated, Henry now decided to break Becket. He summoned him before the royal court to answer trumped-up charges. The Archbishop was found guilty and sentenced to the forfeiture of all his estates. In a hopeless position Becket fled across the Channel and appealed to the Pope for protection. By

taking a stand on principle and then wavering Becket had reduced the English church to confusion.

Once he had succeeded in driving Becket into exile Henry concentrated on more important matters for the next five years: Brittany was conquered and the English judicial system overhauled. Then in 1169 the question of the coronation of the heir to the throne, Prince Henry, led to the interminable negotiations between King, Pope and Archbishop being treated as a matter of urgency. In 1170 Becket returned to England determined to punish those who had taken part in the Young King's coronation. His enemies lost no time in telling Henry of the Archbishop's ostentatious behaviour. 'Will no one rid me of this turbulent priest?' Henry's heated words were taken all too literally by four of his knights. Anxious to win the King's favour they rushed off to Canterbury; and there, on 29 December 1170, Becket was murdered in his own cathedral. The deed shocked Christendom and secured Becket's canonisation in record time. In popular memory the Archbishop came to symbolise resistance to the oppressive authority of the state, but in reality everyone, churchmen as well as princes, was better off with him out of the way. Once the immediate storm of protest had died down it became apparent that the King's hold on the resources of his vast empire had in no way been shaken by the Becket controversy. In the early 1170s Henry stood at the height of his power.

The real threat to Henry's position was to come from within his own family. The Angevin empire was a family possession, not an indivisible state. Henry had no hesitation in planning to partition it among his sons. But his schemes aroused expectations which, while he retained all power in his own hands, he could not satisfy. For example, the Young King (in the whole of English history the only heir to the throne crowned during his father's lifetime) wanted something more than just a royal title.

Thus from 1173 onwards Henry was plagued by rebellious sons. Each new scheme caused new discontents since there was always at least one son who felt hard done by. The rebels, moreover, could always count on a warm welcome at the court of the King of France. After 1180 this was a serious matter for in that year the mild-mannered Louis VII was succeeded by his son Philip II, a shrewd and unscrupulous politician who was determined to destroy the Angevin Empire. The deaths of two of his sons, the Young King Henry in 1183 and Geoffrey in 1186, ought to have simplified Henry's problems, but this was offset by the old King's obvious preference for John, a preference which alarmed Richard. In the autumn of 1188 Richard and Philip came to terms. Throughout the winter the King's health deteriorated and by next summer he was in no condition to resist their invasion. On 4 July 1189 he was forced to accept a humiliating peace. When he was given a list of those who had fought against him he was shocked to find John's name on it. For John's sake he had pushed Richard to the point of rebellion and now John had silently joined the winning side. On 6 July the old King died at Chinon.

Only in the last weeks of his life had the task of ruling his immense territories been too much for Henry. A man of boundless energy he rode ceaselessly from one corner of his empire to another. He travelled so fast that he gave the impression of being everywhere at once – an impression which helped to keep men loyal. He never seemed to be still; when he was not working, he was out hunting. He cared little for appearances; he dressed simply and enjoyed plain food. Although the central government offices, the Chancery, the Chamber and the Constabulary travelled around with him, the sheer size of the empire inevitably stimulated the growth of localised administrations which could deal with routine matters of justice and finance in his absence. In England, where there was a strong administrative tradition going back to Anglo-Saxon days, government became increasingly complex and bureaucratic.

This development, taken together with Henry's interest in rational reform, has led to him being regarded as the founder of the English common law, and as a great and creative king. There is much to be said for this view of Henry, but in his own eyes these matters were of secondary importance – whatever their consequences in the long run may have been. To him what really mattered was family politics and he died believing that he had failed. But for over thirty years he had succeeded.

⨍ RICHARD I ⨍

r. 1189–99

RICHARD, THE SECOND surviving son of Henry II and Eleanor of Aquitaine, was born on 8 September 1157. He spent most of his youth at his mother's court at Poitiers – a court famous for its troubadours and their songs of chivalry and courtly love. Here he was sufficiently well educated to be able to speak Latin and to write verse in French and Provençal. But above all he was educated in the art of war. To this end he took an active part in tournaments and knightly exercises.

In 1169 he did homage to Louis VII for Aquitaine and was betrothed to the French King's daughter, Alice. As the second son Richard was

Kex anglie d'morte ofachions accusar . quod abnegans
se enfina manu excusaturu pmictic.

canden uenia peters litt absoluat

Richard I in Germany from the *Chronicle of Petrus de Eboli*. At the top he is arrested by Duke Leopold's soldiers. Below, he kneels at the feet of Emperor Henry VI and asks for pardon.

to have his mother's inheritance while the patrimony was to go to his elder brother. But Henry II was still only in his thirties and had no intention of allowing his young sons to govern for themselves. Frustrated, Henry, Richard and Geoffrey broke out into rebellion in 1173. In May 1174 Richard took command of his first serious campaign but at the age of sixteen he was still no match for his father and he was soon forced to ask pardon. For the next few years Richard concentrated on bringing to heel the unruly barons of Aquitaine. The unstable political situation and the numerous hill-top castles made it a hard school of warfare, but Richard came out of the course with flying colours. In 1183 the Young King died leaving Richard as heir to the throne. Henry II hoped that Richard would be willing to pass Aquitaine on to John, but Richard had spent too long subduing Aquitaine to give it up now. Whenever these tensions flared up into open hostility, Richard could count on the support of the new King of France, Philip II. In the summer of 1189 Richard and Philip battered Henry II into submission and then, in his moment of defeat, the old King died. On 3 September 1189 Richard was crowned at Westminster.

He stayed in England only long enough to make the necessary financial arrangements for his crusade. In 1187, under the impact of the news of Saladin's advance into the Holy Land, he had taken the Cross. For two years family feuds had prevented him from going on crusade and he was impatient to be off. He and Philip II agreed to travel together and to divide equally any conquests they might make. They set out in the summer of 1190 but transport difficulties led to the decision to spend the coming winter in Sicily. Not surprisingly, the new King of Sicily, Tancred, was somewhat alarmed by the prospect of having a large army encamped for months outside the walls of Messina, but since they were crusaders he could hardly deny them. He and Richard were not on the best of terms. Richard felt that Tancred had

been less than just in his treatment of Richard's sister Joan, the widow of the previous King of Sicily. When fighting broke out between the crusaders and the people of Messina Richard stepped in and took the city by storm. He now held a counter with which to bargain with Tancred and he exacted very profitable terms from the hapless Sicilian. But during the enforced idleness of that winter Richard and Philip quarrelled. In Philip's view it was high time that Richard married his sister, Alice of France, but Richard, who may have believed that the girl had been his father's mistress, refused. His mother then arrived in Sicily with an alternative bride, Berengaria of Navarre, so in anger Philip sailed on ahead to the Holy Land.

When Richard left Sicily (April 1191) he took Berengaria and Joan with him. Unfortunately the ship carrying the two princesses became separated from the main fleet and was nearly captured by the Greek ruler of Cyprus. Richard came up in the nick of time and then became involved in fighting which ended, less than a month later, with the whole of Cyprus in his hands. Militarily it was a brilliantly successful operation; strategically Cyprus was to be invaluable to future generations of crusaders. While at Limassol the wedding of Richard and Berengaria took place. Early in June 1191 Richard completed the short sea trip from Cyprus to Acre where a Muslim garrison had been under siege since August 1189. The army outside Acre was the only Christian force of any size in the whole of Outremer, yet it was itself hemmed in by a still larger Muslim army commanded by the great Saladin. If there was to be any hope of recovering Jerusalem it would first of all depend upon the outcome of the siege of Acre. Encouraged by Richard's arrival the besiegers pressed harder and a month later Acre fell. The moment of triumph was, however, clouded by the quarrel over the spoils which broke out between Richard and Duke Leopold of Austria. The crusaders suf-

fered a further setback when Philip decided to return home.

Richard ordered the slaughter of prisoners taken at Acre and then led the army down the coast to Jaffa. They were harassed all the way by Saladin's troops even though Richard did manage to relieve the pressure slightly when he won a fine victory at Arsuf. From Jaffa it was possible to advance cautiously inland towards Jerusalem. But neither then in January 1192, nor later in June 1192, could the crusaders come any nearer to the Holy City than Beit Nuba, some twelve miles away. Richard's crusade ended when he and Saladin made a three years' truce in September 1192. Inasmuch as Jerusalem had not been recaptured the crusade had failed. On the other hand Richard had probably done as much as was possible. The reconquest of the coastal strip and the settlement of the chaotic political affairs of the kingdom of Jerusalem were unquestionably very considerable military and diplomatic achievements.

Disturbing news from home had forced Richard to curtail his crusade and return as quickly as possible. But a combination of shipwreck and anxiety to be on his way ended with the King falling into the hands of Leopold of Austria in December 1192. For more than a year Richard remained in prison while kings and princes bargained for possession of his person. Eventually the regents of England were able to free him in return for a ransom of £100,000, but not before his treacherous brother John had joined forces with King Philip. As a result some of the most important castles on the borders of Normandy and Touraine were lost. After a second brief visit to England from March to May 1194, Richard

devoted the next five years to the hard grind of recovering the territory lost so rapidly while he was in prison. By 1199 this had been accomplished, and with the building of fortresses like Château-Gaillard the defences of Normandy were in better shape than ever. Richard had won back the initiative against Philip when, in an obscure sideshow at the little castle of Chalus in the Limousin, he received a fatal wound. On 6 April 1199 he died.

His nearest male relative was his brother John, for his marriage to Berengaria had been unsuccessful and he had left no legitimate children. By the standards of his own day he had been an ideal king, preoccupied above all with the crusade and the defence of his ancestral lands. For this reason he spent only a few months of his reign in England. Unlike his father and younger brother he was uninterested in the judicial and financial detail of government, but on his return from Germany he found a minister of outstanding ability, Hubert Walter, justiciar and Archbishop of Canterbury, a man who stood for harmonious co-operation between church and state. In Hubert Walter's hands the domestic business of the empire was efficiently and profitably administered. It was he who raised the money to pay for Richard's ransom and Richard's wars – and vast sums were needed. A generous lord and a shrewd politician Richard was, above all else, a great soldier. His own individual prowess in battle was an inspiration to his men. In the end his indifference to his own safety cost him his life, yet it was precisely this reckless quality which added the attributes of legendary heroism to a man who was also a competent king and a prudent general.

PREVIOUS PAGES Saladin's army illustrated in the *Roman de Godefrey de Bouillon* produced c. 1187. The Turkish cavalry was more mobile than the Franks and could wreak great damage by manoeuvring at a distance and firing a hail of arrows. But in a straight charge the heavy Frankish knights carried all before them.

RIGHT Two illustrations of the Crusades from the fourteenth-century *Chroniques de St Denis*.
ABOVE Christian knights give alms to Saracen beggars, unaware of treacherous soldiers hiding behind them.
BELOW Richard attacking Philip Augustus outside Gisars in 1198, when, although outnumbered, he put to flight the French army.

62 The effigy of King John on his tomb at Worcester Cathedral.

JOHN

r. 1199-1216

JOHN WAS BORN on Christmas Eve 1167, the last of the children born to Henry II and Eleanor of Aquitaine. After his birth his parents drifted apart. He was brought up partly in the household of his eldest brother, so that he could learn to be a knight, and partly in the household of his father's justiciar, Ranulf Glanvil, presumably in order to learn something of the business of government. As the fourth son it was not easy to provide for him; thus the nickname 'Lackland'. Henry II's attempts to remedy this situation usually drove one or more of his other sons into rebellion. Richard's refusal to hand over Aquitaine in 1184 led to the first armed clash between John and his elder brother. Not surprisingly John came off much the worse. Then the old King devised a more promising scheme. In 1185 he sent John to rule Ireland, but although none of John's brothers had any prior rights to Ireland, the expedition ended in fiasco within six months. John and the other, equally frivolous, young men in his train were out of their depth. They rapidly alienated both the native Irish and those Anglo-Norman conquistadors who were in the process of carving out new lordships for themselves. In September 1185 John crawled back home, blaming others for his failure.

Despite everything which his affectionate father had done for him, John seems to have been in no way grateful. When, in 1189, it at last became clear that the old King was a beaten man, John secretly and cynically betrayed him, bringing despair as well as defeat to his father's last days. Then, in the hope of keeping him quiet while he was away on crusade, Richard gave him vast estates: the Norman county of Mortain, the honour of Lancaster, the revenues of six English counties, and the heiress to the earldom of Gloucester. The bribe did not work.

As soon as Richard was at a safe distance John began scheming to overthrow William Longchamp, the man whom Richard had placed in charge of the administration. But news of these intrigues reached Richard while he was in Sicily and he sent back Walter of Coutances, Archbishop of Rouen, to investigate and if necessary to take over. To John's dismay this is precisely what Walter of Coutances did and by October 1191 John, who had enjoyed himself as leader of the opposition to an unpopular minister, found himself left out in the cold.

He began to conspire with King Philip of France. Their discussions began to have a real point when they heard that Richard was a prisoner in Germany. John went to Paris to do homage to Philip and then returned to stir up rebellion in England, while Philip launched his armies against Normandy. John's revolt went badly yet he still hoped for success, indeed he and Philip nearly persuaded the German emperor to sell them Richard for £100,000.

But in February 1194 Richard was released and John was forced to sue for pardon. It was granted at once, casually and contemptuously. 'Don't be afraid, John. You are a child. You have got into bad company and it is those who have led you astray who will be punished.' (The 'child' was now twenty-seven years old.) For the next five years John remained very much in his brother's shadow, but he conducted himself well enough for the dying King to nominate him as his heir in April 1199.

Richard's wishes were respected in England and Normandy, but not in Anjou, Maine and Touraine. There the local barons chose John's twelve-year-old nephew, Arthur of Brittany, as their lord. John had to pay a high price in order to persuade King Philip to abandon the young prince but by May 1200 he had ousted

Neustria Johis huit indefensa sub armis
Cum qui religuit Gallis possessa religuit

Johannes rex genuit videlicet

Arthur and was lord of all the Angevin dominions. Later that year he had his marriage to Isabella of Gloucester annulled and married instead Isabella of Angoulême, an heiress whose estates would help to knit together the northern and southern parts of his empire. Yet this apparently sensible marriage set in train the events which were to lead to the loss of Normandy. Isabella had been betrothed to Hugh of Lusignan; he protested against the sudden loss of his fiancée and when he got no justice from John he appealed to the court of King Philip. When John refused to answer Philip's summons, the French King declared all of his continental fiefs forfeit in April 1202.

It now remained to carry out the sentence, but at first John put up a stiffer resistance than had been expected. Indeed, by displaying an astonishing turn of speed he was able to capture Arthur of Brittany and several of the leading rebels, including the Lusignans. Arthur vanished into one of John's prisons, never to emerge again. Men had already learned to distrust John and as rumours of Arthur's fate began to percolate through Normandy and Anjou, the suspicion and the fear mounted. In this atmosphere no effective defence was possible. In December 1203 John abandoned the attempt and crossed over to England, leaving his castellans to make the best terms they could. By spring 1205 the last of his strongholds in Normandy and Anjou had fallen; Poitou also stood on the verge of surrender. These humiliating military reverses earned for John a new nickname; he became 'Soft-sword'.

From now on John's one overriding aim was to recover the lost territories. An expedition to Poitou in 1206 proved sufficient to stop the slide, but also showed John that it would require careful preparation and an immense concentration of resources before he could tackle the French King directly. For the next eight years he made his preparations, and force of circumstances meant that most of the work was carried out in England. Not since 1066 had a king of England spent so long in the country. The weight of John's presence was even felt in the north where men were not accustomed to seeing English kings. The extent of their resentment can be measured by the number of Northerners who opposed John in 1215-16. But it was not just in the north that John's rule seemed to be oppressive. Scutage which had been levied eleven times in the forty-five years between 1154 and 1199 was imposed eleven times in the sixteen years up to 1215. A recently devised tax on rents and chattels brought in huge sums. Levied at the rate of one thirteenth it yielded £60,000 in 1207 – perhaps twice the total annual revenue of the crown in the twelfth century. The forest laws were tightened up, and also proved very profitable. The King was exerting more pressure than ever before – and all this at a time of economic and social uncertainty when prices were rising at a rate never before experienced. Many families and religious houses were in deep financial trouble and they found it easier to blame the King than to understand the underlying economic forces.

The tension spilled over into the sphere of church-state relationships. A disputed election to the see of Canterbury in 1205 led to a clash between John and the most masterful of popes, Innocent III. In 1208 Innocent laid an interdict on England and Wales; all church services were suspended and remained so for six years. In 1209 John himself was excommunicated. Neither John nor lay society in general seem to have been very worried by this state of affairs; indeed since John's response to the interdict was to confiscate the estates of the church it even helped to ease his financial problem. But in 1212 a baronial plot and Philip's plans to cross the Channel served to remind John that an excommunicated king was particularly vulnerable to rebellion and invasion. So he decided to make peace with the church in order to have a free hand to deal with his more dangerous enemies. By agreeing to hold England as a fief of the papacy in May 1213 he completely won

LEFT King John hunting a stag from an early-fourteenth-century manuscript.

The Angevin Empire c.1174

BRABANT

FLANDERS

HAINAULT

VERMANDOIS

EU
Rouen
VEXIN
Caen • Lisieux
NORMANDY   CHAMPAGNE
Paris
Mortain
R. Seine
BLOIS
MAINE
BRITTANY
Le Mans
ANJOU   Blois
Nantes Angers   Tours   BURGUNDY
TOURAINE
POITOU   R. Loire
Poitiers   BERRI
La Rochelle   Lusignan   THE EMPIRE
SAINTONGE   ANGOUMOIS   LA MARCHE
Angoulême   Limoges
LIMOUSIN   AUVERGNE
PERIGORD
Périgueux
R. Dordogne
Bordeaux
AGÉNAIS
Agén
Montauban   PROVENCE
GASCONY   TOULOUSE
Toulouse
CASTILLE
NAVARRE
ARAGON
BARCELONA

Held by Henry II

| | Controlled after brother's death | | Inherited from parents |

	Acquired by marriage		Duchy of Aquitaine
	Loosely attached
	Claim to overlordship

Held by the French

| | Dependences of French Crown |
| | Lands of the French Royal House |

Scale ▭▭▭ Miles
0   50

over Innocent and assured himself of the Pope's support in the coming struggles.

All now turned on the result of the two-pronged attack on Philip launched by John and his heavily subsidised allies in 1214. At first all went according to plan but then, in July 1214, Philip won the vital Battle of Bouvines. When news of this defeat reached England discontent turned to rebellion. Only success in war could have justified the measures which John had taken in the last eight years, and that success was still denied him. In May 1215 the rebels captured London, forcing John to make peace. In June, at a meeting with the rebel lords at Runnymede, he agreed to the terms laid out in a document later to be known as Magna Carta. In essence it was a hostile commentary on some of the more objectionable features of the last sixty years of Angevin rule – and as such clearly unacceptable to John who regarded it merely as a way of buying time. The attempts to implement the terms of this peace treaty only led, in fact, to further quarrels and the renewal of war. Seeing that they could get no more from John the rebels elected Louis of France, King Philip's son, as an anti-king of their own. In May 1216 Louis invaded and made an unopposed entry into London. When John died, in October, the country was torn in two by a civil war which was going badly for the Angevins.

John possessed some good qualities. Few kings took such a close interest in the details of administration and the daily business of the law courts, but in his own day this counted for very little. John was suspicious of other men and they of him. He inspired neither affection nor loyalty and once he had shown that, no matter how hard he tried, he lacked Richard's ability to command victory in war, then he was lost. 'No man may ever trust him', wrote the troubadour Bertrand de Born, 'for his heart is soft and cowardly.' Not even the Angevin governmental machine could sustain him against that damning verdict.

The King John Cup, believed to be part of the King's treasure, most of which was lost in the Wellstream during his march from King's Lynn to Newark. The cup is now in the Guildhall at King's Lynn.

3 THE PLANTAGENETS 1216-1399

Paintings of Henry III and Edward I on the sedilia to the right of the high altar, erected in the reign of Edward I, in Westminster Abbey.

THE PLANTAGENETS

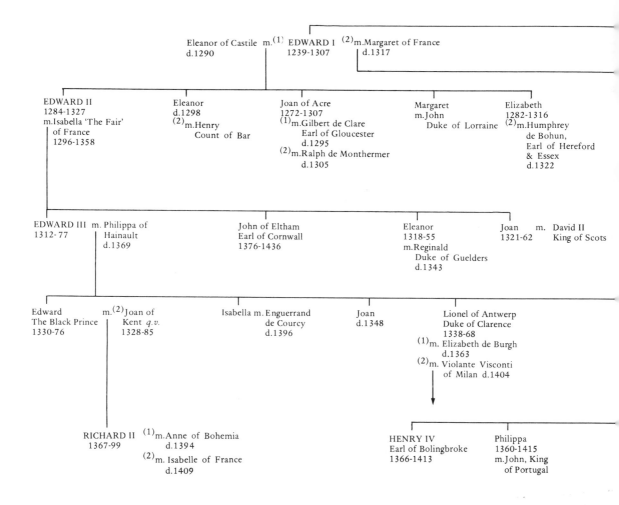

Eleanor of Castile m.(1) EDWARD I (2)m.Margaret of France
d.1290   1239-1307   d.1317

EDWARD II
1284-1327
m.Isabella 'The Fair'
  of France
1296-1358

Eleanor
d.1298
(2)m.Henry
  Count of Bar

Joan of Acre
1272-1307
(1)m.Gilbert de Clare
  Earl of Gloucester
  d.1295
(2)m.Ralph de Monthermer
  d.1305

Margaret
m.John
Duke of Lorraine

Elizabeth
1282-1316
(2)m.Humphrey
  de Bohun,
  Earl of Hereford
  & Essex
  d.1322

EDWARD III m. Philippa of
1312-77   Hainault
                         d.1369

John of Eltham
Earl of Cornwall
1376-1436

Eleanor
1318-55
m.Reginald
  Duke of Guelders
  d.1343

Joan   m. David II
1321-62   King of Scots

Edward   m.(2)Joan of
The Black Prince   Kent q.v.
1330-76   1328-85

Isabella m. Enguerrand
              de Courcy
              d.1396

Joan
d.1348

Lionel of Antwerp
Duke of Clarence
1338-68
(1)m. Elizabeth de Burgh
   d.1363
(2)m. Violante Visconti
   of Milan d.1404

RICHARD II   (1)m.Anne of Bohemia
1367-99   d.1394
             (2)m. Isabelle of France
                  d.1409

HENRY IV
Earl of Bolingbroke
1366-1413

Philippa
1360-1415
m.John, King
  of Portugal

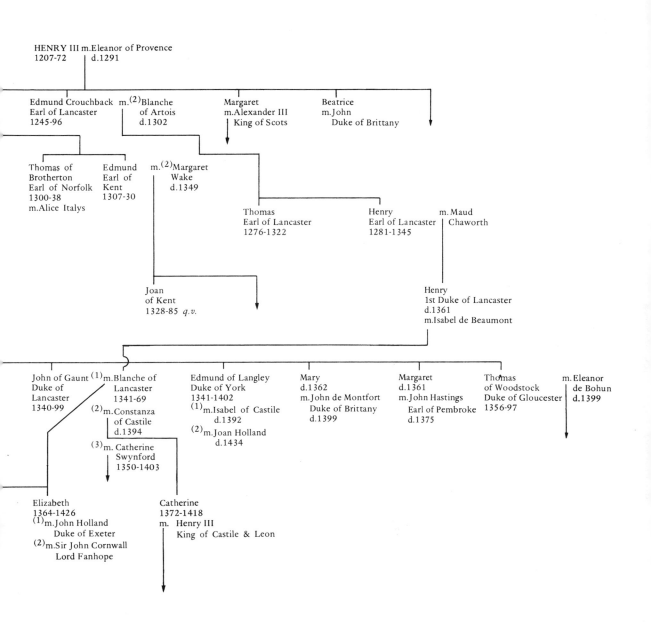

HENRY III m.Eleanor of Provence
1207-72 | d.1291

Edmund Crouchback m.(2)Blanche   Margaret   Beatrice
Earl of Lancaster   of Artois   m.Alexander III   m.John
1245-96   d.1302 | King of Scots   Duke of Brittany

Thomas of   Edmund   m.(2)Margaret
Brotherton   Earl of   Wake
Earl of Norfolk Kent   d.1349
1300-38   1307-30
m.Alice Italys

                              Thomas   Henry   m.Maud
                              Earl of Lancaster   Earl of Lancaster | Chaworth
                              1276-1322   1281-1345

                 Joan
                 of Kent
                 1328-85 q.v.

                                                        Henry
                                                        1st Duke of Lancaster
                                                        d.1361
                                                        m.Isabel de Beaumont

John of Gaunt (1)m.Blanche of   Edmund of Langley   Mary   Margaret   Thomas   m.Eleanor
Duke of   Lancaster   Duke of York   d.1362   d.1361   of Woodstock   de Bohun
Lancaster   1341-69   1341-1402   m.John de Montfort m.John Hastings Duke of Gloucester d.1399
1340-99   (2)m.Constanza   (1)m.Isabel of Castile Duke of Brittany Earl of Pembroke 1356-97
                   of Castile   d.1392   d.1399   d.1375
                   d.1394   (2)m.Joan Holland
              (3)m. Catherine   d.1434
                   Swynford
                   1350-1403

Elizabeth   Catherine
1364-1426   1372-1418
(1)m.John Holland   m. Henry III
    Duke of Exeter   King of Castile & Leon
(2)m.Sir John Cornwall
    Lord Fanhope

HENRY III

r. 1216-72

HENRY III WHO SUCCEEDED HIS FATHER, John, as king of England in 1216 inherited, apart from a passion for lampreys and a perhaps connected tendency to plumpness, a very disorganised kingdom. Much of the magnificent Angevin Empire of his grandfather, Henry II, had disappeared in the reign of his father and in England itself the nine-year-old boy could claim little as his own. London and most of the south-east was in the hands of the French Dauphin Louis, while much of the north of the country was occupied by rebellious barons. Only in the south-west and a broad belt of the Midlands were there supporters prepared to recognise the child as king. Yet within a year he was undisputed king of England and at his death fifty-six years later he was to leave to his son a kingdom more united, more prosperous and more prepared to accept the rule of an autocratic king than anyone in 1216 could have imagined possible. And this in spite of the fact that he has been almost universally castigated by historians as fickle, cowardly, incompetent and totally lacking in wise judgment. Indeed most writers are happy to describe Henry in Dante's words as 'the simple king who sat apart' and then to hurry on to his more glorious son, Edward I.

Henry's ultimate success owes little to his own character. He maintained his kingdom as a boy because he had good men to help him and he handed over a strong kingdom to his son because, in the long run, most people preferred a legitimate king to anarchy or usurpation, and because virtually every institution and everybody with any real power in thirteenth-century Europe was behind him. The English had not yet acquired that remarkable habit of killing their kings in the name of progress and good government that was to make them so notorious to later generations of Europeans, and although it is with Charles I that it is easiest to compare Henry III, he was never in any danger of suffering his descendant's fate.

Even in 1216 when the boy was crowned at Gloucester with his mother's chaplet, things were not as bad as they seemed. The death of King John had taken much of the point out of

William the Marshal, protector of the young Henry III, fighting Baldwin of Guise at a tournament. As a landless young man William had gained fame and fortune through his success in the lists and had been a loyal supporter of King John.

the baronial revolt and had made the Dauphin's presence in the country take on the appearance of an usurpation. The Pope and the church were on the young King's side and crusading vows could be commuted to fighting to restore his inheritance. And the boy King had good men to fight for him. Foremost amongst these was the aged and loyal William the Marshal, now in his seventies, who swore when he agreed to take on the office of Rector of the kingdom that 'if need be, he would carry the King on his shoulders from land to land, rather than give in'. But this was not to be necessary. In two battles, one at Lincoln and the other at sea off Sandwich, William and the Justiciar, Hubert de Burgh, were able to destroy the opposition. The subsequent Treaty of Kingston provided for a general amnesty, very liberal terms for the former rebels and a handsome bribe to the Dauphin to leave the country.

The old Marshal died in 1219 and the government of the country largely devolved on Hubert de Burgh. A few years more were necessary to bring the country back to complete normality, but by 1227 when King Henry, now nineteen, declared his majority, something like a consensus had been reached by King and barons on the basis of Henry's acceptance of his father's Magna Carta.

Such agreement was not to last long. After ten years of tutelage the young King was eager to enjoy the realities of power. An opportunity came after the disgrace of Hubert de Burgh in 1232 on patently trumped-up charges. His successor was the very experienced and competent Peter des Roches, the Poitevin Bishop of Winchester, who actively encouraged the King to rule without the aid of his magnates. Very soon the great men of England had cause for alarm. No longer were they allowed access to the King; no longer was their advice sought. To make matters worse a stream of the Bishop's fellow-countrymen made their way to England to take advantage of his elevation to power. Jobs and privileges which had previously been the perquisites of Englishmen were now eagerly seized by the grasping foreigners.

Not for the last time in his reign King Henry was to discover the limits of his magnates' patience. In 1234 a united opposition and the threat of civil war led to the dismissal of Peter des Roches and the repatriation of the Poitevins. From this time on it was clear to Henry that there were limits to the exercise of autocratic rule. He might think, like most kings, that the magnates were his subjects as much as anyone else and should no more restrict his prerogative or criticise him than their own servants would them. But in fact such a view was incompatible with the decentralised nature of feudal society. No king had sufficient cash or military power under his immediate control to defy completely the desires of his greater subjects. To rule effectively a king had to lead his magnates and persuade the great council, or Parliament as it was increasingly called, that his way was the right way. A king who managed to do this had to be hard-working, strong-willed, consistent and admired.

Henry had none of these qualities. He was unmartial, untrustworthy and inconsistent and as a result, although he kept out of serious trouble with his barons for the next quarter of a century, his rule was weak and came in for almost continuous criticism. The adjective most used by contemporaries to describe him was 'simple' and a good example of what was meant by this is the story told by an Italian Franciscan of the jester who compared Henry to Christ. The King, a very pious man, was flattered and asked the jester to explain the comparison. 'Because Our Lord was as wise at the moment of His conception as when He was thirty years old; so likewise our King is as wise now as when he was a little child' was the devastating reply.

Henry's desire to be his own master, coupled with his political weakness, led to constant squabbles with the barons, if not yet to more serious opposition. These squabbles brought out another characteristic of the King, the famous Plantagenet temper. But Henry was essentially a mild man and such outbursts were as often as not followed by equally rapid reconciliation. Nonetheless nobody quite knew where they were and the King gave his barons ample opportunity to indulge in their natural suspicion and jealousy. At home the King's main policy, if indeed he had one, was to try to expand and make more efficient the system of administration within the royal household. In this he had some success, but such activity was sure to make the barons suspicious. They disliked the secretive and inquisitive practices of the King's personal council. They also disliked its personnel, subordinate and insignificant persons rather than the King's natural-born counsellors – themselves. They hated even more the enormous number of foreigners who surrounded the King and seemed to monopolise all the favours being distributed, while remaining apparently immune from the law of the land.

Many of these foreigners were the kinsfolk of the Queen. Henry married Eleanor of Provence, the younger sister of the Queen of France, in 1236. Their family life seems to have been a very happy one, but the union brought problems for the English baronage. For the Queen's relatives, finding no joy at the court of the prudent Queen Blanche of France, swarmed over to England to make their fortunes. They were joined by the King's half-brothers, the children of his mother's second marriage to a Frenchman. Indeed, mid-thirteenth-century England appears to have been almost proverbial as the place to make one's fortune, replacing that former sanctuary for younger sons, the Holy Land, now reconquered by the Moslems. In such circumstances the hospitable and cosmopolitan King Henry

Henry III sails to Brittany to defend his French possessions in 1230. On the sail of the boat are emblazoned the lions of England.

who was so fond of his kinsfolk must have seemed a godsend.

The English baronage resented competing with high-born foreigners and low-born bureaucrats, and grumbled accordingly. The standard way of avoiding trouble from discontented barons was to lead them to war, but Henry was a poor soldier and his tendency to lose battles did little to attract the fighting men of England to his standard. He did make somewhat desultory attempts to recover what his father had lost of the great Angevin Empire, but the complex series of truces, alliances with ambitious nobles in western and southern France, and occasional expeditionary forces were of no avail against the expansionist policies of the French monarchy. Finally, in 1259, Henry ratified the Treaty of Paris by which he renounced all his rights in Normandy, Maine and Anjou. He retained Gascony but only as a fief held from the King of France to whom he was bound to do homage. Further afield Henry was no more successful. He took the cross in 1250 but was not destined to emulate the feats of his uncle, Richard Coeur-de-Lion, nor indeed of his sainted contemporary, Louis IX of France, in that year a prisoner of the Saracens in Egypt. The money raised for Henry's crusade was diverted to an unrealistic and ultimately unsuccessful attempt to acquire the kingdom of Sicily for his second son, Edmund. Sicily finally went to one of the greatest adventurers of the age, Charles of Anjou, younger brother of St Louis, who built up an impressive if short-lived empire in the central Mediterranean. Henry was left with an enormous debt to the Pope, who had been the instigator of the Sicilian campaign, and mounting discontent among those whom the King expected to pay for his dreams.

If Henry's foreign adventures cost money and gained nothing, there was one field in which he did good service both to himself and to England. Henry III was the great champion of Gothic art in England, and one of the greatest of our royal connoisseurs. His most outstanding

Henry III pictured with one of the churches he built, from the *Chronicle of England* by Peter Langtoff.

achievements are seen in the detailed instructions and records of payment to his craftsmen, and in the surviving works of art of his reign. Perhaps his greatest memorial was the new Westminster Abbey built to house the shrine of his favourite saint, Edward the Confessor. A royal saint is a good advertisement for monarchy and Henry III, like Charles I, was clearly aware of the value of art as propaganda. All over the country the King's builders were at work and the great majority of the royal castles underwent structural alterations during his reign. Wherever the King went his observant eye would pick out what needed to be done to improve or beautify his buildings and detailed orders would go out for the work to be put in progress. Inside, his halls and castles were becoming increasingly decorated. A common theme was the Wheel of Fortune, beloved of the thirteenth century, which was painted above the King's chair in at least two of his castles. But a study of the images that appear on tiles, stained glass, walls and furniture in King Henry's buildings shows that the King's tastes were extremely wide-ranging. Maps of the world, cities, seasons, saints, crusaders and kings, stories from the bible and the romances of chivalry kept an army of skilled craftsmen busy for most of the reign. An order survives from 1256 giving instructions to pay a craftsman for painting a picture of the King rescued from his rebellious subjects by his dogs; this has a certain irony in view of what the future held, and the painting itself may have given the King a wry confidence in the early 1260s.

For by the late 1250s the fairly friendly relationship between the King and his great council was becoming increasingly strained. The main issue was the same as it had been for the last quarter of a century, the freedom of the King to choose his own counsellors and be master in his own household. But now it was given a new urgency by what seemed to the barons the enormous waste and folly of the King's Sicilian adventure. In 1258 the King was compelled by the threat of force and his lack of cash to yield to the barons and he swore to submit to their advice. It was agreed that a new council, half chosen by the King and half by the magnates, should be set up to reform the state of the realm, and that Parliament should meet three times a year. The term Parliament was used at this time to describe irregular gatherings of the lay and ecclesiastical lords and the King's legal advisers.

At first it looked as though the King was sincere in his submission to the barons. But in fact it seems clear that he never intended to abide by his oath and hoped that by dividing the opposition he could maintain the royal supremacy. The period between 1258 and 1265 was a see-saw as first the magnates, then the King, rose to the top in the game of power. But in the long run the King had everything on his side. The most respected ruler of his time, St Louis of France, though a genuine peacemaker keen to resolve the differences between his brother-in-law and his vassals, was too much of a king to deny royal rights. The popes, not yet the tool of party and nation that they were to be in the next century, were also clearly behind Henry. The weapons of dispensation and excommunication were powerful ones that would be used for the King and not against him. Most serious of all, the barons' cause was doomed by the inconstancy of its own members. The King needed to make little effort to divide the opposition who, with an eye to the main chance or in a genuine belief that they had gone too far, were constantly changing sides.

Much of the drama of the contest comes from the character of Simon de Montfort who emerged as the leader of the magnates. A younger son with comparatively poor prospects, he came from France to England in his early twenties to try and make good a somewhat tenuous claim to the earldom of Leicester. Fortune smiled on Simon as on so many Frenchmen at the English court. Not only did he obtain his earldom but in 1238 was secretly married to King Henry's widowed sister. From then onwards his close relationship and his obvious abilities brought him into constant contact with the King, a contact which developed into the love-hate relationship so typical of Henry. At one moment the King would be shouting at Simon, accusing him of treachery, seduction of his sister and other terrible crimes; later he would praise him for the good work he had done in his service and shower rewards upon him. The seeds of Simon's opposition to the King clearly lie in the ambition that brought him to England in the first place, but there is little doubt that he genuinely believed in the need to curb royal pretensions to absolute power and provide for a more effective process of consultation with the great of the land. The degree of popular support for Simon's cause gives some indication of the truth of the baronial claims of royal misrule and lawlessness. This was not just another sordid baronial revolt and it is an indication of both his personality and his cause that his name is remembered today by many who would be completely unable to identify the King he opposed.

The political struggle broke out into open war early in 1264 when the barons refused to accept the French King's arbitration in favour of King Henry. After early successes for the royalists, Simon rose to the peak of his power with the complete defeat and capture of the King at the battle of Lewes in June. In his year of triumph Simon held a conference of leading supporters and summoned two burgesses and two knights from a number of boroughs and shires to attend it. But success brought on Simon much of the opprobrium formerly reserved for the King. Now it was the royalists who were able to attract support by attacking the evil customs of the government and by demonstrating the irony of a movement, one of whose main features had been an attack on aliens in high places, being led by an alien in the person of Simon de Montfort. The dramatic escape from custody of King Henry's eldest son, the Lord Edward, provided a new leader who swore in his turn to reform the realm. Desertions from Simon's cause soon followed and on 4 August 1265 came the end of the great movement. Surrounded near Evesham by the royalist forces, Simon de Montfort and his closest supporters formed a ring around their King and prepared to fight to the death. In the midst of the battle the King formed a pitiful spectacle, in danger from friend and foe alike, as Simon's men were hacked to death and that great fighter, Simon himself, was at last brought down and decapitated.

The last years of King Henry's reign belong more to the story of his son, who after his success at Evesham took over much of the rule of the kingdom before his departure on crusade in 1270. Henry, secure now from baronial opposition, carried on with his patronage of art and his building programme and lived to see the relics of his favourite saint, Edward the Confessor, carried to their new shrine behind the altar in Westminster Abbey in October 1269. Three years later, after one of the longest reigns in English history, the old King went to join them. A rather shadowy figure as a politician, who gained no glory in war, his chief merit was to open England up to the cosmopolitan influences emanating from the continent. King Henry gloried to emulate in England the greatest of French art and architecture, and he was a great admirer of international institutions such as the papacy and the friars, who first came to England in his reign. After his death England began to be more insular, turning its back on the continent, only to return again some seventy years later as a terrifying aggressor. Perhaps we give too much glory to our martial kings and too little to those, like Henry III, who have made England a more civilised country.

EDWARD I

r. 1272-1307

ENGLISH NATIONALIST HISTORIANS turn with relief to Edward I after discussing the reigns of Henry III and John. Here at last is a man who has the personality to prevent the thirteenth century passing away with no English glory at all. Edward was a magnificent creature, standing head and shoulders above the ordinary man of his time, healthy, athletic, with a fine head of hair and a handsome face marred only by a drooping eyelid inherited from his father. He seemed to embody all the traditional qualities of a great medieval king. If his chief delight was in war and tournaments, he was also notable as an imaginative law-maker and a just law-enforcer, as an administrator whose authority was able to make real many of his father's attempts to strengthen and improve the royal household, and as one of those kings who have pushed forward that institution so beloved of historians, the British Constitution. No wonder that he is often claimed as the greatest of the Plantagenets.

Such reputations are bound to be vulnerable to modern criticism and Edward I, like other great men, has been demoted in recent years. Much has been made of a quotation from the Song of Lewes, written during the Barons' war of his father's reign, which described him as inconstant and treacherous. 'When he is cornered', the author wrote, 'he promises anything you like, but once he has escaped he goes back on his word. The lying by which he gains his end he calls prudence; whatever he wants he holds to be lawful and thinks that there are no legal bounds to his power.' Lest this should be merely the inconstancy of youth, the rest of his career has been examined and as a result shorn of some of its nobility. Edward, 'the maker of laws and maintainer of the rights of the weak', has been indicted of manipulating the law to disinherit some of his greatest subjects in favour of himself and his kin. Edward the warrior has been accused of shabby tricks in winning his battles, and Edward, the man, of lack of generosity in rewarding those most faithful to him. What seems clear from this reassessment is that Edward was not quite the god-like figure of romance, but was an extremely tough man, able to keep his contemporaries in order, and like other tough men not above a certain amount of bullying, disregard for law and desire for personal enrichment. On the other hand, he brought a period of firm and, on the whole, just government to a country which had known only too little of such things in the previous half century.

Edward was born at Westminster in 1239. All the evidence suggests that his childhood and relationship with his parents were very happy and this domestic tranquillity was repeated in his own marriage with Eleanor of Castile which took place in 1254. Edward's Court, like his father's, was orderly with none of the grossness of some of his forebears. When Eleanor died in Nottinghamshire in 1290, Edward was to write, 'my harp is turned to mourning, in life I loved her dearly, nor can I cease to love her in death'. He vowed to raise a cross to her memory at every town where her body rested on the way to Westminster and these memorials, three of which survive, are evidence of a much tenderer side to Edward than the character normally projected by historians. The marriage was a diplomatic one to protect the southern borders of Gascony and it was in Gascony that he first took on public duties, the duchy being settled on him together with other outlying lands of the English Crown in Ireland and Wales. He showed little evidence of either military or administrative competence during

Londoners, against whom he felt he had a particular grievance, as his mother had formerly been insulted in the city. Breaking their ranks, he chased them miles up the hill outside Lewes, only to discover when he returned to the battle that the royal cause had been lost. In the following year, after escaping from the custody of the barons, he emerged as the royalist leader, and it was his quick thinking that cut off Simon de Montfort from his reinforcements and brought him to the end of his adventure in the murderous battle of Evesham. But even there the young Lord Edward sullied his honour by the unchivalrous trick of displaying as his own the banners of some baronial supporters who had recently been captured, and thus luring Simon de Montfort to his doom. After the defeat of the barons much of the work of government fell on Edward but he showed little of that leniency which had healed wounds so quickly after the defeat of the barons in Henry III's minority. Leading rebels were savagely fined, as was Edward's bête noire, the City of London, and confiscations from the de Montforts and the Earl of Derby went to build up the enormous patrimony of Edward's brother, Edmund of Lancaster.

With the kingdom secure and his aging father safe in his royal office, Edward was free in 1270 to fulfil a long ambition and set off on crusade with the French king, St Louis. Louis himself died that same year of fever in Tunis and Edward's crusade achieved very little, but it is during his four-year absence from England that Edward's somewhat chequered youth is forgotten and he emerges with an international reputation as a great man and a fine warrior, the 'greatest lance in the world'.

Edward received the news of Henry III's death in Sicily on his way home from the Holy Land, but he made no haste to return to his inheritance, once assured of his peaceful proclamation as king. After a magnificent passage through Italy he proceeded to Paris to visit the new French king, Philip III. Here he did homage

Edward I rides into London on his return from the Crusades.

this period and various stories of youthful injustice and bullying led the chronicler, Matthew Paris, to feel that the prospects for the future of England under his rule were gloomy. Edward did not improve his reputation during Henry III's struggle with the barons between 1258 and 1265. He changed sides twice, broke his sworn promise on more than one occasion and was at least partly responsible for the royal disaster at Lewes. Commanding the right of the royal forces he was faced by an ill-armed body of for his French lands but he phrased his submission in the vague formula 'I do you homage for all the lands which I ought to hold of you'. Twenty years of somewhat uneasy peace were to follow before a new burst of expansionist policy in France led to a fresh outbreak of warfare in Gascony. This was to cause Edward great embarrassment as it coincided with his Scottish wars. A settlement finally came after a truce in 1297 and was later confirmed by Edward's second marriage to the French king's sister, Margaret, and by the betrothal of his son, Edward of Caernarvon, to Philip's daughter, Isabella.

On 2 August 1274 Edward landed at Dover after his four years of travel and adventure. His first task was to reassert the royal authority. Commissioners were appointed to tour the whole country to obtain evidence on such matters as the abuse of the law and local power. After so many years of weak central government, they found plentiful evidence of corruption and extortion, and many royal officers, especially sheriffs, found that their careers of easy pickings had come to an end. Although Edward's enquiry was concerned with abstract justice, its main function was to determine more clearly the boundaries between royal and private power and thus to maximise both royal authority and revenue. He disliked in particular the widespread powers in private hands, with no better warrant than long custom. Edward was unable to do much about such entrenched privileges, but he was able to define the 'time immemorable', in which so many people claimed their rights had been granted, as before the accession of Richard I. Anything granted after then needed rigid proof. All rights now had to be clearly defined and it was shown that their extension without grant was not to be tolerated. Edward followed up his investigations in the country by considerable legislative activity, mainly under the direction of his Chancellor, Robert Burnell. In doing this he was careful to carry the great council or

parliament with him and the result was a considerable extension and clarification of the law, which has earned him the somewhat inflated title of the English Justinian.

Edward's programme of reform was interrupted in 1277 by a long-standing problem of the English monarchy, trouble in Wales. Welsh independence and power depended on the control of the inaccessible area of Snowdonia and the island of Anglesey which served as a granary. From here raids could be made south and east into the more settled areas occupied by Welsh and Anglo-Norman alike. To control this potentially explosive force the king of England depended on the marcher lords who, in their castles in South Wales and the border counties, enjoyed a state of near independence of the English Crown in return for keeping North Welsh tendencies to expansion in check. Relations between the two cultures ebbed and flowed, depending on the strength of the lords of Snowdonia, the political condition of England and the chronic state of private war existing between the marcher lords. Edward had had a somewhat unsatisfactory apprenticeship into the gangster politics of the region as a young man and, now that he was feeling his strength as a king, he was reluctant to allow the former state of near anarchy to continue. By the time of his accession to the throne Welsh power was in the ascendant. The Lord of Snowdonia, Llewelyn ap Gruffydd, had taken advantage of the political disturbances of the previous reign to build up a position of considerable strength, and, by the treaty of Montgomery in 1267, had been acknowledged as Prince of Wales and lord of nearly all the Welsh chieftains.

He now sought a greater degree of independence and refused repeatedly to do homage to Edward, on the grounds that the King had refused to hand over for justice his brother, David, suspected of a plot against him. Edward, aware of the problems of Welsh campaigns, was at first reluctant to take action against this

Statues of Edward I and his beloved first Queen, Eleanor of Castile, from Lincoln Cathedral.

challenge to his feudal overlordship, but in 1277 he decided to exert his authority. In a remarkably well-organised campaign he cut off the Prince from his supply base in Anglesey and forced him to surrender. The settlement was very mild. Llewelyn lost his lands outside Snowdonia and Anglesey, but retained his title as Prince of Wales.

Five years later the Welsh were up in arms again and Edward was forced to repeat his previous campaign. This time he was at first not so successful and the attempted invasion of Snowdonia from Anglesey was foiled. However, the death of Llewelyn after a skirmish led to the collapse of Welsh resistance and the complete conquest of north Wales. Edward took this opportunity to reorganise completely the government of this troublesome area. By the Statute of Wales of 1284, the area was transferred to the King's dominion and divided up into shires on the English pattern. Although the basis of law and custom under the new administration continued to be Welsh, those features which the English did not like were removed and in fact during the next century the whole region underwent a steady process of anglicisation. To secure his new dominion Edward ordered the building of that great ring of castles on the coast surrounding the mountains of Snowdonia which remain today as an impressive, if somewhat grim, monument to his most successful enterprise as king.

Edward I's successes as a general depended heavily on efficient organisation, both of supply and of recruitment. During his Welsh and Scottish wars he was able to bring into the field armies which were not to be exceeded in size in England till the Civil War of the seventeenth century. Admittedly, most of these men were infantry, poorly armed and eager to desert, but their sheer numbers were often sufficient to intimidate the enemy, and they included large numbers of Welsh archers whose skill foreshadowed the English military successes of Edward III's reign. Most battles, however, were still won by cavalry, not archers. The Crown still had the right to unpaid feudal service for forty days but this was now often more of an embarrassment than an asset. Both the King and his magnates began to supplement their feudal levies with paid retainers with whom they had made contracts specifying the nature and length of service and the rate of pay that they should receive.

Edward's wars and the large armies with which he fought them put an enormous strain on the royal revenue. His reign sees a considerable expansion of taxation which resulted, as so often in the reigns of financially embarrassed kings, in a parallel expansion of the effectiveness of the parliaments which granted the extra taxes. Regular meetings of Parliament became an established feature of British political life in Edward's reign and sometimes knights and burgesses were summoned to attend, following the precedent set by Simon de Montfort.

However, taxation was not enough for Edward's needs. The traditional source of extra revenue was to tallage the Jews but, by Edward's reign, the extortions of the past had so impoverished them that this was hardly worth the effort. In 1290 he killed the golden goose for good, expelling the Jews from England and seizing most of their remaining assets. Their place as royal creditors was taken by Italians, papal bankers and wool exporters, who exchanged loans for trading privileges and left Edward at his death in considerable debt.

The arena in which most of this money was spent during the last decade of Edward's reign was Scotland. Relationships between England and Scotland in the thirteenth century were similar to those between England and Wales, although the Scots had a far greater degree of real independence. Nonetheless the King of England claimed the overlordship of the northern kingdom, a claim which at times the Scots were prepared to accept. A chance for Edward to exercise this claim, and if possible to reinforce it, came in 1286 when King Alexander III of

LEFT Edward I makes his sixteen-year-old
son Prince of Wales. This act,
designed to win the loyalties
of the defeated Welsh, became
a tradition of the royal line.

ABOVE Caernarvon Castle was the chief of several castles built by Edward I to preserve his subjugation of the Welsh. Edward had been impressed with the fortifications of the Holy Land, and his architect, James of St George, copied some features of the crusaders' castles. Instead of the traditional Norman system with the keep as focus of defence, Caernarvon was designed as one defensive area divided by a wall into two wards, encircled by walls 8 to 14 feet thick, linking stout towers. The work was completed in 1327 at a cost of £19,000.

John Balliol does homage to Edward I.

Scotland died, leaving as heir his six-year-old grand-daughter, the Maid of Norway. Edward's first plan, which was accepted by the Scots and would have saved much bloodshed, was to marry the girl to his son, Edward, born at Caernarvon in 1284. But sadly, in 1290, the girl died in the Orkneys on her way from Norway to Scotland, leaving the Scots with the horrors of a disputed succession. Edward, as overlord, was called in to adjudicate between the three main claimants. After careful consideration he finally chose John Balliol, a decision which most historians have considered to be fair and just. What was less fair was the advantage Edward took of the needs of the Scots and the weakness of Balliol to establish his supremacy over the northern kingdom. Ultimately Edward's demands pushed the

Scots into accepting in 1295 an alliance with Philip of France with whom Edward was now at war. This clever move came just a little too late. The Welsh too had tried to take advantage of Edward's troubles in France and had risen in the winter of 1295. But Edward had time to quell the Welsh rebellion and then in the spring of 1296 to strike at Scotland. Berwick was stormed and sacked by the King in March, and in late April the main Scots army was crushed by Earl Warenne of Surrey at Dunbar. Edward made a grand passage through Scotland, accepted the submission of the great men and the abdication of Balliol, seized the Stone of Destiny from Scone Abbey and was back in Berwick in August. As a contemporary put it, he 'conquered the Kingdom of Scotland and searched it through in twenty-one weeks'. He then left the country to be ruled by Earl Warenne and went home.

Edward had seriously underestimated the Scots. His contemptuous treatment of them led to bitter hatred of their English conquerors which flared up in the year after Dunbar into a war of independence which was long to outlast his reign. Such hatred was soon matched by the English who were subjected to the horrors of continuous raiding and whose instinctive dislike of their northern neighbours was fed by stories of savage atrocities.

In the face of English military superiority, much of the Scots resistance took the form of guerilla fighting from bases in the hills and forests. The first great leader to emerge was the gigantic outlaw, William Wallace, whose dramatic exploits play such a large part in Scots legend. Supported mainly by peasants and outlaws like himself, Wallace was able in 1297 to score a decisive victory over Earl Warenne at the battle of Stirling Bridge. Although Edward had his revenge the following year, when he returned to Scotland with the greatest army he

had ever assembled to destroy Wallace at the battle of Falkirk, the outlaw himself was not captured till 1305 and he was to be succeeded in the following year by a new leader who was ultimately to inflict on England the most devastating defeat in her history. Robert Bruce was the grandson of one of the claimants to the Scots throne at the death of the Maid of Norway. Like most of the nobles he had made his peace with King Edward, but in 1306, after putting himself beyond the law by murdering a rival for the forfeit throne, he decided to make a bid for popular support and had himself crowned King of Scotland. His early career as king was a disaster and he spent most of that summer hiding in the heather from Englishman and Scot alike. But he remained alive and his threat was sufficient to force the ailing King of England to undergo one last campaign to conquer Scotland. The old King never got there. On 7 July 1307, aged 68, the 'hammer of the Scots' died at Burgh-on-Sands within sight of the Scottish border. His last command was that his son should carry his bones at the head of his armies until the last Scotsman had surrendered.

The assessment of Edward's expansionist policy depends ultimately on one's view of the benefits of the union of the whole island. Traditional English historiography, with its firm roots in the British world empire of the nineteenth century, saw such a union as part of England's manifest destiny. Today opinion is not so unanimous. Edward's legal justification for his attempt to bring both Wales and Scotland under the direct dominion of the English crown is dubious and his failure in Scotland was to give rise to three hundred years of intermittent warfare and almost continuous border-raiding. In return for this devastation and mutual slaughter it can hardly be said that either kingdom received much benefit.

EDWARD II

r. 1307–27

No King of England has had such a consistently bad press as Edward II. Squeezed in between his two warrior namesakes he seemed to justify contemporary suspicion that he was a changeling. Yet the outward appearance was quite clearly that of a Plantagenet. He was as tall, strong, golden-haired and good-looking as his father in his prime, but inside this magnificent shell there was no king as the fourteenth century understood that word. He made no effort to rule or impress his subjects. He cared nothing for the duties of a king. His only desire was to use the advantages of his position to enrich his friends and amuse himself. Such behaviour of course was not all that uncommon among kings, but in addition both Edward's friends and his amusements were themselves suspect. The King had no taste for jousting and the other martial pursuits of his class. Instead he preferred to test his strength in activities of a distinctly plebeian sort, such as digging or rowing, or to learn and practise the manual crafts of his subjects like thatching and farming. Today we would hardly condemn such activities with the intensity that Edward's contemporaries did, but even now they hardly fit our conception of a medieval king. Edward compounded his faults by the low company he kept in pursuing his rural amusements. But even worse was the company he kept at court. He systematically avoided his natural counsellors, the magnates of the land, and gave his heart and all the spoils that flowed from the royal office to upstarts. Edward was a very good friend and his loyalty to his friends is one of the most attractive features of his character, but a policy of continually antagonising the magnates was certain to lead to trouble.

The amateur psychologist that lurks within most historians has made much of Edward's upbringing to explain his unroyal behaviour, which could well have been in part the reaction of a weak son to a strong-willed and increasingly tyrannical father. If Edward I bears some responsibility for his son's character he certainly left him other problems which such a character would be unable to solve. His powerful personality had been able to subdue a serious threat to his autocracy in 1297, but there were many of the magnates who felt that the spirit of the royal concessions of the earlier thirteenth century had been forgotten and who were now only waiting for the death of the terrifying old man to impose themselves on his son. More immediate was the chaotic legacy in Scotland of a war that already looked as if it would never be won. The young King's reaction to his father's last command that he should pursue the Scottish war to the bitter end was very much in character. After a perfunctory march across the border, he gave up the north to civil war and the triumph of Robert Bruce and returned to London to enjoy himself.

Here he was joined by the best of his friends, Piers Gaveston, a handsome Gascon knight with an eye to the main chance, who had been his close companion since childhood. So extravagant were Edward's demonstrations of affection for his 'brother Perrot' that it is generally assumed that there was a homosexual relationship between the two young men. It is clear that Edward I shared these suspicions and Gaveston had twice been banished by the old King. But now there seemed nothing to stop Edward II from showing to the world how much he loved his favourite. Less than a month

RIGHT Edward II and Isabella of France from the treatise written by Walter de Milemete in 1326, and later presented to Edward III.

The marriage of Edward II to Isabella, daughter of Philip IV, at the Church of Notre Dame, Boulogne, in 1308. Edward presented to his favourite, Gaveston, the finest of Isabella's jewels and some of the wedding presents.

after Edward I's death, Gaveston was made Earl of Cornwall, a title formerly held only by the sons of kings. Shortly afterwards he was married to the King's niece, and a further insult to the magnates came early in 1308 when the King left Gaveston as regent when he went over to Boulogne to bring home his young bride, Isabella of France. Edward soon made it plain that the delights of marriage were not going to cool his love for Gaveston. Many of his wedding presents were given away to the favourite and at his coronation he shocked the Court by demonstrating that he preferred the couch of Perrot to that of the Queen.

Gaveston did nothing to quell the hatred and jealousy that the King's generosity aroused in the hearts of the magnates. Indeed he went out of his way to ridicule them, inventing derisive nicknames for them and, even worse, inviting them to a tournament and then demonstrating that his sword was as keen as his tongue by decisively defeating them.

Edward and Gaveston were playing a dangerous game. No king had the military resources to fly in the face of the united opposition of the earls in those days of private armies. Total unity was, of course, unlikely and the number of opponents of the King ebbed and flowed, but the King's behaviour ensured that they were usually sufficient to put very considerable pressure on him. Within a year of Edward's accession, the threat of force from a strong baronial group drove the King to agree to the exile of Gaveston. Edward made strenuous efforts to appease and divide his opponents but had to agree to a programme of reform undermining the royal prerogative before his favourite was reinstated. However, Gaveston's insufferable arrogance speedily reunited the nobility against him. A committee calling itself the Lords Ordainers enforced Edward's agreement to detailed reforms and the perpetual exile of Gaveston. But Edward had no intention of implementing anything or honouring any of his promises. All he wanted was to go on as he had before with Gaveston by his side. Within two months of his second exile the favourite appeared openly at the Christmas Court at Windsor. This was too much for the earls. After a short struggle, Gaveston was captured and murdered by his enemies, despite a promise that he should be allowed to plead his case before Parliament.

In many ways the murder of Gaveston was a tactical mistake, since it removed the main focus of opposition and, by marshalling opinion against the murderers, put Edward in a stronger position than he had so far enjoyed as king. This royalist reaction, however, was only superficial and there still existed an opposition movement determined to reduce the King to a mere figurehead to carry out their wishes. The leader of this group and the most consistent opponent of the King was his first cousin, Thomas of Lancaster. The fortunes of his house had been built up on the confiscated estates of the de Montforts after the battle of Evesham in 1265. By 1311 Lancaster had become a classic over-mighty subject with five earldoms in his

possession and an immense private army at his command. In a rather fanciful way he now saw himself as a second Simon de Montfort who would control the King in the interest of his greater subjects. There are of course parallels between the two situations but Lancaster was unfortunately no de Montfort. By all accounts he was a thoroughly nasty man, grasping and vicious, and on many occasions in his career the idealism involved in opposition to the King was tarnished by his only too obvious desire to divert the benefits that the King was giving elsewhere to himself. To make matters worse, when power did come into his hands he seemed incapable of using it, preferring to stay within his castles and leave the country in a state near to anarchy.

Lancaster's defiance of the Crown came out into the open in 1314 when he and three other earls refused to accept the King's summons to military service against Scotland, on the grounds that the expedition had not been approved by Parliament. It proved to be a wise decision. Edward had hoped to lead his disgruntled barons to a great victory and bring a little glory to his reign but his efforts brought only disaster and the triumph of the stay-at-home Lancaster. On Midsummer Day 1314, after a display of incredible incompetence by both the King and his military advisers, the English were totally defeated at the battle of Bannockburn by Robert Bruce and a Scottish army only one-third their strength. In one day Bruce had assured the independence of Scotland. Edward was to make other expeditions to Scotland but none had any real success.

The next three years must be amongst the worst in English history. After the disaster of Bannockburn, Edward II gave up even the pretence of ruling and became a mere puppet in the hands of Lancaster. But as the royal power collapsed, Lancaster did little to replace it. The Scots ravaged the north of England, levying ransoms from the towns, while private warfare broke out in many other parts of the kingdom.

qui deuoient demourer a chx

Providing a grim background to this situation of chaos was the worst famine in European history.

In 1318 some semblance of normality returned. A measure of reconciliation between Edward and Lancaster was engineered by the so-called middle party under the leadership of the Earl of Pembroke, the most honourable and competent of the earls. But Edward still remained a king in name only, his every act to be controlled by a standing council. Nonetheless by exchanging one master for many he had returned to the position of being able to play them off against each other. For, despite his weakness, Edward was still determined to reassert the royal prerogative and avenge himself on his enemies.

Any hopes that Edward had been tamed for ever were quashed by the rise of new favourites at court. The two Despensers, father and son, were Marcher lords whose greed and ambition were as great as those of Gaveston, but whose ability and sense of political responsibility were far greater. To begin with their story was a repetition of the events of the early part of the reign. Supported by the Despensers the King cast off the control of the magnates and in return for their support they were rewarded with a flow of estates and hard cash. Jealousy led to an inevitable baronial reaction, particularly from the other Marcher lords who resented the expansion of the Despensers' power in South Wales. In 1321 a combination of the Marcher lords and Lancaster forced Edward to agree to the exile of the new favourites.

Here the similarity to the story of Gaveston ends. For in the following year Edward was to act with more resolution than ever before in his reign and completely break the main centres of opposition to royal power. Supported by a movement of moderate opinion in his favour, Edward was able to strike at the Marchers in Wales and force them to surrender. Then he turned his attention to Lancaster whose failure

to support his allies had been the major cause of their defeat. The now isolated Lancaster ruined his chances by asking Robert Bruce to come to his aid with a Scottish army. This act of treachery made him a target for the hatred of the long-suffering north-country men who defeated what was left of Lancaster's great private army at Boroughbridge. At last Edward had the chance to revenge the murder of Gaveston ten years earlier and to pay back his cousin for the years of humiliation after Bannockburn. Lancaster's head was hacked off and the King and the returned Despensers ruled the land.

The long tail of deceit, incompetence, treachery and violence which is the story of the reign of Edward II has a fitting end. The key figure was that of the Queen, Isabella of France. We have seen how shabbily she was treated at her marriage and in the days of Gaveston, but from his death until the early 1320s there seems to have been little discord between the royal couple. They had certainly done their duty in providing for the succession. The future Edward III was born in the year of Gaveston's murder and he was followed by a second son and two daughters. The Queen herself was well looked after and her occasional interventions into politics were those of a peacemaker. But after the defeat of Lancaster in 1322 there were increasing rumours of troubles in the marriage and the Queen emerges as the focus of a new opposition movement determined to overthrow the Despensers. The Despensers returned the Queen's dislike, but seem to have been too confident of their own security and power to do much to check her political ambitions. In 1325 they made a very bad mistake. Relations between England and France had once again come to a head and it was suggested that Isabella, sister of the King of France, might be the best person to re-establish peace. Edward and the Despensers unwisely agreed and the lady who was soon to be known as the 'she-wolf of France' sailed away to find her rather sordid place in the history books.

LEFT Edward III attacks Scotland.

LEFT The citizens of Bristol welcome the arrival of Isabella with the young Prince Edward and her army.

BELOW Isabella and her army at Hereford; in the background is the execution of Hugh Despenser the Younger.

RIGHT This wheel of fortune turned by a queen may well be a comment on the fall of Edward II since it was drawn in the mid-fourteenth century for the Holkham Bible. The King's four sayings are: 'regno, regnavi, sum sine regno, regnabo'. ('I am king, I have been king, I am without a kingdom, I will be king.')

Isabella's court in Paris became a centre for exiles eager to destroy the regime of the Despensers. Amongst these, one of the most powerful was Roger Mortimer, a great Marcher lord, who had been defeated by the King in 1322 but had later escaped from the Tower. To the horror of her brother, the King of France, Isabella openly took Mortimer as her lover and the couple prepared for the invasion of England. The Queen's position was greatly strengthened by the arrival of her eldest son, Edward, to do homage for Aquitaine in the name of his father. Isabella now refused to allow him to return to England and openly defied Edward II and the Despensers.

In 1326 Isabella was forced to leave France as her brother was no longer prepared to put up with the scandal of her liaison with Mortimer. Undismayed, Isabella and Mortimer went to Hainault whose count was persuaded to support her cause with a body of mercenaries by the proposal that his daughter Philippa should marry the young Prince Edward. At last all preparations had been made and, on 23 September, the Queen, her son and Mortimer sailed to Suffolk to invade her husband's kingdom.

That kingdom, long tired of the rule of the King and his favourites, welcomed the Queen with open arms. There was virtually no resistance and Edward II retired with the Despensers to the main base of their strength in the west. The tragedy was slowly played out. One by one the Despensers and the other supporters of the King were captured and executed in various horrible ways.

The King himself was not so easy to deal with. After his capture on 16 November he was persuaded to hand over the great seal of England so that writs could be issued in his name for a parliament. But parliament without a king is no parliament and, in order to give some semblance of legality to the deposition on which nearly everyone was set, it was necessary to persuade the King to renounce the Crown in favour of his son. Edward at this time was a well-treated prisoner of Lancaster's brother, the Earl of Leicester, at Kenilworth Castle. He put up a spirited resistance to the deputation who came to see him, but the threat that his son too might be repudiated persuaded him at last to agree to the terrible demand.

The continued existence of the deposed King was both an embarrassment and a threat to the Queen and Mortimer. Mortimer's solution was to have him secretly and shamefully murdered in the dungeon of Berkeley Castle. Here his gaolers, having failed to starve him to death, satisfied their orders to leave no mark on his body by thrusting a red-hot spit into his bowels. Two months later he was buried in Gloucester Abbey in a lavish ceremony which was attended by both the Queen and the new King.

Edward must always arouse sympathy for the horror of his death and indeed it is easy to feel some sympathy for his whole predicament as king. He is really a standing indictment of hereditary monarchy. He clearly did not have the ability to be a king but yet simply because he was his father's eldest surviving son England had to endure twenty years of his reign. Since these two decades were years when the monarchy was faced with particularly difficult problems and when most of the great earldoms were filled with particularly unpleasant men, the reign of Edward II was one that most people would be glad to forget.

RIGHT Perhaps remorseful for the part he had played in his father's downfall, Edward III erected a splendid tomb at Gloucester Cathedral with a beautiful alabaster effigy of Edward II, depicting him in a pose of serene majesty. Within a few years pilgrims were flocking to the tomb and revering the late king as a saint.

EDWARD III

r. 1327-77

ENGLAND EXPECTS HER MONARCHY to produce at least one great king each century. But even chauvinists like a surprise. Who would have thought that the pathetic Edward II, who presided over England's fortunes for two decades of military failure and baronial quarrels, could have spawned such a magnificent son? And who could have foreseen that this son, the pawn of his scandalous mother and the grasping Mortimer, would not only restore harmony to the English upper classes but would also become the greatest warrior king in Christendom who, thirty years after his accession, was to entertain two captive kings at a series of feasts that were said to be the most splendid since the days of his model, King Arthur?

Edward III was fourteen when he was crowned King of England in 1327, the first king to rule by a parliamentary title. The child who had been born a few months after the murder of his father's favourite, Gaveston, showed no signs that he had inherited his father's low tastes. In every way he appeared to be a conventional representative of his class and there is no evidence that he had any reluctance in joining with his mother to forward his father's deposition. Later he was to make a rather half-hearted attempt to bolster up the royal dignity by building a splendid tomb over his father's grave and encouraging the cult which brought simple pilgrims to the last resting place of a king who had been brought so low, but there seems little doubt that Edward could feel little respect for the man who had brought the English monarchy to its lowest ebb.

Edward's first task was to restore once more the shattered dignity of that monarchy. At first, still a boy, he found himself under the dual control of a regency council of barons led ·by Henry of Lancaster and a court dominated by the arrogant Mortimer, his mother's lover, who was clearly angling for the throne himself. But Edward grew up fast. By 1330 he was ready to strike. With Lancaster's connivance, the King's servants seized Mortimer at Nottingham Castle, as he lay in the Queen Mother's chamber. His supporters disappeared and he was charged before his peers in Parliament with an appalling range of crimes, of most of which he was quite clearly guilty, and executed. Isabella was forgiven and allowed to retire to live a quiet life on a reduced income at Castle Rising in Norfolk.

Following his successful coup Edward pursued a very sensible policy of toleration. There was no wholesale slaughter of Mortimer's followers and most of them were absorbed without difficulty into the life of the kingdom. Mortimer's grandson was later restored to all his grandfather's titles and was to prove a faithful supporter of the King. In this he was no exception for everyone was a faithful supporter of Edward. It was his most remarkable achievement that he was able to turn the baronage into one great happy family with himself as their leader and their friend. It was in fact a family in more senses than one, for Edward strengthened his position by marrying many of his own children to the sons and daughters of magnates, thus tying great houses such as Mortimer and Lancaster to his own dynastic ambitions.

Edward was able to keep the loyalty of his barons because for the most part his tastes were their tastes. Indeed with a diet of war, wine, women, good parties and just enough cultural activity to satisfy the more literate of his colleagues, he could hardly go wrong, especially when the wars provided victory and loot.

Edward presides over jousts held in honour of Catherine, Countess of Salisbury.

Edward was obviously not only a great leader and a great soldier but also a superb host whose court was fully appreciated by the barons. The ethos of the court derived from the romances of chivalry and Edward took great care to promote the knightly image enshrined in the cult of St George and King Arthur. A central feature was the new-style tournament in which the formal, but still highly dangerous, single combat in the lists had replaced the mock battles of the thirteenth century. The culmination of Edward's glorification of the knight and of his promotion of baronial harmony came in 1348 with the establishment of the Knights

3 The Arms of Edward III and Richard II

OPPOSITE ARE ILLUSTRATED the arms of Edward III (top) and
Richard II. It will at once be apparent that a new element
has been introduced into the simple heraldry of their predecessors.
This is the crest.

At the beginning of the fourteenth century it became fashionable to have a modelled device affixed to the top of the helm.
This was called the crest. It was not long before this, like the arms,
came to be regarded as a hereditary symbol. When a man's full
armorial bearings were displayed, as in a picture or on a seal, it
became customary to show the arms on the shield surmounted by
the crest on the helm. As the helm had a short cloak or mantle
attached to it, possibly to deaden the effect of sword blows on the
the neck, this too was depicted. It is referred to as the 'mantling'.

The third seal of Edward III shows an equestrian figure with a
crested helm. The crest is a golden lion *statant* (standing, as
opposed to walking) *guardant*, crowned with an open crown and
standing within a chapeau. The chapeau is an ancient cap of
dignity, the royal chapeau being of crimson velvet lined with
ermine. The royal mantling was also red and ermine.

It may seem curious that the lion in the crest is *guardant*, whereas
if modelled in the round it would naturally look forward over the
front of the helm. This must be regarded as early artistic licence.
The seal engraver must have wanted the lion to look as it did in
the arms and so committed a solecism which has continued down
the centuries. In fact, as the helm of Edward, Prince of Wales, the
eldest son of Edward III, has been preserved at Canterbury
Cathedral, we know that in reality the lion looked forward and
not over his shoulder as he does symbolically in heraldry.

In 1337 Edward laid claim to the throne of France. He symbolised this claim in his royal style, *Rex Angliae et Franciae*, and by
assuming the blue field powdered with gold fleurs-de-lys, which
was the arms of France. He quartered his shield and placed the
French arms in the first and last (France was the senior kingdom in
the medieval hierarchy) and the English in the second and third
quarters.

I have mentioned that Richard II used the attributed arms of
St Edward. This he did in personal rather than formal representations and in the manner illustrated.

R   P

of the Garter, whose twenty-six members were to be 'co-partners both in peace and war'.

This was no idle boast for, if Edward is remembered chiefly for his success in leading his barons to war, he was equally successful in absorbing their natural instinct for criticism of their king in the political arena. Apart from one quickly settled constitutional crisis in 1341 when he learned the lesson that even a popular monarchy has limits, Edward achieved a remarkable record of acceptable government, combining an executive that was sufficiently independent not to make him feel unroyal, with a parliament which was consulted often enough to make its members feel that this was indeed a consultative monarchy and not a tyranny.

To be a successful knightly king it was important to succeed in war, a condition that England had not known for some time. Edward himself had been forced to sign the humiliating Treaty of Northampton in 1328, by which Robert Bruce was at last recognised to have won his long war for Scottish independence. But the great Bruce was to die the following year, leaving his son David, still a child, as king. Here was a chance to play the old game of supporting a Balliol against a Bruce. Meanwhile the standing grievance of Scots presence in the north and continued Scots raids could only be removed on the battlefield. In 1332 Edward went north to York and at the end of the year lay siege to Berwick with a well-trained army. A new spirit and a new professionalism could be seen in the English and when the Scots came south to raise the siege in the following year they were convincingly defeated at the battle of Halidon Hill. Edward had avenged the military failures of his father's reign. More alarming to those who could appreciate it was the method of Edward's victory, for Halidon Hill was the first of those great victories which were to ensure English military

supremacy for the next century by coupling the firepower of the archer with his longbow to the skill of the dismounted man-at-arms.

The English victory forced the Scots back into the hands of their old ally, the king of France. That pattern of encircling alliances already used so adroitly by Philip the Fair against Edward I now once again threatened English possessions both at home and abroad. Indeed there were few English possessions left abroad. Ever since Henry III had signed the Treaty of Paris in 1259 and had agreed to do homage for Gascony, the expansionist policies of the kings of France had tended to nibble away at what remained of the great Angevin Empire. The feudal relationship implied that Gascon subjects of England had a right of appeal to the English king's overlord in Paris. If this right were accepted then the English were sure to lose in the French courts. If it were refused then such disobedience to a feudal superior could mean that Gascony itself was forfeit. By the time that Edward III came to the throne French lawyers and English weakness had reduced the English possessions in southwest France to a narrow coastal strip. Once these last lands had disappeared there was every evidence that a Franco-Scottish alliance might try to nibble away at England as well.

Dynastic accident gave Edward a chance to slip out of this feudal noose. The legal problem would at once be solved if he himself was the king of France. It so happened that the death without male heir of Charles IV in 1328 gave Edward a very respectable claim to the French throne through his mother, Charles's sister. Nothing was said at the time and Edward paid homage to Charles's cousin, Philip VI of Valois, who seized the crown without opposition. But an English claim to the French throne was a useful background to the aggression that was being planned to recover the lost English lands in France, as well as providing a good excuse

RIGHT The battle of Sluys depicted in Froissart's *Chronicles*. The figure of Edward III can be seen aboard his cog *Thomas* on the left.

Quant le roy dan
gleterre z ses ma
reschaulx eurent
ordonnees leurs
batailles et leurs nauires
moult richement z sangemt
Ilz furent tendre et traire
les voiles contremot et vin
drent au vent de quartier
sur destre pour air lauantaige
du souleil qui en venant
leur estoit ou visaige. Si
sauserent que ce se poient
troy nuyre et destyreret vng

pou et tournoyrent tant qz
leuent aleur voulente. Les
normans qui les voyent
tourner se merueilloient
pourquoy ilz le faisoient z
disoient ilz resongnet et
reculent Car ilz ne sont
pas gens pour combattre a
nous. bn voyent les nor
mans sur les bannieres q le
roy dangleterre y estoit per
sonnelement. Si myrent
leurs buisseaulx en bon estat
Car Ils estoient saiges en

for other discontented vassals of Philip to change their allegiance. And of course the withdrawal of the English claim could be a useful bargaining counter in the future.

By 1337 Edward felt strong enough to come out into the open. His plan was to advance into France from the north-east and defeat Philip VI in open battle. Not yet realising quite how significant for the future his tactics at Halidon Hill were to be, Edward felt the need for an offensive alliance of princes from the east and north-east of France to support his invasion. Many of these princes were themselves the victims of French aggression and Edward's diplomacy at first appeared to have been very successful. Meanwhile a great propaganda campaign in England proclaimed Edward's unjust treatment by the French and his rightful claim to the throne of France. The support, both in money and men, was very encouraging and in 1338 Edward crossed over to Antwerp to round up his allies and invade France.

The results of this first stage of what was to become the Hundred Years' War were very disappointing. The only real success was a naval victory in 1340 over a combined French and Genoese fleet at Sluys. But success in the field seemed far harder to achieve. Nothing would induce Philip to come to battle. Nor would he accept Edward's chivalrous invitation to decide the issue by single combat. Meanwhile Edward's allies proved to be hideously expensive and ultimately unreliable. By 1343 it was clear that his attempt to recover his French fiefs had been a very expensive failure. The long years of disappointment ended, however, in 1345 when Henry of Derby, Edward's greatest soldier, recaptured most of Gascony in a whirlwind campaign. Much encouraged, Edward prepared a vast army to invade France.

Edward III was to encounter none of the difficulties met by his ancestors in raising armies to serve abroad. The old feudal element in the army had now been almost entirely replaced by contractual relationships made between the king and his captains. Such captains were for the most part the great of the land and they in turn had no difficulty in raising men to serve under them. The prospect of being paid to fight under so popular a king was an attractive one, soon to be made even more attractive by the realisation that English military superiority would allow them to plunder, burn and rape their way through the richest country in Europe with little danger. The reality of the *chevauchée* was a long way from the ideal of chivalry implied in the cult of King Arthur.

On 12 July 1346 Edward landed with his army of men-at-arms and bowmen on the Cotentin peninsula in Normandy. The orgy of burning and destruction that followed, as Edward moved through France's most prosperous province on his way to link up with his allies in Flanders, was too much for even Philip VI to ignore. The flower of French chivalry was summoned, the oriflamme unfurled and on 26 August Edward III, after crossing the Somme with great difficulty, was brought to bay in a defensive position at Crécy. Confident in their enormous superiority in numbers the French attacked just as the sun was beginning to set. But then 'the English archers stept forth one pace and let fly their arrows so wholly together and so thick that it seemed snow'. Attack after attack broke down under the hail of fire and the steadiness of the dismounted men-at-arms until, by midnight, there was a great wall of dead before the English lines and Philip fled from the field with the remnant of his army. It was the end of the old wars of chivalry.

After the battle Edward led his victorious army to Calais, which after a long siege surrendered in the face of starvation and thus gave the English a base for further assault much nearer to home. The final seal on English triumph came with news from the north. The Scots had taken advantage of Edward's departure to march across the border, only to be crushed by the fighting Archbishop of York, William de la Zouche, in a terrible battle in

LEFT The body of Richard II was brought back to London, on the orders of Henry V in 1413, and interred in the magnificent tomb Richard had prepared for himself and his first Queen, Anne of Bohemia.

thick fog at Neville's Cross near Durham. Amongst the prisoners was King David who was taken to London as the most convincing evidence of the might of English arms.

The next three years are dominated in European history by the first onslaught of the Black Death which is estimated by many historians to have killed one-third of the population of western Europe. The social changes brought about by such a calamity were ultimately to pose new problems for the English monarchy, but its immediate impact on the biography of Edward III was surprisingly small. Normal history did not stop in the face of such clear evidence of God's displeasure with man. The truce made after the battle of Crécy was extended till 1350, but then, with the death of Philip VI and the accession of the optimistic King John, hostilities broke out once more. The English strategy was similar to that of the Crécy campaign. Large-scale raids from both Gascony and Calais filled English pockets and at last drew the French once again to battle. This time success was to fall to the King's eldest son, Edward, the Black Prince, already at the age of twenty-six a warrior with an impressive military reputation. In 1356 he won his astonishing victory at Poitiers in which King John himself was captured and sent back to England to join King David of Scotland in captivity.

After Poitiers the government of France broke down and the country dissolved into virtual anarchy. Peace could still not be made on terms acceptable to both sides and in the winter of 1359-60 Edward III sailed to France to try and impose his will in one last terrible raid. Edward's men suffered terribly in what were appalling climatic conditions and the expedition was a military failure. But it was enough to force the issue. In 1360, by the Treaty of Brétigny, all Edward's original claims were satisfied. His sovereignty over Calais and the whole of Aquitaine, nearly a quarter of France, was recognised and in return he renounced his claim to the French crown.

This remarkable recovery of the English position in France after the disappointments of the last century-and-a-half marks the peak of Edward's achievement as king. As if to demonstrate the vanity of such triumphs the plague returned in 1361 and from then onwards the English hold on French territory was steadily undermined. Delay and incompetence meant that the most important term of the treaty, French acceptance of English sovereignty in Aquitaine, was never ratified. The position was wide open once again. And in 1364 the Dauphin, a very different man from his father, came to the throne as Charles V. He was determined to recover all that had been lost, not in the glory of a great battle, but by steady erosion as English taxation and the indignity of being ruled by Englishmen led the French in Aquitaine to take up arms against their new masters. Castle by castle, town by town, all that the English had won was lost again. English numbers were now too small to hold so great a territory and there was little loot left to attract new adventurers. Many of the great captains were dead and the King's fourth son, John of Gaunt, was a poor military replacement for the ailing Black Prince. By 1374 all that was left was Calais and a coastal strip of south-west France that was smaller than that in English hands at Edward's accession.

Military failure was paralleled at home by a breakdown in the harmony which had been such a characteristic feature of Edward's long reign. The King himself had lost the will to control his kingdom and, as he grew older, sank into a long dotage and increasing dependence on his able but grasping mistress, Alice Perrers. So great a king was still regarded with respect, but popular dislike of the mismanagement of the war and the high taxation that it involved led to increasing criticism of his advisers. The discontent exploded in 1376 with a successful attack by the Commons of the 'Good' Parliament on the King's servants and his mistress who were accused of corruption and pecula-

RIGHT The funeral effigy of Edward III appears to have been taken from his death mask as it shows one side of the mouth twisted with paralysis.

tion. Later that year this unprecedented seizure of initiative by the Commons was reversed and punished by John of Gaunt, now head of the great House of Lancaster, and with the death of his brother the Black Prince in the same year by far the strongest man in the kingdom. Many felt him to be too strong and feared that he planned to disinherit the Black Prince's son, Richard of Bordeaux, and seize the crown himself at his aging father's death.

Gaunt's loyalty was soon to be put to the test for Edward III died the following year. His fortunes had sunk low after the glories of the middle years of his reign but the least that could be said for him was that his reign was one of the few half centuries of the later middle ages that saw no civil war in England. Unfortunately his recipe for harmony was to leave a dangerous legacy. His policy of curbing aristocratic restlessness by leading the barons to war was to involve England in hostilities for many years to come. And his policy of building up the fortunes of his sons was to create a new generation of over-mighty subjects who would attempt to subdue his grandson, Richard II, just as Thomas of Lancaster had tried to subdue his father.

RICHARD II

r. 1377-99

AN UNEASY HARMONY lay over the country when Richard of Bordeaux came to the throne at the age of ten. Court, Commons, Lords and Londoners had played out a somewhat undignified power game as authority slipped from the hands of his aging grandfather, Edward III, in his long dotage. Umpire of this game had been Richard's eldest uncle, John of Gaunt, unpopular but all-powerful, once suspected of coveting the crown himself but now apparently the loyalest supporter of his young nephew's hereditary rights. For the next two decades Gaunt lies like a dark shadow over the land, always suspected of ulterior ends, but always in fact a loyal prop to the Crown, a man whose absence from London was a sure harbinger of trouble. Now, in 1377, it was Gaunt, as Steward of England, who organised Richard's coronation. an impressive affair specifically designed to emphasise the sanctity and magnificence of the hereditary monarchy and to usher in a new period of harmony. The chronicler Walsingham described it as 'a day of joy and gladness ... the long-awaited day of the renewal of peace and of the laws of the land, long exiled by the weakness of an aged king and the greed of his courtiers and servants'. This was to prove a rather optimistic prediction, since the new King, being a minor, was bound to be weak and there was little likelihood that his courtiers and servants would give up that greed which was the hallmark of their trade. Moreover these were troubled times. Forty years of intermittent warfare had left their mark. Great lords now had large private armies tempered in battle which they were prepared to use against other enemies than France. The country was full of disbanded soldiers skilled in the use of the longbow and keenly aware of its power to lay low the mighty. But the war itself had been going badly for a decade. The French celebrated Richard's coronation by raiding the English coast and the people grumbled at the incompetence of their leaders and even

Richard II enthroned, a
portrait by an
unknown fourteenth-
century artist in
Westminster Abbey.
Richard was only ten
years old when he
succeeded his grand-
father, Edward III.

more at the mounting cost of that incompetence. Some were soon to go even further and question the assumption that there should be leaders at all. For had not God made all men equal in his own image?

The boy who had just been crowned was to go the furthest of all England's medieval kings in trying to assert the opposite contention – that God had sent the king to rule the people – a belief that was to cost him his life at the age of thirty-three. Perhaps he could have been successful if he had carried the people behind him as a great warrior. But Richard, son of the Black Prince, inherited only his father's outward appearance and none of his skills at war. Not that he was the coward or weakling of legend – on many occasions in his reign he was to display outstanding courage – but his was the courage of pride, not military prowess.

After his father's death in 1376 the main influences on the young Richard were his gentle and much-loved mother, the thrice-married Joan of Kent, and his tutor, Robert Burley, a knight of his father's household. Soon these influences for moderation and sense were to be overshadowed by his great admiration for his hereditary chamberlain, Robert de Vere, Earl of Oxford, who as the recipient of the King's affection and bounty was to play a part in Richard's reign similar to that of Piers Gaveston in the reign of Edward II. For the moment, however, the influence of the King's court was effectively shackled by the appointment of a regency council chosen specifically so that no one person or group could gain permanent control of policy. Not of the council, but supervising this recipe for weak government, was John of Gaunt.

In 1381 the council was faced with the terrifying challenge of the Peasants' Revolt. This threat to the establishment was extremely well-timed. Most of the army was far from London, in Scotland, France or Wales, and John of Gaunt himself was absent in Scotland negotiating a truce. As the two main armies of peasants marched on London from Kent and Essex, there was therefore little readily available force to resist them. The council had no option but to play for time by appeasing the rebels and standing aside as they took their vengeance on those who seemed to be the authors of their grievances. The young King, 'very sad and sorry', shut up in the Tower with his council and watching his city go up in flames from a garret window, makes a pathetic picture. But in reality he was in no personal danger and the watchword of the rebels was 'King Richard and the True Commons'. This misguided faith in the King as the champion of the people against the cruel hand of authority was to last the whole reign.

Richard, still only fourteen, rose to the occasion. With a great company of nobles he rode out to Mile End to meet the rebel spokesman, Wat Tyler, face to face. Here he carried out his council's policy of appeasement by consenting to every one of Tyler's demands – the abolition of serfdom, a fixed, low rent for all land, and a general amnesty for the rebels. Satisfied, many of the rebels now went home but a hard core of more desperate men remained. There still seemed to be no plan to disperse the rebels by force. The government's only action was to summon yet another meeting with the rebels.

Here at Smithfield Richard played the most dramatic part of his life. Wat Tyler, puffed up with his earlier successes, rode out from the main body of the rebels and in an insulting manner made further demands of the King. But he had gone too far, and the King's retinue attacked and killed him. Realising that they had been betrayed, his supporters began to string their bows, when the young King rode out straight towards the rebels. 'Sirs, will you kill your King?', he cried, 'I am your King, I your captain and your leader. Follow me into the fields.' And the King rode out of the square, followed by the rebels.

The death of Tyler marked the end of the Revolt in London – and ultimately in England.

On the right Richard addresses the army of rebellious peasants; on the left the Lord Mayor strikes down Wat Tyler.

The sheep-like men who had followed their King were rounded up and for the most part sent home. None of the King's promises was fulfilled, though some of the rebels' demands were later implemented by the pressure of economic realities. For the King himself, apart from the enormous boost to his reputation, the Revolt had two lessons. The power of deceit in dispersing trouble had been quite clearly demonstrated, and the almost mystical faith of the rebels in their King was later to stir memories in a man who was to have an almost mystical faith in his own ability to rule.

But the King was not yet a ruler and later in the year an attempt was made to bring some more order to his household. Two experienced men, Richard, Earl of Arundel, and Sir Michael de la Pole, were appointed to attend the King and to counsel and govern his person. This sensible move was to have little effect. The King was growing up and, with the encouragement of de Vere, was beginning openly to resent his leading reins. Very soon there developed an almost inevitable polarisation between the immediate court circle and the magnates which was reflected even between the King's two

Richard greets his second wife, the young Isabella of France, whom he married in 1394.

counsellors; de la Pole winning his friendship, while Arundel, whom he had always disliked, became the leading critic of the court.

Such criticism took a familiar form. The court group were monopolising the King's ear and the flow of bounty from the royal office. They were effeminate, preferring love to war, and were indifferent to the prosecution of the struggle against France and Scotland. The King himself did little to win respect. He threw out insults on all sides, on one occasion threatening the Archbishop with his sword and on another telling the Earl of Arundel to go to the devil when he complained of misgovernment. His reputation sank even lower when in 1385 he led the one major military expedition of his reign to Scotland. The result was a fiasco in which the

Scots army was never encountered and Richard returned to England after about a fortnight, tired of the whole business. The only factor preventing an open break was the continued presence of John of Gaunt and Richard had even had a quarrel with him.

In 1386 events moved to a climax when Gaunt sailed from Plymouth to try and make good a claim to the throne of Castile. In his absence the critics of the court moved into action and demanded the dismissal of de la Pole, the Chancellor. Richard's high-handed answer was to say that he would not dismiss a single man from his kitchen at their insistence. But power lay in his critics' hands and a thinly-veiled threat of deposition from their leaders, Arundel and Thomas of Gloucester, the King's youngest uncle, was sufficient. De la Pole was impeached and the government was placed in the hands of a commission of thirteen.

Richard's first instinct was to try and thwart the opposition by getting the impeachment declared illegal and at the same time raising retainers to fight for him if the situation developed into civil war. This advance notice of his intentions brought matters to a head. Late in 1387, Gloucester and Arundel, now joined by the Earl of Warwick, mustered their men to the north of London and forced Richard to agree to the trial of five of his friends, including de Vere and de la Pole, at a parliament to be held in the New Year. Richard may have agreed, but he did nothing to arrest his friends and de Vere immediately fled to the north-west where he raised an army to impose the King's will on his critics. But to no avail. On 20 December de Vere's army was trapped at Radcot Bridge in Oxfordshire by the forces of the magnates, now augmented by Gaunt's son, Henry of Bolingbroke, and Thomas Mowbray, Earl of Nottingham. De Vere escaped in the mist to die in exile, but others of the King's friends were not so lucky and now had to face the vengeance of their victorious critics.

The Merciless Parliament of 1388 was dominated by the five Lords Appellant, as the leaders of the opposition were called, who, dressed in golden surcoats, led a full-scale attack on the King's household. Those of their original five victims who had not fled suffered the hideous penalties for treason and this fate was shared by other members of the court party, including the King's old tutor, Sir Robert Burley. The King was stunned by this judicial murder of his friends. For the moment there was little he could do but obey the Lords Appellant, now the real sovereigns of the land, but it is clear that for the rest of his reign his deepest wish was to avenge himself for his loss. He was, however, quite prepared to take his time.

The first move came in the following year when the King, now aged twenty-two, an-

nounced his intention to rule as a monarch of full age. No one could query his right to do so and indeed the King made no attempt at this stage to be provocative. Minor changes were made in the household but there was no victimisation and the King went out of his way to be friendly with the Appellants. A further sign of the return to normality came with the arrival of John of Gaunt back from Spain. This atmosphere of peace was to last for six years. During this period Richard as a statesman had some success. In 1394 he scored a personal triumph by bringing a settlement to anarchic Ireland and in 1396 he concluded a very successful twenty-eight years' truce with France.

As the quiet years passed by, Richard was surreptitiously building up his power as king. The most obvious illustration of this was in his creation of a magnificent court, designed to soothe the great and to impress his lesser subjects with his own regality. It was rather different from previous English courts and owed much to continental example, partly as a result of Richard's two foreign marriages, to Anne of Bohemia in 1382 and after her death in 1394 to Isabella of France. Earlier English courts had tended to be geared to war; Richard's court was more peaceful, and though the knightly ideals remained, they tended to be more those of the courtly knight than the knight in the field. Presiding over all was an increasingly flamboyant and dilettante King. But there was nothing dilettante about Richard's activities outside the court. For while faction was hushed in luxury at court, Richard was preparing for future trouble by recruiting in Ireland, Wales and Cheshire a substantial private army who received his pay and wore his famous badge of the white hart.

In 1397 he was ready to strike. Without warning, Gloucester, Arundel and Warwick were arrested, Gloucester being sent to Calais where he was quietly strangled. In September Richard's old enemies were tried before Parliament in a deliberate parody of the Merciless Parliament. Arundel was executed, but Warwick, who pleased the King greatly by making an abject confession of his guilt, was banished for life to the Isle of Man. Now it was the turn of the two younger Appellants, Bolingbroke and Mowbray, to fear for their safety. Both of them had recently been the recipients of the King's favour but they must have been uneasy. In 1398 Mowbray confided his uneasiness to Bolingbroke and the latter, on the advice of his father, John of Gaunt, reported Mowbray's treasonable remarks to the king. Mowbray stoutly denied the accusation of treason and, since there had been no witnesses to the conversation, it was decided that the truth could only be determined by trial by combat. For Richard it seemed a god-sent opportunity to rid himself of the last two of his old enemies at one go. Elaborate preparations had been made for such an exciting contest and the battle was just about to begin, when Richard in the most dramatic way stopped the combat and exiled both the contestants, Bolingbroke for ten years and Mowbray for life.

Now Richard was free to act as he liked. With his enemies dead or in exile and with a large private army at his command, he began to demonstrate the powers of an absolute King. Those who offended him were forced to purchase pardons at a high price. Arbitrary taxes were demanded. The records of Parliament were altered to condemn his enemies as traitors. The rule of law was overridden. Richard himself took on megalomaniac airs, spending recklessly and building a great throne from which on feast-days he could look down on his guests – any who caught his eye being forced to kneel to his majesty. Hatred of the King's Cheshire archers and fear of his power was widespread but there was little that anyone could do. Armed power was controlled by the King and by a group mainly of his kinsmen who had been rewarded with the forfeit estates of Arundel and Gloucester.

In February 1399 John of Gaunt died. In his last years he had been once again a loyal prop to Richard; as Steward he had been in the forefront of the procedure which led to the destruction of Gloucester, Arundel and Warwick, and when in turn his own son was banished he had said not a word. Gaunt's death would have been a good opportunity to pardon his son and maintain the power of Lancaster as a support to the Crown. Instead Richard took the step which was to lead to the rapid curtailment of his arbitrary exercise of power. Bolingbroke's exile was increased to life and his inheritance was seized. No longer could any magnate feel secure in possession of his lands and the determination of the lords to resist the King now only awaited a leader.

Richard was still sublimely confident of his power and that summer he set off to Ireland where the settlement of 1394 had once more dissolved into rebellion. With him he took nearly all his supporters, leaving behind his last remaining uncle, the incompetent Edmund of York, as keeper of the realm. A few weeks later Bolingbroke sailed from Boulogne to claim his inheritance. As he made his triumphal progress from Ravenspur on the Humber across the middle of England, all resistance disappeared and his small number of followers was soon swollen by the retinues of lords eager to greet him. Richard's Cheshire archers, whose arrogance and depredations had been the prop of his power, slunk off to their homes, stripping off their white hart badges as they went. Richard himself, whose personal courage had never been in doubt, left Ireland for the region in which he had most personal support, North Wales. It was a hopeless mission. Betrayed and deserted, he soon found himself a prisoner of Bolingbroke in the Tower, later to be removed to the fatal safety of Lancastrian Pontefract.

So successful had Bolingbroke's enterprise been that he decided himself to seize the throne. The precedent of 1327 could be used to depose King Richard, though he proved more difficult to coerce into abdicating than Edward II.

During his Irish campaign, Richard knights Henry of Monmouth (Henry v), son of the exiled Henry of Bolingbroke who took advantage of Richard's absence to return to England and usurp the throne.

Somewhat more tricky was the fact that Bolingbroke was not the heir of the childless Richard, whose most plausible successor was the eight-year-old Earl of March. But this was no time for a minor, and after much debate Bolingbroke successfully challenged the Crown, 'through the right that God of his grace hath sent me, with the help of my kin and of my friends.' Richard, like Edward ii, was now too dangerous to live, a fact which was made self-evident when on Twelfth Night, 1400, a group of Richard's friends tried to murder Henry iv and all his family preparatory to restoring their captive King. So Richard was secretly murdered in Pontefract Castle and for the rest of his life Henry iv was to be haunted by guilt and doubt – guilt for the murder of an anointed king, and doubt on the part of interested persons that Richard was really dead. It was left for Henry v to lay the bogy for ever when, secure in his Lancastrian inheritance, he removed the remains of the murdered King from their inglorious resting place to the tomb that Richard had built for himself in Westminster Abbey.

4 THE HOUSE OF LANCASTER 1399–1471

Henry IV (in the tall black hat) claims the throne before
Parliament. On the left sit the bishops and abbots, on the
right the lay lords.

HENRY IV

r. 1399–1413

IN SHAKESPEARE'S PLAYS Henry IV is a king condemned to a sterile reign, beset by rebellious barons and an ailing body, punished by divine retribution for his usurpation of Richard's throne. This view is not far off the mark. The King who ruled England and Aquitaine for thirteen troubled years from 1399 to 1413 was a sad contrast to the brilliant, energetic and chivalrous figure of Henry Bolingbroke, Earl of Derby.

Henry was born in April 1366 at Bolingbroke Castle in Lincolnshire, the only son of John of Gaunt and his first wife, Blanche of Lancaster, to survive infancy. His parents were cousins: John was the third surviving son of Edward III and Blanche was the great-great-granddaughter of Henry III. She brought to her husband the vast estates and ducal title of Lancaster, as well as the earldoms of Derby, Lincoln and Leicester. It was in Blanche's memory that Chaucer wrote his *Book of the Duchesse*. She died in her early twenties when Henry was only three.

With his mother dead and his father usually absent on affairs of State, Henry's upbringing was entrusted largely to a group of Lancastrian retainers, some of whom remained his most trusted servants when he became king. He proved himself an able pupil, well equipped to fulfil the ideals of chivalry. With his stocky build and vigorous health he excelled at the martial arts; he was also devout, well read, a pleasant talker and an accomplished musician. Since he was so clearly destined to play an important role in the affairs of State, Henry was not permitted the obscurity of childhood. When Edward III died in 1377, he bore the sword of mercy at the coronation of his young cousin, Richard II, and was afterwards styled Earl of Derby. Three years later, at the age of 14, he

was married to Mary de Bohun, co-heiress of the late Earl of Hereford and Essex, a match which cost his father 5,000 marks. Mary bore him four sons and two daughters, the first being the future Henry V who was born at Monmouth in 1387; the last was Philippa whose birth in 1394 brought about her mother's death. Like Henry's own mother, Mary was in her early twenties when she died.

In the year that saw the birth of his first son Henry also made his precocious entry into the political arena. By joining his name to the cause of the Lords Appellant in their semi-treasonable enterprise to unseat the King's closest counsellors, and by taking arms to block the crossing of the Thames at Radcot Bridge to Richard's special favourite, Robert de Vere, Henry sowed in his royal cousin's mind the mistrust and the thirst for vengeance that was to cost Richard his crown and his life. Indeed there is some evidence that the Appellants meant to depose Richard after Radcot Bridge, but changed their minds when they failed to agree whether Henry or his uncle, Thomas, Duke of Gloucester, should replace him. Instead the Appellants concentrated on the persecution of Richard's servants at the Merciless Parliament of 1388. Here Henry showed a more generous spirit than his fellows by speaking up for at least one of the luckless victims, Sir Simon Burley.

Henry's initiative cannot have pleased his father who remained until his death a faithful servant of the crown, and it would never have taken place unless Gaunt had been absent in Spain, pressing his claim to the throne of Castile. When Gaunt returned to England late the following year (1389) his son retired to the wings and occupied himself for a while with the administration of his estates. But the conventional life of an itinerant nobleman could

In 1398 Richard II exiled Henry Bolingbroke and Thomas Mowbray just as they were about to resolve their quarrel in combat. The sad-faced man in black to the right of the King is probably his elderly uncle, John of Gaunt, a loyal supporter of Richard but father of the rebellious Bolingbroke.

not contain his energies for long, and the autumn of 1390 saw Henry in command of a privately mounted expedition – part adventure, part crusade – to distant Lithuania, where he fought side by side with the Teutonic Knights at the siege of Vilna. The campaign was not arduous – Henry's band of two hundred lost only one knight killed and two captured before returning to Königsberg for Christmas, and he was accompanied throughout by a band of six minstrels. All embarked safely for England in the spring of 1391. In 1392 Henry undertook a more ambitious journey to Jerusalem, travelling overland through Frankfurt (Oder), Prague, Vienna and Venice, and then by ship to Jaffa by way of Corfu and Rhodes. On the return journey he visited Cyprus, Rhodes, Venice, Milan and Paris. This grand tour occupied nearly a year and gave Henry the opportunity to enjoy the hospitality of King Wenceslas of Bohemia, Duke Albert of Austria, the Doge of Venice, the Grand Master of the Knights Hospitaller of St John, King James I of Cyprus (who presented him with a leopard) and the Visconti Duke of Milan. Along the road he impressed his hosts with his handsome appearance, his courtesy and his fluency in English, French and Latin. Now at the age of twenty-seven he could boast the European reputation of a seasoned warrior and courtier.

The five years between Henry's return from Jerusalem and his banishment in 1398 gave little scope for the exercise of these talents. There are signs that he grew restive, for in 1396 it was said that his father forbade him to accept an invitation from William of Hainault, a distant cousin, to join him in a campaign against Friesland. More serious is the story – admittedly unsubstantiated – that Henry was party to the conspiracy, concocted by Gloucester, Arundel and Warwick in July 1397, to imprison both Gaunt and the King for life. Whatever the facts about Henry's complicity, he stood by the King when the three former Appellants were subsequently convicted of treason in Parliament, and shortly afterwards, in September 1397, he was created Duke of Hereford. The motives behind the events that followed are equally obscure. Henry's own account is that Thomas Mowbray (Earl of Nottingham and Duke of Norfolk), the man who apprised King Richard of the conspiracy, told Henry that the two of them were marked men, whom the King would bring down just as he had already brought down the other three Appellants. Mowbray apparently went on to reveal another conspiracy aimed at eliminating all the barons close to the King, including Gaunt and Henry himself. Henry then reported the conversation to his father, who in turn repeated everything to the King. In February 1398 Henry accused Mowbray of treason to his face in the King's presence: in April a court of chivalry at Windsor ordained that the two Dukes should resolve their dispute in a trial by battle, to take place at Coventry in September.

The contest never took place, for Richard decided at the last moment to banish both parties, Henry for ten years, Mowbray for life. Although Henry's sentence was subsequently reduced to six years, he now had ample reason for believing Mowbray's warning that the King meant to undo him. Nevertheless, while Gaunt lived he had no choice but to go. In Paris he was warmly greeted as one of royal rank and resided at the Hotel Clisson. Henry had only been there for four months when he heard the news, in February 1399, of his father's death. It was then that Richard made his literally fatal

mistake of altering Henry's sentence to perpetual banishment and declaring all the possessions of the House of Lancaster forfeit to the crown.

This decision opened Henry's path to the throne. No man could feel safe when the laws of inheritance could be so arbitrarily flouted, and the lifelong service of the father so shoddily repaid in the punishment of the son. Henry's prospects were enhanced by two other recent demises: that of his uncle Gloucester who had reputedly fancied himself as Richard's replacement in 1387 and again in 1397; and that of Roger Mortimer, Earl of March, whom the childless King had recognised as his heir. Mortimer's heir was a seven-year-old boy, Edmund.

When Richard compounded his error by departing on a punitive expedition to Ireland at such a critical juncture (May 1399), Henry gathered his followers and struck. Early in July three small ships bore him and a band of perhaps three hundred men to Ravenspur in Yorkshire. His progress to Pontefract was more of a triumph than a campaign, for he met no opposition, and while the Duke of York, Richard's ineffectual uncle and Viceroy, dithered in the South, Henry's ranks were swelled by Lancastrian retainers and, more significantly, by the heads of the two baronial dynasties who dominated the North, the Percys and the Nevilles. The Percys later claimed that Henry swore an oath at Doncaster declaring that he had come only to claim his inheritance, not to molest the King. If this is true it was more probably a stratagem to broaden the base of his support than a statement of his real intentions.

When the Duke of York, with a small royalist army, gave in to the inevitable and threw in his lot with Henry at Berkeley Castle on 27 July, the outcome was no longer in doubt. Richard, returning from Ireland on the same day, allowed himself to be gulled by assurances that Henry would be content with the restitution of his duchy, and fell into an ambush laid by the Earl of Northumberland's men near Flint. In less than six weeks Henry had made himself master of England. It now remained to take the giant step from de facto master to anointed King.

The manner in which Henry presented his claim was all important, for any loopholes would quickly be seized upon by Richard and his heirs or by any malcontent baronial clique seeking a respectable pretext for rebellion. Many of Henry's subsequent misfortunes stemmed from precisely the fact that his claim was paper-thin by any measure. He could give out that Richard, now a prisoner in the Tower, had abdicated of his own free will and designated Henry his successor by giving him his signet ring, but how could the story be proved? He could claim by right of conquest, but such a right found no sanction in law. He could claim to have been elected by Lords and Commons, but then he might find his prerogative shackled by conditions imposed in return. He could even fall back on the old wives' tale that his Lancastrian ancestor, Edmund, was the elder, not the younger, brother of Edward I, and the crown was being restored to the senior branch of the Plantagenets. In the event, a deliberately vague mixture of all these claims was put before Parliament at the end of September 1399.

Henry's coronation on Monday, 13 October – the feast of the translation of Edward the Confessor – was celebrated in the traditional form, with his eldest son, Henry of Monmouth, bearing the sword of mercy which the new King had himself borne at Richard's crowning. If we are to believe Adam of Usk, a Welsh councillor who wrote a history of Henry's reign, the ceremony was attended by three ill omens for the future: 'First, in the procession, he lost one of his coronation shoes: whence, in the first place, the Commons who rose up against him hated him ever after his whole life long. Secondly, one of the golden spurs fell off: whence, in the second place, the soldiery opposed him in rebellion. Thirdly, at the banquet

Richard imprisoned in the Tower, where he signed a deed of abdication on 30 September 1399, owning himself to be insufficient and useless and asking that his cousin should be a good lord to him.

a sudden gust of wind carried away the crown from his head: whence, in the last place, he was set aside from his kingdom and supplanted by Prince Henry.'

It was the soldiery, or rather the barons whose badges they wore, who struck first. Barely three months of the new reign had elapsed before Henry had to flee from Windsor to London to escape from a rebel coup plotted by the Earls of Kent, Huntingdon and Salisbury and Lord Despenser. All were closely associated with the deposed King and three had recently been deprived of the titles conferred on them by Richard in 1397. But their cause was not yet a popular one and they were beheaded by the mob before they fell into Henry's hands. Some thirty other rebels were executed after the King had presided over their trial at Oxford. Their corpses were chopped up and carted to London in sacks. The ferocity of Henry's response bears witness to the near-panic caused by the revolt of the Earls, a revolt that came so soon after an almost bloodless usurpation. It proved that it was easier to win the throne than to keep it. It also sealed Richard's fate. Although we do not know exactly how or when he died, it must have been with Henry's connivance, if not at his orders. In February 1400 the Council recommended that the body should be publicly exposed in London to scotch any rumours of escape.

The autumn of 1400 saw the beginnings of an intractable guerrilla war in Wales. It began as a purely local quarrel between a Welsh squire, Owen Glendower and his English neighbour, but quickly flared into a national uprising. Glendower's successful resistance was certainly one of the causes of a far more serious crisis which erupted in 1403 with the revolt of Henry's hitherto most powerful supporters, the Percys. The Earl of Northumberland's son, Henry Percy, better known as Hotspur, had taken umbrage when the King refused him the ransom of an important Scottish prisoner, the Earl of Douglas. He also had some grievances about the lack of support he had received while serving as Henry's lieutenant in North Wales. These seem slender grounds for revolt, but Hotspur was a vain, impetuous man and he carried the rest of his family with him. To make matters worse, the Percys were connected with Glendower by marriage. Glendower's daughter

was married to Edmund Mortimer, uncle of Richard II's heir and brother of Hotspur's wife.

It was the most testing crisis of Henry's reign and he solved it with his usual speed and decision. He at once marched west to Shrewsbury, which was held by Prince Henry, and there brought Hotspur and his uncle, the Earl of Worcester, to battle before they could join forces with Glendower or receive help from the Earl of Northumberland. The savage battle fought near Shrewsbury on 21 July 1403 ended in a royal victory when Hotspur himself was slain. Worcester was executed two days later but Northumberland was spared after promising to surrender his castles and his office as Constable. Henry's restraint earned him little credit, for the Earl proved an implacable conspirator. Early in 1405 Thomas Mowbray, the Earl Marshal and son of the late Duke of Norfolk, was involved in a plot to spirit the Earl of March away from Windsor to Wales. The fugitives were caught by Henry himself at Cheltenham. The nineteen-year-old Earl of March was pardoned and promptly made off to join Northumberland in another armed rising. In the meantime Northumberland was said to have signed a compact with Glendower and Mortimer partitioning England between them. Richard Scrope, Archbishop of York, was also persuaded to join the plot, and posted on the Church doors a manifesto accusing Henry of usurping the throne against his oath, murdering King Richard, and levying taxes he had promised to abolish. The rebel army was dispersed and the Archbishop and the Earl Marshal captured by the Neville Earl of Westmorland before Henry arrived. This time there was to be no mercy. A great scandal ensued when not only Mowbray but also the Archbishop were executed, and the unidentified illness which partially paralysed Henry shortly afterwards was said to be God's punishment for this impiety. Northumberland fled to Scotland and was not finally called to account until February

The coronation of Henry IV. His eldest son, Prince Henry, carries the sword of state.

1408 when he died in a skirmish with the Sheriff of Yorkshire's men on Bramham Moor.

After Northumberland's death Henry's throne was secure. The Scottish border had been relatively quiet since 1406, when the young King James I was captured on his way to France. Even the Welsh revolt gradually petered out when Harlech Castle was starved into submission in 1409. The French who had sent troops to Glendower's aid in 1405 were preoccupied with civil war between the rival factions of Burgundy and Armagnac. But the King's health had been broken. From 1406 onwards he was frequently immobilised or bedridden by a mysterious disease that contemporaries called leprosy, and in the winter of 1408-9 there were fears for his life. A famous physician was summoned from Lucca, and Henry made his will. No doubt the campaigns of 1399 to 1405 had taken their toll. So too had the burdens which these campaigns imposed on his administration. To wage war in Scotland

and Wales was prodigiously expensive and lack of money proved a constant headache. No less than ten treasurers in thirteen years struggled to balance the books, but none succeeded. 'There is not enough money in your treasury to pay the messengers', wrote one of them in 1401. Almost annually between 1400 and 1407 Henry had to endure a running battle with his Commons over the granting of taxes and customs dues. Making capital of Henry's political weakness, the Commons aired all their grievances about the extravagance of his household, the membership of his Council, the grants made to his followers and the uses to which previous subsidies had been put, before assenting to taxation. The Commons did not hate Henry, as Adam of Usk implied, but they certainly treated him to more outspoken criticism than any other medieval king had to face. If Henry resented this, he seldom showed it. He met their demands with patient moderation, always careful to avoid a confrontation.

Adam of Usk's third point – that Henry was set aside and supplanted by his son – is an exaggeration, but it has a kernel of truth. Until 1407 the Prince had his hands full campaigning in Wales, and enjoyed his father's complete confidence. In the later years of the reign there were signs of tension, and sometimes even of opposition. As the King's health failed his eldest son expected to play a more prominent role in government. At first, however, Henry IV preferred to entrust his affairs to the veteran Archbishop Arundel, whom he appointed Chancellor. During this time the Prince emerged as the nucleus of an opposition within the Council.

In December 1409 the Chancellor was pressured into resignation and Prince Henry took over as the Council's president. For two years the Prince remained in control, but in November 1411 a serious quarrel with the King brought about the dismissal of his Council and Arundel's return. The causes of the quarrel are obscure, but it seems likely that Henry was goaded into action by the suggestion that he should abdicate

in the Prince's favour. Polite formality was observed on both sides, but unhappily the matter was not allowed to rest there. In the following May there were rumours that the Prince was raising an army to depose his father, and he felt compelled to write a long letter from Coventry denying the charge. He then came before the King in London with a large following to demand the punishment of his slanderers.

Any further development of this sordid family quarrel was cut short before the year was out by the fact that Henry was obviously dying. By now his face as well as his body was badly disfigured. The end came on 20 March 1413 at Westminster Palace. The Prince was at his side and received his blessing.

So died the first of the Lancastrian kings; an old man at 47, wasted by disease and worn out by the cares of State. The crown so easily won in 1399 had brought him little joy since. For a king who strove so hard to do the right thing and a man whose strict piety in Church matters is well attested, his misfortune must have seemed a divine punishment for the sin of usurping Richard's throne. 'I Henry, sinful wretch,' he wrote in his will of 1408, '... ask my lords and true people forgiveness if I have misentreated them in any wise.' But his reign cannot be judged a failure. The fact remains that he founded a new dynasty and passed his kingdom intact to his heir. For a usurper this was a considerable feat, particularly in an age when legitimism lay at the heart of political theory and action. The rebel barons had been defeated, Scotland and France neutralised, and the Welsh restored to their allegiance. Even the Commons, for all their reluctance to pay taxes, never questioned Henry's title. Though he was seldom the master of events, he ruled with a mixture of decision, perseverance and tact that few kings could have matched in his place. This achievement goes a long way towards meeting the claim of at least one chronicler, Thomas Walsingham, that Henry IV 'for thirteen and a half years less five days reigned gloriously'.

HENRY V

r. 1413–22

HENRY IV SUCCEEDED, against the odds, in founding a royal dynasty; his son, against incalculably greater odds, conquered an empire. Two years from his father's death Henry V destroyed the chivalry of France at Agincourt. Within eight years he entered Paris as Regent of France. Within nine he was dead.

Henry V is a rare example of the men who shape history to their own design. The spectacular achievements of his reign are in a very real sense the achievements of one man. Well before he came to the throne in March 1413 his ability was proven beyond doubt. Created Prince of Wales at his father's coronation in 1399, shortly after his twelfth birthday, he was soon taking an active part in the administration of the principality. When Owen Glendower's rebellion signalled the beginning of a national Welsh uprising in 1400, the Prince's household was established at Chester with Henry Percy as his guardian. Hotspur, a seasoned campaigner in his late thirties, provided Henry's early lessons in the art of war. These stood him in good stead three years later, in 1403, when the fifteen-year-old Prince fought his first pitched battle, with Hotspur, now turned rebel, commanding the opposing army. The Battle of Shrewsbury was a viciously contested action, lasting several hours. Henry commanded his father's right and showed his mettle by fighting the day out despite being wounded in the face by an arrow.

The royal victory at Shrewsbury ended Hotspur's career, but Glendower's revolt absorbed the Prince's energies for the next five years. Here he learned the value of a small mobile striking-force to harry his enemy and at the siege of Aberystwyth in 1407 he first experienced the tedium of starving an impregnable fortress into surrender. Constantly short of funds with which to pay his troops, he also

Portrait of Henry V by an unknown artist.

learned the importance of putting war on a proper financial footing.

The Prince did not spend all his time at war in the valleys. From 1406 onwards he was also making his presence felt at meetings of the Council, the body of advisers whom the King selected to run his administration. It was in this year that rumours first began to circulate about the Prince wanting his father to abdicate because of his ill-health. In the winter of 1408-9 Henry very nearly got his way when a particularly bad attack of illness almost killed Henry IV. The Prince had to wait and chafe until the spring of 1410 when he took over as the acknowledged leader of the Council in place of Archbishop Arundel. His father seems to have accepted this situation with some reluctance, and when there was more talk of abdication in the autumn of 1411 he reacted smartly by sacking his son and bringing the Archbishop back as Chancellor. However, the Prince had made a very good impression during his year and a half of office, and afterwards the Commons thanked him handsomely for his efforts.

The differences between the Prince's supporters and Archbishop Arundel's party owed more to temperament and personal loyalties than to political issues. The Archbishop and the Neville Earl of Westmorland represented the older generation, long-time associates of Henry IV, who probably found the Prince's impatience to rule as galling as did the ailing King. They were backed by most of the senior clerics who formed the backbone of any medieval administration. Among the Prince's councillors were two young earls who shared his taste for military adventure – the Archbishop's own nephew Richard, Earl of Arundel, and Thomas Beauchamp, Earl of Warwick. But Prince Henry's chief support came from his Beaufort half-uncles, Henry and Thomas – John of Gaunt's sons by his third wife, Katherine Swynford. Thomas Beaufort acted as Chancellor while the Prince headed the Council, but his younger brother Henry, Bishop of Winchester, was the abler of the two, a financial and administrative genius destined to play a leading role in the next two reigns. The Beauforts were shrewd enough to recognise that the future lay with the Prince and backed him accordingly. It was Bishop Henry who took it upon himself to suggest Henry IV's abdication.

There was, however, one political issue with broad implications for the future, on which Prince Henry took an opposite line to Arundel and his father. It concerned France. From the beginning of Henry IV's reign relations with France had been hostile. Charles VI of France, whose daughter had married Richard II, refused to recognise Henry IV as King, and when Henry sent the widowed Isabella back to France in 1400 he declined to part with her jewellery. The French renewed their claims to the Duchy of Aquitaine, raided Calais and sent help to Glendower in Wales. But these attacks were ill coordinated and half-hearted. Charles VI suffered from frequent bouts of insanity during which his brother, the Duke of Orleans, and his cousin, the Duke of Burgundy, fell to quarrelling. In 1407 the quarrel degenerated into civil war when the Duke of Orleans was assassinated at the instigation of his Burgundian rival, John the Fearless. For the English, hitherto paralysed by their own internal problems, this was a heaven-sent opportunity to divide and conquer. The only problem was which side England should choose as her ally against the other. Henry IV favoured the Orleans faction who called themselves the Armagnacs; his son preferred the Burgundian alliance.

In October 1411, while the Prince still controlled the Council, an English expedition commanded by the Earl of Arundel sailed to Burgundy's aid. But when the Prince was dismissed English policy went into reverse, and in 1412 his brother, Prince Thomas, crossed to Normandy at the head of a much larger army to help the Armagnacs. This second expedition was intimately bound up with the ill feeling between the Prince of Wales and the King. Prince Thomas, now created Duke of Clarence, had sided with his father and was thus chosen to command in his elder brother's place. Prince Henry refused to go and was accused of staying behind in order to stage a coup. His opponents at court also charged him with misappropriating funds intended for the defence of Calais.

The Prince responded by sending a stream of messengers to important people explaining his case, and won from his father a promise to have the accusations against him examined in Parliament. In September 1412 he appeared in London with such 'an huge people' of retainers that fears of an armed take-over were again aroused.

Whatever we make of the poorly documented events of Henry IV's last year, it does seem that the King's final illness and death defused a potentially dangerous situation, with the royal family and the aristocracy splitting into factions, mutual accusations of disloyalty and malpractice, and retainers gathering to protect their lords. It also appears that Prince Henry behaved with an arrogance born out of the absolute conviction that he was in the right.

When the old King was finally dead and the Prince crowned Henry V, the atmosphere changed markedly for the better. Among the new King's first concerns was to extend the olive branch to those who had suffered under the previous reign. The Earl of March, whose father had been named as Richard II's heir, had his estates restored to him, the Earls of Huntingdon and Oxford were returned to favour, and the body of Richard II was reburied with pomp at Westminster. Perhaps Henry retained some affection for the murdered King who had taken him to Ireland in 1399 but declined to use the boy as a hostage when his father came to seize Richard's throne. But it was also a shrewd piece of propaganda, a call to bury old grievances and rally round to Henry's grand design – the conquest of France. The policy paid off, for two years later the only aristocratic conspiracy of Henry's reign was reported to the King by the Earl of March himself.

Clarence's expedition of 1412 had achieved nothing: as soon as he landed the Armagnacs changed their minds about seeking English help and bought him off. Henry still preferred the Burgundian alliance, but this time he was less eager to show his hand. He negotiated with the Armagnacs as well, forcing them to outbid their rivals for England's support or neutrality. Early in 1415 the Armagnacs offered him substantial territorial concessions in Aquitaine and the hand of Charles VI's daughter, Catherine, along with a dowry of 600,000 crowns. But Henry wanted much more than that. He told them he would settle for nothing less than the whole of the old Angevin Empire, lost in the reign of King John, including Normandy, Maine and Anjou. The extravagance of this claim, which no French government could possibly accept, suggests that the negotiations were just diplomatic window dressing. Henry had already made up his mind to go to war. By the time negotiations were broken off in June 1415 Parliament had already voted a double subsidy for the campaign, an army had been raised and the necessary transport requisitioned.

On 11 August Henry sailed from Southampton with an army of about 10,000 archers and men-at-arms. The army landed on the Norman coast and spent the first month of the campaign besieging Harfleur which surrendered on 22 September. By now the season was too far gone for a march on Paris, and Henry settled for a cross-country march to Calais. Shortly after crossing the Somme he found his way blocked at Agincourt by a French army that outnumbered his own by three to one. On 25 October the two armies faced one another in a pitched battle, the French cavalry attacking the English archers in a massed charge on a narrow front. These disastrous tactics ended in a bloodbath for the chivalry of France, who lost perhaps 6,000 men dead and many more captured. Henry lost less than 400, including the Duke of York and the Earl of Suffolk.

The march to Calais had been a grave strategic risk, again the action of a man who never experienced an iota of self-doubt. The rewards were stupendous, not only in France where his bargaining position was immensely strengthened, but at home too where his people were now united to a man behind their victorious King. Agincourt achieved in a single day the

goal that Henry IV had laboured for thirteen years to attain. For the next five years England's energies were harnessed exclusively to the completion of Henry's French conquests.

The task that confronted the King was still formidable. Pitched battles were rare in medieval warfare and after Agincourt the French were far too respectful of Henry's prowess to risk a second annihilation. The conquest of Normandy was to be a lengthy and tedious catalogue of sieges, of towns battered, starved or terrified into submission. This was a radical departure from the traditional forms of the Hundred Years' War – the large-scale mounted raids or *chevauchées* which devastated the countryside in search of plunder. From the very beginning Henry came in the guise of France's rightful King, determined to establish a permanent English presence in the country he subdued.

Before the second expedition sailed in 1417 the King achieved a notable diplomatic triumph. For four months in 1416 Henry entertained the Holy Roman Emperor, Sigismund, who arrived as a mediator and departed as an ally after putting his name to the Treaty of Canterbury. The Treaty is proof of how well Henry argued his claim to the French crown and dispelled the notion that he was a military adventurer taking advantage of the civil war distracting his neighbours. In October 1416 the two monarchs conferred with Duke John of Burgundy at Calais.

On 1 August 1417 Henry set foot in Normandy again. Caen fell in September, followed by Verneuil and Falaise before Christmas. John the Fearless fulfilled his part of the bargain struck at Calais by threatening Paris from the north. By August 1418 the English controlled the whole of Lower Normandy and Henry had invested the key target of Rouen. The Norman capital was too strong for an assault, but the city finally succumbed to starvation in January 1419. The remainder of the resistance throughout Normandy crumbled and by spring Henry was master of the whole Duchy.

At this point diplomacy again took precedence over military affairs. In July 1419 Henry's successes were seriously threatened by a reconciliation between the Burgundians and the Armagnacs (now known as the Dauphinists). But Henry's luck held. The murder of the Duke of Burgundy by the Dauphin's men on 10 September 1419 showed that the mutual hatred of the French factions was still more powerful than their fear of the English aggressor. The Burgundians were now ready to pay any price for Henry's alliance. By Christmas Philip, the new Duke of Burgundy, had given way to all Henry's demands: the mad Charles VI would retain the crown during his lifetime but Henry would be recognised as his heir and would marry his daughter Catherine. In return Henry was pledged to avenge the Duke's murder and make war on the Dauphin, who still controlled most of France south of the Loire. These terms were embodied in the Treaty of Troyes in May 1420. On 2 June the King and Catherine were married at the altar of Troyes Cathedral, and on 1 December the royal couple entered Paris in triumph.

Henry had been absent from England for three and a half years when he returned in February 1421 for the Queen's coronation. A royal progress followed which took the couple through Bristol, the Welsh Marches and Leicester to the northern capital of York, then back to Westminster by way of Lincoln and Norwich. It was a brief and doubtless welcome respite, during which the Queen conceived the future Henry VI. But whatever pleasure it gave the King was cut short by the news of his brother Clarence's death on a raid in the Loire country – a bitter and timely reminder that his task in France was still only half done.

In June he returned to the wars, and the winter months passed in the protracted siege of Meaux, one of the last Dauphinist strongpoints north of the Loire. The town's capitulation in May 1422 was to be Henry's last triumph. During the winter he contracted an illness – probably dysentery – which he could not shake

LEFT A detail from Henry V's chantry chapel in Westminster Abbey showing him in full armour at the battle of Agincourt.

off. In July he had to be carried in a litter to the siege of Cosne on the Loire. A few days later he had to turn back, and in the early morning of 31 August he died at Bois de Vincennes.

How can one assess the tremendous achievement of Henry v's nine short years as king? Certainly he owed a great deal to luck and circumstance. At Agincourt the blundering tactics of the French contributed as much to the English victory as did Henry's generalship. His subsequent successes could not have been achieved without the internecine hatred of the two French factions. As one contemporary cynic noted, the English entered Paris through the hole in the Duke of Burgundy's skull.

But Henry was much more than a soldier with fortune on his side. He was a statesman with a range of exceptional talents that enabled him to bend fortune to his ends. Like Napoleon, Henry v was a glutton for hard work and no detail concerning the administration of his conquests was beneath his notice. The logistical effort of supplying the army of 1417 on foreign soil for more than three years was a feat in itself equal to the victory of Agincourt. During his campaigns in France he insisted even on dealing personally with all petitions forwarded from his Parliaments in England. Contemporaries, his enemies as much as his friends, were profoundly struck by Henry's sense of justice, which was linked with a strict adherence to the tenets of Catholic piety. As Prince of Wales he had personally presided over the funeral pyre of an unrepentant Lollard – one of those proto-Protestants who foreshadowed the Reformation of the succeeding century. On the way to Agincourt he had a man hanged for robbing a church. 'He was a Prince of Justice', wrote the Burgundian chronicler Chastellain, 'he gave support to none out of favour, nor did he suffer wrong to go unpunished out of regard for affinity'. Underlying all Henry's qualities was his ironclad will-power which not only drove

him but also provided the inspiration for others. He gathered around him a team of outstanding military and administrative ability, most notably his Beaufort uncles and his brothers, Thomas the soldier and John, Duke of Bedford, who became Regent of France on Henry's death. No other fifteenth-century king was so ably or so devotedly served, and indeed most found more reason to fear their relatives than to favour them. Another Frenchman observed shrewdly that Henry did not look like a soldier at all, but rather possessed the gravity of a cleric. This view is confirmed by his portraits which reveal a lean, hatchet face dominated by sombre brown eyes, pursed lips and a long, thin nose. The face contains more than a hint of the fanatic, so impatient to supplant his father and subordinate himself to the single obsession of conquering France. He certainly had little time to spare during his reign for any private life or domestic comforts. Even on his deathbed he was immersed in plans and provisions for his son's minority, without seeking or receiving a visit from the child's mother. There is a frightening quality about this all-conquering, all-competent zealot, which could account for the legends that sprang up after his death of his wild and boisterous youth as Prince of Wales. These tales lend his character a posthumous humanity not apparent in his life.

Perhaps Henry was lucky that he died young and passed straight into legend. Even before his death there are indications that his heroic designs were parting company with his country's interests. The Commons were complaining of his prolonged absences. From 1420 Parliamentary grants to prosecute the wars were proving harder to come by. The Dauphin was still master of more than half of France and future success depended on the continuing split between his party and the Burgundians. It was a heavy inheritance to leave in the care of the nine-month-old infant, Henry VI.

Henry encamped at the siege of Rouen, in 1418. The siege lasted for nearly
six months before starvation forced the city to submit.

HENRY VI

r. 1422–71

SOME FIFTY YEARS AFTER Henry V was laid to rest, a lonely old man was quietly done to death in the Tower of London after he had lost his wits, his two kingdoms and his only son. Everything about the reign of Henry VI is in stark contrast to that of his father. But the first and most striking contrast is that whereas the father had to wait with ill-concealed impatience for his inheritance, the son had his thrust upon him before he was one year old.

From the earliest age Henry was frequently paraded at public ceremonies, either seated on his mother's lap or tottering on his own feet between his royal relatives. As he grew up he saw progressively less of the Queen, who had formed a liaison with a Welsh squire named Owen Tudor and was busy raising a second family. In 1428 he was placed in the care of Richard Beauchamp, Earl of Warwick, and one of his father's most trusted lieutenants. Warwick was instructed to 'teach him nurture, literature, language and other manner of cunning, to chastise him when he doth amiss and to remove persons not behoveful nor expedient from his presence'. Henry proved himself a precocious child. At the age of ten, so his governor reported, he was questioning whether he, a king, should be chastised for his misdemeanours and taking an interest in matters 'not behoveful'. The Council was called in to read the riot act.

At a tender age the boy-King was introduced to the most intractable problems of his early reign – the deteriorating situation in France and the unedifying squabbles of those closest to the throne. The emergence of Joan of Arc and the crowning of the Dauphin as Charles VII at Rheims in 1429 heralded the Valois revival. Bedford, the English Regent in France, was sufficiently worried to call for his nephew's own coronation and to bring him over to France for

a state visit. On 2 December 1431 Henry was crowned King of France at Saint Denis in Paris. However, the tide had turned against the English. Duke Philip of Burgundy knew it and was looking for a way out of his alliance. In 1435 he made his separate peace with Charles VII at Arras; in the same year the valiant Bedford, whose earlier successes had almost matched those of Henry V, breathed his last. From that point it was all downhill. When Henry heard of Burgundy's desertion he burst into tears.

At home the trouble was caused by Henry's other and infinitely less able uncle, Humphrey, Duke of Gloucester. Gloucester was a fine scholar but a poor statesman. Though he was nominated Regent of England in Henry V's will, his peers distrusted him sufficiently to insist that he govern with the advice of the Council, not as Regent but as Protector. He quarrelled incessantly with that other pillar of the Lancastrian establishment, the portly Bishop Beaufort, and twice, in 1425 and 1432, their animosity threatened an outbreak of violence. In 1434 Gloucester even picked a quarrel with his brother Bedford, accusing him of mismanaging the war. Henry, in an early display of well-meant but flat-footed conciliation, attempted to mediate between his uncles in person and declared both parties innocent of blame.

Despite their differences the Council did see Henry safely through his minority, which came to an end without a formal declaration to that effect in 1437. The story of the next thirteen years is such a dreary record of infighting at court, disorder in the shires and reverses in France that one is tempted to dwell instead on the anecdotes of Henry's Christian virtues compiled by his biographer and one-time confessor, John Blacman. It is true that he displayed qualities that would have done credit to a monk or a

LEFT The birth of Henry VI at Windsor Castle on 6 December 1421.

mendicant friar and that his two great foundations at Eton and King's College, Cambridge,
in 1440 and 1441 still preserve his memory. He
was chaste, pious and generous. He abhorred
all forms of bloodshed, and intervened frequently to spare the lives of criminals and traitors. On one occasion, while riding through
Cripplegate into London, 'he saw over the gate
there the quarter of a man on a tall stake, and
asked what it was. And when his lords made
answer that it was the quarter of a traitor of
his ... he said, "Take it away. I will not have
any Christian man so cruelly handled for my
sake"'. This story, and others like it, have been
much quoted by Henry's admirers, who see
him as a man dragged down by the coarse
spirit of his time.

But the truth is that even Blacman's eulogies
sometimes cast Henry in a faintly ridiculous, if
not downright foolish, light. He stormed out
in a huff one Christmas when 'a certain great
lord brought before him a dance or show of
young ladies with bared bosoms.' He rebuked
the scholars of Eton for visiting his own court
over the Thames at Windsor 'bidding them not
to do so again, lest his young lambs should
come to relish the corrupt deeds and habits of
his courtiers.' As a youth he spied on his servants
'through hidden windows of his chamber, lest
any foolish impertinence of women coming
into the house should ... cause the fall of any
of his household.' 'From his youth up he always
wore round-toed shoes and boots like a farmer's
... a long gown with a rolled hood like a
townsman, and a full coat reaching below his
knees, with shoes, boots and footgear wholly
black, rejecting expressly all curious fashion of

clothing.' On feast days, when custom demanded that he wear the crown, Henry atoned
with a hair shirt next to his skin.

So it goes on. These were not the attributes
of a king and the truth is that Henry had no real
wish to act like one. His impatience with secular affairs emerges from another Blacman story:
when 'a certain mighty duke' knocked at his
door the King complained to his confessor 'they
do so interrupt me that by day or night I can
hardly snatch a moment to be refreshed without disturbance.' There lay one half of the
coming tragedy. The King was the linchpin of
medieval government. It was not just a quaint
custom that even during Henry's infancy official documents referred to him as King in fact
as well as name. His job was to initiate, to unite,
to inspire – the very things that made Henry v
such a success. Henry vi proved himself incapable of all three.

There was, however, one regal function that
Henry could not lay aside. A vast range of
patronage – from the great offices of state to the
smallest perks of feudal law – lay at his disposal
and had to be disposed. This was the other half
of the tragedy. Henry gave too freely and he
often gave to the wrong people. The result was
that after 1437 the executive power of the
Crown fell into the hands of a narrow clique of
men who had access to Henry. Two of these
were William de la Pole, fourth Earl of Suffolk,
and William Ayscough, Bishop of Salisbury.
Both rose to eminence because of the key positions they occupied in the King's household.
Suffolk, a veteran soldier with fourteen years'
continuous service in France to his credit, became Henry's Steward in 1435 and the Bishop

The English claim to the French throne is shown in this genealogy of the ancestry of Henry vi. On the right are his
English forbears beginning with Edward i; in the centre is the direct French line and on the left the collateral line.
Edward ii is shown married to Isabella of France, whose three brothers, Louis x, Philip v, and Charles iv all died
childless. The English claimed that the throne should then have passed to Isabella's son Edward iii. The French invoked
the Salic Law which debars women from the throne and the French crown passed to a nephew of Charles iv, Philip of
Valois, whose line leads down to Catherine, wife of Henry v and mother of Henry vi. Thus Henry vi is offered two
crowns by the angels. The figures at the foot of the page are two regents of the young king: left, Richard, Duke of
York, father of Edward iv and Richard iii and, right, Humphry, Duke of Gloucester, brother of Henry v.

When he was nine years old Henry VI was taken to France and crowned in St Denis in December 1431. He is the only sovereign to have been crowned both in England and France.

was his confessor. Henry's great-uncle, Bishop Beaufort, also retained his influence until his retirement from political life in 1443 at the ripe old age of sixty-seven. These men were soon under attack for their excessive influence over the King, and resorted to some fairly shady manoeuvring in order to retain their monopoly. In 1439 Gloucester complained to the King that Beaufort and his friends had cut off 'me, your sole uncle, together with my cousin of York ... and many other lords of your kin from having knowledge of any great matters that might touch your high estate and realm.' In the summer of 1441 the King's advisers replied with an accusation of sorcery against Gloucester's wife, Eleanor. The Duchess was forced to undergo public penance in the streets of London, and Gloucester, though not directly involved, was neatly discredited.

France was still the burning political issue of the day, with Henry's advisers favouring a peaceful accommodation while Gloucester followed a hawkish line that endeared him to the London mob. The doves of course prevailed and in 1444 Suffolk secured his ascendancy at court by arranging for Henry to marry Charles VII's niece, the fifteen-year-old Margaret of Anjou. The King gratefully added a marquisate to the long list of Suffolk's preferments. Unhappily the result of the marriage was not a lasting peace with France but the renewal of war which led speedily to the loss of all English territories in France save Calais. Margaret was carefully briefed before arrival to work on her future husband and persuade him to surrender the county of Maine. Henry duly promised to do so, but without telling anybody. When the news leaked out, it was greeted with a surge of patriotic outrage. The spring Parliament of 1447 had to meet in Bury rather than risk the fury of the Londoners, and Gloucester was arrested on arrival to be charged with planning an uprising. His death in confinement a week later quickly gave rise to rumours that Suffolk had ordered his murder. To retrieve his tarnished reputation at home, Suffolk suddenly turned hawk in France and launched a provocative attack on Charles VII's ally, the Duke of Brittany. Charles at once retaliated by invading Normandy. Rouen fell in October 1449, Caen in the following July, and by September the whole duchy was in French hands. In 1451 Charles turned on Gascony and took Bordeaux. Two years later a relieving force under the Earl of Talbot was cut to pieces at Castillon. The Duchy of Aquitaine, after nearly 300 years in England's possession, was lost forever.

Not even Henry could save Suffolk from the repercussions of the loss of Normandy. In February 1450 the King's 'priviest and best trusted' adviser was impeached in Parliament, charged with every sort of mismanagement and embezzlement. Henry did his best to get him out of harm's way by banishing his favourite, but the ship carrying him to safety was intercepted in the Channel and Suffolk was executed on the spot. In truth he deserved little better, and not only because his bungling brought about the catastrophe in France. For years he had been feathering his nest while Henry's Exchequer plunged into debt. He had presided over a general slackening of control at the centre which in turn bred lawlessness, corruption and unrest throughout the kingdom. His most fitting memorial is the Kentish rising known as Cade's Rebellion which exploded shortly after his death in May 1450. The rebels'

Henry VI as a young man. His pointed chin and nose bear a marked resemblance to the portrait of his father on page 125 but his face looks sensitive and weak in comparison.

chief demand was for the punishment of 'the false progeny and affinity of the Duke of Suffolk'. 'His false council', they concluded, 'has lost his (the King's) law: his merchandise is lost: his common people are destroyed: France is lost. The King himself is so placed that he may not pay for his drink.' 'In this same time', wrote a later chronicler, 'the realm of England was out of all good governance, as it had been many days before, for the King was simple, and led by covetous counsel, and owed more than he was worth.'

It would be foolish to follow the polite fiction of the time and exonerate Henry of all blame for these events. Government was in the hands of the men he himself had chosen. There was no lack of critics to tell him what was wrong. Nor was he incapable of action: he would intervene readily enough when his favourites came under fire. The best that can be said of Henry is that he was quite exceptionally naive.

The disaster which overtook Suffolk did nothing to open the King's eyes. In August his defeated lieutenant in France, Edmund Beaufort, Duke of Somerset, returned to London and stepped into the vacant niche of court favourite. Somerset was a nephew of the departed Bishop and associate of Suffolk. It was bad enough that the new favourite should be tainted by failure in France and friendship with Suffolk's circle: but more serious in the long term was Somerset's long-standing personal feud with Richard, Duke of York, the greatest landowner in England after the King, who had long been at the losing end of a running fight with the Beauforts over the conduct of the war. As a supporter of the Duke of Gloucester he had been excluded from Henry's charmed circle, and in 1449 his opponents had him appointed Lieutenant of Ireland for ten years in order to get him out of the way. In 1450 he returned from his post without permission to take up the cudgels with his rival duke.

Their rivalry was all the keener for the fact that both dukes stood a good chance of inheriting the throne. Margaret had as yet borne no children. Somerset was descended from John of Gaunt and although the Beauforts had been barred from the succession by Parliament in Henry IV's reign, the Act was not immutable. York was descended from Gaunt's elder brother, Lionel, through his mother, Anne Mortimer, and from Gaunt's younger brother, Edmund, through his father, Richard, Earl of Cambridge. From the confrontation of these two men sprang the Wars of the Roses.

For the next three years (1450-53) the court party, headed by Somerset, successfully resisted all York's attempts to dislodge them. When the Member for Bristol suggested in the Commons that York should be recognised as Henry's heir, he was promptly sent to the Tower. In the spring of 1452 York actually marched on London with an army at his back. Somerset quickly assembled a larger force and blocked the way at Dartford. On this occasion bloodshed was avoided by trickery. York agreed to dismiss his force on condition that Somerset should be arrested and called to account for his misdoings in Normandy. But when York allowed himself to be brought into Henry's tent, he found himself a prisoner. Somerset wisely refrained from putting his enemy on trial, for popular sympathy favoured York. The Duke was released after swearing never again to take up arms against any of Henry's subjects.

In 1453 came several dramatic reversals of fortune. First, the Hundred Years' War came to an end with Talbot's annihilation at Castillon, and Henry's government was once more held to blame. In August the King suffered the first of those bouts of insanity which were to recur at intervals throughout the rest of his life. His illness reduced him to a state of paralytic melancholia, depriving him of memory, speech and reason. For this he had to thank the genes inherited from his mad grandfather, Charles VI of France. It is ironic that only two months later the House of Lancaster was blessed with the birth of a male heir. After eight barren years of marriage Queen Margaret presented her afflicted husband with a son. Prince Edward was shown to the King for his blessing at Windsor on New Year's Day 1454, 'but ... in vain, for they departed thence without any answer or countenance, saving only that once he looked upon the Prince and cast down his eyes again, without any more'.

Henry and Margaret were in many respects a most ill-suited pair. In contrast to his ineffectual, other-worldly nature she was a tigress, quick-tempered, courageous and passionate both in her likes and dislikes. She cannot have found Henry a very attentive husband. In the early years of their marriage the rumour was that the King's confessor and councillor, Bishop Ayscough, was responsible for dissuading him from having 'his sport' with the Queen, advising Henry not to 'come nigh her'. Given Henry's prudish views on sex and nudity it is doubtful whether he needed much persuading. When he recovered from his first madness he himself expressed bewilderment at the birth of his son, who, he said, must have been conceived by the Holy Ghost.

Notwithstanding their incompatibility, the Queen was a powerful force in the world of politics. Henry was putty in her hands when she wanted something done, and she developed a fierce, almost partisan, loyalty to his chief ministers: first Suffolk, whom she treated as a father; then Somerset, who was accused of being her lover. Equally fierce was Margaret's dislike of York, whom she saw not as the self-styled victim of Somerset's wiles, but as an arrogant aggressor intent on destroying herself, her husband and her son. She was, as it happened, proved absolutely right, but it was her own implacable hostility towards York which converted him from the one to the other.

Ironically, York had his first taste of power soon after Prince Edward's birth knocked him out of the succession. With the King clearly unfit to rule there was nothing Margaret or Somerset could do to prevent York's appointment as Protector in March 1454. Somerset was arrested (in the Queen's apartments), impeached and committed to the Tower. Towards Christmas the King recovered, and in February 1455 York was dismissed, Somerset restored. Mutual hatred and suspicion were by now so deeply entrenched that a recourse to arms became inevitable. York's appeals to the King were suppressed by Henry's courtiers. On 22 May 1455 a Yorkist force confronted Somerset and the King at St Albans. Parleying broke down when Henry refused point-blank to surrender the Duke of Somerset. Within an hour the battle was lost, Somerset was dead, and the King, his neck grazed by an arrow, meekly allowed the victor to renew his oath of allegiance.

Despite the bloodshed a settlement should now have been possible. It would be wrong to think that the peerage was irrevocably split into two hostile factions, the Yorkists on one side, Lancastrians on the other. The men who backed York – including the powerful Richard Neville, Earl of Warwick – did so not because they wanted to make him King in Henry's place, but because of their various private grudges against members of the court circle. With Somerset out of the way most peers favoured conciliation, and Henry himself certainly had no wish to propagate a blood feud.

Queen Margaret unfortunately took a very different view, and it was she who prevailed. The heirs of the men who had fallen at St Albans readily supported her and soon the two leading Northern families, the Nevilles and the Percies, were at each other's throats again. In March 1458 Henry, on his own initiative, made a remarkable effort to forestall another explosion of violence. At a special ceremony of reconciliation all the chief protagonists, including Margaret and York, marched hand in hand to St Paul's behind their King.

This was all a charade. In the summer of 1459 Margaret raised another army and marched on York's stronghold of Ludlow in the Welsh Marches. This time the Yorkists were routed: the Duke fled to Ireland, the Earl of Salisbury, his son Warwick and York's heir Edward, Earl of March, to Calais. The Calais contingent reappeared in the summer of 1460 and in turn routed the royal army at the battle of Northampton. This time York was in no mood for further compromise. It was clear that while Margaret ruled the King any compromise would simply be undone the moment the court party felt strong enough to renege on it. Accordingly, in October, York submitted to Parliament his claim to the throne of England.

It looked as though a repeat performance of 1399 was about to be enacted. However the

Lords, including even the two Neville Earls, were not yet ready to sanction such a revolutionary move. It was agreed instead that Henry should remain king for life, but recognise York as his heir. Henry seems to have acquiesced in the disinheriting of his son. Not so Margaret who had eluded capture at Northampton and taken refuge with the Prince behind the battlements of Harlech Castle. In a fine display of martial courage she took ship for Berwick on the Scottish border and appeared in mid-December at the head of a new Lancastrian host. York and Salisbury hurried north with a small force to meet the threat and rashly committed themselves to battle without waiting for reinforcements. On 30 December 1460 York's army was crushed at Wakefield. The Duke himself died on the battlefield, and his head was later displayed on the gates of York wearing a paper crown.

In 1461, the final year of Henry's reign, events came thick and fast. As Margaret marched on London, St Albans was the scene of a second battle at which Warwick was defeated and the King restored to his wife. Nevertheless, London's gates remained closed, its citizens fearful of the looting that might ensue if Margaret's northerners gained admittance. Warwick managed to join his mauled troops with those of York's eldest son, Edward, who entered London in triumph, and was installed as King in Westminster Abbey on 4 March. Henry and Margaret withdrew towards Yorkshire, with Edward at their heels. On 29 March the two armies fought it out near Towton in a blizzard of wind and snow. It was a bloody engagement and ended in the massacre of Margaret's soldiers. The King and Queen took refuge over the border in Scotland.

Nine years were to pass before Henry regained his throne. The story is briefly told, for it is really an epilogue to his reign. For three years he hovered on the outskirts of his lost kingdom at Harlech and at the Northumberland fortress towns of Berwick and Bamburgh,

while Margaret schemed to enlist the Scots and the French in his cause. Some minor successes were achieved in the north with the help of Piers de Breze, a renowned French captain on loan from Margaret's cousin Louis XI, but there was not enough money or manpower to pose a serious threat. By the summer of 1463 even Margaret was sufficiently discouraged to return to France with her French allies and her son, leaving Henry precariously ensconced at Bamburgh. Hopes flared again the following spring when the dwindling rump of Lancastrian leaders attempted a rising in Northumberland, but they were trounced at Hexham by Warwick's brother, Lord Montagu. The fall of Bamburgh in the summer deprived Henry of his last stronghold and he seems to have spent the best part of the next year as a wandering fugitive. He was finally picked up near Clitheroe, Lancashire, in July 1465: whence, in Blacman's words, 'he was brought as a traitor and criminal to London, and imprisoned in the Tower there; where, like a true follower of Christ, he patiently endured hunger, thirst, mockings, derisions, abuse and many other hardships'.

And so at last to the bizarre episode of Henry's restoration, the so-called Readeption of Henry VI. The background details belong more properly to the reign of Edward IV. Suffice it to say that on Wednesday 3 October 1470 the astonished Henry – 'not cleanly kept as should seem such a Prince' – was suddenly transferred to the luxuriously furnished apartments of Edward IV's Queen and addressed once again as King. Three days later his former adversary, the Earl of Warwick, knelt before him to ask forgiveness. Later Henry, dressed in a long blue gown, was conveyed to St Paul's

RIGHT An illustration from a law treatise of Henry VI's reign showing the Court of the Exchequer at Westminster. Dressed in red robes and a turban the Lord High Treasurer presides with two judges at either side. Around the tables are clerks and officers, two counting gold coin. In the foreground are two prisoners.

THE HOUSES OF LANCASTER AND YORK

showing their descent from Edward III and the Tudor claim to the throne

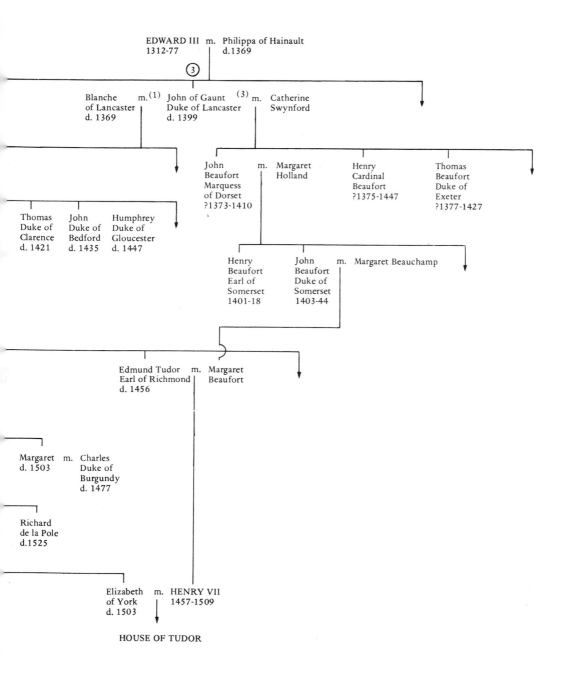

EDWARD III m. Philippa of Hainault
1312-77   d.1369

③

Blanche   m.(1) John of Gaunt   (3) m. Catherine
of Lancaster   Duke of Lancaster   Swynford
d. 1369   d. 1399

John   m. Margaret   Henry   Thomas
Beaufort   Holland   Cardinal   Beaufort
Marquess   Beaufort   Duke of
of Dorset   ?1375-1447   Exeter
?1373-1410   ?1377-1427

Thomas   John   Humphrey
Duke of   Duke of   Duke of
Clarence   Bedford   Gloucester
d. 1421   d. 1435   d. 1447

Henry   John   m. Margaret Beauchamp
Beaufort   Beaufort
Earl of   Duke of
Somerset   Somerset
1401-18   1403-44

Edmund Tudor   m. Margaret
Earl of Richmond   Beaufort
d. 1456

Margaret   m. Charles
d. 1503   Duke of
               Burgundy
               d. 1477

Richard
de la Pole
d.1525

Elizabeth   m. HENRY VII
of York   1457-1509
d. 1503

HOUSE OF TUDOR

to give thanks for his delivery. At his new quarters in the Bishop of London's palace in Fulham Henry learned from Warwick the details of the Earl's quarrel with Edward IV, of Edward's flight to Burgundy and of the Kingmaker's reconciliation with Queen Margaret at Angers Cathedral. In the following month Warwick's episcopal brother George opened Parliament with an address on the text, taken from the Book of Jeremiah, 'Return, O backsliding children'. In December came news from France that Prince Edward had married Anne Neville, Warwick's fifteen-year-old daughter.

Throughout the readeption Henry remained, as always, a puppet, while Warwick pulled the strings. In the words of one chronicler, 'the King was as mute as a crowned calf'. His one act was to send food and clothing to Edward IV's abandoned wife who was about to give birth in the Sanctuary of Westminster Abbey. He never saw his own family again. In March Edward IV landed in Yorkshire, and on 11 April, having outmanoeuvred Warwick, he re-entered London. Two days later Henry was compelled to join Edward's army on the road to Barnet, where on Easter Sunday, Warwick's army was put to flight and the Kingmaker slain. On the same day Queen Margaret landed too late at Weymouth, to be defeated in her turn some three weeks later at Tewkesbury. The seventeen-year-old Prince Edward was among the dead. Margaret was brought back to London and lodged in the Tower, though not in Henry's company.

Henry's captivity ended on the night of 21 May, the day Edward returned to the capital from his victory at Tewkesbury. The chronicler Henry Warkworth recorded that he 'was put to death ... between eleven and twelve of the clock, being then at the Tower .. : the Duke

of Gloucester ... and many other; and on the morrow he was chested and brought to St Paul's, and his face was open that every man might see him ...'. Later he was buried in the Lady Chapel at Chertsey Abbey.

Henry was killed because the magic of his name could still inspire the respect and loyalty that men like Warwick needed as a cloak for their ambitions. His execution was an act of state designed to prevent further rebellion in his name. Even in those blood-soaked days it aroused a shiver of horror among contemporaries, who pointed to Henry's blameless conduct, his charity and his devotion to God. His burial-place soon became a shrine, and it was later said that Richard III moved the body to St George's, Windsor, to put a stop to the pilgrimages and the talk of miracles. Yet Henry must take his share of responsibility for the events that brought him down. The Wars of the Roses sprang from his failure to meet the enormous demands of medieval kingship. If the man was a saint, the King was a political simpleton, who would neither provide leadership nor delegate it to those who could.

A fitting epitaph is the poem Henry wrote himself:

> Kingdoms are but cares,
>   State is devoid of stay,
> Riches are ready snares,
>   And hasten to decay.
>
> Pleasure is a privy prick
>   Which vice doth still provoke;
> Pomp, imprompt; and fame, a flame;
>   Power, a smouldering smoke.
>
> Who meanth to remove the rock
>   Owt of the slimy mud,
> Shall mire himself, and hardly scape
>   The swelling of the flood.

The battle of Agincourt, 1415, from a fifteenth-century
miniature. Henry v's resounding victory established his
reputation for his life and for posterity.

5
THE
HOUSE OF
YORK
1461~85

Anthony Woodville, Earl Rivers, presenting *The Dictes and Sayenges of the Phylosophers* to his brother-in-law Edward IV. Elizabeth Woodville, the Queen, stands on the right with her eldest son Prince Edward. Rivers had translated the *Dictes* from a French manuscript; it was one of the first books printed by William Caxton at his press near Westminster Abbey.

EDWARD IV

r. 1461–83

'WORDS FAIL ME to relate how well the commons love and adore him, as if he were their God. The entire kingdom keeps holiday for the event.' So wrote an Italian observer who witnessed the coronation of Edward IV on 28 June 1461.

The euphoria which greeted Edward is not difficult to understand. Over six feet tall and exceptionally good looking, he had the physical presence of a king. At nineteen years of age he had already proved himself a brave and resourceful general. After the disaster of Wakefield which claimed the lives of his father, the Duke of York, his brother Edmund and his uncle, the Earl of Salisbury, he had defeated Jasper Tudor at Mortimer's Cross in Wales, saved London from Queen Margaret's northerners and won his crowning victory at Towton. With his prodigious feats on the battlefield he combined an instinctive grasp of political showmanship. He loved to be seen in public, dressed always in the latest fashions, and treated all his subjects, high and low, with the same easy familiarity. Among his many accomplishments was his reputation for being able to remember the names and fortunes of all his subjects of any importance throughout the kingdom.

He understood, too, the reasons why successive parliaments under Henry IV and Henry VI had proved so stubborn in opposition to the sovereign. Edward won the approval of his Commons by adopting the policies once voiced in opposition. He saw it as his first priority to make the Crown solvent. The Crown lands were put in the hands of salaried officials rather than doled out at ludicrous rents to fortune-seeking courtiers and their clients. Many recipients of Lancastrian largesse found their lands confiscated or resumed by Act of Parliament.

Detailed ordinances were set down for the control of the royal household expenses. The King also showed a keen interest in foreign trade and backed a number of successful commercial ventures as a merchant in his own right. Such measures testified not only to Edward's acumen but to the fact that the Yorkists owed a great deal of their support to the promise of better government and financial reform. Edward meant it when he told the Commons in 1467 that 'I purpose to live of mine own and not to charge my subjects but in great and urgent causes'.

However, these achievements really belong to the second part of Edward's reign. The first ten years were dominated by his relationship with his power-hungry cousin, Richard Neville, Earl of Warwick. Although Edward wore the crown it was initially Warwick, fourteen years his senior, who called the tune. The Earl's pre-eminence was the supreme example of what inspired matchmaking could do for a family. Warwick's grandfather, Ralph Neville, had married Joan Beaufort, daughter of John of Gaunt. He could thus claim to be of royal blood as a great-great-grandson of Edward III. His father, also called Richard, acquired the earldom of Salisbury by marriage to the former earl's daughter, Alice. This inheritance passed to Warwick when his father was captured and executed at Wakefield in 1460. Warwick himself married an even greater heiress, Anne Beauchamp, and through her acquired his earldom along with a vast inheritance in Wales and the West Midlands. His manors and castles spanned more than half the counties of England. Warwick's numerous brothers, sisters, uncles and aunts had also married well, none more so than his aunt Cicely Neville, a famed beauty who married the Duke of York and in

Edward IV at the battle of Mortimer's Cross in 1461 when he defeated a Lancastrian force under Owen Tudor.

April 1442 gave birth at Rouen to the future Edward IV.

Without the Neville connection the Yorkists could not have triumphed over the majority of the baronial houses who remained loyal to Henry VI. Warwick, a domineering, short-tempered and ambitious character, expected and received the rewards to match his services. He held office as Chamberlain of England, Captain of Calais and Warden of the Cinque Ports. The upbringing of Edward's youngest brother, Richard, was also entrusted to his care (at the ancestral Neville stronghold of Middleham in Yorkshire).

For the first four years of Edward's reign Warwick and his brother John continued their labours on the King's behalf. While they were mopping up the last pockets of Lancastrian resistance in the North, the King tasted the pleasures of court life at Westminster and Windsor. In 1464, after the decisive Battle of Hexham, John Neville was rewarded with the hereditary Percy earldom of Northumberland and another brother, George Neville, became Archbishop of York.

But in the autumn of 1464 there arose the first signs of dissension between the great Earl and his royal cousin. Two issues – sex and diplomacy – lay at the root of the trouble. Edward was an insatiable womaniser with, it appears, a special taste for older ladies. According to the contemporary French historian, Philippe de Commynes, Edward 'thought upon nothing but women and that more than reason would'. Another foreigner, Dominic Mancini, who visited England towards the end of Edward's reign records that 'he pursued with no discrimination the married and the unmarried, the noble and lowly: however he took none by force. He overcame all by money and promises, and having conquered them, he dismissed them.' Early in the reign Edward ap-

parently entered into a marriage contract with the widowed Lady Eleanor Butler, a daughter of old Talbot, 'the terror of the French', in order to coax her to his bed. In May 1464 another reluctant widow, Lady Elizabeth Woodville, refused to submit until Edward actually married her. With extraordinary lack of foresight the King agreed to her terms and the couple were secretly made man and wife, 'after which spousals ended, he went to bed and tarried there for four hours'.

At about the same time Warwick was negotiating with France's King Louis XI for a treaty of friendship which was to be sealed by the

Richard Neville, Earl of Warwick, and his wife, Anne Beauchamp, from the *Rous Roll*, an account of the Earls of Warwick written during the reign of Richard III by a chaplain, John Rous.

marriage of Edward IV to a French princess. These negotiations, which Warwick conducted off his own bat, meant a great deal to the Earl who was flattered by Louis's overtures and given to understand that he would receive French lands and titles as his reward. The revelation of Edward's secret marriage was therefore both a personal affront and a blow to Warwick's grandiose diplomatic ambitions. To rub salt in the wound the King's bride was the widow of a Lancastrian knight, and brought with her to Court a swarm of relatives – two sons, five brothers and seven sisters – eager for advancement. Within two years of the marriage three of the sisters were in their turn married to the heirs of great baronial houses and one of her sons was married to the Duke of Exeter's daughter, previously pledged to a nephew of Warwick. The most notorious match was reserved for the Queen's brother, John: as one chronicler put it, 'Catherine, Duchess of Norfolk, a slip of a girl about eighty years old, was married to John Woodville, aged twenty years. A diabolical marriage.'

Over the next four years (1464-68) Edward made it abundantly clear that he no longer regarded himself as Warwick's protégé. The King favoured an alliance with Burgundy, England's traditional ally and trading partner, and backed the proposal that his sister, Margaret, should marry Charles of Burgundy. At the same time he did not feel strong enough to put a stop to Warwick's flirtation with Louis XI. England's diplomacy thus had two masters, each pursuing contradictory aims while interested spectators, like Sir John Paston, placed bets on the outcome. In the spring of 1468 Edward had his way and Margaret married the Duke of Burgundy. This match tipped Warwick from sullen opposition into undeclared rebellion. He had made one king; why not another? A new puppet was ready in the wings in the shape of Edward's own brother, George, Duke of Clarence. The foolish Clarence nursed exalted notions of his own importance which the King did not apparently

share. He had already aligned himself with Warwick over the Burgundian alliance and in 1467 Edward had to scotch his proposed marriage to Warwick's elder daughter, Isabel Neville. The prospect of a crown made Clarence an easy prey to the King-maker's new conspiracy.

It started early in 1469 with a series of Neville-inspired risings in the North and Midlands. In July Warwick and Clarence slipped across the Channel to Calais, where Clarence was married to Isabel. In the meantime Edward was bottled up at Nottingham, where he confronted a rebel army easily outnumbering his own. On 26 July 1469 a relief force coming to the King's aid was cut to pieces near Banbury. With disaster staring him in the face, Edward now decided on a strategic capitulation. He dispersed his army and allowed himself to fall into Warwick's hands.

This was a crucial gamble and it paid off. Warwick, who had intended to depose Edward with the assent of a compliant Parliament, found himself beset by a breakdown of local order reminiscent of the worst years of Henry VI's reign. The conspirators lost their nerve and far from deposing Edward they were compelled to release him so that order could be restored in the shires by the King's authority. The rebels were formally reconciled with their King and in October 1469 Edward returned to his capital. It was a brilliant recovery whereby military disaster was transformed into a political victory. However, it was abundantly clear that accounts would have to be settled. Edward could not contemplate a permanent truce with the man who had rebelled against him, executed the Queen's father and brother and turned his own brother against him. Warwick knew it too, and in the spring of 1470 rebellion broke out again in Wales and in Lincolnshire at the King-maker's instigation. This time Edward put the rebels to flight, and Warwick, with the wretched Clarence still in tow, had to flee to France.

For Europe's master spinner of diplomatic

webs, the 'universal spider' Louis XI, this was a god-sent opportunity. The once-mighty Earl of Warwick, so assiduously courted over the years, was now sufficiently humbled for Louis to pull off his cherished ambition: the reconciliation of the Kingmaker with Margaret of Anjou. On 22 July 1470 Warwick made his submission to Henry VI's Queen at Angers Cathedral. In September he was in England again accompanied by two Lancastrian stalwarts, the Earl of Oxford and Henry VI's half brother, Jasper Tudor. Their landing caught Edward ill prepared in York; marching south he was very nearly captured by Warwick's brother, John. The King, accompanied by his brother, Richard of Gloucester, Lord Hastings and a few retainers, dashed acrosss country to Lynn and embarked for Burgundy. While Warwick brought Henry VI out of the Tower and put him back on the throne, Edward's future lay in the hands of the Duke of Burgundy. Charles was at first reluctant to embroil himself in his brother-in-law's problems, but he changed his mind when first Louis XI and then Warwick declared war on him. He finally agreed to lend his brother-in-law a fleet and some 1,500 Burgundian troops, and on 11 March 1471 Edward set sail for the reconquest of his kingdom.

One month later the Kingmaker fought his last battle at Barnet. Apart from his superior generalship Edward owed his victory to the lingering suspicions between the old-guard Lancastrians and their new-found ally. Margaret of Anjou did not land in England until the very day of Warwick's defeat and death. On 4 May Edward caught up with her at Tewkesbury, and defeated her army as decisively as he had dealt with Warwick's. Thus Edward regained his crown and Louis forfeited, for the time being, his chance to swallow up the Duchy of Burgundy. As an added, if rather dubious, bonus Edward also recovered the allegiance of his brother Clarence, whose expectations of a crown had been quietly put aside when War-

The handsome widow Elizabeth Woodville who captured the heart of Edward IV but refused anything less than marriage.

wick restored Henry VI. Henry himself fell victim to the power game in which he was no more than a befuddled bystander. On Edward's return to London from Tewkesbury, he was put to death in the Tower of London.

If the second half of Edward's reign lacks the drama and excitement of the first, it is because his authority remained unchallenged until his death. With the deaths of Warwick, Henry VI and his son Prince Edward, there was no need

153

to proceed against the small fry. In contrast to the 113 Acts of Attainder passed on individuals after Towton in 1461, there were none after Barnet and Tewkesbury. Moreover the Queen, whom Edward had left behind in his precipitate flight to Burgundy, had now presented him with a son and the kingdom with an heir. In the twelve years left to him Edward was able at last to deliver the reforms promised in the Yorkist manifestoes of the 1450s. Contemporaries were greatly impressed by his efforts to suppress brigandage on the roads and prevent local magnates from taking the law into their own hands. The Crown was gradually freed from its burden of debt and Edward was able to make do for several years without asking Parliament for taxation measures.

There was one other aspect of the Yorkist programme which the King fully intended to carry out, and that was the reconquest of France. Louis XI had done his best to unseat Edward: now it was Edward's turn to try his luck against France. Edward's diplomacy during the years 1472-74 aimed at building up a grand alliance of Louis's enemies – the Duke of Brittany, the King of Aragon and, most crucial to its success, the Duke of Burgundy. In July 1475 Edward finally embarked for Calais with an army of 10,000 men, the largest and best-equipped host ever led into France by an English king, according to Commynes. Duke Charles, however, failed to meet his side of the bargain and arrived to meet his ally without any troops at all. He had left the Burgundian army far away at Nantes embroiled in another campaign on behalf of the Holy Roman Emperor. As Commynes again remarked, 'God had troubled his senses'. Deserted also by Francis, Duke of Brittany, and now confronted by Louis's formidable French army, Edward decided to abandon the whole enterprise in exchange for a hefty annual pension. On 29 August 1475 Louis and Edward met at Picquigny to seal the terms of a seven-year truce. The French entertained the entire English army at Amiens, after which Louis was heard to boast that he had evicted his would-be conquerors with venison pies and good wine.

The French peace provoked some grumbles of complaint in the English ranks, most notably from Edward's straightlaced brother, Richard of Gloucester. But it was the other brother Clarence who gave the King most cause for concern after his return to England.

A summons from Edward to the great men of the kingdom in 1475, calling on them to supply men for the French war. Heraldic symbols are drawn next to the names: a black bull for the Duke of Clarence, a boar for Richard of Gloucester, a white lion for the Duke of Norfolk, a gold lion with a forked tail for Suffolk and a Stafford knot for the Duke of Buckingham.

His unstable behaviour had long been a thorn in Edward's side. Although forgiven for his involvement with Warwick, Clarence had quarrelled with Richard of Gloucester over the division of Warwick's lands and breathed hints of treason when compelled to share the spoils. The crisis came in 1477 when Clarence, now a widower after Isabel's death in childbirth, wanted to marry the Duke of Burgundy's daughter, Mary. Edward refused point-blank to sanction this plan. Following her father's death in battle earlier in the year, Mary had become a great heiress and far too important a match for the unreliable Clarence. The enraged Clarence immediately plunged into fresh treasons. This time Edward had had enough. First a member of Clarence's household was accused of plotting the King's death by necromancy and executed; and when Clarence failed to heed the warning, he was arrested, attainted of treason in Parliament and sentenced to death. Egged on by the Queen, who had not forgotten Clarence's part in the death of her father and brother John in 1469, Edward permitted the sentence to be carried out on 18 February 1478. Tradition has it that Clarence met his end in a butt of Malmsey wine and certainly his daughter, Margaret Pole, wore a model of a wine cock on her wrist in remembrance.

In reality Clarence was more of a nuisance than a threat. His execution was an unnecessary act of cruelty and points to the coarser side of Edward's nature. Three decades of warfare, treason and betrayal could not fail to leave their mark. It was an age of endemic violence which bred strange contradictions. Edward's former Constable, John Tiptoft, Earl of Worcester, who was executed during the Readeption of Henry VI is a good example; a widely travelled humanist scholar, he introduced with Edward's approval the practice of impalement for traitors and was nicknamed 'the butcher of England'.

Perhaps Edward's addiction to the pleasures of the flesh was another reaction to the temper of his age. 'In food and drink', wrote Mancini, 'he was most immoderate: it was his habit ... to take an emetic for the delight of gorging his stomach once more. For this reason, and for the ease which was especially dear to him after his recovery of the Crown, he had grown fat in the loins.' Nor did he lose his taste for female company: towards the end of his life his particular favourite was the mercer's wife, Jane Shore. 'For many he had, but her he loved', wrote Sir Thomas More. In this curious blending of energy with laziness, ability with self-indulgence, Edward's character foreshadows that of his Tudor successor, Henry VIII.

In his leisure hours Edward also found time for artistic and cultural pursuits. He collected a fine library and spent considerable sums on the copying of manuscripts. During his Burgundian exile he was much taken with that recent invention, the printing press, and later became the friend and patron of William Caxton. In November 1477 Edward received from the Queen's brother, Anthony, Lord Rivers, a copy of *The Dictes and Sayenges of the Phylosophers*, the first dated book to be printed in England.

During the last years of his reign, when war erupted again on the border with Scotland, Edward's robust constitution showed signs of giving way. In 1481 and again in 1482 elaborate plans to lead a great army north had to be postponed and the job was left to the King's able brother, Richard of Gloucester. In the winter of 1482-83 an even more ambitious project was mooted when Louis XI finally came to terms with Burgundy and cut off the annual payment to the English. Edward planned to invade France in person once again, and Parliament voted a generous subsidy. But it was too late. Edward contracted a fever and died on 9 April 1483. The crown passed to his twelve-year-old heir, Prince Edward, and in his will the King appointed Richard of Gloucester as Protector.

4 The Royal Arms in the Fifteenth Century

IT IS SAID THAT in 1376 Charles V of France formally altered the royal arms of France by reducing the number of fleurs-de-lys to three. Various theories have been put forward as to why he did this. The most romantic is that in 496 Queen Clothilde was given a holy cloth embroidered with three lilies, symbolising the Blessed Virgin and that she gave this cloth to her husband King Clovis. It is suggested that Charles adopted the three fleurs-de-lys in order to give official sanction to this popular legend.

Whatever the reason and at what exact moment it happened, from the end of the fourteenth century the French royal arms contained but three lilies and, when a new great seal was struck for Henry IV in 1405 he followed the French king's lead and reduced the number of lilies in the French quarterings in his arms to three.

Henry V, Henry VI, Edward IV, Edward V and Richard III used more or less the same arms. The only small difference occurred in the detail of the crest. Basically it remained the same but minor variations are to be found. For example, Edward IV at one time used an uncrowned lion standing within a crown on a chapeau, as illustrated, whilst in his third Great Seal the crown is shown with arches. Eventually, with Henry VIII, the chapeau and coronet gave way to an arched crown and the lion was similarly crowned. This is essentially the crest of England as borne by the Queen today.

Towards the close of the fifteenth century, representations of the royal arms are found, although not on the Great Seal, with supporters on either side of the shield. These supporters seem to have their origin in artistry. Seal engravers, sculptors and wood carvers took the liberty of adding favourite beasts or badges to representations of arms so as to obtain a more interesting artistic effect. This custom must have pleased the nobility and more and more of them began to affect these adornments to their arms. The kings were no exception and there are examples of the arms of Henry VI, Edward IV and Richard III supported by a variety of beasts chosen from their family, rather than their royal heraldry.

It was not long before the heralds began to take official notice of supporters and, as it were, admit them to the field of official heraldry, recording them, assigning them and making rules for their depiction and devolution.

RICHARD III

r. 1483–5

KING RICHARD III reigned for only two years and two months before he went down fighting at Bosworth Field. Nevertheless his reign has acquired an importance out of all proportion to its length. Richard was the last of thirteen kings of the Plantagenet line, which had ruled England since 1154. He was the last English king to die on the battlefield. His death in 1485 is said to mark the boundary between the medieval and the modern age. And he is the chief suspect in the longest and most emotive murder investigation in English history – the problem of who murdered the Princes in the Tower.

Richard's career also exemplifies the pitfalls confronting the biographer of any medieval figure. The records preserve the facts, but not the motives. In Richard's case no court history, no personal correspondence, not even a contemporary portrait survives to illumine his personality or his appearance. His image has been blackened in caricatures compiled in the reign of his successful rival, Henry VII, and later adapted by Shakespeare to give birth to the monster portrayed in his play, *Richard III*.

Before seeking to untangle motives, it is therefore best to start with the unembroidered facts. Richard, fourth and last surviving son of Richard, Duke of York and Cecily Neville, was born at Fotheringhay Castle in Northamptonshire on 2 October 1452. His childhood was soon affected by all the vicissitudes of the Wars of the Roses. When York and the Nevilles were put to flight at Ludlow in 1459 he and his brother George were placed in the custody first of the Duchess of Buckingham and then of the Archbishop of Canterbury. After York's death at Wakefield in December 1460 the Duchess of York took refuge with her two younger sons in the Burgundian Netherlands, where she remained until Edward's great victory at Towton made it safe to return. On the eve of Edward's coronation in June 1461 Richard, aged nine, became a Knight of the Garter and four months later the King created him Duke of Gloucester. For the best part of the next four years Richard's home was in the Yorkshire castle of Middle-

A sixteenth-century version of the standard portrait of Richard III, probably taken from life but now lost.

ham, favourite residence of the Earl and Countess of Warwick. It was the custom among the nobility to farm out their children among families of equal rank, and, as the King's brother, Richard naturally rated the King's greatest subject. But when the great Earl's quarrel with Edward erupted into violence, Richard, unlike his brother George, remained steadfastly loyal to the King. In 1469 he was appointed Constable of England and charged with the suppression of a rising in Wales.

Richard's apprenticeship was now at an end: from 1469 until Edward's death Richard was to play a key role, both military and administrative, in the affairs of the kingdom. In 1470 he accompanied Edward in his flight to Burgundy, while the Warwick-Lancaster alliance restored Henry VI to his throne. At the battles of Barnet and Tewkesbury in 1471 Richard commanded with distinction a wing of the Yorkist army. There is no foundation for later stories that Richard was present at, or took part in, the death of Henry VI's son, Prince Edward. Contemporary accounts simply state that Edward was killed during the battle. He was probably present at the Tower on the night Henry himself was put to death, but so were many other Yorkist leaders.

With the Yorkists safely restored to power, Richard was chosen to take up Warwick's former task of pacifying the lawless northern counties and sealing the border against Scottish incursions. This commission was to keep Richard occupied intermittently until 1475 and almost exclusively thereafter. In the autumn of 1471 Richard married Anne Neville, the sixteen-year-old widow of Prince Edward and younger daughter of the Kingmaker. As co-heiress of the Beauchamp estate, which Warwick had held in his wife's right, Anne brought her husband a valuable inheritance; but there is reason to suppose that Richard's intentions were not exclusively mercenary. He had grown up with Anne during his stay at Middleham, and subsequently treated her mother with kind-

ness and generosity. This much cannot be said for George, Duke of Clarence, the husband of Warwick's other daughter, Isabel. George was in fact so keen to keep his hands on the whole of the Countess's estates that he put every obstacle in the way of Richard's marriage, including the attempted abduction of the intended bride. With Edward's mediation it was agreed that the marriage should go ahead, but that most of the Beauchamp estates would be reserved for Clarence. Early in 1473 Anne bore Richard a son, whom they christened Edward. Though he fathered at least two bastards before his marriage, he was faithful to her afterwards.

In 1475 Richard took part in the inglorious but profitable French campaign that ended with the Treaty of Picquigny. We are told that the Duke of Gloucester opposed this betrayal of the Agincourt spirit and earned thereby the distrust of France's king, Louis XI.

The last act in Clarence's pitiful career provided the occasion for Richard's next visit to court in the autumn of 1477. Continually threatened by the disloyalty of Clarence, Edward at last had him tried for high treason. Despite the earlier rancour over the Warwick-Beauchamp inheritance Richard was, according to one contemporary account, 'overcome with grief for his brother' when the death sentence was carried out. Three days after Clarence had been drowned in a wine butt the Duke of Gloucester procured a licence to set up two religious foundations to pray for his dead brother and other members of the royal family. Our source, the level-headed Italian cleric, Dominic Mancini, goes on to say that 'thenceforth Richard came very rarely to court. He kept himself within his own lands and set out to acquire the loyalty of his people through favours and justice. The good reputation of his private life and public activities powerfully attracted the esteem of strangers ... Such was his renown in warfare, that whenever a difficult and dangerous policy had to be undertaken, it would be entrusted to his discretion

and generalship. By these arts Richard acquired the favour of the people, and avoided the jealousy of the Queen, from whom he lived far separated.'

Clearly there was no love lost between Richard and his sister-in-law, the Woodville Queen. Like many of the aristocracy he probably resented the favour shown to her innumerable relatives, and it is possible that he also held her responsible for Clarence's death. In any event he preferred a life of service in the North to the intrigues and luxury of Edward's court. Nor is there any doubt that his lieutenancy in the North merited Mancini's complimentary remarks. The records of the City of York contain many references to his activities – from suppressing illegal fish traps to commuting taxes in times of need – and record the gratitude of the city fathers: 'The Duke of Gloucester shall, for his great labour ... be presented ... with six swans and six pikes.' His legal commissions also toured the West Riding, Cumberland and Westmorland dispensing 'good and indifferent [i.e. impartial] justice to all who sought it, were they rich or poor, gentle or simple'.

As Warden of the West March Richard was also responsible for the defence of the border country, and from 1480 conducted several hard-fought campaigns against King Louis's ally, James III of Scotland. These culminated in 1482 with the recapture of Berwick and an unopposed entry into Edinburgh. Edward's gratitude for this victory and the ten solid years of service preceding it was expressed in 1483, when Parliament made the Duke of Gloucester's Wardenship of the West March a hereditary office and granted him all the royal manors and revenues in the county of Cumberland. This palatinate state within a state which Richard now controlled was a fitting reward for a brother who had more than fulfilled the promise of his adopted motto, *Loyaulté Me Lie*, loyalty binds me. Parliament approved the grant in February: two months later Edward IV died.

So passed the first thirty of Richard's thirty-three years. Had he, rather than Edward, died in 1483 he would no doubt have earned a respectable footnote in history as an able soldier, a conscientious administrator and a self-effacingly loyal brother; a man whose old-fashioned sense of honour led him to disapprove of Picquigny-style diplomacy as much as the free-wheeling sexual mores of Edward's Court; a blameless husband who remained faithful to his wife and shielded her relatives from the consequences of Warwick's fall. And yet, within six months of his brother's death he had bastardised Edward's children, executed Edward's closest friend, seized the crown for himself and driven Edward's Queen into an improbable alliance with an obscure Lancastrian pretender named Henry Tudor.

Events came quickly to a head after Edward IV's death on 9 April 1483. The Woodville clan, led by the Queen, knew that they had many enemies including Richard of Gloucester whom Edward had named Protector in his will. They therefore opted for attack as the best means of defence. While Richard was still in the North they passed a resolution through the Council to replace Gloucester's protectorship with a Regency Council. They also arranged for the young Edward V to be brought from Ludlow to London as quickly as possible for his coronation. Once he was crowned the protectorship would lapse in any case. Clearly the Woodvilles were aware from the start that Richard might opt to grab the throne for himself. As Mancini says, 'they were afraid that if Richard took the crown, or even governed alone, they who bore the blame of Clarence's death would suffer death or at least be ejected from their high estate.'

Lord Hastings, an intimate friend of the late king, but no lover of the Queen's affinity, let slip these plans to Richard. With the help of another Woodville opponent, the powerful Duke of Buckingham, Richard promptly intercepted Edward V on the road to London and

LEFT A new knight of Bath rides through the courtyard of the Tower of London to present himself to the king in the royal lodging. His squire carries his sword and spurs and trumpeters and heralds lead the procession. The miniature comes from *Writhe's Garter Book c.* 1490.

arrested his guardian, Anthony Woodville, Earl Rivers. When the news reached London on 1 May, the Queen immediately took Sanctuary at Westminster with her younger son, Richard. The Dukes of Gloucester and Buckingham entered London unopposed on 4 May.

It is not strictly relevant to ask who was the aggressor in this situation, for the answer is that both parties acted in self-defence for fear of the other. The situation itself was a legacy of Edward IV's marriage, which created the rift between the Woodvilles and the older aristocracy. Richard came out on top because the Woodvilles, without Edward's protection, were no match for their enemies. However, the Protector's position was still decidedly tricky. At the age of twelve his nephew was by contemporary standards nearly an adult, and his coronation could not be indefinitely postponed. Preparations were in fact going ahead for the coronation to take place on 24 June. Once deprived of his authority as Protector Richard could not expect Edward V to side with him against the boy's own mother and his former guardian. The logical conclusion was simple enough: to survive Richard must rule, and to rule he must be king.

By the second week of June Richard had decided to make his pitch for the throne. His faithful Yorkshiremen were summoned to 'come unto us to London ... with as many as ye can make defensibly arrayed, there to aid and assist us against the Queen, her bloody adherents and affinity'. On 16 June Prince Richard was removed from Westminster Sanctuary with threats of force and joined his elder brother in the Tower. All this was done under the pretext that the Queen's 'bloody adherents' were hatching a murderous plot, but in the meantime Richard was sounding out his principal supporters on the idea that he should be crowned in place of his nephew. Buckingham, a headstrong man with a special grudge against the Woodvilles, was willing enough; but some of the old guard from Edward IV's reign, notably

Lord Hastings, would not stomach the disinheritance of Edward's children. Without hesitation Richard had him arrested at a Council meeting and beheaded on the spot. Two days later, on 22 June, the Lord Mayor's brother, Dr Ralph Shaw, preached a sermon at Paul's Cross on the text 'bastard slips shall not take deep root': his message was that Edward IV had made a marriage contract with Lady Eleanor Butler before his subsequent marriage to Elizabeth Woodville. Under canon law this would have invalidated the Woodville marriage and made bastards of their children. The true heir to the throne was therefore none other than the Duke of Gloucester. At the end of June Parliament met and assented to a document petitioning Richard to take the throne. The petition was brought to Richard at Baynard's Castle, where he graciously accepted after a show of reluctance. Richard's coronation on 6 July was attended by virtually the entire peerage, including Henry Tudor's mother, Margaret Beaufort.

Despite the exemplary speed and efficiency with which Richard carried out his *coup d'état*, he was soon prey to the same sort of troubles as the Lancastrian usurper Henry IV had encountered some eighty years earlier. He was on a royal progress at Lincoln in October 1483 when he learned that his chief accomplice, Buckingham, was now in arms against him, having come to terms both with the Woodvilles and with the exiled Henry Tudor. Buckingham's revolt seems as gratuitous as that of the Percys in 1403: according to Henry VII's historian, Polydore Vergil, Buckingham had encouraged Richard's usurpation simply as the stepping stone to his own elevation. Whatever the motives behind it, the whole carefully co-ordinated rebellion ended in fiasco. After heavy rainstorms melted his army, the Duke was taken without a battle and executed on 2 November at Salisbury. Henry Tudor's little invasion fleet turned back to Brittany without attempting a landing and Richard's able lieutenant, the Duke

A piece of parchment with the signature *Edwardus Quintus* at the top with Richard's motto, *Loyaulté me lie* and his signature in the centre. At the bottom is the motto of the Duke of Buckingham *Souvente me souvene* and his signature. This was probably written at St Albans where the young King halted on 3 May on his way to London with Richard and Buckingham.

of Norfolk, dispersed scattered risings in the south-east.

Richard had won the first round; but the revolt had crystallised the pattern of opposition to his rule and left little doubt that a second round would follow. Elizabeth Woodville, by now convinced that she would never see her sons alive again, had made an agreement with Henry Tudor that he would marry her eldest daughter, also named Elizabeth. Since Henry was the sole surviving heir to the Lancastrian claim and Elizabeth was the eldest daughter of Edward IV, this alliance was just as dangerous as the earlier *rapprochement* between Warwick and Margaret of Anjou. The Wars of the Roses created some strange bedfellows.

1484 was for Richard a year of watching and waiting for the expected invasion. It was also witness to a personal tragedy and a diplomatic failure both of which seriously undermined his position. In April his only son Prince Edward died at Middleham. In the words of one chronicler, 'you might have seen his father and mother in a state almost bordering on madness by reason of their sudden grief.' Without a direct heir Richard was a far less likely prospect to the many who had tacitly supported his coup in the hope of avoiding a trouble-ridden minority. In the summer the King narrowly failed in his attempt to extradite Henry Tudor from Brittany. Henry escaped and found refuge at the court of a far more powerful friend,

Painted wooden panels from St George's Chapel, Windsor, portraying from left to right Henry VII, the uncrowned Edward V, and Edward IV. The panel was commissioned by a loyal servant of Henry VII, Oliver King, who wished to portray Henry in the legitimate royal line.

King Charles VIII of France. The year ended with only one success, a three-year truce with the Scots, which was sealed with great solemnity at Nottingham Castle in September. At Christmas the King learned from his agents in France that the invasion was definitely scheduled for the following summer.

The campaigning season of 1485 opened with a propaganda war. The death of Queen Anne in March – another blow to the be-

leaguered King – gave rise to rumours that he had poisoned her in order to marry Henry Tudor's intended bride, Elizabeth of York. It was not until 7 August that the Tudor made his landing at Milford Haven in South Wales. The final battle took place on Monday 22 August a few miles west of Leicester, near the village of Market Bosworth. Anxious as ever to settle the affair by direct action, Richard led a cavalry charge directed at the person of his rival and was slain in the mêlée. The Earl of Northumberland, who commanded Richard's rearguard, watched the proceedings as a spectator, while the Stanley brothers threw their levies into battle on Henry's side. When it was over Richard's naked body was strung over the back of a pack-horse and taken to Leicester for burial in the Grey Friars' chapel.

The country as a whole probably shared the Earl of Northumberland's view of the conflict. It mattered little who won at Bosworth because the issue at stake was simply a dynastic one. Even the dynastic issue was confused by the split within the Yorkist camp and the promised marriage of the Lancastrian Henry to Elizabeth of York. In the earlier stages of the Wars of the Roses, when the Yorkists promised good government in place of Lancastrian incompetence and corruption, there had been real issues to fight over. In 1485 it came to a choice between a childless usurper and a little-known Welshman who had spent most of his life in exile. Richard's only mourners were the knights and squires of his personal following – many of whom fell at his side – and those who remembered his administration in the North: 'King Richard, late mercifully reigning upon us, was ... piteously slain and murdered, to the great heaviness of this city.' A brave tribute from the civic records of York.

Richard's career is too often judged on the issue of whether or not he had the Princes in the Tower murdered. The evidence is not conclusive, but it seems highly probable that he did. The Princes were not seen alive after the autumn of 1483 and Mancini feared they might already be dead when he left the country at the end of June. Had they still been living in 1484 or 1485 Richard would surely have produced them to scupper Henry Tudor's marriage plans. The murder of two innocent children was a

horrible crime even by fifteenth-century standards, but it is difficult to see how Richard could have let them live without risking needless conspiracies in their names.

Richard's real failing as a king was his inability to win over the great magnates whose support was crucial to any medieval regime. For all his solid virtues as an administrator and his undoubted courage in battle, Richard lacked Edward IV's knack of making friends and he was a bad judge of character. He allowed Buckingham to lead him by the nose, and made an enemy of his erstwhile supporter, Lord Hastings. The Earl of Northumberland was his close associate in the North for ten years, but not, it seems, his friend. Lord Stanley was close at Richard's side for two years but turned his coat at the vital moment. Louis XI found him unsympathetic, and Sir Thomas More, admittedly a biased witness, described Richard's nature as 'close and secret'. Ill at ease with his peers, Richard preferred to put his trust in boyhood friends or able lieutenants who owed their positions to his favour. Three of these, William Catesby, Sir Richard Ratcliffe and Francis Lovell, are unflatteringly commemorated in the famous doggerel verse:

> The Cat, the Rat
> And Lovell our Dog
> Rulen all England
> Under an Hog

Yet it was a military rather than a political verdict which settled Richard's fate. Bosworth was the supreme test of his right to rule, just as Shrewsbury was for Henry IV, Towton for Henry VI, and Barnet and Tewkesbury for Edward IV. Richard failed and the crown, reputedly retrieved on the battlefield from under a gorse bush, was placed by Lord Stanley on the head of the first Tudor king.

6
THE
TUDORS

1485~1603

Henry VII and Elizabeth of York with St George and the Dragon. Kneeling behind them are their seven children, three of whom did not survive infancy. On the tents behind are the Tudor rose and the Beaufort portcullis. Henry VII's mother, Margaret, was the last of the Beauforts.

HENRY VII

r. 1485–1509

THOUGH IT DID NOT SEEM SO at the time, 22 August 1485 remains a seminal date in the history of English monarchy, for it ushered in the House of Tudor and, ever since, the crown of England has remained in the line of the heirs of Henry Tudor, the victor at Bosworth Field. A dynasty was born. Henry was head of the House of Lancaster through his remarkable mother, Margaret Beaufort, and he soon strengthened his claim to the throne of England by Parliamentary approval and by his marriage with Elizabeth of York who was destined to bear him three sons and four daughters, though only their second son, Henry, and their eldest and third daughters, Margaret and Mary respectively, were to survive their parents. Henry VIII was to become so desperate to beget a healthy male heir that he divorced his first wife to the consternation of Christendom and beheaded the second before embarking on four further marriages, the last three of them childless, and left, like his father, a son and two daughters. These all died without issue, yet their combined reigns lasted from 1547 to 1603, when James VI of Scotland, great-grandson of Henry VII's daughter Margaret, came south to inaugurate the rule of the House of Stuart. Such was a notable legacy of the first Tudor, who throughout his reign was haunted by the fear that an army no larger than the one which he had himself led against Richard III might overthrow him. His son, too, was threatened by Yorkist pretenders and his grandchildren troubled by rival claimants of 'the blood royal', yet they all died in their beds. The principle of legitimacy had triumphed.

The only son of Edmund Tudor, Earl of Richmond, and Lady Margaret Beaufort, the future Henry VII was very much a child of the civil wars of Lancaster and York, for his father had been taken by the Yorkists in the summer of 1456 and died a prisoner in Carmarthen Castle, leaving a widow of no more than thirteen years who pinned her hopes on giving birth to a son. Edmund's brother, Jasper Tudor, Earl of Pembroke, brought Margaret to his stronghold of Pembroke Castle, where Henry was born on 28 January 1457. In after years when he had achieved all her ambitions for him, she would write to him on his birthday, 'This day of St Agnes, that I did bring into this world my good and gracious prince'; but before then there were to be many tribulations. Henry was only four when, following Edward IV's seizure of the Crown in 1461, Pembroke fell to the Yorkists and mother and child were placed under the guardianship of William Herbert, the new owner, who was granted Jasper's earldom, while Jasper himself fled abroad. Henry was now parted from his mother, who married a Lancastrian knight, Sir Henry Stafford, but he received a sound schooling and was intended as a husband for Herbert's daughter.

When he was twelve his guardian was executed for alleged treason by Warwick, the Kingmaker, yet the following year, when Henry VI was restored to his throne, Jasper could return from exile and bring his nephew to the Lancastrian court. Henry VI, seeing the youth from Wales for the first time, greeted him, 'This truly, this is he unto whom both we and our adversaries must yield and give over the dominion'. Those were prophetic words, for within a year the King had died, his own line became extinct and the young Henry Tudor became the true heir of the House of Lancaster. Edward IV recovered the crown at the battle of Barnet on Easter Day 1471, and as it was no longer safe for Henry and his uncle to remain even in wild Wales they found political asylum in north-west France, which then formed the independent Duchy of Brittany. Henry was destined to remain here for fourteen impressionable years. We know little about his years of exile, though by all accounts he was tall for a Welshman, and if his hair was dark he had a fair complexion; he was athletic and rode well.

What was the strength of Henry's claim to the throne? On his father's side it was weak. His grandfather, Owen Tudor, had secretly married Catherine of Valois, widow of Henry V, and when Henry VI came of age his step-father and his half-brothers, Edmund and Jasper Tudor, were high in favour, until civil war broke out in 1461. On his mother's side the claim went much deeper, for her great-grandfather was John of Gaunt, who had a number of children by his mistress, Catherine Swynford, who were subsequently legitimised; they were known as Beauforts, after Beaufort Castle in France where they were brought up. The second boy, Henry Beaufort, became a cardinal and for a time ruler of England, but the elder boy was created Earl of Somerset, and his own son John, who came to the earldom, left at his death a daughter of three years, Margaret Beaufort, who ten years later gave birth to Henry Tudor. With the deaths of both Henry VI and his son Prince Edward in 1471, Henry Tudor became head of the House of Lancaster. As such, he was a potential threat to the Yorkist regime, and Edward IV made various attempts to lay hands on him.

Richard III's usurpation of the throne in June 1483 had antagonised many of the Yorkist nobility and subsequent rumours of the murders of Edward V and his brother brought Henry appreciably nearer the throne. Later that year the Duke of Buckingham had prematurely staged a rebellion in favour of Henry, which was easily suppressed, though the conspirators who escaped from England came to swell Henry's tiny court in exile. He took a solemn

Lady Margaret Beaufort, mother of Henry VII, at her prayers. In the canopy above and around her are the Tudor rose and the Beaufort portcullis. The painting now hangs in St John's College, Cambridge, founded in 1511 in accordance with the Lady Margaret's will.

oath in Rennes Cathedral at Christmas 1483 that once he became king of England he would marry Princess Elizabeth, heiress of the House of York. His greatest asset was his Welsh blood and the bards fervently proclaimed his just cause, so that when he landed in Pembrokeshire in August 1485, he attracted a large following. His army marched north via Shrewsbury and thence to Stafford and Tamworth to face Richard III south-west of Market Bosworth in Leicestershire. Only nine peers had answered Richard's summons but they included Howard of Norfolk. It was Henry's good fortune to have the support of Oxford, a most experienced soldier, while Richard found himself deserted by Northumberland. As Richard rode down Ambien Hill with his household knights to charge at Henry's bodyguards, he was surrounded by Stanley's horsemen and toppled from his horse to death. In a brief engagement, Henry became master of the realm.

Henry's weak claim to the crown was of small moment compared with the outcome of the day's fighting. He had accepted the invitation of Richard's rebellious subjects to put his claim to the test of trial by battle, and had slain the reigning king. Without doubt, he was *de facto* sovereign and on the last day of October was crowned in Westminster Abbey. Eight days later Parliament assembled to greet him as a second Joshua, sent to rescue his people from tyranny, and an Act was speedily passed declaring the inheritance of the crown to have come as of right to Henry and the heirs of his body. Pope Innocent VIII subsequently threatened any who challenged his legitimate kingship with excommunication. Early in 1486 Henry married Elizabeth to unite the rival houses.

Elizabeth was eight years younger than her husband and a woman of considerable beauty. She was tall, of fair complexion with long golden tresses, and her funeral effigy indicates most graceful features. There was no role for her to play in politics beyond becoming Henry's queen and the mother of his children. By contrast, her mother, the Queen Dowager Elizabeth Woodville, was a mischievous woman and Henry suspected her of being thick with the Yorkist conspirators in 1486, so he persuaded her to withdraw to Bermondsey Abbey, a religious house to which kings of England had the right to present their relatives. Her dower lands were settled on Elizabeth of York; she

died in 1492 and was buried at Windsor beside Edward IV.

Henry's consort was gentle and devout in the tradition of the great ladies of medieval chivalric poetry, and brought out the best in her husband. After years of exile – almost his whole life until his accession – he had a settled home and soon a growing family. The moral laxity of continental courts was a byword, yet Henry remained faithful to Elizabeth. Theirs had been a political marriage, not a love match, but they grew together; he came to show her exceptional tenderness and consoled her in a most moving way when their eldest child tragically died in 1502. When, the following year, she died in childbed, Henry was stricken with grief and 'privily departed to a solitary place and would no man should resort unto him'. Thomas More wrote an elegy in which the dying Queen addresses her husband:

Adieu! Mine own dear spouse, my worthy lord!
The faithful love, that did us both continue
In marriage and peaceable concord,
Into your hands here I do resign,
To be bestowed on your children and mine;
Erst were ye father, now must ye supply
The mother's part also, for here I lie.

Until then, domestic happiness, with the future of the Tudor dynasty assured, had enabled Henry to weather the storms of internal disaffection and foreign intrigue.

In September 1486 Henry had chosen Winchester, the ancient capital of Saxon England, for Elizabeth's lying-in and here she was delivered of a son who was named Arthur 'in honour of the British race'. He was hailed as a prince who would inaugurate a golden age, this scion equally of Lancaster and York, and heir to a united England and a unified Wales. Whom he married was to be of fundamental importance. As early as 1489 Henry planned that Arthur should be betrothed to Catherine of Aragon, the daughter of Ferdinand and Isabella of Spain. It was recognition of England's new status that he should succeed in ally-ing his family with those powerful sovereigns of Aragon and Castile and, despite the perils of diplomacy and mutual suspicion of the two Kings, a marriage treaty was ultimately signed so that Catherine left Spain for good and landed in Plymouth in October 1501. Anxious until he had set eyes on his son's bride, Henry was delighted with the graceful princess and Arthur declared that 'no woman in the world could be more agreeable'. They were married in St Paul's Cathedral and after a month of court celebrations, set out for Ludlow; yet here in March the Prince of Wales and hope of England died of consumption in his sixteenth year.

Margaret had been born in 1489 and, two years later, another son Henry, Duke of York, who was intended for the Church, but Margaret and Mary (born in 1495) were expected in that age of matrimonial diplomacy to marry into royal houses to strengthen England's alliances. Princess Margaret was to marry James IV of Scotland at Holyrood House in 1503, an event celebrated by William Dunbar in his poem, *The Thistle and the Rose*, which prophesied in a mysterious way the union of the Crowns of the two warring kingdoms which would come about exactly 100 years later, when James VI travelled south to succeed Elizabeth I. The younger princess, Mary, was to be the subject of a series of conflicting treaties of betrothal, but remained single until 1514.

To the end of his reign Henry was troubled by Yorkist claimants to the throne and by pre-tenders. Immediately after his victory at Bos-worth he had sent to the Tower of London the ten-year-old Earl of Warwick (the son of Edward IV's brother, the Duke of Clarence) for he was the chief Yorkist competitor, yet King Henry could not feel secure until another claimant, John de la Pole, Earl of Lincoln, who had fled from the battlefield, was also in custody. In the autumn of 1486, not long after Arthur's birth, came disturbing news of a pretender,

claiming to be the young Warwick, who, it was rumoured, had escaped from the Tower. Lambert Simnel, who had been carefully groomed for this impersonation, swiftly be-came the hope of the White Rose and even those, such as Lincoln, who were satisfied that Simnel was an impostor saw him as a useful puppet. With aid from Margaret of Burgundy, an implacable foe of Henry's, there seemed enough support for the Plantagenet cause 'to give the King's grace a breakfast'. Once the conspirators had toppled the throne, Simnel could be cast aside for either the real Warwick, if he were still alive, or for Lincoln himself. Lincoln and Francis Lovell were able to hire 2,000 German mercenaries as the nucleus of an army, which sailed to Ireland where Simnel was crowned 'Edward VI' on Whit Sunday 1487. (Long afterwards Henry mocked an Irish dele-gation by saying 'My lords of Ireland, you will crown apes at last'.) Yet in 1487 the threat seemed very real when the rebels landed in Lancashire and made their way towards the heart of England, for the King had no standing army and no mercenaries. At the battle of Stoke, however, the pretender's army was routed, Lincoln being slain and Lovell drowned while attempting to escape. Simnel received unexpected clemency, for he was put to work as a turn-spit in the royal kitchen.

The White Rose did not, however, die at Stoke, for there was soon to be another im-postor, Master Perkin Warbeck from Tournai, whom the men of Cork felt convinced was Richard of York, the younger of the Princes in the Tower. His cause was soon supported by the Kings of France and Scotland, by Margaret of Burgundy and by the Emperor Maximilian, all of them anxious to embarrass Henry Tudor. The King at first made derisory comments about 'this lad who calls himself Plantagenet', yet Perkin Warbeck was to trouble him for six years. After Lincoln's treachery, Henry felt he could trust no-one and his minute enquiries established that Sir William Stanley and others

in high places were prepared to throw in their lot with the pretender. Their execution took the heart out of the Yorkist disaffection and when Warbeck landed at Deal in Kent, he found no supporters, so he sailed on, first to Ireland, and then to Scotland, where he was fêted at court. The large-scale invasion of England planned by James IV degenerated into a border raid, yet Henry was bent on humbling the Scots and forcing the surrender of Warbeck, so he summoned Parliament to vote heavy war taxation.

The men of Cornwall resisted the collection of the subsidy and under Michael Joseph, a smithy, and Thomas Flamank, a lawyer, raised an army, it was said, of 15,000 men to march on London and force Henry to dismiss his financial ministers, Archbishop Morton and Sir Reginald Bray, who had advised him 'to pill and poll the people'. Lord Audley agreed to lead the Cornish rebels who made their way across England to camp on Blackheath. On 17 June 1497 they were defeated by the royalist troops under Lord Daubeney. Joseph, Flamank and Audley were executed, but the rest were pardoned on condition they returned peaceably to Cornwall.

The problem of Perkin Warbeck remained. Henry sent an embassy to James IV to demand his surrender, but the pretender had already left by the West Coast; instead of making straight for Cornwall he foolishly wasted precious weeks in Ireland and did not land in England until early September. For a time Henry looked like having to fight on two fronts, but when James crossed the border to begin the siege of Norham Castle he was repelled by a massive force under the Earl of Surrey and speedily agreed to a truce. In Bodmin, meanwhile, Warbeck had himself proclaimed 'Richard IV' and attracted a strong following. Exeter re-

sisted the rebels, but they made for Taunton where the pretender learnt that the King's army was only twenty miles off. In panic he tried to find a boat in Southampton Water, but the coast was too well guarded, so he threw himself on Henry's mercy. As with Simnel, Henry showed great clemency and merely required Perkin to reside at court, but when he abused his freedom he was sent to the Tower. In 1499 there were rash plans to rescue his fellow prisoner, Warwick, and Henry decided he would take no further chances; both Warbeck and the Earl of Warwick were executed. It is hard to acquit the King of the charge of judicial murder over the latter's end, for Warwick had been a close prisoner since the accession and was guilty of no crime beyond his Yorkist blood.

Even with Warwick out of the way, Henry still felt uneasy, because Edmund de la Pole, Earl of Suffolk, the brother of Lincoln, had picked up the Yorkist gauntlet as the century closed and fled abroad to seek help from the Emperor Maximilian. Eventually in 1506 Henry succeeded in forcing the Archduke Philip to send him back to England and 'the White Rose of England' was confined in the Tower until seven years later he was summarily executed by Henry VIII.

Henry Tudor's dynastic success was exemplified by two buildings, Richmond Palace and his Chapel at Westminster Abbey. The small palace of Sheen in Surrey, by the River Thames, named after the Old English word for a beauty spot, had been a favourite residence of Edward III and Henry found it a pleasant retreat from London. He planned to keep Christmas here in 1498, but a few days before the palace was seriously damaged by fire and, surveying the ruins, he decided to replace Sheen manor with a splendid residence in the Gothic style, built

LEFT Henry VII and Queen Elizabeth witness the betrothal of their eldest son Arthur to Catherine of Aragon. This detail from an early sixteenth-century Flemish tapestry hangs in Magdalen College, Oxford. The President of the College, Richard Mayhew, was one of the envoys sent to meet the Spanish princess.

Henry's great palace at Richmond drawn by Anthony van Wyngaerde in 1555. To the right lie ruins of the former palace of Sheen which was burnt out at Christmas 1498. Only the gatehouse of Richmond Palace still survives.

round a paved courtyard. Within two years the new building was ready for occupation. The privy lodging for the royal family was decorated with fourteen turrets and it boasted an exceptional number of windows, yet the main architectural feature was a great tower. To crown his achievement Henry gave the palace a new name – Richmond – which perpetuated the title of the earldom and honour of Richmond in Yorkshire which had been his until he became King. Richmond Palace was to become a favourite residence of both Henry VIII and Elizabeth I.

Despite the union of the Red rose with the White, depicted in the emblem of 'The Tudor Rose' worn by the Yeomen of the Guard which he had established, Henry was at pains to emphasise his own Lancastrian heritage by glorifying the name of the martyred King Henry VI who had predicted his own triumphant accession. Accordingly he decided to enlarge Westminster Abbey, pulling down the Lady Chapel behind the high altar to make way for an impressive new chapel to house a shrine to

Henry VI. Negotiations were opened with the Pope for a formal pronouncement on the claim for the King's canonisation, by submitting evidence about miracles performed at his tomb, though the affair had made little progress by 1509. There was also an unseemly dispute between the canons of St George's Windsor and the monks of Chertsey and of Westminster about the custody of the relics of Henry VI, for the offerings of pilgrims at important shrines added significantly to a monastery's income. In the end Henry's coffin remained at Windsor. Work on the memorial chapel at Westminster had been going steadily forward since 1503 and Henry had drawn up an elaborate series of foundation statutes for what had in effect become his own chapel. The stately proportions of the building owed much to Sir Reginald Bray's plans, but it was not to be completed until 1519 by the master mason Robert Vertue. In his will Henry charged his executors with the task of commissioning a sculptor to work on the tombs of his wife, his mother and himself and, as a result, the Florentine Pietro Torrigiano

RIGHT A procession to Parliament drawn in the reign of Henry VIII but believed to represent a procession of Henry VII's reign since the King is depicted as an old man.

was invited to England to execute these tombs with their life-like effigies.

Overlooking Henry's tomb is a carving of the red dragon of Wales, which had been his personal standard in 1485. He had recognised the importance of paying due honour to his Welsh heritage in a way that would satisfy the ambitions of the men from the Principality who had been swayed by the Anglophobia of the bards to rise for 'Richmond's cause'. Some of them later complained that after Bosworth Field there had been no vengeance meted out to the English foe and though minor posts were found at court for a number of Welshmen, and Rhys ap Thomas of Dynevor – affectionately called 'Father Rhys' by the King – was given the Garter, Henry had no wish to revive the troublesome Marcher lordships which had so weakened the Crown in the Wars of the Roses. The government of South Wales he left to his uncle Jasper and when he died without heirs, his extensive chain of lordships passed to the Crown. To give the Welsh people pride in the Tudor dynasty Henry created Arthur Prince of Wales and on his marriage he was sent to

keep his court at Ludlow, where he received the homage of the Griffiths, Vaughans and Herberts, whose families were to provide the backbone of local government. Henry had become a thoroughly 'English' King and resisted all moves for Welsh vengeance across the Marches. Indeed, he began a series of reforms which forshadowed the Act of 1536 for incorporating Wales into the English administrative and legal system.

Henry VII was much less of an innovator than was once thought, for he built on the foundations of Yorkist experiments in autocratic, efficient government and there was much continuity in the servants of both regimes. But although he did not create the 'new monarchy' in England, he certainly strengthened the power of the Crown and succeeded in taming the great landed aristocracy so that his writs ran throughout the realm. The Lancastrians had a reputation for financial incompetence, but Henry knew the importance of exploiting the Crown's revenues. He had set out to make himself solvent as the surest way of keeping his throne, and personally audited accounts. He took a keen interest in trade, especially with the Netherlands, where the great port of Antwerp was the unrivalled centre for European trade, and through his commercial treaties secured special privileges for the English Merchant Adventurers. He also financed the Cabots' voyages of exploration to Newfoundland. As Henry became fully aware of his strength he cowed the baronage by fines and bonds. Perhaps in re-establishing royal power and a strong administration he had pressed too hard, for once he was gone his principal ministers, Empson and Dudley, were thrown to the wolves.

After Elizabeth's death Henry became almost a recluse and his court sombre. He seemed prematurely an old man, yet was reluctant to instruct Prince Henry in the science of government. To the end he was fearful that those foxy diplomatists, the Emperor Maximilian and King Ferdinand of Spain, might outwit him, and yet he seemed more of a pilgrim, seeking a crown of glory in the next world, in the tradition of the medieval church, with his obsession for his new foundation at Westminster Abbey. Although he was never popular, when he died in April 1509, aged fifty-two, Henry Tudor had brought internal peace and prosperity to England and given her a reputation in Europe she had not enjoyed for a century.

Gilt-bronze effigies of Henry VII and Elizabeth lying on a black marble tomb in Westminster Abbey. These were made by Pietro Torrigiano, a Florentine sculptor who was called to England to carry out the detailed instructions of Henry's will. The tomb is the first Renaissance monument in England.

HENRY VIII

r. 1509-47

AFTER THE PERVADING GLOOM of Henry Tudor's last years, Henry VIII came to the throne on the crest of a wave of popularity, for this handsome, beardless youth of seventeen embodied a new age and seemed the antithesis of his father. He was tall and well-proportioned, with a 'fine calf to his leg', had a fair complexion and auburn hair 'combed short and straight in the French fashion'; indeed he was 'altogether the handsomest potentate I have ever set eyes on', wrote an envoy not given to exaggeration, and there was no hint that this young man with the figure and features of a Greek god would one day swell into a gross Goliath. He was athletic, riding well, accurate in his marksmanship in the butts and determined to shine in jousts; but if he had led a sheltered life and was quite unprepared for the tasks of kingship, he had nonetheless received an enviable general education, understanding Latin easily, speaking French fluently, a boy with a profound interest in theological questions and in the problems of scholarship which worried his friend Erasmus, and possessing a flair for music-making of all kinds. He dressed superbly and by natural grace commanded the stage with an easy authority. There was no question that here was a strong personality, who would leave an indelible mark on his country. 'Hitherto small mention has been made of King Henry', commented a Venetian in London, 'whereas for the future the whole world will talk of him', and that shrewd commentator Machiavelli (who never met him) described Henry by repute as 'rich, ferocious and greedy for glory'. Here was a Renaissance prince to his fingertips, who was determined to make his court a centre for the arts and humane studies. Unlike Henry VII the new King showed himself to his people everywhere, for he knew that showmanship was a most necessary branch of statesmanship.

On his deathbed his father had advised him to marry Catherine of Aragon, the widow of his ill-fated elder brother Prince Arthur, to whom he had been betrothed since his twelfth birthday, to preserve the Spanish alliance. She was now twenty-three, petite beside Henry, but dainty and graceful, with fine eyes, and since he was young enough to be in love with love, he became captivated by the Princess it was his duty to wed. They were married at Greenwich six weeks after the accession, to enable the coronation in Westminster Abbey on Michaelmas Day to be a double crowning. There was prolonged merry-making at court in those early weeks. Henry had inherited a full Treasury and was open-handed; there were lavish banquets, masques, dances and tournaments. 'Our time is spent in continual festival', wrote the Queen. Much more mature than her husband, Catherine's sense of dignity corrected his flamboyance and added a note of seriousness without dampening his high spirits.

Henry had been content to leave the direction of affairs to Archbishop Warham, who was Lord Chancellor, Bishop Foxe and Surrey, the Lord Treasurer, though he had sacrificed his father's hated ministers Empson and Dudley to popular demand. The death of his grandmother, the remarkable Lady Margaret Beaufort, Countess of Richmond, a devout woman and a great patroness of learning, snapped a link with the past and before long Henry would be playing a more independent role, especially in foreign affairs. Since he was anxious to earn a reputation as a military commander no less than to back a righteous cause, he joined the Holy League, formed by Pope Julius II with Venice and Spain against France, whose conquests in Italy had destroyed the balance of power, and

An illustration from the Great Tournament Roll of Westminster shows Henry jousting before Catherine of Aragon at the celebrations on the birth of a son. Sadly the child died within two months. The initial 'K' and the motto 'Coure Loyall' (True heart) are embroidered on Henry's surcoat and the trappings of his horse.

in 1513 he himself led an expedition across the Channel, resuming the Hundred Years' War. Even if he missed the battle of the Spurs, his presence at the sieges of Thérouanne and Tournai gave him a taste for campaigning he never lost; fighting an enemy was in quite a different category from jousting in Greenwich tiltyard, and even as an old man of 'chronic disease and great obesity' he insisted on taking the field again in 1544. While Henry was away in France, Surrey won a signal victory over the Scots at Flodden, leaving Henry's elder sister, Queen Margaret, regent for the infant James V.

The preparations for the French campaign and the advantageous peace secured from Louis XII owed most to the King's almoner, Thomas Wolsey, who so impressed Henry by

his ability that he was promoted Archbishop of York in 1514, a year later was appointed a Cardinal and soon afterwards succeeded Warham as Lord Chancellor. From 1515 to the summer of 1529 Wolsey's rule was undisputed. He had won the King's confidence and Henry delegated more and more to him, while he followed his own bent in field-sports and music. From time to time he would bestir himself to take greater interest in diplomacy and administration, yet for all his talents he was lazy, found paperwork distasteful and lacked powers of concentration, so that increasingly the partnership with the Cardinal became one-sided. Wolsey was the last English ecclesiastic to rule in the medieval tradition, and perhaps the greatest. He amassed benefices, holding in

RIGHT Henry sends his doctor to attend Wolsey, lying sick in bed. (Bodleian Ms Douce 363, f 76)

succession the richest bishoprics in addition to his archbishopric and was also Abbot of England's wealthiest religious house, St Alban's Abbey. With these enormous revenues he indulged in his passion for building at York Place in Whitehall and at Hampton Court, of which Henry grew envious, and lived in great pomp. Though granted special powers as a papal legate, the Cardinal took little interest in reforming the church; he stood for the status quo and seriously underestimated people's dissatisfaction with clerical control, and while he was a skilled diplomatist he neglected domestic affairs. Men talked of him as if he were more powerful than the King himself, yet he was entirely dependent on Henry's favour and when he lost it he was finished.

Under the peace treaty with France in 1514 Henry's younger sister Mary, 'a nymph from heaven' of seventeen, was married off to the aged King Louis XII, still anxious to be father to a son, but he died soon afterwards and Mary impetuously made a runaway match with Charles Brandon, Duke of Suffolk, a boon companion of Henry's. They were pardoned, on being required to pay a crippling fine, and after long exile in the country Suffolk returned

to court to become Wolsey's severest critic. From this marriage sprang the Suffolk line to the succession, for their elder daughter Francis married Henry Grey, to give birth to Lady Jane Grey and her sisters.

The old Europe was changing, and changing much faster than England. The rapid expansion of Spain's empire in the New World and Portugal's exploitation of the eastern spice trade were to revolutionise the economies of the European nations. With these discoveries Europe was ceasing to be a Mediterranean continent, for there was a shift of balance to north-west Europe. Humanism, which embraced a fearless search for truth and beauty, questioned the purpose of man, and the search led inevitably to dispute with the authority of the church. Yet England remained surprisingly orthodox. The contacts of John Colet and other scholars with Italy had made them anxious to reform the church from within, much as Erasmus desired, but in England, if pockets of Lollardy remained and anticlericalism increased under Wolsey, there was no incident approaching the issue of Luther's theses at Wittenburg, which launched a specifically Protestant Reformation. England was regarded by popes as a most loyal member-state of Christendom and her King an apostle of orthodoxy. Indeed, Henry felt it his mission to write a tract against Luther, the *Defence of the Seven Sacraments*, and though Thomas More and John Fisher helped him, the book was turned by his pen in 1521 into a most effective essay in Catholic polemics. In later life he regretted some of his statements here about the indissolubility of marriage and about papal power: 'What serpent so venomously crept in as he who calls the most Holy See of Rome "Babylon" and the Pope's authority "Tyrannical"?' Dedicated to Leo X, that all might see Henry 'was ready to defend the church not only with his armies, but with the resources of his

mind', the book caused a great stir and became a best-seller on the continent; not until Queen Victoria's *Leaves from the Journal of Our Life in the Highlands* would an English royal author be so successful.

In recognition of his championship of the church Henry was given the title *Fidei Defensor*, which was confirmed by the golden bull of 1524, and though this did not make the title hereditary, its use by subsequent kings and queens of England was to be warranted by an Act of Parliament in 1544.

In France the dashing Francis I had replaced Louis XII, while in Spain Charles of Ghent had succeeded the foxy Ferdinand. The Emperor

Maximilian, who had transformed the Habsburg monarchy and strengthened its hold on the Netherlands, was approaching his end. He had recently contemplated resigning the headship of the Holy Roman Empire to Henry VIII and when Maximilian died in January 1519, Henry, no less than Francis, decided to stand for election, for he was captivated by the mystique of the Empire and wanted to be recognised as the leader of Christendom; he was the most experienced of the contestants, and the senior, being six years older than Francis and nine older than Charles. But the seven imperial electors wanted only a Habsburg to rule the confederation of German states and Charles V became the

victor. Personal rivalry between the three sovereigns, each of whom regarded himself as the embodiment of Renaissance chivalry, dominated European politics for another thirty years. Habsburg-Valois disputes in Italy, Flanders and the Rhine Valley made each turn to England for support, and despite Wolsey's aim to preserve neutrality as a method of holding the balance of power, Henry found it hard to overcome his own animosity towards Francis I and his inherited conviction that France was the traditional enemy.

Wolsey's finest hour was the glittering gathering of the Field of Cloth of Gold which he devised for Henry to meet Francis, near Guisnes. This was intended as a summit meeting to guarantee the peace of Europe. The two Kings were supported by the greatest in their realms who spent four weeks from midsummer 1520 in banquets, jousts and other contests to celebrate the rebirth of chivalry, but the burial of old animosities never succeeded. Both before and after the Field of Cloth of Gold, Henry had private meetings with Charles V at Dover and then at Gravelines, but there was no duplicity on his part. Under Wolsey's guidance he hoped to extend the entente to the Empire, but Valois-Habsburg rivalry proved too strong.

Another opportunity for Henry to become 'arbiter of Europe' came with Pope Leo X's death, and he was anxious that Wolsey should be elected, for only once before had there been an English Pope – Nicholas Brakespeare in the twelfth century. Despite much diplomatic activity and fair promises from both Charles and Francis, he failed and the Emperor's tutor, Adrian of Utrecht, become pope. His pontificate was brief and Henry again pushed forward Wolsey's candidature with no better success.

Dynastic problems soon became enmeshed in the trammels of international politics. Henry

Henry VIII arrives at the Field of the Cloth of Gold in June 1520. At the top of the picture is shown the meeting of Henry and Francis I of France.

had been overjoyed on New Year's Day 1511 when Catherine had presented him with a son, but the Prince Henry survived for no more than six weeks to their intense grief. Thereafter there was an unhappy series of miscarriages and still-births, but in 1516 the Queen gave birth to the Princess Mary, who seemed a healthy enough infant. 'The Queen and I are both young', Henry told the Venetian ambassador, 'and if it is a girl this time, by God's grace boys will follow.' Alas, the Almighty withheld his blessing and with the passing of the years it became painfully clear that no further children would be born to Catherine. Until marriage Henry had been shy with women, but Catherine had given him confidence and now he cast a roving eye at the beauties at court. In 1519 his mistress Bessie Blount, who 'excelled all other damsels in singing, dancing and goodly practices', gave him a son, Henry Fitzroy, who was subsequently created Duke of Richmond and groomed for the succession, but a natural son was a poor substitute for a prince born in the purple. The Duke died in 1536, after marrying the Duke of Norfolk's daughter.

Henry began to think that his marriage to Catherine was unfruitful because it was against God's law, despite ample papal dispensations, for he had disobeyed Holy Writ by marrying his deceased brother's wife and the more he dwelt on the matter the clearer it seemed to him that under canon law he was a bachelor who had been living in sin. No word of consolation, not even from the Pope himself, would satisfy him; Catherine was not, had never been, his lawful wife. He desperately wanted a son born in wedlock who could ultimately succeed to his throne unchallenged. Dynastic need and the burden on his conscience had become unsupportable by the beginning of 1527 and he prayed for the church to give him the relief that was his due, requiring Wolsey to use his influence with Rome to declare unequivocally that his marriage with Catherine had been invalid so that he could marry again. Dissatisfac-

tion with Catherine as a wife preceded his infatuation with Anne Boleyn, who was not content like her elder sister Mary to be a royal mistress, but wanted to be Queen consort, while Henry wanted a legitimate heir. Thus developed the 'King's Great Matter'.

Anne, the younger daughter of Sir Thomas Boleyn and Lady Elizabeth Howard, had been brought up in France in the household of Queen Claude and perhaps Henry first set eyes on both Boleyn girls at the Field of Cloth of Gold, when Anne was thirteen. She did not develop as a dazzling beauty, as Bessie Blount had been, yet she came to exercise an unprecedented fascination over the King. Her strongest points were her almond-shaped eyes and her raven hair, but she also possessed remarkable vivacity and acquired in France a flair for fashion that made Catherine seem downright dowdy. Her enemies remarked on the rudimentary sixth finger on her left hand – a sure sign, they said, of a sorceress. Before Henry had tired of her sister Mary, four years her senior, Anne had charmed Sir Thomas Wyatt, the poet, who lived near her parents' home of Hever Castle; and then came a more serious suitor, Sir Henry Percy, Northumberland's son, who was a ward of Wolsey's, but the Cardinal, sensing the King's interest in her, asked the Earl of Northumberland to call home his son. Sensual love letters survive from 1527 in which Henry assures Anne of his undying devotion: 'I would you were in mine arms or I in yours, for I think it is a long time since we kissed.' He somehow saw himself as a chivalrous knight, protecting that same 'virtue' that she so vigorously defended. It was marriage or nothing. In February 1528 he told her that with the negotiations Wolsey had in hand 'shortly you and I shall have our desired end'. Neither foresaw the difficulties ahead in his achieving a separation from Catherine, but each setback over the next five years made him long more fervently for Anne as his true wife.

The sack of Rome by imperialist troops in 1527 made Pope Clement VII a puppet of

Charles V, who would never consent to his aunt Catherine being cast aside, and despite great activity Wolsey failed to secure a satisfactory verdict from Rome. The most Clement would do was to issue a commission jointly to Cardinals Campeggio and Wolsey to hold a court in London which could hear the parties but make no judgement. Queen Catherine refused to acknowledge the authority of the court, but in a moving speech appealed to her husband: 'This twenty years I have been your true wife ... And when ye had me at the first I take God to be my judge, I was a true maid without taint of man.' At the end of the law-term Campeggio adjourned the court, to procrastinate further before the suit was removed to Rome, and this signalled Wolsey's fall. Parliament was summoned for the autumn, when the cry was 'Down with the Church', and after a period of ineffectual shadow-boxing with the papacy, Henry hearkened to the advice of Thomas Cromwell that England must break away from papal allegiance as the necessary preliminary for him to be legally rid of his wife. Wolsey was spared an attainder and allowed to retain his archbishopric. He had never visited his province and on the eve of his enthronement in York Minster in November 1530 he was arrested on suspicion of treason, but died on his journey south to face his accusers. As Cardinal legate and Lord Chancellor he had combined the reins of government in both church and state and now, under Cromwell's astute guidance, the Reformation Parliament made Henry Pope, as well as King, in his own dominions. He became Supreme Head of the Church of England, a national church that retained its medieval organisation but lacked a firm confession of faith.

Henry secretly married Anne in January 1533 and, following Archbishop Cranmer's judgement at Dunstable that Henry's marriage to Catherine had been null and void since its beginning, she was crowned Queen in Westminster Abbey at Whitsun, the folds of her robes concealing her pregnancy. She was imperious and unpopular, for there was great sympathy for Catherine of Aragon, who now reverted to her former title of Princess of Wales and lived out her remaining days at Ampthill and Kimbolton manors with a tiny household, whose wages were always in arrears. She was heart-broken, but remained firm in her Catholic faith and died in January 1536. Henry celebrated her death by dressing from head to foot in yellow.

The King had confiscated the Cardinal's residences and made extensive alterations to them. York Place, with which Anne was enchanted, was transformed into Whitehall Palace and it soon covered twenty-four acres, the largest palace in the Western world, symbolising, no less effectively than Holbein's portraits, the power of the new monarchy. At the same time he took over the neighbouring site of the Hospital of St James, where he built St James's Palace; the royal initials 'H.A.' are still depicted in the brickwork of the Clock Tower. Before long, out of the spoils of the monasteries, Henry embarked on the Palace of Nonsuch in Surrey, a fantastic pleasure dome, with its strange turrets and pinnacles and the intricate carving and plasterwork of the inner court, which was dominated by a massive statue of the King.

It was Greenwich that Anne had chosen for her lying-in and here she gave birth in September 1533 to Princess Elizabeth. Henry treated mother and child coldly; it was not for another daughter that he had broken with Rome and made Anne his Queen, but the child was healthy and precocious and he hoped a son would follow. To distract himself he took immense personal interest in the legislation Cromwell was devising to make him supreme in his own domain and to make government more efficient; there was brought about an administrative revolution to modernise the workings of the old medieval departments of state even while the Reformation Parliament was still in session. The King was adamant that his

5 The Arms of Henry VII and Henry VIII

THE FIRST KING seriously and consistently to use supporters was Henry VII. He favoured the dragon and greyhound. The dragon was traditionally associated with Cadwalader, the last native ruler of Britain, from whom Henry claimed descent. Certainly it was a favourite beast of the first Tudor king, who used it freely as a badge and motif in decoration and even created a new pursuivant (a junior herald) and named him Rouge Dragon.

The greyhound appears to have been a badge or beast associated with the House of Lancaster, from which line came Henry VII's drop of royal blood, his mother being a great-grand-daughter of John of Gaunt, Duke of Lancaster. It was later associated with the Earldom of Richmond and Henry VII's father, Edmund Tudor, used it as a supporter after being created Earl of Richmond. Although there are examples of early mottoes, Henry VII was the first king to use the motto *Dieu et mon droit* (God and my right) more or less consistently. For this reason it has been shown in the illustration. The archaic spelling of *droict* has been used below.

In the illustration of Henry's arms it will be seen that the shield is the fluted and scalloped tilting shield. There is no significance in this except that it was fashionable at the time. Arms may be shown on any shape of shield, just as the mantling may be drawn in any way the artist pleases. In heraldry only the actual objects (called charges), their disposition and colour remain unalterable.

The other coat illustrated is that of Henry VIII. He sometimes used a greyhound supporter but preferred the crowned lion of England for it must not be forgotten that the Lancastrians and the Beauforts would have had less significance for the son of the heiress of the House of York, for Henry's mother Elizabeth was Edward IV's eldest daughter.

Henry VIII was the first monarch consistently to use a crown of crosses formy and fleurs-de-lys with arches. There are some representations of his father's arms ensigned with such a crown but Henry and succeeding sovereigns always used it.

They also encircled their arms with the insignia of the Order of the Garter; a blue garter garnished with gold and embroidered with the motto of the Order *Honi soit qui mal y pense* (Evil to him who evil thinks).

An anti-papal allegory of the death-bed of Henry VIII, painted *c.* 1548. Henry indicates Edward VI as his successor. To Edward's left are members of the Regency council: Edward Seymour, John Dudley, Cranmer and William Russell. The pope sinks beneath the prayer book and in the background soldiers are destroying religious statues.

decisions over Anne and the church, ratified by Parliament, should be unreservedly supported by all his subjects, through the taking of an oath to the Succession. Sir Thomas More, who had been close to Henry and had succeeded Wolsey as Lord Chancellor, would only swear if the oath could be so framed that it did not imply his own sanction to the repudiation of the Pope's authority or the invalidity of Henry's first marriage. Neither More, nor Bishop Fisher of Rochester, the two men whose support Henry wanted most, would go against their conscience; they were tried for treason and executed, yet the King feared their stand on principle would be interpreted abroad as a powerful witness against his rule.

The month that Catherine died, Henry had a serious accident while riding in the lists and his life seemed in danger. Norfolk brought the news to his royal niece and, according to her, the shock was so great that it brought on a miscarriage of a male child. Henry was so angered that nothing could save her; he talked about being 'seduced by witchcraft' when he married her, and others said the Queen must have a defective constitution. Already Jane Seymour was waiting in the wings. There was enough circumstantial evidence that Anne had behaved indiscreetly and in the highly-charged atmosphere at court, chivalrous attention could be transformed by a gesture into passionate devotion. First Mark Smeaton, a lutanist, confessed on the rack to adultery with the Queen; then Henry Norris was implicated, two other gentlemen of the Chamber and finally her own brother, Lord Rochford. Henry was convinced of the guilt of all five men and his own profligacy assured him that Anne's own behaviour had been utterly libidinous – an English Messalina. She was tried after her alleged lovers had all been found guilty and was executed on Tower Green on 19 May 1536. The same day Cranmer issued a dispensation allowing Henry to marry Jane Seymour.

Jane was the daughter of Sir John Seymour, a Wiltshire knight who had served with Henry in France in 1513, while her mother, a Wentworth, was descended from Edward III. She was now twenty-five, fair, of medium height, rather pale-faced, and with a reputation for modesty and an inclination towards the Reformed faith. She was married to Henry in the Queen's Chapel, Whitehall, on 30 May, but her coronation, arranged for the autumn, never took place because of the plague. She chose as her motto 'Bound to obey and serve' and realised her essential role was as mother of England's heir, but first she acted as peacemaker between Henry and Princess Mary. On Trinity Sunday 1537 a *Te Deum* was sung 'for joy of the Queen's quickening of child' – an unprecedented step in the development of the liturgy – and on 12 October in Hampton Court she was delivered of a son in a difficult confinement that cost her her own life. In dynastic terms Jane had achieved all that had been expected of her and, alone of Henry's Queens, she was buried in St George's Chapel, Windsor. When ten years later he was called to his Maker he ordered that his coffin should be laid beside hers, for Jane had given him, after twenty-eight years of ruling, the Prince he had wanted, Edward, Prince of Wales.

Cromwell had enriched Henry beyond his wildest imaginings through dissolving first the smaller religious houses and then the greater monasteries, provoking the one serious threat of the entire reign, the Pilgrimage of Grace. The insurgents were suppressed as ruthlessly as the abbots who refused to surrender their houses. At the same time an authoritative English Bible based on the work of Coverdale and Tyndale was required to be placed in all churches and Cromwell and Cranmer began doctrinal discussions with the German Lutherans. Isolated in Europe Henry cast about for an ally, for when Francis I and Charles V signed a ten-year truce Henry feared they would join forces to invade England to put into practice the papal bull deposing him. This search for an alliance with Protestant states became caught up in Henry's search for a further wife and as a result he married Anne of Cleves, whose portrait by Holbein had been so flattering, in January 1540. Fearful of the consequences of the Cleves alliance if he were not to proceed with the marriage he went through with the ceremony, but found his bride from the Rhenish principality impossible; she spoke no English, had no accomplishments and, worst of all, was the antithesis of beauty. Their marriage was never consummated and once more he turned to Cromwell, the minister who had arranged the match, to secure a divorce.

While the Cleves marriage negotiation had been in progress, a Catholic reaction had begun in England, through the initiative of Stephen Gardiner, Bishop of Winchester, and Treasurer Norfolk. They had the King's ear and Henry himself came down to the Lords for the debate on the Act of Six Articles; persecutions of Anabaptists followed, though Cromwell endeavoured to mitigate the operation of the law. Henry had barely created him Earl of Essex, when he was arrested at the Council table as a result of a well-planned conspiracy of Norfolk and Gardiner. He had not attempted to procure a royal divorce because he knew that once free from Anne of Cleves Henry would marry the beautiful and orthodox Catherine Howard, niece of his enemy Norfolk. He was condemned for treasonable heresy and for the

moment even the King believed he was a sacramentary and had been too close to the Lutherans. With the Habsburg-Valois struggle renewed his policy was out-dated.

Norfolk might have profited from Cromwell's fall had the young Catherine Howard not proved such a liability. She had, like Anne Boleyn, been schooled for court and the royal bed but then it came out that she continued adulterous relations with Francis Dereham, an old flame, and with Thomas Culpeper. Henry vowed he would cut off her head with his own sword, and then self-pity overcame rage and he 'regretted his ill luck in meeting with such ill-conditioned wives'. She was executed on 13 February 1542.

After such experiences few imagined Henry would embark on a sixth marriage, yet the next year he married Catherine Parr, who had already buried two husbands, Sir Edward Burrough and Lord Latymer. She was a blue-stocking of thirty-three, who though childless had successfully brought up three step-children. She was amazed at Henry's proposal, but loyally responded it was 'the greatest joy and comfort' to look after him and his children. By now lonely, and much troubled by his ulcerous leg that had developed from his fall in 1536, Henry wanted an intellectual companion who

could make a home for his family. She succeeded in meeting his expectations as nurse and stepmother, though he disapproved of her friendship with the Cambridge Reformers. Edward, Mary and Elizabeth were all brought to court and she took the closest interest in their education. Catherine also encouraged Henry's foundation of Trinity College, Cambridge, and his transformation of the rump of Wolsey's Cardinal College, Oxford, into Christ Church.

In those last few years of the reign Gardiner fought for Catholic dogma, while Henry supported Cranmer in a much more broadly-based church. At the political level there was a struggle for the regency when Edward should succeed, in which the main contestants were Norfolk and the Prince's uncle, Edward Seymour, Earl of Hertford. It was Hertford who won the final laurels of the French war, while Norfolk was compromised by his son Surrey's treason. Here, as in the doctrinal dispute, Henry aimed at a consensus. By his will no single minister would direct affairs after he had gone, but a balanced Council of Regents. The colossus who had founded the modern English nation state died in the early hours of 28 January 1547 in Whitehall, with Thomas Cranmer at his side, but his wife and children were deliberately kept away. He wanted no farewells.

EDWARD VI

r. 1547-53

'GOD'S IMP', Henry VIII's son by his third wife Jane Seymour, was born at Hampton Court on 12 October 1537 as a result of a Caesarian section. As Bishop Latimer remarked, 'We all hungered after a prince so long that there was as much rejoicing as at the birth of John the Baptist'. His mother never recovered

from the ordeal of childbirth, but died 'through the fault of them that were about her, who suffered her to take great cold and to eat things that her fantasy in sickness called for'. Yet the fact that the boy lived and seemed healthy enough quite put his mother's death in the shade.

LEFT A portrait of Henry VIII attributed to Hans Holbein.

Elaborate precautions were taken to safe-guard Prince Edward's health to protect him from the slightest risk of infection and no less elaborate rules were drawn up for his education and his spiritual development, so that in the fulness of time he would be fully prepared to succeed his father as King and Supreme Head of the Church in England. In March 1538 the Prince was assigned a separate establishment at Hunsdon in Hertfordshire in which the key figure was Lady Bryan, a woman of long ex-perience of royal nurseries. His father remained torn between having Edward at court to lavish affection on him and show him off as a proud parent who, after twenty-eight years as King, had at last solved the intractable problem of the succession, or leaving the child safely at a manor house in country air. The motherless boy's relations with his father before Henry's final marriage to Catherine Parr were non-existent; as he later wrote in his personal chronicle, until he was six years he was 'brought up among the women' – including his half-sisters Elizabeth, four years his senior, and for some of the time, Mary, a grown woman of twenty-one. Cathe-rine Parr, however, felt it would be in the Prince's best interests to spend longer periods at court, since his whole education was being framed to help him in his future responsibili-ties. At last she had her way and this extra-ordinary family became re-united.

On Catherine Parr's recommendation Rich-ard Cox, a Cambridge humanist, was given formal charge of Edward's studies while John Cheke, professor of Greek in the same univer-sity, was appointed his regular tutor. Cox told King Henry that his six-year-old charge 'under-taketh and can frame pretty Latins ... and is now ready to enter into some proper and profitable fables of Aesop and other wholesome and godly lessons'. Cox and Cheke were both scholars in the Erasmian tradition – humanists concerned with learning, not ministers preaching a gospel – and neither would have dared to indoctrinate the Prince with the advanced views of some of the Cambridge reformers during the years of Catholic reaction that came with Cromwell's fall. Little Edward heard Mass daily, for 'every day in the mass time he readeth a portion of Solomon's proverbs', learning from them 'to fear God's commandments, to beware of strange and wanton women, to be obedient to father and mother and to be thankful to him that telleth him of his faults'. The precocious child was schooled in conscientious duty, 'in part to satisfy the good expectations of the King's Majesty' – he himself put it; *in part* because he could never hope to be wholly satisfactory to his father, nor to God, and the Almighty must have seemed to him as a heavenly version of his earthly father.

His was an unbending curriculum which, as he described it himself, included 'learning of tongues, of the Scriptures, of philosophy and the liberal sciences'. Perhaps it is fitting that Edward's name is chiefly remembered today as the nominal founder of a score of grammar schools, such as Birmingham and Southamp-ton, when a small proportion of chantry and other ecclesiastical revenues were diverted to educational purposes during his reign. If he appears as rather a prig, it is worth remember-ing that on occasion Dr Cox beat him for failing in his lessons and also that the life of the school-room was leavened by riding, archery and music making. Nor was Edward alone, for Catherine brought in boys of much the same age to share his lessons and sports, including Henry Brandon, Duke of Suffolk, Lord Thomas Howard and Barnaby Fitzpatrick, son of an Irish peer, who was Edward's closest friend, and one girl, Jane Dormer, with whom he would dance.

Edward was not yet ten years old when his father died on 28 January 1547, leaving as he believed careful constitutional arrangements for the government of the realm during his mi-nority. However, the new King's uncle, Edward

RIGHT Prince Edward as a baby painted by Holbein.

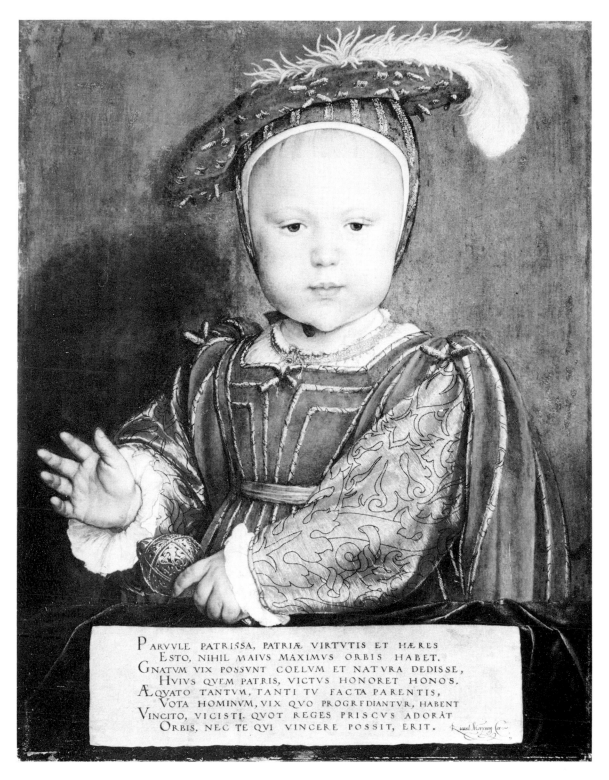

PARVVLE PATRISSA, PATRIÆ VIRTVTIS ET HÆRES
ESTO, NIHIL MAIVS MAXIMVS ORBIS HABET.
GNATVM VIX POSSVNT COELVM ET NATVRA DEDISSE,
HVIVS QVEM PATRIS, VICTVS HONORET HONOS.
ÆQVATO TANTVM, TANTI TV FACTA PARENTIS,
VOTA HOMINVM, VIX QVO PROGREDIANTVR, HABENT
VINCITO, VICISTI. QVOT REGES PRISCVS ADORÀT
ORBIS, NEC TE QVI VINCERE POSSIT, ERIT.

Seymour, Earl of Hertford, seized power, over-turning the Council of Regency to establish himself as Protector of the realm and sole guardian of the boy King, who soon created him Duke of Somerset. Edward became puppet of a faction for under Somerset's rule England became established unequivocally as a Protes-tant state. The Catholic Act of Six Articles of 1539 was repealed, the Chantries were abolished and an English Prayer Book was issued in 1549 which owed most to the genius of Thomas Cranmer. This new Reformation was enforced by an Act of Uniformity for public worship and it was to take an even more radical turn with the preparation of a Second Prayer Book in 1552, in which the central doctrine of the service of Holy Communion was declared to be no more than a commemorative rite. Gone were the veneration of saints and the remembrance of the departed; in churches there was widespread iconoclasm, for monuments were defaced, wall-paintings covered with whitewash and stained-glass windows removed if they betrayed any hint of medieval superstition. The Bible was enthroned and the glosses of the Early Fathers of the Church cast down. Henry VIII's attempt to pursue a middle course had been abandoned with a vengeance, and King Edward's tutors and chaplains so influenced his development that despite his tender

The coronation procession of Edward VI marches from the Tower along East Cheap, past Bow Church into Cheapside, past the spire of old St Paul's, and down the Strand to the embankment and Westminster. The watercolour was painted by Grimm from a wall painting in Cowdray House, destroyed by fire.

years he was in the vanguard of the movement for Protestant truth.

It is a bizarre thought that Somerset sought to enforce the 1543 treaty with Scotland under which Edward was to have been betrothed to the infant Mary, Queen of Scots, for these Tudor and 'Stuart' royal offspring were poles apart in their beliefs and general attitudes. Somerset defeated the Scots army at Pinkie near Musselburgh and then captured Edinburgh, but the Catholic Mary was sent into France to be educated as a French princess and was betrothed to the Dauphin. The Protector explored the possibility of a union of England and Scotland without success.

The summer of 1549 saw two serious threats to the regime, the rising in the West Country in protest at the English Prayer Book, which was suppressed by Lord Russell, and Kett's Rebellion in Norfolk, largely a movement against the enclosure of common fields, where the insurgents were routed by John Dudley, Earl of Warwick, son of Henry VII's finance minister. Warwick exploited his success by challenging the autocratic rule of Protector Somerset, who was outmanoeuvred, sent to the Tower and subsequently executed. Although the Duke of Northumberland (as Warwick became in 1551) never took the title of Protector, he concentrated offices and power in his hands and was ambitious for his family.

Edward VI had been kept busy at his studies. By 1550 the 'Royal Imp' had read the *Ethics* of Aristotle in the original Greek and was translating Cicero's *De Philosophia* from Latin into Greek. Even more so than the great seal of England, the boy King was *clavis regni*, the Key to the Kingdom. To establish control over his person was to become the effective ruler. Sir Thomas Seymour, the Lord Admiral and Somerset's younger brother, had married the Queen Dowager, Catherine Parr and tried to bribe Edward with pocket money. Now Northumberland sought to persuade him to use his undoubted power and rule as his father had, sure that Edward would not go against his wishes. Princess Elizabeth sewed shirts for her half-brother and wrote him touching little letters in Latin, yet Mary stayed aloof from court, very conscious of the pitfalls. Edward did not return their affection and showed no emotion when his uncles, the Protector and Admiral Seymour, were executed, nor when his stepmother, Queen Catherine, died in childbed.

The King became fanatically Protestant, as his mentors had intended, yet the future of Protestantism in England hung on the slender thread of the sickly boy's life. If he died without issue the Crown would pass to his elder sister Mary, the child of Catherine of Aragon, who was no less fanatically Catholic in her beliefs. By mid-1552 there was no doubt about the King's frailty and even courtiers regarded him as a living corpse. Northumberland was led to make his desperate gamble to alter the succession in favour of Lady Jane Grey, the eldest daughter of Henry Grey, Marquess of Suffolk by Francis Brandon, who was the daughter of Mary, younger sister of Henry VIII. Northumberland hurriedly married his son Guildford Dudley to Lady Jane and easily obtained King Edward's signature to the document to alter the succession in her favour, which was witnessed by twenty-six peers. Recent research suggests that in this Edward was not the innocent dupe of Northumberland's scheming, but was himself most anxious to preserve the Protestant succession. The salvation of England was for him more important than the doctrine of legitimacy embodied in his half-sister Mary. The consumptive, delirious youth died at Greenwich on 6 July 1553 in his sixteenth year, assured that as he had done his duty, the gates of Hell would not prevail, while good Bishop Ridley told the crowds at Paul's Cross that Jane must be acknowledged as the rightful Queen.

⌒◍⌒ MARY I ⌒◍⌒

r. 1553-8

Mary painted in 1541 when she was in her twenty-seventh year.

THE ONE SURVIVING CHILD of Henry VIII by Catherine of Aragon, Mary, was born at Greenwich Palace on 18 February 1516 and there was much rejoicing that the baby lived, even though she was a girl. She was christened at the Friary Church, outside the palace gates, where her parents had been married, and her godparents were Cardinal Wolsey and the Duchess of Norfolk, wife of the victor of Flodden. From her birth King Henry looked on his daughter as a useful pawn in the great game of dynastic diplomacy and in 1518 the first of a long series of proxy marriages for her took place when she was formally betrothed to the Dauphin of France. When Wolsey lifted the little girl in his arms to place a tiny ring on her finger, leaving it to the French Admiral Bonnivet to 'pass it over the second joint', Mary said to the Admiral, 'Are you the Dauphin? If you are, I want to kiss you'. Alas, Mary was destined to take part in several abortive betrothals to foreign princes and by the time she was twenty-eight feared she would always remain a spinster, for she had longed for a husband and children of her own. When suitors came, she said, 'there was nothing to be got but fine words and while my father lives I shall be only the Lady Mary, the most unhappy lady in Christendom'.

Mary was to remain devoted to her mother's memory, yet the later parallels drawn between Catherine of Aragon and her daughter have tended to obscure the characteristics which the Princess inherited from her father. She had the same precociousness of all Henry's children and he was proud of her. She could play the virginals when she was four and soon began a most strict regimen of study on plans drawn up by Vives, the Spanish philosopher, so that she was sent from court under the care first of the Countess of Salisbury and then of Lady Shelton, following the philosopher's precept that 'cherishing marreth sons, but utterly destroyeth daughters'. She was by nature stubborn and strong-willed and, as she developed, failed to regard compromise as anything but a betrayal of weakness.

Once the rift between Henry and Catherine developed, Mary was sent to Ludlow as Prin-

6 The Arms of Philip and Elizabeth I

EDWARD VI AND MARY I, until her marriage to Philip of Spain, used the same arms as their father. After her marriage half of Philip's complex quartered coat was placed side by side with the quartered royal arms on a single shield supported by Philip's black eagle crowned with a golden crown and a lion of England, for it must be remembered that Philip was King of England although he had to demit his regal powers when Mary died childless.

As the illustration shows, Philip's arms were divided into four grand quarters so that when just the two on the left hand side were shown conjoined to Mary's arms no symbolism was lost. The first and last grand quarters are the castle of Castile and lion of Leon quartered and repeated. Side by side in the other quarters are the coats of Aragon and Sicily. In the second and third grand quarters are four coats, namely Austria (the white band on red) Burgundy modern (the French royal arms with a border), Burgundy ancient and the lion of Brabant. Over all is a shield on which the lion of Flanders is shown side by side with the eagle of Tyrol. The pomegranate in the point in base symbolises Granada.

Elizabeth I, whose arms are shown beneath Philip's, added an extra touch of splendour to the royal arms. She adopted a gold barred helmet facing outward and substituted a gold for a red mantling. From her reign onwards this helm and mantling have been a coverted privilege of royalty. Queen Elizabeth also affected her own motto *Semper eadem* – always the same.

I have, in passing, mentioned badges. Badges, unlike arms, were usually simple devices employed to mark retainers and property. They also appeared on the long rallying flag, the standard. In the middle ages the badge was more often associated with a place than a person or family. The royal family, having vast possessions, have used a multiplicity of badges. The Tudor rose, crowned thistle, white boar and gold portcullis are among the best known.

The badges illustrated are the falcon badge, which was a favourite badge of Elizabeth and had been previously used by her mother Ann Boleyn, and the crowned Tudor rose. This famous badge symbolised the coming together of the houses of York and Lancaster in the Tudor dynasty. It was used by all the Tudors and, uncrowned, has remained a popular heraldic symbol.

SEMPER EADEM

cess of Wales (as Arthur had been by Henry VII, though for very different reasons) and was agonisingly deprived of her mother's company. Inevitably she took her mother's side in the King's Great Matter and Anne Boleyn hated her for it. Once Anne, as Queen, had produced a rival Princess, she demanded that Mary's ears be boxed 'for the cursed bastard she is' and at Hatfield the seventeen-year-old girl was now assigned the pokiest room in the house, deprived of her personal maids and made to serve as lady-in-waiting to her baby half-sister. The animosity between Catherine and Anne was understandably to be continued in the next generation by their respective daughters. Mary was heartbroken at her mother's death. In her last hours Catherine had written to Henry, pleading with him to be a good father to Mary and to preserve her rights to the succession.

With Anne Boleyn's fall, there was a chance of *rapprochement*, for Jane Seymour desperately wanted to reconcile Henry with Mary. She was now twenty, with a mind of her own, and she persistently refused to recognise her father as Supreme Head of the Church, for such contradicted all she had learnt about religion from her earliest years. The Duke of Norfolk told her if she had been *his* daughter he would have knocked her head 'against the wall until it was as soft as baked apple'. At last Cromwell, with the help of Chapuys, the imperial ambassador, succeeded in bringing home to Mary the peril in which she lay. He sent her a draft letter in grovelling terms which he told her to copy out word for word and sign, making her submission to Henry. This she did, making mental reservations about the Pope's authority, and when summoned to court to acknowledge her faults personally before her father, 'most humbly laying at his feet', the worst of their estrangement was over. Above all Mary wanted to be taken back within his family circle: 'I would rather be a chamberer, having the fruitions of Your Highness' presence than an empress away from it.' Henry was overjoyed that

his 'chiefest jewel' was again living with him, though Mary was still under the slur of bastardy. Prince Edward's birth brought the two sisters together, for both must now give way to a brother; yet there was seventeen years between them. At Hunsdon Mary taught Elizabeth to play card games for stakes and encouraged her fool to amuse her with his antics.

King Henry's final marriage meant much to Mary, for she was now more regularly at court than at any time since 1530 and she regarded Queen Catherine Parr as more of a sister than yet another step-mother. Catherine showed her many kindnesses and for the first time the Princess had an adequate allowance for clothes. The Queen suggested Mary should undertake a translation of Erasmus's paraphrases of the New Testament, which she began and Nicholas Udall completed when her ill-health made serious study impossible. Mary suffered much illness throughout the 1540s.

On Edward VI's accession the Protector's brother Admiral Seymour attempted to make a bid for Mary's hand before turning his attentions to the Queen Dowager, when he implored the Princess to use her influence with Catherine Parr to accept him. Mary wisely refrained – 'I being a maid am nothing cunning' in love affairs. Such circumspection did not desert her throughout the reign, when the revolution in religion was anathema to her. No-one, not even her royal half-brother, knew how they might 'turn her opinions'. She resided quietly, outside London, waiting for sickly Edward's demise, but praying for him fervently. When Northumberland had Lady Jane Grey proclaimed Queen in London, Mary was in Suffolk and the country rallied to her, content to allow the succession to take its proper course, even if the sovereign were a woman, single and at heart a Catholic.

The key question was whom should Mary, England's first Queen Regnant since Matilda challenged Stephen's accession in 1135, marry? She secretly sought the advice of Simon Renard,

A prayer for a woman with child from Mary's prayer book. It is said to be blotted with her tears.

Charles v's ambassador, telling him she had 'never felt that which is called love, nor harboured thoughts of voluptuousness'. His list of eight possible bridegrooms was rapidly reduced to a single name, Philip II of Spain, now a widower, and reports of his religious orthodoxy delighted her no less than his portrait. In her private oratory, accompanied by Renard and a lady-in-waiting, Mary led the saying of the *Veni Creator* and then solemnly declared she would marry Philip and 'love him perfectly'. A marriage treaty was signed in November. By then Parliament had begun to dismantle the Edwardian Reformation settlement and the Roman Mass was again celebrated. In due course Cardinal Reginald Pole would return to England to absolve Mary's subjects from their sin of heresy and reconcile them with the Church of Rome.

The Spanish marriage proposal alarmed many Englishmen and there were widespread plans for a rising to force Mary to abandon her

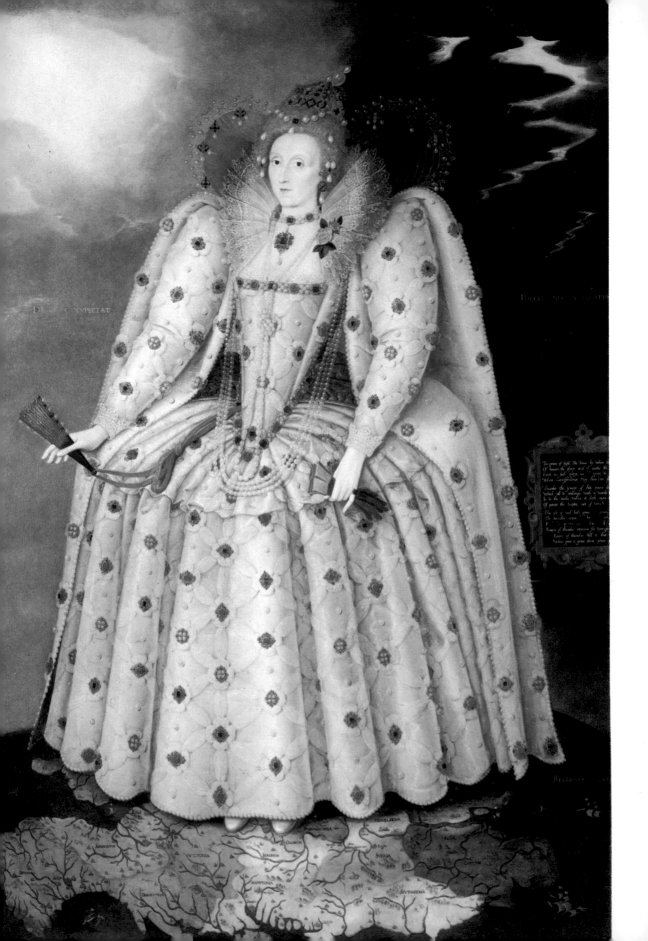

betrothal to Philip, but they were mishandled and only Kent rose, under Sir Thomas Wyatt in January 1554. Wyatt, with a following, succeeded in crossing Kingston Bridge to march on London, but he was routed, while the Queen stayed impassively at St James's Palace. Mary was convinced that her sister was in league with Wyatt and sent her to the Tower, but no evidence could be found to incriminate her so she was moved to Woodstock Palace to be out of the way when Philip arrived, for Elizabeth was the obvious focus for opponents to Mary's regime.

Philip and Mary were married in Winchester Cathedral in July 1554 and proceeded to Hampton Court for their honeymoon. It was to Hampton that she returned the following May, convinced she was pregnant. Midwives were engaged and announcements of the happy event were prepared, ready signed, with blanks left for the sex and the date, to send to foreign courts. The weeks passed, yet no child was delivered, for Mary had mistaken the symptoms of dropsy for signs of pregnancy. So desperately did she want a child, for its own sake quite apart from the need to maintain the Catholic succession, that next year there was a plot at court to pass off a suppositious prince, though it never reached her own ears.

Mary Tudor felt deserted by Philip, whose sole interest in marrying her had been to secure England's support for his continental designs. Besides Spain, he now had the government of the Netherlands, Milan and Naples assigned to him by his father, Charles v, who was abdicating, and there was the growing problem of the Spanish Empire in the New World. Philip could not believe it when Parliament refused to have him crowned 'King of England'. His

Queen was sure the ill-success of their marriage was due to divine vengeance – a punishment for the heresies still practised in England, and so the fires of Smithfield began. Hooper, the deprived Bishop of Gloucester, was burnt at the stake in February 1555 and later in the year Archbishop Cranmer and Bishops Ridley and Latimer followed him. Many clergy and lay folk who would not be turned from their Protestantism escaped to Geneva or Zurich to await safer, saner times, but the militants who remained faced persecution and risked death. Their heroism is enshrined in John Foxe's 'Book of Martyrs' as his *Acts and Monuments* soon became familiarly termed. The burnings provoked utter disillusionment with Mary's regime and her leading minister Cardinal Pole.

England had entered the war with France as Spain's ally and despite an early success at St Quentin, there came in January 1558 the great national disaster of the loss of Calais, England's last possession in France to which it had hung tenaciously since the end of the Hundred Years' War. Mary bore the brunt of the blame and she knew that instead of raising the stature of England by her marriage to Philip, she had brought national prestige to the lowest point in memory.

Mary's illness became progressively worse and Philip's absence caused her to turn to her step-sister and achieve in her final months some measure of reconciliation. Elizabeth was at Hatfield when Mary died at St James's on 17 November 1558. It was in the Chapel Royal at St James's that Mary's heart and bowels were buried, though her corpse was laid to rest at Westminster Abbey. Perhaps this symbolises her torn interests. Half Spanish by birth and married to a Spaniard, she never understood her native people.

LEFT A portrait of Elizabeth I painted in 1592 to commemorate the Queen's visit to Sir Henry Lee, her Champion of the Tilt, in September 1592. The Queen's feet stand on Ditchley in Oxfordshire where Lee staged a magnificent entertainment.

ELIZABETH I

r. 1558–1603

THE DAUGHTER OF HENRY VIII and Anne Boleyn came into her inheritance on 17 November 1558, a day to be marked by celebrations even after the close of her long reign some forty-four years later. The 'crown imperial' was hers of right, and for this she had never known a mother's love, had carried the stigma of bastardy, had faced the terrors of suspicion when Somerset and Northumberland ruled for her young brother Edward and had endured the peril of the Tower and the ignominy of exile at Woodstock in her sister Mary's reign. Elizabeth had triumphed over endless difficulties and at the age of twenty-five learnt at Hatfield that her reign had begun: 'This is the Lord's doing; it is marvellous in our eyes', she quoted from the Psalms. Throughout the land there was rejoicing; bonfires were lit in thankfulness that the burnings at Smithfield were over, tables were brought into the streets of London for folk to 'eat and drink and make merry for the new Queen' and in York when the accession proclamation was read, her name was greeted as a true sovereign 'of no mingled blood of Spaniard, or stranger, but born mere English here among us'. She saw it as her mission to unite a divided people and she came to embody a truly national consciousness with such success that she gave her name to an age.

Her early years had been spent chiefly at Hunsdon and Hatfield manors under the care of Lady Bryan, but when she was four Catherine Champernowne was appointed her governess and quickly won her confidence. Catherine gave her a remarkable grasp of languages and classical scholarship; by the time she was six one courtier reckoned that if her formal education ceased forthwith 'she will prove of no less honour and womanhood than shall be seen her father's daughter'. Though she saw little of him,

Elizabeth was devoted to King Henry and later on would revere his memory for what he had achieved in church and state. At last, after he married Catherine Parr in 1543, the three royal children were brought to court for long periods, so with a room at Whitehall Palace next door to the Queen's she felt she had a settled home. Catherine encouraged her studies so she now had Greek lessons from John Cheke, learnt Italian from Battisti Castiglioni and, to her father's delight, made excellent progress on the virginals. Godly learning in the Erasmian tradition was varied by riding, archery and dancing in all of which Elizabeth excelled. There was much practical relevance in the curriculum for a future ruler, though at the time no-one expected the Princess to become more than the consort of a foreign sovereign.

The earliest portrait shows a pale-faced girl of thirteen, with auburn hair and innocent eyes, regal and confident in her bearing, seriously reflecting on the book she is holding. Those final years of Henry's reign were perhaps the most peaceful of times. He had been the one constant factor in her life and once he died there would be endless difficulties for her. The Act of Succession had settled the crown in turn on Edward, Mary and Elizabeth and although Henry had confirmed this in his will, he went on to provide for the remote possibility of all three of his children dying childless, in which case the crown should descend to the heirs of his younger sister Mary (the Suffolk line) instead of the heirs of his elder sister Margaret, who had married James IV of Scotland in 1503 (the Stuart line). In the event Elizabeth was to override his preference, just as Edward Seymour, Earl of Hertford, immediately abrogated the dying King's plans for a Council of Regency by seizing power himself.

Elizabeth stayed with her stepmother in Chelsea but soon the Protector's brother, Lord Admiral Seymour, had intruded on their household to marry the Queen Dowager and then to flirt with the fourteen-year-old Princess. He would barge into her bedroom to tickle her and snatch kisses, but for all his charm he became repulsive to her and she was relieved when Catherine sent her to stay at Cheshunt, where she had the company of 'Kat' Ashley (her governess had married John Ashley, the friend of Roger Ascham). Soon Ascham himself became her tutor, extending her scholarship by his method of 'double translation'. Later in life Ascham remarked on her industry, her prodigious memory and her modesty. She was not entirely free from Thomas Seymour, for when Catherine Parr died in childbed he was indeed free to marry her; rumours were rife, but the Princess dismissed the topic – 'it was but a London news'. The Admiral's plans to overturn his brother were tumbled and he was sent to the Tower. In the investigations both Mistress Ashley and Thomas Parry, the Princess's cofferer, were themselves examined in the Tower to wring from them any incriminating evidence, while Elizabeth was cross-questioned by Sir Robert Tyrwhit who was amazed at her circumspect answers. For a time she was denied Kat Ashley's service but made such a fuss that the Council relented. The list of treasons alleged against Seymour, which sent him to the block, included craftily attempting to marry Elizabeth; long afterwards she spoke of him as 'a man of much wit and very little judgement'. She survived by steering clear of politics under Northumberland and, despite her Protestantism, was relieved at the failure of the attempt to place Lady Jane Grey on the throne, for the establishment of the Suffolk line would have ruled out her own right to succeed, and with Mary's accession she became heir apparent.

With Mary's re-establishment of Catholicism and betrothal to Philip of Spain, the real test began for Elizabeth. Opposition to Mary

The earliest portrait of Elizabeth, by an unknown artist.

naturally focussed on her sister, who was popular, and she had to be on her guard to avoid entanglement in the plots woven about her. Suspected of complicity in Wyatt's revolt, she was summoned from Ashridge to court and, as she was ill, was brought in a litter by easy stages to Whitehall Palace where Mary refused to see her. After a month she was taken by barge to the Tower in terror of being quietly put out of the way, but she bravely told her warders she was no traitor 'but as true a woman to the Queen's Majesty as any'. Mary suspected much and could not believe Elizabeth was being frank when she swore that though Wyatt might have

The succession of Henry VIII, painted in Elizabeth's reign, shows Mary and Philip followed by Mars, the god of war, and Elizabeth followed by Flora and the fruits of prosperity. Edward VI kneels beside his father.

written to her, 'on my faith I never received any from him'. Yet since the Queen had no evidence to send her for trial she had no justification for confining her, even though the political situation required her to be under close surveillance. At last after eight weeks in the Tower she was moved to Woodstock in Oxfordshire in the custody of a stiff-necked Norfolk squire, Sir Henry Bedingfield. Here Elizabeth remained for ten months, to all intents a prisoner, while Mary married Philip and Cardinal Pole reconciled England with the Church of Rome.

At Woodstock there were pin-pricking restrictions about her books, about letter-writing and about her devotions. When she was ill, Mary refused her request for a royal physician to attend her and said an Oxford doctor would do just as well. This brought a characteristic outburst – 'I am not minded to make any stranger privy to the state of my body, but commit it to God'. The Queen gave way and sent Dr Owen to her, and his treatment reduced the swellings in her face and arms. She kept up her spirits by her duel of wits with Bedingfield and remained ambivalent about her conversion to Catholicism; some said she only heard mass daily 'to give the impression that she had changed her religion. However she is too clever to get herself caught.' At last in April

1555 she was allowed to return to court and though she stubbornly denied there had been any fault in her behaviour, which angered Mary as it made plain that Elizabeth felt she had been wrongfully punished, there came a reconciliation between the half-sisters when the Princess unreservedly professed her undying loyalty. For the rest of the reign she remained chiefly at Hatfield, with Sir Thomas Pope, who proved a much more cultivated and endearing guardian than Bedingfield. Proposals for her hand had come thick and fast, from Habsburg princes, from the Duke of Savoy and from the King of Sweden's son, but Elizabeth said 'she had no wish to marry'. In the summer of 1557 Queen and Princess kept midsummer together at Richmond and later in the year Mary paid a state visit to Hatfield. In her last illness Mary agreed with the Spanish ambassador and her Council that only Elizabeth could succeed her and sent word imploring her to maintain the old faith.

As Queen, indeed, the most urgent problem was the religious settlement. From the beginning Elizabeth was determined to avoid the extremes of both her brother's and her sister's reigns, so that her people could live together in unity and concord and she strove hard to establish a church that was broadly based with a doctrine sufficiently elastic to satisfy the vast majority of her subjects. This middle way naturally antagonised the Protestant exiles returning from Geneva and Zurich who had greeted Elizabeth as Deborah, the restorer of Israel, and hoped that the doctrine embodied in the 1552 Prayer Book would be reintroduced, but episcopacy abolished, for they had drunk deeply at the wells of Calvinism. Such partisan views were anathema to the Queen and, despite the pressure of Protestants in Parliament, the *via media* was to be pursued. She would not, she said 'open windows in men's souls'. Outward conformity by attendance at church of a Sunday was enough; if men chose also to hear the Roman mass privately or to attend a sectarian

meeting there would be no harm done. Alas, because she was both Queen and Supreme Governor of the Church of England, 'nonconformity' would come to be interpreted as 'disloyalty' to the regime and after 1570, when the Pope had the effrontery to issue a bull deposing her and absolving her subjects from their allegiance, practising Catholics were turned into potential traitors. In a similar way the Puritan wing of Protestantism came to undermine royal authority. Under the pressure of political events Elizabeth's ideal of a golden mean could not be achieved, but there is no denying her abhorrence of persecution and her fundamental dislike of extremes.

From the first Elizabeth placed exceptional trust in William Cecil, who had helped to administer her properties as Princess, and he was destined to serve her devotedly until his death in 1598, first as Principal Secretary, then as Lord Treasurer – a remarkable partnership. Matthew Parker, whom she selected as Archbishop of Canterbury, fulfilled all her expectations of him in moulding the Church of England, though she never approved of his having a wife. These two men were links with the past, for Cecil's grandfather had fought for her grandfather at Bosworth, while Parker had connexions with the Boleyns.

At the outset of the reign de Feria, the Spanish ambassador, had noted that Elizabeth was 'much attached to the people and is very confident that they take her part'. Her popularity was indeed most obvious during the festivities accompanying the Coronation on 15 January 1559, a date which the astrologer John Dee had helped her to select. The post of Lord High Steward of England at the Coronation went to Henry, Earl of Arundel, a widower who fancied his chances of becoming consort. Another English candidate was Sir William Pickering, a diplomat whose swagger upset everyone, but there was no shortage of foreign princes offering their hands – Philip of Spain himself, the Duke of Holstein, Eric of Sweden and two Habsburg Archdukes. It was taken for granted in England and abroad that Elizabeth would marry and that marriage would solve the problem of the succession; her marriage and the succession were the twin topics on which Parliament continued to press her, to her extreme annoyance – they would never have dared to treat her father thus, she growled.

The problem of the succession was the more acute since, immediately on Mary's death, her cousin Mary, Queen of Scots, wife of the Dauphin of France, had claimed to be rightful Queen of England in Elizabeth's place, and when the Dauphin succeeded to the throne as Francis II in July 1559, England looked most vulnerable; never had the 'auld alliance' between Scotland and France been so menacing, for both were controlled by the Guise faction. That winter the English fought over the border as allies of the Protestant Lords of the Congregation to expel the French and, by the Treaty of Edinburgh that followed, the Scots fully recognised Elizabeth's right to her throne and undertook that their own Queen, still in France, should relinquish her claims. The sudden death of Francis II in December 1560 increased Elizabeth's difficulties, since Mary would now reside in Scotland. Mary consistently refused to ratify the Treaty of Edinburgh, unless Elizabeth would name her as her successor, and Mary's search for another husband, in England and on the continent, further aggravated the matter. The two Queens, enemies to the end, would never meet each other.

Elizabeth caught smallpox in 1562, and seemed near to death. Ministers discussed who might succeed her, which was no longer an academic question, especially as there were 'nearly as many different opinions as there were councillors present'. When the Queen recovered she said that in case of a like emergency, Lord Robert Dudley should be made Protector of the realm. Dudley, Northumberland's fifth son, had been appointed Master of the Horse and had come to high favour by April 1559; he

was so much with the Queen that men said that had he not already a wife Elizabeth would have married him, and exaggerated tales of their relationship were related in foreign courts. Then Dudley's wife, Amy Robsart, died in suspicious circumstances and though the coroner's inquest cleared Lord Robert – he was with the Queen at Windsor at the time – the tragedy at Cumnor made all the difference to the question of marriage. Dudley was in any case too controversial a figure in personality and politics for her to take him as a husband without dividing her court and people, though she remained emotionally tied to 'sweet Robin' till his death. The request that he might become 'protector' if anything happened to her indicates the strength of their special relationship. 'The Queen would like everyone to be in love with her', commented a shrewd ambassador 'but I doubt whether she will ever be in love with anyone enough to marry him.' Though there were to be other suitors from abroad, notably the Archduke Charles and then the French Duke of Alençon, Dudley long cherished the hope of marrying the Queen, nor was he the only Englishman with this ambition.

Christopher Hatton, who had caught her eye at a masque by his fine dancing, became one of the corps of Gentlemen Pensioners, her personal bodyguard of which in 1572 he became Captain. While she nicknamed Robert Dudley 'Eyes', Hatton became 'Lids' and wrote her passionate love letters: 'To serve you is heaven, but to lack you is more than hell's torment'. He wept when she spurned him and vowed to stay celibate for her sake, dreaming of the idyll that might have been, and she loved him for it. She forced the Bishop of Ely to give him his house in Holborn, while the favourite built Holdenby House in his native Lincolnshire as a 'shrine' for her. He was to become Lord Chancellor. There developed a curious bond between Dudley, Hatton and also Heneage through their rival devotion to the Queen, but none of them could stand the outsider,

Walter Raleigh, who made his début at court in 1581.

Though the society in which she lived at court was essentially masculine, Elizabeth succeeded in dominating it, evoking a genuine emotional response from courtiers in general because she was a woman as well as a Queen. She charmed those about her into participating in the sophisticated allegorical fantasy of the Virgin Queen, contriving to live out a mystical romance on a public stage. The musicians and poets praised her as Fair Oriana or as the immortal shepherdess of a pastorale and the older she grew the more she delighted in the cult. Her household resembled a large family, often on the move between residences, and as a family it had its feuds, when factions formed around strong personalities. It was not out of malice that Elizabeth opposed her maids of honour's plans to marry, but because marriages broke up her own family circle. Like her father Elizabeth wanted her court to become a great cultural centre, an academy where scholars, musicians and artists could find fellowship and patronage, although she was not prepared to spend as freely as Henry VIII. Musicians such as William Byrd fared much better than the poets, and Edmund Spenser failed to find a post at court even when he had dedicated *The Faerie Queene* to his sovereign.

To solve the problem of Mary of Scotland, Elizabeth had suggested that Mary might marry her own Dudley, whom she created Earl of Leicester. Mary, however, had set her heart on Lord Darnley, descended from Queen Margaret's second marriage with the Earl of Angus. The fact that Darnley was an English subject made him even more unsuitable in Elizabeth's eyes, yet in July 1565 their marriage took place. 'King Darnley' fathered the future James I and VI, but soon showed himself a worthless sot and he was murdered at Kirk-o'-Field, probably on the Earl of Bothwell's orders. Next month Mary married Bothwell, provoking the Lords

of the Covenant to arms; they defeated Bothwell at Carberry Hill and forced Mary to abdicate. In May 1568, however, she escaped from Lochleven Castle, to throw herself on Elizabeth's mercy, but the Queen decided she had no alternative but to keep her in close custody. Unwillingly she found herself acting as arbiter between Mary and her subjects and while she could never forgive a claimant to her throne, she would not lightly sacrifice an anointed queen to rebellious subjects.

Mary's presence in England provoked the Northern Rebellion of 1569 in which the Earls of Northumberland and Westmorland aimed to restore Catholicism and place Mary on the throne. The rebels were defeated by Hunsdon, the Queen's cousin, but another cousin, Thomas Howard, fourth Duke of Norfolk, was found to be deeply implicated in the rising and in 1572 was executed for his share in the Ridolfi conspiracy. Elizabeth would have preferred to pardon him, but Cecil pointed out to her the inexorable logic of statecraft. Thereafter a further series of conspiracies were planned by Catholics to carry out the papal bull deposing Elizabeth; all hinged on foreign aid and saw the Queen's death as a preliminary to Mary Stuart's accession. In this atmosphere of plot and counterplot Elizabeth showed remarkable courage and forbearance, trying hard to reduce the severity of the Draconian laws against her Catholic subjects. Francis Walsingham, now Secretary of State, longed for her to take a positive role in opposing the forces of the Counter Reformation in Europe by supporting the Dutch Protestants against Philip of Spain and intervening on the side of the Huguenots in the French religious wars, but she was anxious to be at peace with her neighbours, hating the waste and inhumanity of war, even if she profited by the marauding of Hawkins and Drake against Spanish possessions in the New World. In 1572, however, England at last found an ally in France and to preserve this alliance Elizabeth undertook a protracted courtship of the Duke of Alençon, throwing herself into the role of lover with gay abandon.

François Alençon was half her age and diminutive beside her, yet he had remarkable charm and she fell for his flattery. During 1579 it seemed as if she would really marry him, but there was a Puritan outcry against the Duke's 'unprince-like, French kind of wooing'. The discovery that Leicester had secretly married the beautiful Lettice Knollys, while still protesting his undying love for Elizabeth, would almost have driven her into Alençon's arms, had it not been for Protestant fervour; the match eventually failed, as the Habsburg marriage negotiations had also foundered in 1567, because the potential bridegroom was a Catholic. Her head overcame her heart and she let Alençon go, but by now she was in her late forties and knew that it was her last chance of marriage and children.

Her depression was saved by the arrival of Walter Raleigh, a west countryman of singular wit and gallantry, who praised her in verse. Leicester's nose was soon out of joint and Hatton in utter despair, for his rise to favour was meteoric. She was truly fascinated by Raleigh and fed on his adoration; only Raleigh would have tried to plant a colony in North America and name it Virginia, after his Queen. Yet eventually, when he realised that she would never marry him and found happiness with Bess Throckmorton, the Queen was furious and banished them both from court.

War with Spain loomed nearer as Walsingham's agents pieced together plans for Philip

Elizabeth is carried by her courtiers, attributed to Robert Peake. Ahead of the Queen are seven Garter knights: Edmund Sheffield; Charles, Lord Howard of Effingham; George Clifford, 3rd Duke of Cumberland; Thomas Butler, 10th Earl of Ormonde; unknown; George Talbot, 7th Earl of Shrewsbury; Edward Somerset, 4th Earl of Worcester. The Gentlemen Pensioners line the route. The picture was probably painted in 1600, but like most of Elizabeth's portraits, shows the Queen as still young and beautiful.

A map of the British Isles in 1588, showing the course of the Spanish Armada. In the bottom right-hand corner the English and Spanish fleets are depicted off Calais where English fire-ships drove the Spaniards from their anchorage. Further north the English ships are shown pursuing the Spanish fleet off the coast of Holland. The Spaniards sailed home westward around the north of Scotland but were much depleted by storms and disease before reaching Spain.

II's Enterprise against England, and then Mary Queen of Scots was found to be personally committed in the Babington Plot against the Queen's life. Elizabeth hesitated long over sending Mary to her execution at Fotheringhay and then blamed it on her officials. Burghley (as Cecil had become) was in disgrace and for a time feared the Tower. Already, following the murder of William the Silent, she had been persuaded to send an army under Leicester to fight against the Spanish in the Netherlands, though she refused to accept the sovereignty of the Dutch people. Drake and the seadogs, flushed with their successes in the Caribbean, urged open war with Spain, but still Elizabeth held back, preferring negotiation to fighting. Drake's

raid on Cadiz postponed the sailing of the Armada for a year, but at last in August 1588 the great Spanish fleet was in the Channel, endeavouring to gain command of the Straits of Dover to launch a full-scale invasion.

In this moment of crisis Elizabeth was superb. Against her councillors' wishes she went down to Tilbury Camp to exhort the troops under Leicester at the very moment when it was feared an invasion would be attempted. 'Let tyrants fear. I have always so behaved myself that, under God, I have placed my chiefest strength and goodwill in the loyal hearts and goodwill of my subjects ... I know I have but the body of a weak and feeble woman, but I have the heart and stomach of a King.' She spoke for England. The Armada, scattered from Calais Roads by the fireships, was driven into the North Sea, to find its way home by the north of Scotland and Ireland. The Spanish defeat did not bring Philip II to his knees, but it put fresh heart into the cause of Protestantism in Europe, especially in Holland. Through divine intervention, men said, the Colossus of Spain had at last been stayed and Elizabeth was the heroine of the hour. None then predicted that the war would outlast the Queen's reign.

Leicester's death the following month soured the fruits of victory. She locked herself in her room and would see no-one, so that her councillors ordered her door to be broken down, fearing for her safety. The intensity of her feeling for Leicester was revealed only after her own death when in a little casket by her bed was found among her treasured keepsakes the letter he had written to her from Rycote the night before he died, with her own inscription in a shaky hand 'His last letter'.

Old age brought its harsh losses. Soon she was being called to the bedside of Christopher Hatton at Ely Place to feed him 'with cordial broths' as he lay dying, then Walsingham went and finally old Burghley, who had triumphed by bringing in his second son Robert Cecil to share his power. The series of 'Armada portraits' and the splendid painting of Elizabeth standing on the map of England (1592) concealed the ravages time had made on her face and figure. Marvellous in jewels and ruff, Gloriana was almost sixty, and had resorted to an auburn wig to hide her thinning hair, and a liberal use of cosmetics. Still the masquerade went on and the final act was dominated by Leicester's stepson, Robert, Earl of Essex, a handsome youth who fancied himself as a general and looked to the Queen to retrieve him from financial ruin. Robert Cecil outwit-

ted him in Council, yet Essex banked all on success against the Irish rebels. He came home in defiance of the Queen's orders and gambled on saving himself by his charm, but she had decided to teach him a long-overdue lesson and she refused to underwrite his vast debts. In 1601 he drifted into conspiracy, aiming at the throne himself, but his revolt was easily suppressed and Essex was executed for treason. Elizabeth reckoned he had as little judgement as Thomas Seymour, two generations back.

That year she addressed her last Parliament and her touch was as sure as ever. She had always taken great care with her speeches from the days of her earliest Parliaments, but now she delivered what posterity called her 'golden speech', because it epitomised the relationship of sovereign and people in a golden age of monarchy that effectively ended with her death. Being Queen, she told them, was a glorious thing, but it was her people's loyalty and love that mattered: 'There will never Queen sit in my seat with more zeal to my country . . . And though you have had, and may have, many Princes more mighty and wise, sitting in this state, yet you never had, or shall have, any that will be more careful and loving.'

She had never named her successor and even at the last would not do so, for she knew that the careful Cecil was discreetly planning for James VI of Scotland, the son of Mary Stuart and Darnley, to enter upon the seat of Kings on her demise. After Christmas 1602 she began to feel most frail and six weeks later fell ill at Richmond. Insomnia was far worse to bear than sickness and it increased her melancholy. Her work of 'having brought up, even under her wing, a nation that was almost begotten and born under her' (as Thomas Dekker put it) was over. She died on 24 March 1603, the last of the Tudors and the greatest of queens.

7
THE
STUARTS
1603 ~ 1714

James I in Parliament: the Lord Chancellor and Lord
Treasurer stand to left and right; on either side are
bishops and lay lords. His son Prince Charles sits in front
of the Lord Treasurer.

THE TUDORS AND STUARTS

Arthur
Prince of Wales
1486-1502

m.(1)Catherine (2)
of Aragon
d. 1536
(divorced)

m.(1)HENRY VIII
1491-1547

(2)m. Anne Boleyn
d. 1536
(3)m. Jane Seymour
d. 1537
(4)m. Anne of Cleves
(divorced)
d. 1557
(5)m. Catherine Howard
d. 1542
(6)m. Catherine Parr
d. 1548

James IV
King of Scots
d.1513

m. (1)Margaret (2)m. Archibald
1489-1541 / Douglas,
6th Earl of
Angus
d.1557
(3)m.Henry Stuart
Lord Methven
d.c.1551

James V (1)m.Madeleine
King of of France
Scots d.1537
1512-42 (2)m.Marie of
Lorraine-Guise
d.1560

Margaret m. Matthew Stuart
Douglas 4th Earl of Lennox
1515-78 d.1571

MARY I
1515-58
m.Philip II of Spain
d.1598

ELIZABETH I
1533-1603

EDWARD VI
1537-53

François II
King of France
d.1560

m. (1)Mary
Queen
of Scots
1542-87

(2)m. Henry Stuart
Lord Darnley
1545-67
(3)m. James Hepburn
4th Lord Bothwell
d.1578

Anne of Denmark
d.1619

m. JAMES I
(VI of Scotland)
1566-1625

Henry Frederick
Prince of Wales
1594-1612

CHARLES I
1600-49

m. Henrietta Maria
of France
1609-69

CHARLES II
1630-85
m.Catherine of Braganza
d. 1705

Mary
1631-60

m. William II
Prince of Orange
d.1650

Anne Hyde m. (1)JAMES II(2)
d.1671 1633-1701

m. Mary of
Modena
d.1718

WILLIAM III m. MARY II
1650-1702 1662-94

ANNE
1664-1714

m. George of Denmark
d.1708

William, Duke of Gloucester
1689-1700

died
in
infancy

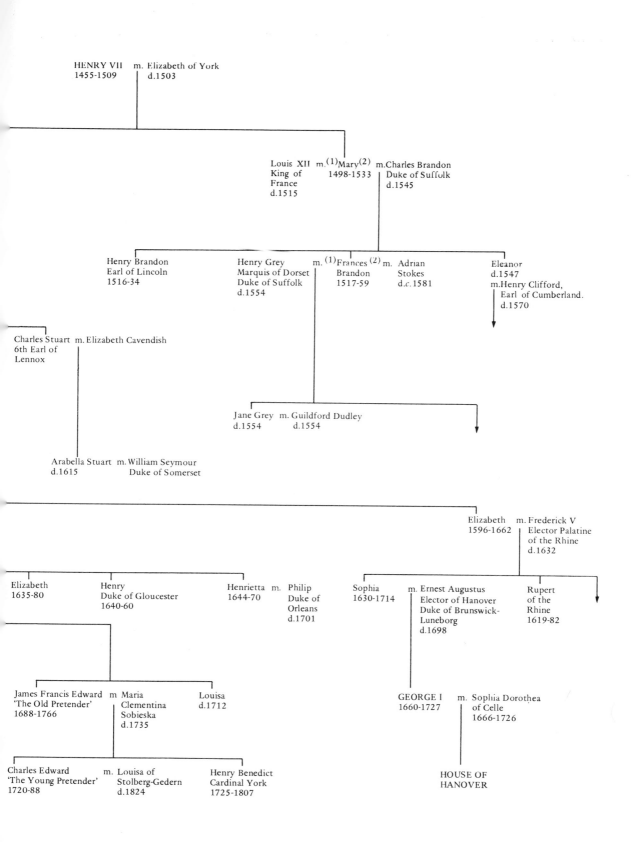

HENRY VII   m. Elizabeth of York
1455-1509   d.1503

Louis XII m.(1)Mary(2) m.Charles Brandon
King of   1498-1533   Duke of Suffolk
France   d.1545
d.1515

Henry Brandon   Henry Grey   m.(1)Frances(2) m. Adrian   Eleanor
Earl of Lincoln   Marquis of Dorset   Brandon   Stokes   d.1547
1516-34   Duke of Suffolk   1517-59   d.c.1581   m.Henry Clifford,
                           d.1554   Earl of Cumberland.
                                                                                   d.1570

Charles Stuart m. Elizabeth Cavendish
6th Earl of
Lennox

                           Jane Grey m. Guildford Dudley
                           d.1554   d.1554

Arabella Stuart m. William Seymour
d.1615   Duke of Somerset

                                                    Elizabeth   m. Frederick V
                                                    1596-1662   Elector Palatine
                                                                     of the Rhine
                                                                     d.1632

Elizabeth   Henry   Henrietta m. Philip   Sophia   m. Ernest Augustus   Rupert
1635-80   Duke of Gloucester   1644-70   Duke of   1630-1714   Elector of Hanover   of the
                1640-60   Orleans   Duke of Brunswick-   Rhine
                                                      d.1701   Luneborg   1619-82
                                                                                   d.1698

James Francis Edward m Maria   Louisa   GEORGE I   m. Sophia Dorothea
'The Old Pretender'   Clementina   d.1712   1660-1727   of Celle
1688-1766   Sobieska   1666-1726
                        d.1735

Charles Edward   m. Louisa of   Henry Benedict   HOUSE OF
'The Young Pretender' Stolberg-Gedern   Cardinal York   HANOVER
1720-88   d.1824   1725-1807

JAMES I

r. 1603-25

WHEN ON 24 MARCH 1603 James Stuart ascended the English throne, he was, as he himself boasted, an experienced king. His ancestors had ruled or at any rate reigned in Scotland since the fourteenth century and James was crowned King of the Scots when he was only thirteen months old in 1567. His father, Lord Darnley, had been mysteriously murdered and his mother, Mary Queen of Scots, had first abdicated, then reclaimed the throne and finally, defeated in battle, fled to England where she was kept a prisoner in honourable captivity until her execution for treason in 1587. A Regent, the fourth Earl of Morton, governed Scotland for fourteen years during James's minority.

Although James grew up in an atmosphere of civil strife he had a sound Presbyterian and classical education. When he became an adolescent, homosexual feelings were first aroused in him by a sophisticated French nobleman, D'Aubigny Lennox. In 1581 Lennox helped engineer the execution of the Regent but his power angered some of the nobility; James was kidnapped by the Earl of Gowrie and Lennox was banished. However, James was soon rescued by his supporters and in 1583, at seventeen, assumed the reins of government. When he was twenty he concluded a treaty with Queen Elizabeth I of England, a year before his mother's death. As Elizabeth was childless and his mother, who claimed to be her successor, was dead, the likelihood of James inheriting the English throne was enhanced. He devoted all his attention to remaining on friendly terms with the Queen of England, although he made formal protests about his mother's execution. In his anxiety to obtain the throne of England he even cultivated the Pope and the English

Roman Catholics. In 1600 he survived a plot on his life by the Gowrie family. After entering into friendly correspondence with Sir Robert Cecil his efforts were finally crowned with success. On the death of Elizabeth I, being the direct descendant of King Henry VII, James VI King of the Scots was acknowledged as the ruler of England and went happily to London.

The conditions of monarchy in England were very different from those in Scotland. There the King was little more than the first among equals. He had twice been kidnapped and held prisoner by his own subjects and though eventually he succeeded in imposing bishops upon the Kirk, the power of the General Assembly of the Scottish Church was great. In England, on the other hand, the King was the chief executive, the Supreme Governor of the Church, the possessor of hereditary wealth, the leader of his subjects in war and peace. But his authority was constitutionally limited by tradition. The English Parliament was more independent than that of Scotland. To wage war or to meet extraordinary expenses the House of Commons had to be asked to vote money for their sovereign.

Three immediate problems presented themselves to James when he reached London. The first was a growing Puritan movement which wished to sweep all Roman Catholic rites from the church services and to revert to what were claimed to be primitive usages which laid stress on preaching and prayer rather than ceremonial and sacraments. Secondly, Parliament had waxed stronger under the Tudors and the rich gentry, who provided most of the members of the Commons, were seeking to play a larger part in state as well as church affairs. Lastly, England was still at war with Spain, a

D·GRATIA
·SCOTORŨ
SUE 40

1583

IACOBVS
DEI GRATIA
REX SCOTO
ÆTATIS SUE

James portrayed with his mother, Mary Queen of Scots, in 1583.
The picture is imaginary since they never met after James was a year old.

war which had continued for some fifteen years. With the last problem James coped expeditiously: he concluded peace without betraying the Dutch who were still fighting for their independence from the Spanish Habsburgs in Madrid. James refused even to sanction privateering, a profitable form of licensed piracy, in which the Elizabethan seafaring heroes from Drake to Raleigh had enthusiastically engaged.

With the Puritans James initially had some sympathy, for he himself had been brought up as a Calvinist. After receiving a petition from a group of representative Puritans, James summoned a conference at Hampton Court Palace between the bishops and leading Puritans, over which he presided in person. Although he was ready to offer some concessions to the Puritans, he was provoked by the suggestion that the episcopacy should be abolished and uttered the famous dictum: 'No bishop, no king.' He ordered the preparation of a new translation of the Bible which became known as the Author-

217

The discovery of the Gunpowder plot in the nick of time was considered miraculous. In this engraving an angel leads the warders to the chamber where the plotters are about to ignite the barrels and another angel surveys the scene from on high.

ised Version or King James's Bible. On the whole, his attitude to religion was fairly tolerant and eclectic. But when the famous Gunpowder Plot by Roman Catholics to blow up the Houses of Parliament on 5 November 1605 was discovered, James became less kind to practising Catholics; having waived the penalties against them for not attending English church services, he reimposed them.

As a result of the Gunpowder Plot James remained for some time on friendly terms with his first Parliament, which had met in March 1604; but he had an irritating way of making exaggerated claims for the rights of the monarchy. In a book which he wrote before he left Scotland called *Basilikon Doron*, printed in 1603, he stressed the patriarchal nature of kingship and compared monarchs to gods; he was fond of addressing Parliament in lofty terms extolling the supremacy of kings. Nevertheless he was a shrewd politician and actually repudiated the argument put forward by a Cambridge professor that he was above the law.

James set himself two constructive tasks: the first was to effect a complete union between the kingdoms of Scotland and England whose crowns he wore; the second was to arrange a financial deal with the House of Commons which would guarantee him a regular and permanent income. His chief minister, Sir Robert Cecil, whom James raised to be Earl of Salisbury, attempted to carry out his master's wishes. Promoted Lord Treasurer in 1608, Salisbury took advantage of a test case to levy additional Customs – known as 'impositions' – to increase the royal revenue. Parliament would not assent to either scheme. Though James assumed the title of King of Great Britain, the Commons were not prepared to concede equal rights to the Scots; nor would they accept a plan put forward by the King's government – the Great Contract – by which, in return for a regular revenue, the King promised to give up all feudal dues belonging to the Crown and not to levy new impositions without the consent of the Commons. Faced by this opposition, James

Detail of a portrait of James I by Paul van Somer, c. 1620. The Whitehall banqueting house, built by Inigo Jones, can be seen in the background.

dissolved his first Parliament in February 1611.

In May 1612 Salisbury died, worn out in the King's service, for though James was willing enough to take decisions, he spent most of his daylight hours hunting stags and falling off horses in the process, while Salisbury had done all the hard work. After Salisbury's death, power came into the hands of royal favourites. James had married Princess Anne of Denmark in 1589 while he was King of the Scots; he had romantically braved the perils of the Baltic in order to meet his wife at Oslo on her way to Scotland. They had six children, two sons, Henry and Charles, and four daughters, two of whom died very young. But basically James was homosexual and grew bored with the frivolity and stupidity of his Queen. His first favourite in England was a Scotsman, Robert Carr, who rose to power in 1610 and in 1613

was married with James's connivance to Frances Howard, daughter of the Earl of Suffolk, after her marriage to the third Earl of Essex was annulled. (Her father was to succeed Salisbury as Lord Treasurer.) But in 1616 Carr, who had been created Earl of Somerset and was made Lord Chamberlain, and his wife were accused of poisoning a former secretary of Somerset while he was imprisoned in the Tower of London. Though both were found guilty neither was severely punished, but Somerset's influence at court came to an abrupt end. James's next favourite was George Villiers who rose rapidly in the King's esteem and in 1623 was created Duke of Buckingham. During the last years of the reign Buckingham's influence on policy, particularly foreign policy, was decisive.

Although it was James's avowed intention to

be a prince of peace, much of the remainder of the reign was absorbed in foreign affairs. In February 1613 his eldest daughter, Elizabeth, was married to Frederick the Elector Palatine who was a Calvinist and prominent among the German Protestant princes. James himself entered into an alliance with the German Protestant Union and regarded himself as a Protestant champion. But at the same time he was anxious for an agreement with Spain, a country then regarded as the strongest in Europe. He aimed to reach an understanding by marrying his son Charles to the Spanish Infanta, sister of King Philip IV of Spain. He also put an end to his alliance with the Dutch, soon to renew their war against Spain, by selling back to them the towns acquired by Queen Elizabeth I.

In 1619 his son-in-law the Elector Palatine accepted the throne of Bohemia offered him by the Bohemian Protestant leaders. This led to war against the Holy Roman Emperor who himself claimed to be the rightful holder of the Bohemian throne. Thus James became reluctantly and at first indirectly involved in what was to be known as 'The Thirty Years War' in Germany, in which the Spaniards engaged on the side of the Emperor against the Elector Palatine who lost his hereditary throne. So James's foreign policy fell to pieces. Nevertheless he hoped that if the Spanish marriage alliance could be achieved he might persuade the Spanish Government to use its influence with the Holy Roman Emperor to conclude a peaceable settlement with his son-in-law. But this elaborate manoeuvre was doomed to failure and on Buckingham's instigation James was forced into a war with Spain and into hiring a mercenary army to fight against the Emperor.

Even before this James had grave financial difficulties. For he was grossly extravagant, spending, for example, a small fortune on his daughter's wedding, besides being lavish to his male favourites. When his second Parliament had met in 1614 he had vainly tried to persuade the Commons to vote him money, but the members expressed many grievances, especially over James's Scottish favourites, so that he was obliged to dissolve Parliament after two months. His third Parliament, which met in 1621, though avid for a war against Spain, thought that such a war should pay for itself and again demanded to discuss grievances before voting supplies. James said that foreign policy and religion were his business; when the Commons entered a protestation in its journal James tore the protestation out of the book and ordered the arrest of three or four of its leading members.

James employed various expedients other than impositions to raise money. Lionel Cranfield, the Earl of Middlesex, was appointed Lord Treasurer and reorganised the royal finances; Sir Walter Raleigh, one of Queen Elizabeth's favourites, was allowed to seek a mythical gold mine in Guiana; James granted commercial 'monopolies' from which Buckingham and his relatives largely profited; and he still hoped to procure money through his son's marriage. But he allowed his ablest servants to be dismissed and punished. His able Lord Chancellor, Francis Bacon, was deprived of all his offices for taking bribes; Raleigh was put to death for conspiracy; and Middlesex was impeached by the Commons after Buckingham was convinced that the Lord Treasurer had failed him. So James's reign ended in confusion and disaster both at home and abroad.

Though James's mental capacities declined towards the end of his life, he was a highly intelligent ruler who did not provoke his leading subjects too far and was ready to withdraw unpopular policies. He was a learned theologian and after an original belief in witchcraft was persuaded finally of its falsity. But he was vain, lazy and too fond of his own voice. He allowed himself to be increasingly imposed upon by men favourites while 'he piqued himself on his great contempt for women'. Before he died on 27 March 1625 he recognised the growing influence of the House of Commons and vainly warned his heir of the dangers that waited him.

CHARLES I

r. 1625-49

THE SECOND SON OF JAMES I and Anne of Denmark was born in Dunfermline Palace, twelve miles from Edinburgh, on 19 November 1600. Charles was a weak and backward child and needed the permission of the royal doctors to be brought south in a curtained litter after his father settled in England. Like his father he was educated by a Scottish Presbyterian tutor, mastered Latin and Greek and showed an aptitude for modern languages. His brother Henry, who was six years his elder and whom Charles admired, died in 1612 when he was eighteen. In the following year Charles's sister Elizabeth departed with her husband for Heidelberg. Thus the shy and reserved boy – he never overcame a stammer – was created Prince of Wales in 1616, becoming important but lonely. In 1619 his mother died, but he struck up a friendship with the Marquis of Buckingham, his father's favourite, while James himself proved a conscientious and loving father. By 1624, going with Buckingham on an incognito mission to Madrid in search of a Spanish wife, Charles was described as having 'grown into a fine gentleman'. He was five feet four inches tall. The flattering portraits of him by Van Dyck and Bower made him appear more dignified than he really was. In fact he was a small man who in due course enjoyed asserting himself.

On 27 March 1625 Charles succeeded to the throne and within two months was married to Henrietta Maria, the sister of King Louis XIII of France. When in Madrid Charles had been attracted by the languorous Spanish princess, who shrank from him as a heretic; at first he thought his French wife disappointing and took a dislike to her train of priests and women she brought over with her from Paris, some of whom he sent packing. For the first years of his reign he was under the influence of Buckingham and found himself at war with both Spain and France. The expeditions against these countries organised and on occasion led by Buckingham were complete failures. Because of their distrust of Buckingham the House of Commons refused to grant Charles the supplies he needed to wage wars, while even the Customs duties (known then as tonnage and poundage) were voted for his use only for a single year. So Charles was driven to a number of financial expedients; he cashed his wife's dowry; he exacted forced loans from his wealthier subjects, imprisoning five knights who refused to pay; he billeted soldiers without paying for them; and he collected tonnage and poundage without parliamentary sanction. Both the Parliaments of 1625 and 1626 showed their distrust of the King and Buckingham.

When Charles's third Parliament met in 1628, after the failure of the campaigns against Spain, the leading members of the Commons were extremely critical of the Government. Not only did they resent the royal financial methods but they complained about the mismanagement of the war against the Spaniards and on behalf of the French Protestants, and also objected to the King's attitude to the Church of England. For although Charles had been tutored by a Scottish Calvinist, he was a man of fastidious tastes who disliked the kind of church services of which the Puritans most approved. He was accused of promoting so-called 'Arminians' or high churchmen who believed in free will rather than predestination to achieve salvation and of appointing clergy who preferred the retention of Catholic ritual and rites in services to long sermons and extempore prayer.

The Commons showed themselves extremely restless; a Petition of Right was drawn up with

(continues on page 226)

Charles I and Henrietta Maria, painted by Daniel Mytens in 1634.

7 The Arms of the Stuarts

WHEN JAMES VI OF SCOTLAND inherited the English throne a
change in the royal arms was necessary in order to include
James's other kingdom. The resultant arms are here illustrated. The
shield has been divided into four grand quarters. The old French
and English quartered arms, as used for about two hundred years,
were put in the first and fourth quarters. The Scottish lion within
its *double tressure flory counterflory* was assigned the second quarter,
whilst the harp of Ireland made its debut in the royal coat in the
third quarter.

Although Ireland had been raised from a lordship to a kingdom
by Henry VIII and although the badge of a harp had been associated with Ireland, no proper arms of dominion existed. This was
put right in the new version of the royal arms.

The supporters of the Scottish royal arms were two unicorns
and so the Tudor dragon supporter was replaced by one of the
Scottish unicorns. As king of Scotland, James and his successors
used the arms in a different manner. The Scottish lion changed
places with the English and French coats; the Scottish crest and
motto replaced the English and the supporters changed sides and
were depicted in a slightly different manner.

When William III and Mary II became joint sovereigns William
as Prince of Orange, could have added a complex quartered coat
but opted for a little shield (illustrated below the arms of the
Stuarts) of the arms of Nassau, which he placed in the centre of
the Stuart coat. These arms are today the royal arms of Holland.

After William's death without issue the crown passed to Mary's
sister Anne but, as she did not succeed her brother-in-law as a
hereditary Statholder in the Netherlands, she dropped the arms of
Nassau and reverted to the Stuart royal arms until, in 1707, the
two kingdoms of England and Scotland were united to form
'one Kingdom by the Name of Great Britain'. As the Act for the
Union with Scotland provided that the arms of the United
Kingdom shall be 'as Her Majesty shall appoint', they were
duly altered.

DIEU·ET·MON·DROIT

the concurrence of the House of Lords in which forced loans, the billeting of soldiers, the imprisonment of subjects without cause shown, and other grievances were condemned. Charles accepted the petition with reluctance, but scarcely abided by it. When the Commons went on to condemn the King's favourite divines and to threaten the impeachment of his friend Buckingham, Charles felt obliged to adjourn Parliament without obtaining the money he needed from it.

The assassination of Buckingham by a fanatic in August 1628 failed to reconcile Charles with his Parliament. Before he again adjourned it in March 1629 the Speaker of the Commons was held down in his chair while resolutions were unanimously passed condemning 'innovations' in religion and the illegal levying of tonnage and poundage. For the next eleven years Charles governed without Parliament and saved money by bringing the wars to an end. In 1633, however, he appointed a leading 'Arminian', William Laud, as Archbishop of Canterbury and with his aid set out to impose a service book drawn up in London on the Scottish Church or Kirk so that the religious practices of his two kingdoms should become uniform. Provoked by this action the Scottish lowlanders turned against their King and swore to uphold a National Covenant embodying loyalty to the Kirk, as exemplified in the public rejection of the new service book. Infuriated by this rebelliousness, Charles raised an army to enforce his wishes on Scotland. He was humiliatingly rebuffed in what was known as the first Bishops' War. To pay for a second campaign he was compelled to summon a new Parliament at Westminster.

This Parliament insisted on discussing their pent-up grievances before voting the King money. So Charles dissolved it after a few weeks, which gave it the sobriquet of 'the Short Parliament'. For a second time Charles sent an army against his Scottish subjects; this time he was conclusively beaten. The King was thus obliged to pay the Covenanter army while it was encamped on English soil in Northumberland and Durham and once more threw himself on the mercy of an English Parliament, which met in November 1640 and was to be called the Long Parliament.

During the long interval before the Short and Long Parliaments met, the King's Government had employed a number of dubious methods of raising money. 'Ship money', a tax which had been used in Tudor times, was imposed on inland towns as well as ports to pay for the upkeep of the navy. Tonnage and poundage continued to be levied illegally. Various irritating medieval imposts, such as fines upon gentry who refused to accept knighthoods, were collected. Thus the whole of the House of Commons, consisting of country gentlemen, lawyers and merchants, were alienated from the King's government which they considered to be acting unconstitutionally. Fears grew that the English army in the north and the garrison of Ireland were going to be employed to enforce the King's absolute will on Parliament. In fact Charles had no intention of doing anything of the sort, but his ablest minister, the Earl of Strafford, Lord Lieutenant of Ireland, whom he had summoned to organise the second Bishops' War, was selected by the Commons as a scapegoat. They reckoned him with Archbishop Laud as the chief of the King's 'evil counsellors' and it was decided to impeach Strafford for treason before the House of Lords.

Charles understood what the Commons had in mind. But he hoped that if Strafford defended himself successfully before his fellow peers the whole absolutist system of government, called by its opponents 'the eleven years tyranny', would be vindicated. However, when the trial for treason faltered, Charles was asked to sign a bill of attainder by which Strafford could be put to death without any legal judgement. The King was subjected to heavy pressures; the House of Lords was menaced by city mobs; the King believed that

RIGHT A Puritan satire shows Charles I and his men cutting down the tree of religion. Charles's unyielding support for the Established Church led him to be venerated as an Anglican martyr after his death.

The five eldest children of Charles I, from left to right: Princess Mary (who married William of Orange), Prince James (James II); Prince Charles (Charles II), Princess Elizabeth and Princess Anne (who died as children).

his Roman Catholic Queen, with whom he had fallen in love since the death of Buckingham, was in peril. Reluctantly he signed the Bill. Afterwards he gave way over ship-money and agreed that this Long Parliament should not be dissolved without its own consent.

Only on two questions did Charles refuse to yield to the pressure of the leaders of Parliament. The first was over the reform of the Church of England, which they held was being catholicised by the King's High Church bishops; the second was over the control of the militia, the only permanent armed force in the kingdom apart from the King's own guards. In the summer of 1641 Charles visited Scotland in the hope that by offering concessions to his subjects there he could rally them to the defence of the throne. When he returned empty-handed from Scotland, he found that about half the members of the Commons were now veering towards his side. A 'Grand Remonstrance', which set out all the grievances against his

government, was only carried by a few votes in November. Egged on by his Queen, the King now attempted to arrest five leading members of the Commons, including his chief critic, John Pym. But when he entered the House in January 1642 he discovered that 'the birds had flown'. He then left London and both sides – the Royalists and the Parliamentarians – prepared for civil war.

During the next seven months negotiations went on between the two parties for a peace treaty. But they broke down on the two principal questions over which the King was willing to compromise but not to yield. Parliament also demanded the right to nominate all his ministers and military officers, even to supervise the upbringing of his children. Gradually hopes of a peaceful settlement faded; and the first civil war began when Charles raised his standard at Nottingham on 22 August 1642.

Charles had many fine qualities. He was temperate and grave, a devoted husband and

Charles I resting during the chase by Van Dyck.

THE
CONFESSION

June 25 OF *1649*

Richard Brandon

The Hangman (upon his Death-bed) concerning His beheading his late Majesty, C H A R L E S the first, King of Great Brittain; and his Protestation and Vow touching the same; the manner how he was terrified in Conscience; the Apparitions and Visions which apeared unto him; the great judgment that befell him three dayes before he dy'd ; and the manner how he was carried to White-Chappell Church-yard on Thursday night last, the strange Actions that happened thereupon; With the merry conceits of the Crowne Cook and his providing mourning Cords for the Buriall.

Printed in the year Year, of the Hang-mans down-fall, 1649.

father, and a sincere Christian. He was an aes-
thete who spent money on beautiful things.
Inigo Jones, to be famous as an architect, and
Ben Jonson, the playwright, designed masques
for the court; Rubens was brought over to
England to paint the ceiling of the banqueting
house in Whitehall Palace in memory of
Charles's father. Van Dyck did portraits of the
royal family, and other artists, such as William
Dobson, an outstanding native portrait painter,
enjoyed the King's patronage. But Charles also
had serious defects. He was lazy and lacked any
sense of humour. Moreover, he thought any
means was justified to win the war and regain
his absolute authority. Consequently he made
all sorts of contradictory promises to Scottish
Presbyterians, English Anglicans, Irish Roman
Catholics and the Puritan leaders of the Parliamentary army, which he had no intention of
keeping. Gradually he forfeited all trust.

As commander-in-chief of the army which
he raised with difficulty from among his loyal
subjects to fight Parliament, he was by no
means negligible as a tactician. He distinguished
himself at the battle of Edgehill in 1642, at
Cropredy Bridge and Lostwithiel in 1644 and
at the relief of Hereford in 1645. But as a
strategist he constantly vacillated. He refused
to march on London after Edgehill or when his
fortunes were high in 1643. He failed to impose
his will on his generals. Towards the end he
could not decide whether to stand and fight in
England or to join his supporters in Scotland.
Eventually, after major defeats, he resolved to
leave his headquarters at Oxford in disguise and
make for the camp of the Scottish Covenanter
army which had allied itself with the English
Parliamentarians and conquered the north-east
of England. As he refused to promise to intro-
duce the full Presbyterian system of church
government in England, the Covenanters
handed him over to the English Parliament, but
in 1647 he fell into the hands of the victorious
Roundhead army led by Thomas Fairfax and
Oliver Cromwell.

Both Fairfax and Cromwell were anxious to
come to terms with the King on the basis of a
written constitution, in which the King's
authority could be harmonised with the wishes
of his leading subjects. A scheme drawn up by
the army commanders known as the 'Heads of
the Proposals' was considered by some of
Charles's advisers to be a cheap way of regain-
ing authority after his defeat.

But rather than come to an agreed settlement
Charles preferred trying to play off his enemies
against each other. He escaped from honourable captivity in Hampton Court and fled to
the Isle of Wight; thence he bargained both
with the Parliamentarians, among whom there
was a substantial peace party, and with his
Scottish subjects, who did not care for the imprisonment of a Stuart king by the English and
were ready to engage themselves in his service
in return for mainly religious concessions.
Charles accepted this 'engagement'; the Scottish 'Engagers' invaded England in 1648 while
earlier in the same year many Royalists, tired of
Puritan restraints and exactions, took up arms
again. The second civil war was quickly over.
Cromwell defeated the Scots and left a garrison
in Edinburgh; Fairfax overcame the Royalist
revolt in south-eastern England. Though part
of the navy deserted the Parliamentarians for
the King, it did not even attempt to rescue him
from imprisonment in the Isle of Wight.

The army leaders determined that the King
should be put on trial for waging war on his
own people. The House of Commons was
purged of the peace party which had vainly
negotiated with Charles in the Isle of Wight. A
high court of justice was erected and the King
brought to Westminster hall in January 1649 to
face his trial. The King conducted himself with
dignity, firmly refusing to recognise the legality
of the court and thus making no real defence of
his actions. The court condemned him to
death. On 30 January 1649 he was publicly
executed outside Whitehall Palace and his body
was secretly buried in Windsor Castle.

LEFT The title page of *The Confession of Richard Brandon*, the executioner
of Charles I, showing the scene of execution on 30 January 1649.

THE ELDEST SURVIVING SON of Charles I and Henrietta Maria was born on 29 May 1630 and sealed his father's and mother's newly-found married happiness. He was brought up as a child in that idealistic atmosphere which was pictured by Van Dyck and described by the Earl of Clarendon in his celebrated *History*, before the clouds that heralded the civil wars began to gather. His first governor was the wealthy and cultivated magnifico, the second Earl of Newcastle, who told him that he would learn more from men than books. He was only twelve when the civil war began and was present at the first big battle, Edgehill. Two years later he accompanied his father on his victorious campaign in Cornwall, and in March 1645 Charles I sent him, when only fourteen, to be nominal commander-in-chief in western England with his headquarters at Bristol.

After being driven for a year from pillar to post by the conquering Parliamentarians, he was forced to leave England together with his council (which included some able men) first for the Scillies, then Jersey, and finally, on his father's orders, he joined his mother in Paris. In 1648 he took command of the warships which had mutinied against Parliament during the second civil war, but was obliged to return to his base in Holland where at the beginning of 1649 he learned of his father's execution. The next eleven years he devoted to trying to regain the thrones of England and Scotland.

Charles arrived in Scotland in 1650 where he was humiliatingly treated by the bigoted Covenanters. However, after Cromwell's victory at Dunbar, his stock rose; he was crowned King of the Scots and allowed to take command of a united Scottish army. In the summer of 1651 he led this army into England only to be conclusively defeated by Cromwell at the battle of Worcester, where he fought extremely bravely. He escaped from the field of battle and after many exciting adventures managed to return safely to France. Next year the first war between England and the Dutch Republic broke out. Charles vainly offered his services to the Dutch and later when Spain was at war with England he succeeded in concluding a treaty of alliance in Brussels which promised that if the Royalists could lay hold of a port in England he would be provided with an expeditionary army. Nothing came of his plans. It was not until after the death of Oliver Cromwell, which was followed by anarchic struggles between Oliver's would-be successors, that Charles was by general acclamation welcomed back to England. He arrived in London on his thirtieth birthday.

Charles had been extremely skilful in the way in which he seized this opportunity. In his Declaration of Breda (4 April 1660) he did not commit himself to any specific undertakings about a constitutional settlement except that he promised 'liberty of conscience' to all Christians and demanded the punishment of his father's murderers. In fact he was relatively merciful, and made earnest efforts to achieve an agreement between the enthusiastic supporters of the old Church of England and the Presbyterians who had helped to procure his restoration. However, negotiations broke down. A new prayer book was drawn up; an act of uniformity was passed; and some two thousand clergy left their parishes. Moreover Charles's second Parliament, elected in May 1661, refused to accept a declaration of indulgence which he issued and for a time showed itself to be more rigidly Anglican than the King.

Charles had been crowned on 23 April 1661 and a year later he was married to Catherine of

RIGHT The adventures of Charles II during his escape after the battle of Worcester. Top left: the battle; top right: Charles and Major Careless hide in an oak tree in Boscobel Wood while soldiers search for them; bottom left: Charles dressed as a servant rides with Jane Lane behind Lord Wilmot on the road to Bristol; bottom right: Charles takes ship for France.

Worcester

 goe to find the King!

Mrs Iane Lane and King:

the Kings escape in the sea Adventure

Nell Gwynne rose from selling oranges outside Drury Lane Theatre to become a leading actress of the day and the most celebrated of Charles's mistresses. She is shown in this detail of an engraving after Gascard with one of her two sons by the King, Charles, Duke of St Albans.

Braganza, the daughter of the King of Portugal. His ministers were chiefly the old Royalists who had served him during his long exile from England together with General George Monck, the man chiefly responsible for the Restoration, who was created Duke of Albemarle. In 1665 the House of Commons pressurised Charles into a war with the Dutch over which he was not at all keen and the causes of which were largely naval and commercial rivalries. Though the King had inherited a big navy from the Cromwellian period, the Dutch more than held their own. The reason for their success was not that Charles lacked good admirals but that the kingdom was distracted first by the Great Plague and then by the Great Fire in London. Furthermore naval warfare was expensive and the Commons did not vote enough money to wage a long war. In July 1667 a peace was concluded which left the position much as it was before the war. Nevertheless the leading subjects of the King were disappointed and to appease them Charles dismissed his chief minister, Edward Hyde, Earl of Clarendon. A group of five men now became the King's closest advisers: Lord Clifford, Lord Arlington, the Duke of Buckingham, Lord Ashley and Lord Lauderdale, known as 'the Cabal', the word formed by the first letters of their names.

The next few years were dominated by questions of foreign policy. Charles decided that he must have his revenge on the Dutch. Though for a time he entered upon a Protestant alliance with the Dutch and the Swedes, he was resolved to become the ally of the French monarchy which had become the strongest single power in Europe. After complicated negotiations in which Charles's youngest sister, Henrietta, played an important part, a secret treaty was signed at Dover in May 1670. By this treaty Charles undertook to wage war against the Dutch together with the French, while by a secret clause he promised to declare himself at an appropriate time to be a Roman Catholic. The French undertook to pay him financial

subsidies and, when the war had been won, to award him Dutch ports. The treaty was concealed from Charles's dedicated Protestant ministers of State such as Anthony Ashley Cooper, Earl of Shaftesbury. One of his Catholic ministers, Lord Clifford, offered by hook or by crook to raise the money necessary to fight the war even if the House of Commons refused. To keep his promise to the French King about helping the English Catholics, Charles published a second declaration of indulgence; then without Parliament being informed the war began.

Although the French army overran much of the Dutch Republic the English navy was kept away from the Dutch coasts where the intention had been to land an expeditionary force to aid the French. The House of Commons showed itself to be increasingly anti-French and anti-Catholic. Charles was asked to withdraw his declaration of indulgence and to agree to a Test Act excluding Roman Catholics from all offices. Though the King did so, he was refused the money he needed to continue the war and so he was compelled to make a separate peace. The next five years were concerned mainly with foreign affairs. Charles tried to act as a mediator between the Dutch and the French, though he was still drawing subsidies from the French King, while the Commons vigorously demanded that he should go to war with France. In the end he was driven to agree to a marriage between Prince William III of Orange, the Dutch Captain-General, and his niece Mary, and to threaten war against France. But his actions had small influence upon the Peace of Nymegen which ended the war in 1678.

In the course of these years Charles had managed to raise a small army; Parliament became afraid that he was aiming at absolutism, though that was not his intention at this stage of his reign. Domestic affairs became difficult for him as an anti-Catholic agitation boiled up. His brother James, Duke of York, was now known to be a Roman Catholic convert because he had resigned all his offices after the passing of the first Test Act; he then married a Roman Catholic Italian princess as his second wife; the Queen was also a Roman Catholic, as was Charles's principal mistress, the French Duchess of Portsmouth; and suspicions arose over what Charles had promised the French by treaty. In the summer of 1678 a 'Popish Plot' was revealed to the Government by perjured informers. Charles insisted that the whole plot was 'a contrivance'. But when the Duchess of York's secretary, named Coleman, was arrested and incriminating letters found outlining Roman Catholic aspirations, Charles was unable to keep the general frenzy under control. Coleman and a number of Jesuits were put to death. The Earl of Danby, who became Lord Treasurer and the King's chief minister when the Cabal broke up in 1674, was threatened with impeachment and the Commons were angered by revelations about Charles's pro-French policy for which in fact Danby had not been responsible. In January 1679 Charles dissolved the former Cavalier Parliament which had sat for eighteen years. Before its dissolution a second Test Act was passed excluding Roman Catholics from sitting in either House of Parliament.

When a new Parliament met in the spring a bill to exclude the Duke of York from succession to the throne was introduced. Charles, now virtually his own first minister, was determined to prevent its enactment. For two years a contest took place between the King's supporters, the Tories, and their opponents, the Whigs, who were led by the unscrupulous Shaftesbury. Charles stopped the passage of an Exclusion Bill by bringing his own influence to bear on the House of Lords. In 1680 the fourth Parliament of the reign met and again the Commons voted for exclusion. Charles dissolved it. In 1681 he summoned a fifth Parliament to meet in Oxford where he exerted military pressure upon the Whigs. He and his brother were now genuinely afraid of civil war, but the King kept

his head. He came to a secret understanding with the French King that he would be given support in the event of a rebellion. A Tory reaction slowly set in, aided by the revelation of what was called 'the Rye House plot', an alleged conspiracy to murder the King on his way from the Newcastle races, engineered by the Whigs. By using his influence to obtain friendly officials in key posts both in the government and in the counties, the King succeeded in crushing the Whig movement and its leaders fled abroad. Shaftesbury died in Holland. The last four years of Charles's reign were peaceable. He had enough money to live on because of the expansion of the receipts from the Customs and Excise, and he had an army on which he could rely. His Roman Catholic brother in effect resumed his post as Lord High Admiral.

Charles thus proved himself an extremely shrewd politician as well as a ready liar. Though like his father and grandfather he was rather lazy, he could exert himself effectively at times of crisis. With the exception of the two Test Acts he made few concessions to Parliament. Like his father he refused to give up control over the armed forces of the kingdom; unlike him, he saved his leading ministers from execution for treason. Charles had charm and a vast sense of humour which caused him to be much loved by ordinary people. The 'Merry Monarch' did not eat or drink to excess but he had a large sexual appetite, enjoying a succession of mistresses – Nell Gwynne is the best remembered – whom he rewarded generously but did not love. He refused to divorce the Queen, though she could bear him no children. His main interest was the navy, but he also enjoyed horse races and fishing. He was very human and, from the point of view of his dynasty, a successful king. Before he died on 6 February 1685 he was received into the Roman Catholic Church, but there is good evidence that since before his restoration he had been a Catholic at heart. He was buried in Westminster Abbey.

RIGHT Detail from a painting of Charles II dancing at a ball at the Hague during his years of exile.

JAMES II

r. 1685-88

T HE SECOND SON OF CHARLES I, James
Duke of York was only twelve years old
(he was born on 14 October 1633) when the
city of Oxford, in which he had been brought
up, surrendered to the Parliamentarians and the
Prince himself was taken as a prisoner to St
James's Palace in London. In April 1648 he
managed to escape dressed as a girl and found
his way to his sister Mary in Holland. After his
father's execution he was appointed Lord High
Admiral by his brother, but Charles II refused
to allow him to sail with the fleet. Instead James
was commissioned as an officer in the French
army. By the time he was twenty-one he had
been promoted to lieutenant-general. He distinguished himself as a soldier, and his conduct

was commended by the famous French marshal
Turenne. But when the French Government
came to terms with the Cromwellian Protectorate James reluctantly resigned his commission. Instead he served with the Spaniards, who
were fighting the French and the English republicans in 1658. That June in the battle of the
Dunes James again fought courageously and
thus by the time that his brother was restored
to the English throne James had earned a high
reputation as a soldier.

Two occurrences, which were kept secret
before the Restoration, were that James had
been attracted to the Roman Catholic Church
and that he had signed a contract of marriage
with Anne Hyde, the daughter of the future

James II with his first wife, Anne Hyde, and their daughters Mary (holding flowers) and Anne. The portrait was begun
in 1669 by Peter Lely and completed by Benedetto Gennari some ten years later.

CONVERTE ANGLIAM

It is a foolish Sheep that makes the Wolf her Confessor

James's marriage in 1673 to the Catholic princess, Mary of Modena, appalled public opinion in England.
In this engraving Mary is portrayed confessing to a wolf.

8 The Royal Arms 1707-1837

THE ALTERATION made in the royal arms to reflect the union of England and Scotland was as illustrated. The arms of the two countries were placed side by side in the first and last quarters, France was assigned the second quarter and Ireland stayed put. No alteration was made to crest nor supporters; these have remained unchanged from 1603 until the present day. It will be noticed that the *double tressure* which surrounds the Scottish lion is discontinued where the coat is joined to that of England. This is an old heraldic convention which affects all forms of border when arms are shown side by side, that is *impaled*.

This new version of the arms was short-lived as Anne died in 1714 and, under the terms of the Act of Settlement of 1701, George, Elector of Hanover, Duke of Brunswick and Luneburg and Arch Treasurer of the Holy Roman Empire, succeeded to the throne. Another reshuffle was called for in order to make reference to his German dominions. This was easily effected by removing the last quartering, which was only a repetition of the first, and substituting a coat divided into three, containing the two lions of Brunswick, the lion and hearts of Luneburg and the white horse of Hanover. The little shield in the centre, which will be seen in the illustration of this coat, has on it a representation of the crown of Charlemagne. This was the badge of office of the Arch Treasurer of the Empire; other members of the royal family never showed this shield.

In 1801 the royal arms were altered yet again in order to reflect better the new kingdom of Great Britain and Ireland created by the Act of Union with Ireland in 1800. The opportunity was taken to remove the French arms, an excision which some might think several hundred years overdue. The three kingdoms were each given a quartering, the arms of England being repeated in the last quarter in the cause of symmetry. The German arms were placed in the centre, thus enabling the Electoral Bonnet, which by right should have ensigned them, to be shown. This shield is illustrated whilst next to it is the same shield ensigned by the crown which replaced the bonnet in 1816. Under the terms of the Congress of Vienna the electorate, which had disappeared when Napoleon overthrew the Empire, was erected into a kingdom.

Earl of Clarendon who had been the Chancellor of Charles II's Exchequer and was afterwards Lord Chancellor. Charles II insisted that his brother should publicly acknowledge the marriage. James took an active part in Charles's counsels and when the first Anglo-Dutch war of the new reign broke out he commanded the navy in person, inflicting a defeat on the Dutch at the battle of Lowestoft in June 1665. But the King refused to let him go to sea again until the second war of the reign. Then he was in the thick of the battle of Solebay fought in May 1672, but, though assisted by a French squadron, failed to defeat the Dutch who were determined to prevent enemy troops landing from the sea.

James's conversion to the Roman Church took place in 1668, but he continued to attend Anglican services for another eight years. When the first Test Act was carried he felt constrained to resign his post as Lord High Admiral, but consoled himself by his second marriage, to the young Mary of Modena. As the anti-Catholic agitation, which culminated in the disclosure of the 'Popish Plot' was intensified, he became the target of the Whigs' wrath. They aimed to exclude him from succession to the throne and Charles sent James into exile first in Brussels and then in Edinburgh to allow tempers to cool. It was not until the Tory reaction set in that the King allowed his brother to return to Whitehall. This was in 1682 when the Duke brought an action for libel against Titus Oates, the fountain-head of the Popish Plot. During the last three years of Charles II's reign James served in the Privy Council and on the Committee for Foreign Affairs and in effect resumed his position as Lord High Admiral. Sir John Reresby noted in January 1682 that 'the Duke of York did chiefly manage affairs, but with great haughtiness'.

When Charles II died in February 1685 James succeeded to the throne unexpectedly peacefully considering the attempts that the Commons had made to exclude him because he was an avowed Roman Catholic. He at once openly attended Mass, but informed the Privy Council and a new Parliament which met in May 1685 that he would protect the Church of England 'whose members have shown themselves so eminently loyal in the worst of times'. The House of Commons consisted for the most part of members who were strongly Royalist and Anglican; it was determined to give James a fair trial as ruler and voted him a generous revenue. Nevertheless the King treated it superciliously and he was annoyed when a resolution was passed asking him to publish a proclamation to put in force the laws against 'all dissenters whatsoever from the Church of England'. For James's intention was precisely the opposite. He was determined to place both Roman Catholics and Protestant dissenters in a position of civic equality with his Anglican subjects.

In June 1685 Scotland was invaded by a rebel force directed by the Marquis of Argyll, while Charles II's eldest illegitimate son, the Duke of Monmouth, landed in the south-west of England. The two rebel leaders had assumed that their countries would refuse to obey a Roman Catholic king but the invasions were defeated without undue difficulty. Parliament showed its loyalty to James and during the summer harmony reigned. Yet by the autumn James's decision to allow Roman Catholic officers to serve in the army in spite of the first Test Act and his insistence on the suspension of the penal laws against nonconformists provoked the Commons to protest. They did not at all care for the idea of a standing army, recently victorious over Monmouth and officered by Catholics, being at the King's disposal. So this Parliament, initially entirely loyal, became so restive that James prorogued it on 20 November 1685, though he did not dissolve it until July 1687. Thus he lost some of his promised revenue, but was able to exploit his royal prerogatives of suspending or dispensing with laws to pursue his policy of introducing complete religious equality.

The seven bishops who defied James's order to read the Declaration of Indulgence are taken to imprisonment in the Tower.

The first thing he did was to appoint an ecclesiastical commission which was intended to prevent Anglican clergy from attacking the tenets of the Roman Catholic religion from their pulpits, which James called 'indiscreet preaching'. This commission proceeded to suspend the Bishop of London from his office because he disobeyed the King's orders. Next a test case was brought before the high court which decided (after the judges had been purged) that it was legal for James to dispense with the law in individual cases. This verdict enabled him to admit Roman Catholics into the Privy Council, freely to employ Roman Catholics as military and naval officers, and even to choose Catholics for positions in Oxford colleges. On 4 April 1687 he issued a Declaration of Indulgence aiming at complete religious

toleration; a second declaration was published a year later. The Anglican clergy were instructed to read it from their pulpits on the following Sundays. Finally James dismissed from office his two brothers-in-law, sons of Clarendon, who as Protestants did not altogether approve of his policies. The unscrupulous Earl of Sunderland then became Lord President of the Council as well as Secretary of State.

The summer of 1688 was the turning point in James's reign. The Archbishop of Canterbury and six other bishops petitioned the King to withdraw his orders about the second Declaration of Indulgence on the ground that Parliaments of Charles II's reign had insisted that the King had no right to dispense with the penal code. James was furious and ordered that the seven bishops should be put on trial before

James leaves Rochester for France; unlike his brother Charles, his exile was to be permanent.

the King's Bench for seditious libel. They were acquitted by a jury and the verdict was celebrated not only in the streets of London but even in the army camp at Hounslow. On 10 June the Queen gave birth to a son – to be known as the Old Pretender. Thus it seemed as if a Roman Catholic dynasty would become permanent. On the same day that the bishops were acquitted the Bishop of London and six laymen – to be called the Immortal Seven – secretly invited James's nephew and son-in-law, William of Orange, to come over to England to protect liberty and property and to sustain his wife's right to succeed to the throne since it was alleged (wrongly) that the birth of the 'Old Pretender' was an imposture.

James was fully aware that he could not ensure toleration indefinitely by the exercise of his prerogative. He therefore devoted much effort to trying to pack a parliament which would be committed to repealing the penal laws and the two Test Acts so that liberty of conscience would continue to prevail even after his own death. How far he might have succeeded is hard to say, but in any case before a new general election could be held, William of Orange landed in south-west England on 5 November 1688 with a considerable army. It now emerged that so dissatisfied had public opinion become with the King's clumsy and arbitrary way of acting that neither his army nor his navy would fight for him. Vainly the King made concessions to Protestant opinion and dismissed the subservient but panic-stricken Earl of Sunderland. Soon after William landed, leading officers deserted the army which was concentrated at Salisbury to prevent a Dutch advance on London, and the entire navy later went over to William. James, who had been so brave when young, lost his nerve completely. He would not take command of the army; he sent his wife and baby son abroad; and after pretending to negotiate with William for the summoning of a free Parliament, he fled from his capital. He was caught attempting to board a ship and bundled back to London, from where William allowed him to flee again. On Christmas Day he arrived in France.

James had shown himself to be impatient, arrogant and, as one contemporary remarked, 'a silly man'. He had little interest in the arts or sciences, was over-sexed and a poor judge of men. Conscious of his father's fate on the scaffold, he surrendered his throne too easily to his son-in-law. Even when he managed to raise a Catholic army in Ireland and had the benefit of French military advice, he lost the battle of the Boyne against William largely through his own incompetence (1 July 1690). He spent most of the rest of his life in some comfort at St Germain, piously regretting his sins. Some historians believe that he was mentally defective in his last years, but there is no firm evidence for that. He continued to hunt and philander until he died after a stroke at the age of sixty-six.

WILLIAM III & MARY II

r. 1688–1702   r. 1688–94

THE MARRIAGE OF THE TWO future monarchs took place in St James's Palace in London on 4 November 1677, which was William's twenty-sixth birthday. They were married for reasons of State. When Mary, the elder daughter of the Roman Catholic Duke of York, was informed that she was to be wedded to a stranger and a foreigner she wept for two days. William, who was asthmatic and slightly hunchbacked as well as reserved and taciturn, was hardly an attractive prospect, although the English public was delighted that Mary was to be 'embraced in Protestant arms'. She was then a pretty girl of fifteen, brought up in the Church of England, and her love life had hitherto consisted of a highly imaginative and platonic affair with an older lady of the Court. Though a strict Calvinist, William had sown

his wild oats, but since the age of twenty had been too deeply engaged in politics and war in the United Netherlands to have much time for frivolity. He had received an excellent education, was a master of languages and a real connoisseur, as Mary was also to be. The marriage worked out as well as most.

William, a posthumous son, had been brought up first by a formidable grandmother and later as a 'child of State'. He was the great-grandson of William the Silent who helped form the independent Dutch Republic. But his father, Prince William II of Orange, who was ambitious, had quarrelled with the powerful Regents who constituted the wealthy governing class of Holland, and they strongly reacted against the House of Orange. The Regents and their leader, John de Witt, the Grand Pensionary of

LEFT A miniature of
William and Mary by
Peter Hoadley.

RIGHT A contemporary
Dutch print shows
William arriving in
England at Bridport;
he told the crowd:
'I come to do you goot;
I am here for all your goots'.

Holland, were determined to prevent the boy prince from being appointed to his father's posts of Captain-General of the United Netherlands and Statholder or chief executive of Holland. De Witt allied himself with the French monarchy in 1662, but when five years later the King of France, Louis XIV, launched an aggressive war upon the Spanish Netherlands (modern Belgium), which lay between France and the United Netherlands, thus endangering Dutch security, the Grand Pensionary formed a triple alliance with England and Sweden to restrain French territorial de-

mands. Although it is doubtful whether Louis XIV concluded peace with Spain because of the formation of this triple alliance, he was angry that the upstart Dutch republicans, whom he had earlier befriended, should defy him. Louis succeeded in detaching King Charles II of England, William's uncle, and the Swedish Government from the Dutch alliance and with the connivance of Charles and the assistance of the English navy directed an unprovoked attack on the Dutch in 1672. Thus threatened, the Dutch overthrew De Witt as a Francophile and called upon the twenty-year-old William

III, Prince of Orange and Count of Nassau, to
lead them against the French as their Captain-
General and Admiral-General. For six years the
young prince resisted French aggression by
every political and military means at his disposal. When peace was eventually concluded
in 1678 the Dutch did not have to make any
concessions whatsoever. William became not
only the hero of his countrymen but also a
Protestant champion in Europe.

William never forgave the French for this
blatant attempt to subdue his small country.
His uncle, Charles II, who withdrew in a
humiliated way from the war in 1674, was
anxious to gain prestige as an intermediary between the French and the Dutch. At first he
aimed to please his nephew by carving a little
kingdom for him out of the dismembered republic, but William was not to be bribed. Then
Charles wanted William to use his influence

with the Dutch States-General to accept a
mediated peace. William refused to discuss the
latter proposal until he had concluded his dynastic marriage with Princess Mary, which
would draw together, at least symbolically, the
English and Dutch peoples in resisting French
ambitions. There is no doubt that this marriage
impressed and annoyed Louis XIV. A mediated
peace came next year. As the elder daughter of
James Duke of York Mary was after her father
the heir presumptive to the English and Scottish
thrones. William soon found himself in an extremely awkward situation because his father-
in-law was an avowed Roman Catholic and the
great majority of the English House of Commons (from which Roman Catholics were
excluded by a Test Act of 1678) were determined that James should be stopped from succeeding. It was even believed that the Popish
Plot had been concocted to murder Charles II

247

A portrait of William II, probably painted after his victory in Ireland at the Battle of the Boyne.

and to replace him by his Catholic brother. There was no such plot; but the Exclusionists or Whigs were committed to preventing James from coming to the throne and to replacing him either by his daughter Mary, William's wife, or by the Duke of Monmouth.

In 1681 William again visited England, Charles II hoping that he would assuage the anxieties of the Exclusionists. William was naturally cautious. He did not want to jeopardise his wife's hereditary rights, but on the other hand he did not wish the English monarchy to be so weakened by internal squabbles that it became a dependant of France. Charles for his part would not accept exclusion at any price and he did in fact count as a last resort on French protection to shield him from rebellion at home. In the end he skilfully defeated the Exclusionist movement, thus enabling William's father-in-law to succeed peacefully to the throne.

William viewed the whole political situation in England not so much from the point of view of religious controversy or personal ambition as in the context of Europe as a whole. By the 1680s the French had overrun much of western Europe and therefore, above all, William wanted to preserve a close friendship with England as a counterweight to Louis XIV's undimmed aims for glorious expansion. Although an Anglo-Dutch treaty was renewed in 1685, the danger was that his father-in-law would alienate his subjects by granting too many concessions to his fellow religionists and thus provoke a rebellion which would paralyse English influence on the continental mainland. His relations with James II were thus ambivalent. James was willing to be friendly only if both William and Mary would give their open support to the repeal of the anti-Catholic Penal and Test Acts. Both refused to do so since they were afraid that the predominance of Roman Catholic Ministers and advisers in England would carry the kingdom over into the French camp even if this did not cause an insurrection. That was

why ultimately William felt compelled to intervene actively in England in 1688 at the time when Louis XIV was launching large armies into Germany.

The revolution of 1688, as it was called, though actually it was a Dutch invasion welcomed by English Protestants, was a bloodless success. To William's relief, since his father-in-law had left the kingdom it could be argued that he had 'abdicated' or 'deserted' his throne. It was not until early February in 1689 that a 'convention' or Parliament met which invited William and Mary to become King and Queen with the executive authority in William's hands. Thus it could be asserted that their reign did not begin until 1689; but in fact William had exercised administrative authority since Christmas 1688. Before they were offered the crown William and Mary were asked to agree to a Declaration of Rights (subsequently converted into a Bill) which condemned the way in which James II had used his prerogative, particularly by dispensing with the laws. They agreed to this in general terms so that in effect a limited monarchy was established. Mary, who came to England in mid-February and put a cheerful face on things (for which she was censured by some as having usurped the throne of her father) had made it clear from the beginning that she had no intention of seeking a superior or even an equal position to her husband. She was content to love and obey him, but was willing to preside over the government during his absences abroad.

In fact substantial constitutional changes took place in the course of William's reign. An Act of Indulgence permitted Christian nonconformists (but not Roman Catholics) to worship freely subject to specific conditions; a Triennial Act required a new parliament to be summoned every three years; a Mutiny Act prevented the employment of a standing army in times of peace without the consent of the Commons; a Civil List Act gave the Commons control over the King's expenditure, and indeed when he

The Royal Palace of KINGSINGTON.

attempted to appropriate money from forfeitures of land in Ireland there was a rumpus. Finally in 1701 an Act of Settlement was passed which among other things not only provided for the Protestant succession, but required future monarchs to be specifically members of the Church of England, and forbade them to leave the kingdom without Parliamentary permission. Judges were not to be dismissed without Parliamentary approval. (William did not in fact try to do so.) Other clauses, which would have hampered the evolution of Cabinet government, did not become effective. But possibly the most important event in the reign of William and Mary was the establishment of the Bank of England, which by enabling the Government to borrow money in a sensible way simplified foreign and colonial problems.

William's main concern was the war which broke out in Europe even before he had become

Kensington Palace in the reign of William and Mary. Wren added four new pavilions to the original house. The King and Queen took a great interest in the grounds of their palaces and set a fashion for neat geometrical gardens.

capture in September 1694 of the heavily fortified town of Namur against a French covering army. The peace of Ryswick, concluded in 1697, reduced French power. Afterwards William devoted his efforts to averting another major European war by negotiating two treaties defining the partition of the Spanish empire when its childless ruler died. Unfortunately neither of them worked and the English Parliament blamed him for his secret diplomacy.

Queen Mary, whose influence had considerable effect on the moral climate of the court and country, died of smallpox in December 1694 at the age of thirty-three. William wrote to a friend just before her death: 'You can imagine what a state I am in, loving her as I do. You know what it is to have a good wife.' Though he was pressed to do so, he did not marry again. William was never a congenial king and indeed his popularity diminished after his wife's death and as memories of the causes of the revolution of 1688 faded. His original attempt to govern by employing more or less non-party men as his ministers did not really succeed, although he had a gift for discovering capable (but not always loyal) administrators. His difficulty was that whereas he could not be called a 'Tory king', he disliked the Whigs because their aim was to limit monarchical authority. Furthermore the Tories were 'Little Englanders' while the Whigs were more anti-French, which better suited his taste. He was able, however, to provide for the succession by reconciling himself to Princess Anne, Mary's younger sister, who had quarrelled with her, and by appointing Anne's friend, John Churchill, Earl of Marlborough, to be commander-in-chief and the architect of a second Grand Alliance against France when the danger of another war over the partition of the Spanish empire loomed up. Before William died on 8 March 1702 his only regret was that he could not live to witness the final defeat of Louis XIV's France.

king. Though the Holy Roman Emperor and the Dutch Republic had agreed to ally themselves in May 1689 so as to prevent the French mastery of Europe, it was not until September that William was able to induce the English people to accede to what became known as the first Grand Alliance. Then he had to campaign in Ireland before himself engaging upon fighting the French in Flanders. He proved himself a fairly capable general, his chief success being the

ANNE

r. 1702-14

THE SECOND DAUGHTER of the future James II by his first wife, Anne Hyde, was born on 6 February 1665. As her likelihood of succeeding to the throne appeared to be remote she was uneducated and untrained for the profession of monarchy, while her husband, Prince George of Denmark, whom she married in 1683 and loved dearly, was an amiable nonentity, who preferred being in the background. On the whole, Anne led an unhappy life. Though she had seventeen children, not one of them survived for long: her son William, Duke of Gloucester, was hydrocephalic and lived for only eleven years.

When Anne became Queen she was in perpetual pain. Modern doctors are not in agreement about her precise maladies, but contemporaries called it gout. Being stout and unwieldy she often had to be moved on chairs or by pullies. Her chief amusements were playing cards, drinking tea and admiring gardens; but she disliked fresh air. Her passionate affection for Sarah Churchill, the future Duchess of Marlborough, which began before she was married, was to give her much pleasure and later much pain. Sarah's voluminous writings have been largely relied upon by Anne's biographers as a basis for assessing her character, but it has to be remembered that what Sarah recorded was chiefly written after they had quarrelled. The fact was that Anne was an extremely conscientious Queen – though she had her personal prejudices – and was also a stout pillar of the Church of England. The bounty which she established out of her private resources for the benefit of the poorer clergy kept her name respected among churchmen long after she was dead.

When William III invaded England in 1688 it had evidently been arranged between Anne's

friends, Bishop Compton and John and Sarah Churchill, that they would all desert her father in favour of her sister Mary's husband. For both Mary and Anne were devout Protestants and genuinely believed that James II had been using autocratic methods to catholicise England. The two sisters were also convinced that the son born to James by his second wife in June 1688 was suppositious. The letters that they wrote to each other sustaining this view are rather revolting. In any case it was a blow to James when both his daughters deserted him. After he went into exile Anne acquiesced in the decision made by Parliament that William should rule England during his lifetime, thus postponing her own right to succeed to the throne until after his death on the assumption, which proved correct, that William and Mary had no children. She rejoiced in an income of £50,000 a year voted her by Parliament and she moved into her own palace known as the Cockpit, on the site of the present Downing Street.

Unfortunately she was to be on bad terms for nearly five years with her sister, Queen Mary. The reason for this was that John Churchill, who had been created Earl of Marlborough by William and who had served him brilliantly during the Irish campaign, did not consider that he had been adequately rewarded for his services at the Revolution and therefore engaged in political intrigue against the King while Sarah remained Anne's closest friend. How far it was Churchill's intention to make use of the Jacobites (the followers of James II) in these intrigues is not clear. But Anne herself was conscious of guilty feelings over the way in which she had treated her father and even appears to have written him a contrite letter. William was fully aware of these intrigues in which not only Marlborough but some of his ministers engaged, but he was magnanimous enough to ignore them. For a short time Marlborough was deprived of his offices and put in the Tower of London. Mary naturally enough sided with her husband, thinking it was monstrous that Anne should keep Marlborough's wife so close to her. When Anne refused to dismiss Sarah from her service, she was obliged to leave Whitehall and sever relations with the King and Queen. It was not until after Mary's death that a reconciliation was effected with her brother-in-law. Then William restored Anne and John Churchill to his favour. Meanwhile Sarah had given birth to four healthy daughters which made her feel very superior to Anne, whom she treated with some condescension. Her eldest

ABOVE Queen Anne with her son William, Duke of Gloucester, painted by Godfrey Kneller c. 1694. Although Gloucester lived longer than her other children, he was only eleven when he died.

Marlborough's great victory at Ramillies in Flanders when the armies of the Grand Alliance lost only some four thousand men against fifteen thousand Frenchmen killed.

daughter, Henrietta, was married to Francis, only child of Sidney Godolphin, one of King William's ablest ministers. Thus Anne, the Churchills and Godolphin became a closely-knit group. When, after William's death in March 1702, Anne became Queen, she wrote to Sarah, whom she appointed her Mistress of the Robes: 'We four must never part until death mows us down with his impartial hand.'

Anne, like William, tried at first to govern with a Cabinet of non-party or all-party ministers. Marlborough, who took command of the English and Dutch armies when war with France began in May 1702, and Godolphin, whom at his suggestion Anne appointed Lord

Treasurer, were really non-party men, though they were often described as Tories. But Anne tended to favour the Tories, first because they were enthusiastic supporters of the established Church and second because they upheld the royal prerogatives. For most of the reign England was involved in the war of the Grand Alliance against France, in which Marlborough won three notable victories as well as planning successful campaigns. The extreme Tories however became critical of Marlborough because they favoured naval warfare rather than the expensive commitment of the kingdom to continental campaigns on land.

Anne was upset by this and showed it. For

sons-in-law, the third Earl of Sunderland, to the important ambassadorship in Vienna.

Anne, though she had her own principles – for example she was a patriot and spoke of 'her English heart' – was strongly influenced by personal likes and dislikes. She could not abide Sunderland, an extreme Whig; she took to Harley, a moderate Tory. Thus she resented it when after Whig compulsion in the House of Commons she was obliged to accept Sunderland as one of her Secretaries of State. Marlborough, Sunderland's father-in-law, and Godolphin became increasingly sure that the war against France could only be won if the support given it by the Whigs in Parliament was reinforced by the presence of all the leading Whigs in the Government. Harley, on the other hand, who had proved himself an able statesman and contributed markedly to the formation of the union with Scotland, of which the Queen approved and which was celebrated in May 1707, professed still to believe in the virtues of a central coalition government. Gradually, partly through the help of Abigail Masham, one of the Queen's ladies-in-waiting, Harley came to exert so much influence over the Queen, visiting her up the backstairs, that Godolphin and Marlborough were perturbed. A keen rivalry between Harley and Godolphin eventually culminated in the dismissal of Harley, mainly because Anne was still dependent on Marlborough's military genius to win the war.

At a general election in May 1708 the Whigs won a majority in the Commons and the Queen was compelled to admit all the members of what was called 'the Whig junto' into her Cabinet. Thus in spite of another victory achieved by Marlborough at Oudenarde, 1708 was a sad year for Anne. In October her beloved husband died. She ceased to trust any members of her government, while her alienation from Sarah Marlborough, which had begun not long after her accession owing to Sarah's haughty attitude to her as Queen, was increased

she at once raised Marlborough to a dukedom, asked that he should be voted a generous income in perpetuity and poured offices and money into Sarah Marlborough's lap. After his great victory at Blenheim in 1704 she presented him with one of the royal estates at Woodstock in Oxfordshire and in the following year dismissed his chief Tory critic, her uncle the Earl of Rochester, while another Tory leader, the Earl of Nottingham, resigned from his post of Secretary of State and was replaced by Robert Harley who was also Speaker of the Commons. Godolphin, Marlborough and Harley became known as 'the Triumvirate' which concentrated on winning the war. After the general election of 1705 the Queen dismissed three more leading Tories and under pressure from Sarah Marlborough appointed another of her

Upon her Knees fam'd *Somerset* receives,
An Office which another D——*ss* leaves.

by the fact that Sarah absented herself from her duties at Court for long periods and devoted herself to pro-Whig propaganda.

But in 1709 the party tide turned. The kingdom was growing tired of the long and costly war, while Anne herself reflected these feelings. Also, she was half persuaded that her Church was 'in danger' especially since she was not allowed to appoint the bishops she herself preferred, who were usually High Churchmen. When in February 1710 a clergyman named Henry Sacheverell, who had delivered an outspoken attack on the Whig settlement after the revolution of 1688, was impeached in Westminster Hall, Anne showed sufficient interest to follow the proceedings in person. Despite being condemned Sacheverell was punished extremely lightly, and a political reaction set in. Harley got in secret touch with the Queen, offering to relieve her from the thraldom of the extreme Whigs. Thereupon she plucked up sufficient courage to dismiss her faithful servant, Godolphin, almost as cavalierly as Charles II got rid of Clarendon or James II of Sunderland. Afterwards she was to regret having done so. Furthermore, as the French had gallantly resisted the threat of invasion in the previous year, heavy losses being inflicted upon Marlborough at the battle of Malplaquet, the war looked as if it were going on forever.

Thus pro-Anglican emotions and anti-war sentiments were expressed in the general election of 1710, which resulted in an overwhelming Tory victory. At the beginning of 1711 Anne dismissed Sarah from all her offices after some painful scenes, and at the end of the year Marlborough was also dismissed. Harley took office and another extremely able and highly ambitious Tory, Henry St John Viscount Bolingbroke, assiduously if unscrupulously devoted himself to securing a separate peace with France. To make certain that both Houses of Parliament approved the peace, Anne agreed to create twelve additional Tory peers at one time. When she opened Parliament in 1713 she was able to give news of the Treaty of Utrecht, which was by no means unfavourable to British interests; it was followed by another general election when once again the Tories won a victory.

But Harley's powers were failing fast and Anne dismissed him from office in July 1713. She distrusted Bolingbroke and preferred, even though her sufferings were culminating in a last and fatal illness, to hand the office of Lord Treasurer, virtually prime minister, to her old and trusted friend the Whiggish Earl of Shrewsbury; she also had a woman friend in the red-headed Duchess of Somerset, another moderate Whig. On 1 August 1714, still perplexed by the exigencies of party politics, the Queen died; her doctor said 'I believe sleep was never more welcome to a weary traveller than death was to her'.

Anne's was a notable reign in British history because it saw not only the Union with Scotland but also the acquisition of territorial gains and economic privileges which led to the foundation of the first British empire. What the Queen's personal contribution was is hard to measure but recently it has been contended that her reign was the first in which Parliamentary elections and party contests were genuinely significant. In her support first of a coalition government then of a moderate Whig government, then her reluctant acquiescence in a purely Whig government, and finally her approval of a peace-making Tory government, it is reasonable to argue that she exemplified the feelings of the majority of her subjects, doing her duty, sometimes reluctantly, sometimes harshly, as she understood it.

LEFT A playing card of Queen Anne's reign illustrates the end of her friendship with Sarah Churchill; the Queen gives to the Duchess of Somerset Sarah's court appointments.

8
HOUSE
OF HANOVER
1714~1901

The triumph of the family of George I in the Painted Hall at
Greenwich. The elderly lady behind the King is his mother,
Sophia, a grand-daughter of James I, through whom he inherited
the throne. To his right is his daughter Sophia Dorothea and his
daughter-in-law Caroline of Anspach (carrying mirror). To his
left stands his grandson Frederick, father of George III. His other
grandchildren, including William, Duke of Cumberland, are
grouped to the left. The figure of justice surmounts the scene with
St Paul's in the background. On the top left is a cornucopia,
signifying a reign of plenty.

THE HOUSE OF HANOVER

GEORGE I
1660-1727
m. Sophia Dorothea of Celle 1666 1726

GEORGE II
1683-1760
m. Caroline of Anspach d. 1737

Sophia Dorothea
1688-1757
m. Frederick William II King of Prussia

Frederick Lewes Prince of Wales d. 1751
m. Augusta of Saxe-Gotha d. 1772

William Augustus Duke of Cumberland d. 1765

Anne d. 1759
m. William IV Prince of Orange

GEORGE III
1738-1820
m. Charlotte Sophia of Mecklenburg-Strelitz d. 1818

Edward Augustus Duke of Albany & York d.1767

William Henry Duke of Gloucester d.1805
m. Maria Walpole

Henry Frederick Duke of Cumberland m. Anne Luttrell

William Frederick Duke of Gloucester & Edinburgh d.1834
m. Mary q.v. 1776-1857

Sophia d.1844

GEORGE IV
1762-1830
m. Caroline of Brunswick-Wolfenbuttel q.v 1768-1821

Frederick Duke of York and Albany 1763-1827
m. Frederika of Prussia 1767-1820

WILLIAM IV
1765-1837
m. Adelaide of Saxe-Meiningen 1792-1849

Charlotte Princess Royal 1766-1828
m. Frederick I King of Wurtemburg 1754-1816

Edward Duke of Kent 1767-1820
m. Victoria of Saxe-Coburg-Saalfeld 1786-1861

Augusta 1768-1840

Charlotte
1796-1817
m. Leopold of Saxe-Coburg-Saalfeld 1790-1865

VICTORIA
1819-1901
m. Albert of Saxe-Coburg-Gotha d.1861

HOUSE OF
SAXE-COBURG-GOTHA

Amelia
d. 1786

Caroline
d. 1757

Mary   m.   Frederick
d. 1772   Landgrave
             of Hesse-Cassel

Louisa   m.   Frederick V
d. 1751   King of Denmark

Augusta
d.1813
m. Charles
   Duke of
   Brunswick-
   Wolfenbuttel

Caroline *q.v.*
1768-1821

Caroline
Matilda
d. 1775
m. Christian VII
   King of Denmark

Frederick
William
d.1765

Elizabeth
Caroline
d.1789

Louisa
Anne
d.1768

Elizabeth
1770-1840
m. Frederick
   Landgrave
   of Hesse-
   Homburg
   1769-1829

Ernest
Augustus
Duke of
Cumberland
King of
Hanover
1771-1851
m. Frederika of
   Mecklenburg-
   Strelitz
   d. 1841

Augustus
Frederick
Duke of
Sussex
1773-1843
m.(1)
   Augusta
   Murray
   (2)
   Cecilia
   Underwood

Adolphus
Frederick
Duke of
Cambridge
1774-1850
m. Augusta
   of Hesse-
   Cassel
   1797-1889

Mary *q.v.*
1776-
1857
m. William
   Frederick
   Duke of
   Gloucester
   d. 1834

Sophia
1777-
1848

Octavius
1779-83

Alfred
1780-2

Amelia
1783-
1810

GEORGE I

r. 1714-27

IN 1701 THE ACT OF SETTLEMENT declared that, after Princess Anne, 'the most excellent Princess Sophia, Electress and Dowager Duchess of Hanover, daughter of Elizabeth, late Queen of Bohemia, daughter of James I, shall be next in succession to the Crown'. It was Sophia's son, George Lewis, born in 1660, who became King when Anne died on the morning of 1 August 1714. George had had his agent, Baron von Bothmar, in London since 1710, but it was not until the dying Anne made the Whig Duke of Shrewsbury her chief minister that the Elector could be sure of the crown. The change of dynasty was surprisingly peaceful – 'not a mouse stirred against him in England, in Ireland or in Scotland'. George took his time in coming to England, stopping for festivities and congratulations at several towns in Holland. It was not until 30 September that the King's barge arrived at the steps at Greenwich. Candles and flares scarcely pierced the swirling fog as courtiers and politicians jostled to ingratiate themselves with their new master.

George was not altogether delighted with his good fortune. He loved the flat north German landscape between the Weser and the Aller; he loved his fine country house, the Herrenhausen, his very own miniature Versailles. George's territory might be small, but his people were obedient and prepared to let him rule as he wished. In Hanover, the Elector decided everything; all expenditure over £12 had to receive his personal sanction whilst the army was regarded as his private property. England, on the other hand, was the most fractious, constitution-ridden country in Europe. George might remember that English ingratitude had often made William III wish that he had stayed in Holland. Like William III, George became king of England for European reasons. The new dig-nity would enormously enhance his prestige amongst the other Electors of the Holy Roman Empire and England's resources would be of incalculable help in resisting any power which might seek to destroy the independence of the German princes.

The new King was welcomed with ecstatic verses:

> Hail mighty George! auspicious smiles thy Reign,
> Thee long we wish'd. Thee at last we gain.

The true feeling of the nation was less enthusiastic. Of course, there was a party – well represented in the Church of England, amongst the country gentry and above all in Scotland – which felt that this 'wee, wee German lairdie' had no right to the crown. George's prospects would have been bleak if the rightful king 'James III' had had the sense to take Henry St John's advice and become a Protestant. In an age when royal power was still enormously strong, the personal abilities of the sovereign were of paramount importance. George may have been an improvement on Anne but no-one could pretend that he was a remarkable man. In many ways, the King closely resembled his father, Ernest Augustus. George was of medium height and build with the usual Guelph features of bulbous eyes and fair complexion. His main interests in life appeared to be food, horses and women. England's new King was a shy, suspicious and unimaginative man who said little and at least gave the impression of being a good listener. Certainly there were good qualities; his bravery was unquestioned and he had fought with great distinction at the siege of Vienna in 1683. Unfortunately, even to an uncensorious age, there was one aspect of George's private life which was discreditable in the extreme.

George's unfortunate wife, Sophia Dorothea, with their two children George and Sophia Dorothea. Her indiscreet affair with Count Königsmark caused the vindictive George to imprison her for the rest of her life.

George's wife, the beautiful but empty-headed Sophia Dorothea of Celle, had soon grown bored with her husband and had become involved with a Swedish Colonel of Dragoons, Philip von Königsmark. On 1 July 1694, Königsmark disappeared and was never seen again; it was rumoured throughout Europe that George had ordered his wife's lover to be hacked to pieces and that his mutilated body had been buried under the floorboards at the Herrenhausen. What really shocked people was George's inhuman treatment of his wife. Sophia Dorothea was divorced, forbidden to see her children again and then imprisoned in the Castle of Ahlden for the rest of her life. Sophia was twenty-eight at the time and was to live for another thirty-two years; perhaps von Königsmark's fate had been kinder.

But what interested people in 1714 was who was going to benefit from the new regime. The extreme Tories under St John had worked for a Jacobite succession and would be lucky to escape impeachment, heavy fines and disgrace. Those who had supported George in and out of season demanded their reward; power and patronage were soon in the hands of a Whig 'Junta' of Halifax, Sunderland, Stanhope, Townshend and a rising young man called Robert Walpole. It was not only English friends who expected their reward; George had to consider 'all his German ministers and playfellows, male and female'. Public opinion was easily roused against foreign favourites. The King certainly took a good deal of notice of the loyal Bothmar, of the prime minister of Hanover, Baron von Bernstorff and of William III's old friend, the Huguenot, Jean de Robethon. Robethon was very unpopular – 'a prying, impertinent, venomous creature, for ever crawling in some slimy intrigue'.

As soon as the King had settled down after his coronation, the English took stock of the situation and started to laugh. George just did not know how to behave like a King; the new monarch never dined in state but had his meals served in his apartments – a set of two rooms. In the early days of his reign the King made many *faux pas*. He issued his guards with new uniforms to celebrate his birthday but the soldiers refused to wear their new tunics on the grounds that the cloth was too coarse. With the best will in the world, George expressed interest in the new craze for agricultural improvements. How much would it cost, he asked, to close St James's Park to the public and plant it with turnips? His Secretary of State replied laconically, 'Only three crowns, sire'.

George's shyness made it hard for him to make new friends. He was determined to surround himself with people who had become part of his routine, people who would not make clever jokes about their master behind his back. The result was a very motley Court. George's

The coronation procession of George I passing St James's Palace, his official residence.

two Turkish servants, Mustapha and Mahomet, were regarded as distinctly odd, but the King's taste for ugly women provoked the greatest ribaldry. One German mistress was very fat and the other German mistress was very thin. The skinny Ehrengard Melusina von Schulenberg, later Duchess of Kendal, was nearing sixty. George's passion for her had cooled but he spent most of his evenings with her, cutting out paper patterns with a pair of scissors. The fat Charlotte Sophia Kelmanns (who may have been George's half-sister) was more vivacious, even though her vast uncorsetted bulk terrified Horace Walpole as a little boy. Both women grew rich taking bribes from those who wanted a favour from the King. They certainly made more like this than they would have done from what was regarded as their real profession – 'old, ugly trulls, such as would not find entertainment in the most hospitable hundreds of old Drury'. The Duchess of Kendal was soon christened 'The Maypole' whilst Charlotte Kelmanns became 'Elephant and Castle'.

George's circle was not the most cultivated in Europe. The King's first language was German but he spoke French tolerably well. With his habitual dislike of clever women, he always described his daughter-in-law, Caroline of Anspach, as 'Cette diablesse Madame la Princesse'. Despite Walpole's story that his father had to 'brush up his Latin' in order to communicate with the King, it is not quite correct to say that George knew no English. The King certainly had unorthodox ideas about grammar and pronunciation; on one occasion he declared roundly 'I hate all boets and bainters'. But if George had none of his mother's linguistic ability or artistic interests, he did have a deep and genuine love of music. George Frederick Handel had been *Kappelmeister* at the Herrenhausen. As soon as his old master became King of England, Handel was able to present concerts at St James's Palace and begin to make his enormous contribution to English music. By the beginning of 1715 then, George was beginning to adjust to his new position, putting down a few tentative roots, finding new reasons to quarrel with his son, acquiring a more presentable English mistress, going to the opera incognito and making up a card-playing circle. Perhaps George was beginning to hope that he could enjoy a quiet life as King of England; any illusions were soon to be destroyed.

George's reign witnessed two major crises – the Jacobite rebellion and the South Sea Bubble. The Jacobite rising began on 6 September 1715 when the Earl of Mar proclaimed James III at Braemar. Although Edinburgh remained loyal, most of the other towns in Scotland welcomed the rebels. From France, Henry St John was directing a superb propaganda campaign against 'the flight of hungry Hanoverian vultures' with their 'cacophonous, outlandish, German names'. Perhaps George should have trembled – there were indeed riots in many English towns – but there is no evidence that the King ever considered packing his bags and returning to his beloved Hanover. The only indication of the King's feelings was in his behaviour after the rebellion had been defeated. Six Scottish noblemen were condemned to death; George attended a ball on the day that Lord Derwentwater and Lord Kenmure were beheaded. It was generally felt that the King's ostentatious gaiety was a slight on the whole order of nobility. George's behaviour to Lady Nithsdale, the wife of another condemned nobleman, provoked even more criticism. When Lady Nithsdale forced her way into the royal apartments

to beg for mercy, George simply seized her, threw her on the floor and then walked contemptuously away. George's boorishness soon left him; when he heard the news that Lord Nithsdale had made a dramatic escape from the Tower of London disguised as a woman, he is alleged to have commented, 'It is the best thing that a man in his situation could have done'.

St John's involvement with the Jacobites meant that the Whigs now had a monopoly of power; George seemed almost the prisoner of his government. The King was not a clever man but he was strong willed, he would be no one's puppet. Above all, it was vital for the interest of Hanover that he should retain a free hand in foreign affairs. George had allied himself with Peter the Great of Russia in order to grab some of the pieces of the crumbling Swedish Empire. Peter's success in the Baltic had been so complete that George had become alarmed and was wondering whether the time had come to change his foreign policy. Peace had come to Western Europe in 1713 but the Great Northern Wars were to continue till 1721. It was a very difficult situation and frequently demanded George's presence in Hanover. If British politicians were to serve his purpose, George would have to break up the Whig unity. In the nature of things, British politicians did not care twopence for Hanover, but if there were a number of rival factions in politics, George would be able to invite bids for office. Those who were most solicitous for the welfare of Hanover were likely to get the contract.

No doubt George was helped by the quarrels and ambitions of his leading statesmen but the King's success is a tribute to his personal shrewdness and an indication of the continuing power of the Crown as an institution. George's poor English meant that he rarely attended meetings of his ministers and thus allowed the beginnings of the modern Cabinet. But although day-to-day decisions slipped out of the hands of the monarch, the choice of who was to hold office remained firmly with the King. By July 1716 there were already stories about 'the heats and divisions betwixt the King's servants'. With things beginning to boil nicely George could go off to Hanover, so happy 'that he seemed to have forgot the accident that happened to him and his family on 1 August 1714'. With the King's encouragement, Sunderland and Stanhope forced Townshend and Walpole out of the government. The administration was now weaker and was more dependent on George's support. Stanhope was told to stop shilly-shallying; he was ordered to join an alliance with France and Holland which would allow Britain to concentrate on Baltic affairs.

George had to pay a high price for his advantage. In the absence of genuine constitutional disputes, political struggles were bound to become personalised. Bitter hatred between the sovereign and his eldest son seems to have been the norm under the Hanoverians. George Augustus was eleven when his mother was hurried off to spend the rest of her life in prison; the young boy never forgave his father. After 1714 the Prince of Wales made it brutally clear that he could hardly wait for George I to die so that Sophia Dorothea might be released. Walpole and Townshend joined 'The Leicester House Set' which did its best to thwart the King and openly looked forward to the next reign. George I came to see that he had made the wrong choice of ministers; he needed Walpole's political skill but this could be had only on condition of a humiliating 'reconciliation' with the Prince of Wales. The meeting duly took place, apparent amity was restored but, as the Prince departed, the King began to mutter, 'Votre conduite! Votre conduite!'

A few months later, George again felt his throne trembling beneath him. The South Sea Company had nothing to do with the South Seas. It was a finance company whose shares reached astronomic levels when it received a contract to manage £30 million of the National Debt. The crash came in September 1720,

the shares became worthless and thousands were ruined. Highly-placed persons at Court, including the hated Germans, appeared to be implicated in gross fraud; the small investors were clamouring for blood, anybody's blood. The South Sea crash was a gift for the Jacobites and for a few weeks the future of the dynasty seemed precarious in the extreme. Walpole's achievement in restoring confidence was his greatest service to the House of Hanover. After the deaths of Sunderland and Stanhope, Walpole had no serious rivals; George had no alternative but to make him Chancellor of the Exchequer and First Lord of the Treasury. With complete control over patronage and mastery of the House of Commons, Walpole was indeed the country's first prime minister. A succession of Jacobite plots, notably Bishop Atterbury's conspiracy, were revealed just in time by the prime minister's agents. Like it or not, George I could not get away from the fact that Robert Walpole was indispensable.

In a way, George had been beaten. Walpole's hegemony meant that there could be no question of Hanover's interests taking precedence over those of England. The King recognised what had happened and spent more and more of his time in Germany. George's divorced wife, Sophia Dorothea, died on 3 November 1726; on the day he received the news the King ostentatiously went to a play at the Haymarket Theatre. For seven months poor Sophia Dorothea was denied burial, but eventually in May 1727 George left for Hanover accompanied by 'the Maypole'. A fortune-teller had once told George that he would not survive his wife by a year. The King's sixty-seven years were beginning to tell and, leaving his mistress at Delden, he set out for Hanover full of anxiety. On 10 June 1727, as his coach neared Osnabrück, George suffered a cerebral haemorrhage. He was carried to the castle at Osnabrück and died in the very room in which he had been born. The English had never loved their German King; when news of his death arrived broad-

RIGHT The battle of Preston, 1715, where the Anglo-Scottish Jacobites were defeated by General Wills.

THE
Battle
of
PRESTON

Robert Walpole's silver salver, incorporating the great seal of George I which was given to him as Treasurer. The figure of Atlas and view of London behind were designed by Hogarth. The silversmith was Paul de Lamerie.

sheets declared 'The Devil has caught him by the throat at last'. The King was out of mind so quickly in England that they even forgot about burying him. No plans were made to bring his body for burial in Westminster Abbey. In the end, George was buried at Osnabrück in Hanover – where his heart had always been.

It is hard to describe George as an attractive man but one should always remember the enormous disadvantages he had to contend with. At least he put his trust in able ministers. The ultimate verdict on George must be favourable; he was very much better than 'James III' would have been.

GEORGE II

r. 1727-60

KING GEORGE II was a tall and well-built man, with prominent blue eyes, a ruddy complexion and a nose which was perhaps a shade too large. The new King was interested in history and genealogy; he had a good grounding in the classics and could speak French, Italian and English tolerably well. George Augustus had a very German passion for detail, uniforms, the pleasures of the battlefield and the minutiae of court etiquette. His was not an enquiring mind; in matters of religion he 'jogged on quietly in that which he had been bred without scruples, zeal or inquiry'. Hatred of his father had long dominated the life of George Augustus, Prince of Wales. As a boy he is alleged to have tried to swim the moat surrounding the Castle at Ahlden in a vain attempt to see his mother. In Hanover, the Elector had steadfastly refused to entrust his son with even the most minor responsibility and constantly denigrated his considerable achieve-

ments at the battle of Oudenarde. Such treatment did nothing to improve George's quick temper; within his own circle he made up for his lack of power by behaviour which was arrogant in the extreme – 'looking upon all men and women he saw as creatures he might kick or kiss for his diversion'.

In 1714 George Augustus was thirty years old and had been married for eight years to Caroline of Anspach. Caroline, an extremely intelligent and lively woman, was a great asset to her husband. She was large, blonde, blatantly sensual and earthy. A tremendous flirt, Caroline knew precisely what she was doing in charming men to advance her own political influence. George was genuinely attached to his wife who, despite her artful and somewhat bawdy ways, was probably never unfaithful to her husband. Caroline discreetly dominated George Augustus and was far too intelligent to make a fuss over his occasional lapses with her ladies' maids.

George II as Prince of Wales with his father and his wife Caroline.

She had readily accepted the situation when Henrietta Howard became her husband's chief mistress in 1710; as the Dowager Duchess Sophia pointed out, Mrs Howard would at least improve George's English.

George Augustus and Caroline soon established a rival 'court' where life was much more fun than in the stupefying boredom at St James's. At any rate Caroline was able to provide a veneer of culture; she collected Van Dycks and as a girl she had had a learned conversation with the philosopher Leibnitz. The stakes at the card tables were higher than at the King's court and there was even dancing – 'the Princess danced in slippers very well and the Prince better than any'. Above all, the Prince and Princess went out of their way to cultivate the English. Caroline's ladies of the bedchamber were all English, although George Augustus was probably rather overdoing it when he declared 'I have not one drop of blood in my veins dat is not English'. The best jokes against George I tended to come from the Prince's circle; the young Lord Chesterfield told a delighted audience: 'The standard of His Majesty's taste, as exemplified in his mistress, makes all ladies who aspire to his favour, and who are near the suitable age, strain and swell themselves, like the frogs in the fable, to rival the bulk and dignity of the ox. Some succeed, and others – burst.'

But it was not all fun and games. For years the only time when the Prince of Wales met his father was at the christenings of his children; on these occasions there were fearful scenes and after one of them the King ordered that his son should be arrested for threatening to murder the Duke of Newcastle. George I firmly refused to allow the Prince to assume the title of Regent during the King's long absences in Hanover and would only grudgingly permit 'Guardian of the Realm' – with virtually no powers attached. Even in death, George Augustus would not trust his father. The Prince of Wales merely suspected a trick when told that

he was now King. When Walpole gave him the news on the evening of 14 June 1727 he is said to have replied 'Dat is one big lie'.

Unlike his father, George II had gained considerable experience of English politics by the time he came to the throne. The new King was forty-four and was to live for another thirty-three years. He had the time and the opportunity to arrange things to suit himself; most people expected that he would reverse everything his father had done. As Prince of Wales, George had been resentful at Walpole's 'betrayal' in rejoining the government in 1720. Few expected 'Robin' Walpole to survive long:

> Unhappy, me amongst the Birds of Prey
> Once I'd a comfort, now he's turned to clay.

Opposition Whigs like Pultenay and even the now forgiven St John believed their day had come. George II did indeed ask his friend Sir Spencer Compton to take over the government but Compton only burst into tears and declared that he was not up to the job. Although George had recently described Walpole's favourite brother Horatio as 'a scoundrel and a dirty buffoon', in the end the old gang remained in power. Walpole's triumph should not be seen as the victory of Parliament over the Crown. The prime minister owed his survival to the influence of Queen Caroline. Despite constant rumours of an affair, Caroline found the twenty-stone Walpole physically repulsive, but his tolerant, worldly and cynical outlook coincided precisely with her own. Whilst the opposition courted George's mistresses, Walpole remained on good terms with Caroline. The ministry was safe when the Queen told George that Walpole was the only man who could get large increases in the Civil List through Parliament. Walpole always appreciated Caroline's ultimate hegemony over her husband; he remarked crudely but perceptively 'I have the right sow by the ear'.

As soon as George I was dead, George Augustus seemed to grow more and more like

ABOVE Frederick, Prince of Wales (wearing Garter star) at the gaming table.

his father. The court was not very exciting; most of Caroline's bright young friends, 'the Virgin Band', had gone off and married disreputable husbands. The new King's concern for the strictest observance of court etiquette and absolute punctuality was fast becoming a mania. Parties like those before 1720 were now very rare; George had decided that economy should be his watchword. In the long boring evenings at court the King reminisced *ad nauseam* about his exploits at the battle of Oudenarde. To some extent things were enlivened by the malice of the strange Lord Hervey, but Hervey scarcely enjoyed his life at Court. 'No mill horse ever went on a more constant track or a more unchanging circle.'

The most striking similarity with the previous reign was the deplorable relationship between the new Prince of Wales and his parents. 'Poor Fred' who was born in Hanover in 1706, did not even look like a Guelph. He had a yellowish complexion and a curved, rather semitic nose. There were stories that he was a changeling but these seem highly improbable. What is certain is that Frederick's father – and even more his mother – hated him from the moment of his birth. George I had wanted his eldest grandson to marry Princess Wilhelmina of Prussia, a match which Frederick appeared to welcome. As soon as George II ascended his throne he broke off the marriage negotiations with the comment, 'I did not think that ingrafting my half-witted coxcomb upon a mad woman would improve the breed'. Later the King exclaimed 'Our first-born is the greatest ass, the greatest liar, the greatest canaille and the greatest beast in the whole world and we heartily wish he was out of it'. Even George I would not have said that about his son.

In some ways Frederick was rather a foolish young man but he was not really vicious. A little extravagance, a little gallantry with the ladies can hardly justify or even explain this intense hatred. Kings certainly do not like being

271

reminded that they too are mortal and that a successor is waiting in the wings. It is probable, however, that the main reason for George's hostility to his son came from the knowledge that Frederick was bound to be the focus of opposition to the royal government. Even as a young man, it was said of George II: 'Whenever he meets with any opposition to his designs, he thinks the opposers insolent rebels to the will of God.'

The King did his best to reduce Frederick's social influence by keeping his allowance down to £24,000 per annum; as Prince of Wales, George II had received £100,000. Queen Caroline suggested that Frederick was reduced to offering Lord Hervey a half share in his mistress in order to raise cash. In the eighteenth century, however, so long as there was an heir to the throne, there would always be a 'Leicester House Set'. Even with his limited resources, Frederick could patronise the Italian opera of Buononcini and sneer at his parents' loyalty to Handel. George II told Frederick sourly that no persons of quality would demean themselves by setting up 'factions of fiddlers'.

The fashionable world thought otherwise, and disappointed politicians, wits and dramatists began to find the Prince's company far more agreeable than that of his parents. Walpole's power appeared to be crumbling with the introduction of the unpopular Excise Scheme, whilst his policy of non-involvement in European affairs was threatened by the outbreak of the war of Polish Succession. George faced the nightmare that Frederick would use the political influence of the Duchy of Cornwall to eject the present ministers and install his own friends – a group derisively described by Walpole as 'The Patriot Boys'.

For the moment, Walpole survived but his power was weakened; the King was compelled to allow Frederick to marry, a step which would entail a separate establishment and a larger income. The King and Queen chose the seventeen-year-old Princess Augusta of Saxe-Gotha as a suitable bride for their son; the future Princess of Wales arrived at Greenwich clutching her doll. George and his wife immediately added their new daughter-in-law to their list of enemies. Ambassadors were forbidden to call on Augusta; the House of Lords, the Armed Forces and officers of the court were told that a visit to the Prince of Wales would incur royal displeasure. Primed by Henry St John, Frederick was making the appropriate noises about the crown being in bondage and exploited by a parasite gang of Whigs. George II had limited his own political freedom because, at the back of his mind, he believed that all Tories were secret Jacobites; his son had no such qualms. Frederick's popularity grew and grew: 'My God', said the King, 'popularity always makes me sick, but Fretz's popularity makes me vomit.'

Eighteenth-century Princes of Wales usually tried to persuade society that their fathers were simply rather unpleasant and disagreeable old men. George II had said it about his father; now he was subjected to the same treatment. Frederick described the King as 'an obstinate self-indulgent miserly martinet with an insatiable sexual appetite'. This observation was sadly close to the truth. When George was fifty-two he had gone over to Hanover to acquire a new mistress. Madame von Walmoden caught his eye and immediately he wrote to the Queen, 'You must love the Walmoden, for she loves me'. Under Walmoden's influence the King became more German-orientated, a trait which the English had always deplored in their Hanoverian monarchs. George became increasingly rude to his courtiers; those who had had the honour of having the King's back suddenly turned on them formed themselves into a Rumpsteak Club. Nothing English would suit now: 'I am sick to death of all this foolish stuff and wish with all my heart that the devil may take all your bishops, and the devil take your Minister, and the devil take your Parliament and the devil take the whole island, provided I can get out of it and go to Hanover.'

Perhaps George had reason to be in a bad mood. The same mocking laughter which had made George I so absurd was beginning to attach itself to him. During one of George's foreign tours, a broken-down old horse was turned loose in the streets of London; the animal bore a placard 'Let nobody stop me – I am the King's Hanover equipage going to fetch His Majesty and his whore to England'. When the government tried to reduce the consumption of gin, mobs stormed round the royal coach screaming 'No Gin! No King!' But there were much more serious blows. Queen Caroline died a lingering and painful death in November 1737. George, who hated illness, was a mixture of irritation and remorse. One moment he asked Caroline how the devil she could expect to sleep when she would not lie still; the next, he was in tears at the prospect of losing his beloved wife. When Caroline died, George was genuinely heart-broken; he had known many women yet 'I never saw one fit to buckle her shoe'.

Caroline's death had serious political implications. Women certainly had a great power over the King; it had been Caroline who had kept royal influence behind Robert Walpole. Which politician would benefit from the new situation? The Duke of Newcastle suggested that the greatest influence in George's life now was likely to be his favourite daughter; the prime minister would do well to cultivate Princess Caroline. Walpole knew what really influenced the King – 'Will she go to bed with her father? If not, I am for Madame Walmoden, I'll bring her over; Lady Deloraine will do as a stop gap.' Disagreement soon appeared between George and the man who was almost deputy king. Walpole's success was not just a matter of exploiting the greed of his opponents with large doses of 'Doctor King's Golden Soporific'. Not enough funds were available to bribe everybody and some did not care to be bribed.

Walpole's policy was one of Whig men and Tory measures; low taxation and peace kept the squires contented. Walpole clung to peace but George II wanted war and a chance to relive the military triumphs of his youth.

The war which broke out on 26 September 1739 – first against Spain and then against France too – delighted the King but it was the beginning of the end for Walpole. It had been the opposition and Prince Frederick that had really wanted war. Walpole resigned on 1 February 1742 but even then Frederick was denied his triumph. George was able to reconstruct the government by retaining some of the existing ministers and fill the other places with men who claimed to be the Prince's friends. The trouble with the Reversionary Interest was that no-one knew how long it would take to mature; faced with the temptation of immediate power many of Poor Fred's erstwhile friends deserted Leicester House for St James's Palace as fast as their legs could carry them. The fortunes of war, too, looked more encouraging. At the age of sixty-one George was again on the battlefield. At Dettingen, on 15 June 1743, the King led a joint army of British, Hanoverians, Hessians, Austrians and Dutch to victory over the French. George was often under heavy fire. 'Don't tell me of danger', cried the King, 'I'll be even with them. Now boys! Now for the honour of England! Fire and behave brave, and the French will run.' They did. Whatever one may say against George II, he was the last British sovereign to risk his life fighting alongside his soldiers. The King's popularity, at a low ebb for years, received a tremendous boost.

The popularity was badly needed when, in the summer of 1745, the Young Pretender, so much more dashing than his father, launched another invasion of Britain. The threat was more serious than in 1715; this time Edinburgh fell, then Carlisle, then Derby. Some of the King's ministers thought they would be lucky to spend the rest of their lives in exile – living in miserable attics in Hanover. George remained

George II at the Battle of Dettingen; he was the last British sovereign to lead his troops into battle.

calm and the rebellion was defeated by his favourite son, the Duke of Cumberland. War at home and abroad meant increasing taxation which in turn meant increasing the power of Parliament. George might rail against the 'republican' features of the British constitution but he never had the nerve to try to get rid of a government he was not keen on. The events of the mid-1740s consolidated the position of the Duke of Newcastle and his relations, the Pelham family. The Pelhams were to remain in control for the remainder of George II's reign.

The King constantly complained that he was 'in toils' to his nominal servants but in fact ministers still needed royal support. After a protracted royal visit to Hanover, the Duke of Newcastle went to Germany to beg his master to return to England and show his approval of the administration. A modern sovereign would be bound to accept such a request; George II not only refused but 'said a great many things I will not repeat'. There were other consolations; although no woman ever took Caroline's place, the King was fond enough of Madame von Walmoden to make her Lady Yarmouth. George also had the satisfaction of outliving the hated 'Fretz'. Poor Fred had spent his life talking about what he would do when his father expired but it was the son who died first – in March 1751. George put on a show of the sorrowing father but many people did not find the performance convincing; at any rate he adamantly refused to pay his late son's debts.

George did not care for the Pelhams and he liked their occasional ally, William Pitt, even less. George's own miscalculations were partly responsible for getting England involved in the

RIGHT A map of 1746 showing the sea journeys and land marches of Bonnie Prince Charlie and his army in the Jacobite rising of the previous year. The Prince's army reached as far south as Derby.

Seven Years' War. England's traditional ally on the continent was Austria; George had substituted Prussia and seriously underestimated the expansionist plans of his nephew Frederick the Great. George may have been at fault, but Pitt, who had begun his career as a 'Patriot Boy', was the man to lead the country in war. Another round with France was probably inevitable after the inconclusive peace of 1748. The King, 'the good old King' – tactless and short-tempered as ever – took his time before accepting Pitt. He swallowed his pride at the end of 1756 and after that, despite reverses in Hanover, most things seemed to go right. 1759 was the year of England's greatest military triumphs – complete command of the sea, conquests in Canada, India and the Caribbean. At seventy-eight the King was beginning to fail; he had always wanted military glory and now it was his. No reign has ended on a grander note.

But somehow George II never quite made greatness; there was about him that hint of the ridiculous which dogged all the Hanoverians. The King's death was mercifully sudden but it was not dignified. For years, George had suffered from constipation; on the morning of 25 October 1760 his exertions to overcome his difficulty were too much for him and brought on a fatal heart attack. Poor King George II died sitting on the lavatory.

GEORGE III

r. 1760–1820

GEORGE WILLIAM FREDERICK, eldest son of Frederick Prince of Wales and Augusta of Saxe-Gotha, was only twelve when his father died. Even the circumstances of the future George III's birth illustrate the bitterness between George II and 'Poor Fred'. George was born in lodgings in St James's Square because the King had evicted Frederick and Augusta from their apartments in the nearby Palace. George's schoolwork was poor, and he was thought young for his years. From earliest childhood, however, he was made conscious of his royal rank. One of his few playmates was the future Lord North, but North's parents told him: 'Bow to the Prince, my son, address him as Your Royal Highness, if you play a game with him, he must win; never, never, raise your hand to him and, who knows, my son, if you play your part well, you may in time get a sinecure post and your father exchange his barony for an earldom.' Under the circumstances, it is astonishing that George had such a pleasant character; he was described as 'silent, modest and easily abashed'.

The main influences in George's life were his rather possessive mother and her close friend, the Earl of Bute. Bute was very much a father figure to George who constantly sought the Earl's approval. In 1759, when it was clear that he would soon be King, George fell in love with Lady Sarah Lennox, a descendant of Charles II and Louise de Kerouaille. The young man wrote to Bute: 'I don't deny having often flattered myself with the hopes that one day or other you would consent to my raising her to the throne.' It was Bute who persuaded George that he must give up the idea of marrying one of his own subjects and should send for accounts of eligible Princesses in Germany. Bute and Augusta were largely responsible for George's views on politics. Ideas that the Prince was deliberately indoctrinated with notions of absolutism can be dismissed – the history dispensed by Bute was impeccably Whiggish – but George was taught that his grandfather was a despicable cipher in the power of corrupt ministers. Bute was a scholarly, cultivated and ambitious man who hoped to follow the example of Cardinal Fleury, Louis XV's tutor who had become first minister of France. George readily supported his friend's plans but neither appreciated that the Earl's lack of experience in practical politics would be an enormous obstacle to the realisation of this project.

George III was proclaimed King immediately after his grandfather's death. The twenty-two-year-old monarch seemed to have many advantages. Horace Walpole said: 'His person is tall and full of dignity, his countenance florid and obliging.' George inherited the family features of prominent eyes and fair colouring. Although not remarkably handsome, the young King was generally regarded as good-looking in a rather Germanic way. Unlike his two predecessors, George had been born and educated in England. He was entirely English in sympathy, never visited Hanover and was the first sovereign since Queen Anne to speak his subjects' language without a foreign accent. Such things mattered with the xenophobic English.

George might not be outstanding in book learning but he was intensely hard working; he would spare no efforts to do the job of king properly. Few monarchs have been more acutely conscious of their duty to God and to their people. The King was a deeply religious young man; unlike George II's half-hearted formal religion, George III's faith was very real. Throughout his life George spent long hours in private prayer; perhaps this enabled the King to remain calm in moments of crisis – like the terrible Gordon Riots of 1780 – when his ministers completely lost their heads. One of George's first priorities was to clean up the disreputable moral tone of his grandfather's court; within a month of his accession, he had issued a royal proclamation for the encouragement of piety

and virtue. It is true that, when nervous, the King tended to speak too fast – a common enough failing – and to fill gaps in his conversations with meaningless patter; it is a gross slander, however, to use this fact to support the contention that the King was already showing signs of mental instability. Compared to George I and George II, George III may seem a little dull and a little priggish. He made his mistakes but, even then, his actions have been subject to greater distortion than those of any other British monarch. The plain fact is that George III was the only Hanoverian who could be called a genuinely decent and good man.

After selecting and marrying an appropriate German princess, Charlotte of Mecklenberg-Strelitz, George III set about destroying the power of the Whig clique which had dominated the government since 1714. George II had indeed chosen his own ministers but he had done so from within the limits of a narrowly defined caste of professional politicians. In refusing to accept this constraint, George was not acting unconstitutionally; he was not planning to establish an enlightened despotism on continental lines but he was attempting something which no British monarch had done for the previous fifty years. Language difficulties, long absences in Hanover and a desire for a quiet life had meant that power had slipped away from the Crown almost imperceptibly. George III was going to stop the rot. The young King eased Pitt out of office, then Newcastle, began peace negotiations with France and installed Bute in power.

Bute was not one of the Whig grandees; he had had Jacobite relations and he came from Scotland, a country still regarded by Englishmen as both foreign and savage. George had a difficult first decade; he had to learn several lessons before he could succeed in politics. He had wanted to abolish corruption, yet in order to keep Bute in power he had to resort to the very tactics he deplored in others. Sadly he concluded, 'We must call in bad men to govern bad men'. Bute managed to get the peace with France through Parliament and then resigned rather than face an all-out attack. Prime ministers followed in rapid succession – George Grenville, Lord Rockingham, William Pitt and the Duke of Grafton. Ministers claimed that political instability was caused by George's failure to give his official advisers proper support; ignoring his constitutional duty to consult them in all things, he 'went behind the curtain' to seek advice from Bute. Grenville had some cause for complaint but, instead of trying to win the King's confidence, he indulged in long lectures upbraiding George for ingratitude. The King declared, 'When he has wearied me for two hours, he looks at his watch to see if he may not tire me for an hour more'.

All the time, George was subjected to crude abuse from the gutter press, whilst the irresponsible libertine, John Wilkes, stirred the London mob to riot and sedition.

George had shown that governments which did not enjoy the monarch's full confidence tended to have a short life but, equally, prime ministers could stay in office only if they had the respect and votes of Parliament. Patronage might help but it was not enough on its own; was there anyone in politics who was genuinely acceptable to both King and Parliament? In 1770 George thought he had found his man – Lord Frederick North, 'the man who lost America' and allegedly the worst prime minister in British history. George's selection of North seems proof of the King's stupidity – 'a

George III and Queen Charlotte with six of their fifteen children in 1770. From left to right: William, Duke of Clarence; George, Prince of Wales; Frederick, Duke of York; Princess Augusta, Princess Charlotte and Princess Elizabeth.

The King returns through Eton to Windsor after the hunt; a painting by Rowlandson.

fool chosen by a fool'. Yet one cannot so dismiss a man who retained a working majority in Parliament for ten years. Within the context of British politics George's judgement was sound. The 'green boy' of 1760 had become a shrewd politician; North was a good Parliament man, an able speaker and would have been an excellent peace-time premier. Claims that George wanted to enslave his colonial subjects are absurd. The King certainly supported his prime minister's attempts to suppress the American rebels; perhaps George III might have shown more imagination but then the same charge can be made against almost all of the political establishment. Those who became advocates of American Independence were converted only very late in the day when the war was virtually lost. Kings are expected to be consistent.

The loss of America was a terrible blow. Catherine the Great of Russia said: 'Rather than have granted America her Independence as my brother monarch, King George has done, I would have fired a pistol at my own head.' The political problems created by the collapse of North's ministry were enormous. Charles James Fox described the King as an arbitrary despot who had squandered his subjects' blood and treasure in his mad lust for revenge. After North, Lord Rockingham took office with a programme of reducing royal influence in politics, but even this was not enough. The country was soon confronted with the astonishing spectacle of Fox joining up with the now discredited North to impose even greater restrictions and humiliations. 'The King's closet had been stormed' by men George had reason to hate. It must have seemed absurd to suggest that anyone short of a political genius could ever recapture for the King the right of choosing his own ministers. To the astonishment of everyone, this is what George proceeded to do.

The Humbug Wedding

On 18 December 1783 the House of Lords rejected the government's East India Bill – at 1 a.m. the King sent out notices of dismissal to all members of the Fox-North coalition. George had chosen his moment carefully; the country would not permit an illegitimate extension of royal power or of ministerial power against the Crown. Influential people felt that Fox was going too far and swung around to support the King. The next prime minister, William Pitt the Younger, was only twenty-four. Pitt was very much George's personal choice; for several months the new government was constantly defeated in Parliament, yet the King refused to think of accepting its resignation. When Pitt felt that the time had come for a general election, George put all the resources of the Crown behind his protégé. The result was a tremendous defeat for Fox. The King's choice of Pitt is probably the best proof of royal sagacity. Pitt was to remain in power for twenty-one years and was to lead England in the terrible struggle with Revolutionary France. In such perilous times it was better that Pitt, rather than the wild Charles James Fox, should be running the country.

The mid-1780s were probably the best years of George's reign. Under Pitt's guidance, Britain was fast recovering her prosperity and self-confidence. George III was in vigorous middle age, his figure kept trim and youthful by a spartan diet and plenty of exercise. Apart from one illness in 1765 the King had enjoyed excellent health throughout his reign. George was a good and faithful husband; although not the most exciting of women, Queen Charlotte was at least contented with her lot. She de-

LEFT A cartoon on the marriage of the Prince of Wales and Mrs Fitzherbert on 21 December 1785. The King and Queen are shown entering his bedroom with the act of parliament forbidding the marriage of royal princes without the King's consent. On the wall is a portrait of Charles Fox, who was believed to have connived at the marriage, though in fact he had been deceived by the Prince's denials.

clared that since her marriage she had never known a moment of real sorrow. There had been no less than fifteen children to the marriage; no-one could say that George had not secured the succession. The atmosphere at court was more relaxed. The King was less prudish than in the early years of the reign and laughed heartily at Cibber's play *She Would and She Would Not*. Absence of political pressure meant that George was able to develop his knowledge of botany and write pamphlets on agricultural improvements under the pen name of Ralph Robinson. Intellectually the King had been a slow starter but he had caught up; in the 1780s he compared favourably with most European monarchs, certainly with Louis XVI.

The one black spot was the growing antagonism between George III and his eldest son, the future Prince Regent. The same conflicts which had soured the relationship between George I and George Augustus and between George II and 'Poor Fred' were appearing yet again. There were faults on both sides; George III's great failing was that he was over-protective. He genuinely loved his son but he wanted the Prince of Wales to remain a child for ever. The 'cotton wool' atmosphere of Kew Palace was far too restrictive for the high-spirited young Prince and the desire to rebel against it led him into all kinds of wickedness. But the King's reaction to his son's follies was more of sorrow than anger; the Prince of Wales really had far less to complain about than Poor Fred had done.

Such was the state of the country and of the royal family when George III 'went mad'. The King had not been well in the summer of 1788; he had an alarming attack of convulsions after riding in the rain on 16 October. George's manner was thought odd and he seemed never to stop talking. It was about this time that the famous Oak Tree incident is alleged to have occurred with the King talking to a tree as if it were the King of Prussia. This story was put about by a page who had been dismissed from the royal service so its veracity must be questionable. On 5 November 1788, however, there were obvious signs of derangement. At dinner in Windsor Castle the King attacked the Prince of Wales and tried to smash his head against the wall. George was talking non-stop gibberish, foam was coming from his mouth and his eyes were so bloodshot that they looked like currant jelly.

When it was clear that the King would survive although he might never recover his reason, he was removed from Windsor and taken to Kew. George's doctors may have thought they were doing the right thing, but there can be no doubt that their treatment was abominably cruel and only served to delay the patient's recovery. George's chief doctor at Kew was Dr Francis Willis, the proprietor of a private lunatic asylum in Lincoln. Lectures, threats and the strait-jacket played a large part in Willis's treatment. If the King refused food or was restless, his legs were tied to the bed and a band strapped across his chest. Later, Willis introduced a special iron chair to restrain his patient; with bitter irony George called this terrible contraption his 'coronation chair'. As the real thing had brought him respect and honour so this travesty brought only humiliation. Willis was not the only tormentor; Dr Warren insisted on putting poultices of Spanish Fly and mustard all over the King's body; the idea was that the painful blisters which resulted would draw out the 'evil humours'. Despite the efforts of his doctors, George III gradually regained his reason and was well enough to attend a service of thanksgiving for his recovery in St Paul's Cathedral on 23 April 1789.

Ever since that time, doctors and historians have argued about the nature of George III's madness. One school believes that the King's illness is best explained in psychological terms, the other thinks that George was suffering from a rare physical illness. If the second explanation is correct then, in the strict sense, George III was never 'mad' at all. It has been variously claimed that George III had an Oedipus com-

plex about his mother, that he suffered from sexual repression by remaining faithful to an ugly Queen, or even that he was burdened with the guilt of a secret marriage in 1757 to 'the Fair Quakeress' Hannah Lightfoot. Others believe that the strains of kingship were too much for George and see the traumatic loss of America as the crucial factor. George III, it seems, might have been an excellent country squire but he was just not up to being King. More recently, attention has been focused on the physical symptoms which accompanied George's illness – rapid pulse, an angry rash, yellow or bloodshot eyes, swollen feet and red-coloured urine. From this, it is possible to argue that George III was suffering from porphyria, an unusual disease which was not properly understood until the 1930s. Porphyria is the name given to a disturbance of the porphyrim metabolism, the process which creates red pigment in the blood. If too much of this pigment is produced, the urine becomes discoloured and the whole nervous system, including the brain, is poisoned. The porphyria explanation may sound too exotic but it does fit the known facts very well. Above all, it has the advantage of demolishing theories that George III was rather unbalanced throughout his life.

George's illness showed how much the people of his country loved and respected him. In November 1788 there was panic on the Stock Exchange when it was thought that the King would die and be succeeded by the Prince of Wales. Most people were delighted that George recovered in time to prevent the implementation of the provisions of the Regency Bill. The Royal Tour of the South of England in the summer of 1789 was a tremendous success, crowds and triumphal arches in every village and a local band wading into the sea to play 'God Save the King' when George went bathing at Weymouth.

George III was less outraged by the French Revolution than some other European monarchs. He felt that the Revolution was Divine

The nightmarish last years of George III are reflected in this portrait
of the King at Windsor, old, insane and uncared for.

'A Voluptuary under the horrors of Digestion', by Gillray, one of the many
scathing cartoons on the extravagance and loose living of George IV when Prince of Wales.

Punishment of the House of Bourbon for its unnatural support of the rebels in the Thirteen Colonies. Of course, the outbreak of the war with France in 1793 brought serious strains and republican ideas were formed in some circles. The King was the object of a number of assassination attempts. On 15 May 1800 George was standing in the royal box of the Drury Lane Theatre when a man in the pit stood on a box and fired two pistol shots at the King. The bullets missed by inches and embedded themselves in the panelling of the box. George ordered the performance to continue and was so calm that he went to sleep in the interval.

The King had two brief relapses into his old complaint in 1801 and 1804 but it is far from true that the King was unimportant by the first decade of the new century. George's main concern now was to prevent the passage of 'Catholic Emancipation', a measure which would allow Roman Catholics to sit in Parliament. The King believed that if he agreed to such a measure he would be guilty of breaking the solemn coronation oath to defend the Protestant religion. Such a view may seem incredibly benighted but it was certainly the opinion of the vast majority of George's subjects.

In his determination to stop Catholic Emancipation George forced Pitt out of office in 1801 and summarily ejected the Grenville ministry in 1807. To the end of his active life, therefore, the King maintained the vital principle that the choice of ministers remained with the Crown.

Until he was over seventy, George III had been 'mad' for less than six months. It was only in 1810 that permanent insanity descended upon him. The last decade of George's life was very sad. He was a blind old man with a long white beard, wearing a violet dressing gown and shambling around an isolated set of rooms in Windsor Castle. Only the Star of the Order of the Garter which he kept pinned to his chest was a reminder that this wreck of a man was King of England. George found release on 29 January 1820; he was nearly eighty-two. The Lear-like figure of the last years was still revered by his people. They knew that 'Farmer George' had been a good man and a good King. Many books have been written to explain why the monarchy fell in France and survived in England; historians would do well to consider whether the personal integrity of King George III did not have a lot to do with it.

GEORGE IV

r. 1820–30

GEORGE IV WAS KING for only ten years, from 1820 to 1830, but, as Prince Regent from 1812 to 1820, he exercised all the powers of sovereign for a total of eighteen years. There can be no doubt that George wasted his great gifts and abilities. As a young man the Prince was outstandingly handsome and charming. He was tall and dignified in his bearing and Mrs 'Perdita' Robinson was only one of the many women who found it impossible to forget 'the grace of his person, the irresistible sweetness of his smile, the tenderness of his melodious yet manly voice'. A taste for gargantuan meals and heavy drinking soon changed that. By the time he had reached his late thirties, George had become very like the repellent creature depicted in Gillray's cartoon 'A Voluptuary under the horrors of Digestion'. This shows George

The Prince of Wales, slender and handsome as he was in his youth, surrounded by friends at Newmarket.

recovering from an enormous meal at Carlton House, his huge belly bursting from his breeches and his florid face on the verge of apoplexy. He is surrounded by empty wine bottles, unpaid bills for which an overflowing chamber-pot acts as paperweight, and various patent medicines including the famous cures for venereal disease, Veno's Vegetable Syrup and Leeke's Pills. There is certainly some justification for Leigh Hunt's damning comments on the occasion of George's fiftieth birthday in 1812: 'A libertine over head and ears in debt and disgrace, a despiser of domestic ties, the companion of demi-reps, a man who has just closed half a century without a single claim on the gratitude of his country or the respect of posterity.'

More than anyone else, the Prince was responsible for the cruel slander that George III spent most of his life insane. When George III was desperately ill in November 1788, his eldest son was going round the London clubs giving intimate details of the King's condition, mimicking his ravings and even speculating on a coup d'état to take over full royal power. The Prince's behaviour to women was no better. His affair with Perdita Robinson ended with a curt note saying that they must meet no more. In 1784, after a brief affair with Lady Melbourne – who exploited her position to get for her husband the appropriate job of Gentleman of the Bedchamber – George met a rather straight-laced Roman Catholic widow. Maria Fitzherbert was five years older than the Prince;

although attracted to the young man, she resolutely refused to become his mistress. In the end, the only way to overcome her scruples was to go through a form of marriage. The Reverend Robert Butt, then confined to the debtors' prison, agreed to perform the ceremony on condition that he was given a bishopric when George became King. Although canonically valid, the marriage was null and void from the beginning under the terms of the 1772 Royal Marriages Act and was to prove a great embarrassment for George's Whig friends who tried to deny its existence in Parliament.

George was genuinely in love with Mrs Fitzherbert – for a while – but it was not long before he left her for Lady Jersey, who was already a grandmother. George's extravagance frequently got him into difficulties; as early as 1783, George III denounced plans to increase his son's allowance as 'a shameful squandering of public money to gratify the passions of an ill-advised young man'. But George's greatest disaster came in 1795 when he agreed to marry his cousin, Caroline of Brunswick, in order to persuade Parliament to write off his debts. George was appalled when he met his bride to be; his first words were 'I am not well, pray get me a glass of brandy'. In turn, Caroline found George 'very stout and by no means as handsome as his portrait'. The Prince was helplessly drunk at the wedding.

Caroline was scarcely an ideal Princess of Wales; she was fat, coarse, vulgar and unwashed. After the birth of a daughter, Princess Charlotte, on 7 January 1796, the couple lived apart. In later years, Caroline spent much of her time in Italy and, according to her accusers lived 'in a most unbecoming and disgusting intimacy' with Bartolomo Pergami, the handsome Chamberlain of the Queen's Household. In 1820 Caroline returned to England to claim her rights as Queen and quickly became a focus of popular discontent against George and his government. Slogans appeared all over London – 'The Queen for ever! The King in the

River!' George forced the government to bring in a Bill which deprived 'Her Majesty Caroline Amelia Elizabeth of the title of Queen' and declared her marriage to the King 'for ever wholly dissolved, annulled and made void'. A great deal of titillating but not altogether trustworthy evidence was produced and the Bill was eventually dropped. Caroline appeared at George's coronation only to be turned away from the doors of Westminster Abbey. Fortunately for the King's peace of mind, his unsuitable Queen died suddenly on 7 August 1821.

George's critics overplayed their strong hand. A great deal of the animosity against the Prince came from political reasons and it was in this spirit that *The Times* could dismiss him as 'a hard-drinking, swearing man who at all times would prefer a girl and a bottle to politics and a sermon'. But there was more to George than that. When he was moderately sober, his conversation was fascinating and full of amusing anecdote. He had a good memory and was an excellent mimic. George (Beau) Brummell said that he could have been the best comic actor in Europe. He was by far the most intelligent of the Hanoverians and could hold his own in the Sublime Society of Beefsteaks, to which he was elected in 1784.

But George's greatest claim to fame was as a man of style, a man of taste. Before George, the Hanoverians had been decidedly philistine. Almost as if they expected to be sent back to Germany at any moment they had virtually camped in the rambling and uncomfortable buildings left by the Stuarts. George was determined to create palaces which would rival any in Europe. Styles varied from the 'Gothick' restoration at Windsor Castle, the 'rustick' of the Royal Lodge to the extraordinary 'Oriental' of the Brighton Pavilion. Of course it was easy to make fun of the Brighton Pavilion; William Cobbett wrote: 'Take a square box, take a large Norfolk turnip and put the turnip on the top of the box. Then take four turnips of half the size and put them on the corners of the box. Then take a considerable number of bulbs of the crown-imperial and put them pretty promiscuously about the top of the box. Then stand off. There! That's a Kremlin.'

Despite Cobbett's jibe, there can be no doubt that the Brighton Pavilion was a success. The mixture of domes and minarets, the Chinese furniture and the lotus and dragon chandeliers could have produced a palace of quite hideous vulgarity. But the Pavilion's exuberance always stops short of vulgarity and it was the personal sensitivity of George IV which prevented this outcome. George did not follow fashions, he set them. One of his most important discoveries was of the seaside resort and the life-style that went with it. The style evolved; in the early days Brighton was a byword for almost every kind of wildness but later the Prince enjoyed a quiet, almost domestic, existence there. Perhaps the change was symbolised by the abandonment

of multi-coloured 'peacock' fashions in favour of the smart black, sombre dress pioneered by George and Brummell in the 1790s. In 1800 Mrs Fitzherbert returned to live with the man whom she regarded as her lawful husband, cut down his drinking and nursed him back to health when he was stricken with inflammation of the stomach.

Politically, George was not to be trusted. As a young man one of his closest companions was Charles James Fox; George had even applauded when Fox had strutted in the uniform of the American rebels. But George's Whiggism was really a means of annoying his father. He supported Fox because Fox was an enemy of William Pitt and Pitt was his father's choice as premier. Politics was a game that became deadly earnest after 1793. The Prince came to the conclusion that the type of Whiggery dispensed by Fox could lead to anarchy and revo-

The coronation banquet of George IV in Westminster Hall, 1821, painted by Jones. The King is surrounded by his brothers and his son-in-law, Prince Leopold. Before them stands the King's Champion attended by the Lord High Constable and the Deputy Marshal. Only the lords were fed at the banquet; the hungry peeresses had to watch from the balcony above.

lution. George had made countless promises to the Whigs but as soon as he gained any real power he told them that they could expect nothing from him and that he intended to keep his father's Tory ministers in office. As King, George came to share his father's views that the concession of the right of Roman Catholics to sit in Parliament would involve a violation of the sacred coronation oath. By the late 1820s, the Whig of the 1780s had become an ultra Tory.

Whigs like Lord Grey never forgave this 'betrayal' of their cause, yet George was not a vicious man. Perhaps he was too worn out even by the time he became Regent for one to expect determined stands. George was a weak and vacillating ruler. He was untrustworthy because he did not like scenes, because he was lazy and because he always took the easy way out. In 1829 he appeared to accept Wellington's decision that the government must grant Catholic Emancipation and then, under pressure from the Duke of Cumberland, denied that he had ever given his consent. Even in his worst moments there was still a streak of kindness in George IV. He might be ferocious in his general pronouncements but it was a different matter when it came to individual cases. When Robert Peel became Home Secretary he was amazed to find himself being woken up at 2 a.m. with messages from the King urging him to reprieve criminals due to be executed the next morning.

George was forty-eight when he became Prince Regent. He put on great spectacles to celebrate his new power; later there were banquets and triumphal arches to celebrate the Allied victory over Napoleon and entertainments for visiting sovereigns. When it came to planning things like this, George forgot his ailments, overcame his laziness and mastered every detail. His coronation was probably the most elaborate of all time, the ultimate in regal splendour, with the new King looking like 'some gorgeous bird of paradise'. In the following year George made enormously successful state visits to Dublin and Edinburgh where he paraded up Princes Street wearing the Stuart Tartan. The visit to Ireland, the most rebellious part of the United Kingdom, was a particularly bold step. There must have been something a little special about a man whose presence could make an old Irishman declare 'I was a rebel to Old King George in '98 but, by God I would die a thousand deaths for his son'.

George was at his best on such occasions. He could behave with superb royal dignity and at least temporarily remove the bad impression his other actions created. In the days of the Regency, *The Morning Post* could still describe George as 'an Adonis of Loveliness' but the picture depended on cosmetics and corsets. The hectic style of the first two years of the reign did not last. George was an old man well before he was sixty. He did not sleep well and his remaining energy was sapped by the large doses of laudanum he took with his brandy. George became a very expensive recluse living at Windsor Castle, his mind filled with fanciful building projects rather than the affairs of state. In his declining years, the King was surrounded by a group of elderly former mistresses and dominated by his sinister doctor and confidant, Sir William Knighton. Visitors from London found the scene pathetic or just plain boring. Occasionally the King pretended that he had played a prominent part in the battle of Waterloo; no-one could tell if it was a joke to annoy the Duke of Wellington or whether George IV, like his father, was going mad. It was a world of fantasy, of 'might have been'; in a way George had been a great man but the sad thing was that his last years were haunted by the realisation that he might have been – indeed should have been – very much greater.

WILLIAM IV

r. 1830-7

IT WAS NOT UNTIL after the deaths of Princess Charlotte in 1818 and the Duke of York in 1827 that people began to pay much attention to William Henry, Duke of Clarence. As third son of George III and Queen Charlotte, it seemed so unlikely that he would ever be King that no-one ever attempted to teach him to behave in a regal way. Unlike George IV, William had been given a job to do. At the age of thirteen he became a midshipman in the Navy. William enjoyed his life at sea and soon became a competent if rather severe officer. His tastes were those of a sailor, his language strong and his opinions forthright. William was certainly an honest man but no-one could call him sophisticated. He followed his eldest brother in rebelling against their father and actually tried to become a Member of Parliament in the opposition interest. Unlike the Prince of Wales, William was not the man to wound his father by some brilliant epigram nor could he put the same intensity of bitterness into the quarrel. William was liked by most members of the royal family but the general opinion was that he was rather a fool – 'Silly Billy' was the inevitable nickname.

From 1791 to 1811 William lived in irregular but very domestic bliss with Mrs Jordan, a famous London actress. The Prince's mistress was thirty, stout and was to be the mother of a large family of Fitzclarences. Perhaps William was genuinely happy in these years but he was certainly angry that no-one thought of asking him to take command of a Fleet, or even a ship, throughout the long struggle against Revolutionary France. The Duke's tactlessness was frequently revealed in his speeches in the House of Lords. During a discussion on the Slave Trade he asserted: 'The promoters of abolition are either fanatics or hypocrites and in one of these classes I rank Mr Wilberforce.' The rest of the speech was drowned by cries of 'Withdraw'.

In the royal scramble to marry and produce an heir to the throne after the death of Princess Charlotte in 1818, William's prize was Adelaide of Saxe-Coburg-Meiningen, an excellent wife but plain, evangelical and much concerned with 'the end'. She must have been dull after Mrs Jordan and, unlike that prolific lady, none of her children lived more than a few hours. As he grew older, William became increasingly eccentric. In 1827 he was appointed High Admiral of England, an entirely honorific post, and caused great scandal by hoisting his standard at Plymouth and taking a squadron to sea in defiance of orders from the Admiralty. Despite his views on slavery, William was more progressive than George IV and after 1827 he was assiduously courted by the Whigs and the more liberal Tories. He was a strong supporter of Catholic Emancipation and intervened in a debate in the House of Lords to deliver a very bitter attack on the Protestant champion, Ernest, Duke of Cumberland. Opinions differed about William. Charles Grenville dismissed him as 'a mountebank bidding fair to be a maniac', but for most people in June 1830 he was an unknown quantity.

William IV heard that he was King on the morning of 26 June 1830 when Sir Henry Halford, physician to George IV, rode out to Bushey to announce his master's death. William had taken care to live to this day – gargling two gallons of water every morning and wearing huge goloshes to guard against chills. The new King could scarcely contain his glee. William was an excitable man and, in the first few days, behaved extremely wildly. On the first day of the reign, this bluff, hearty-looking man of sixty-four was seen racing through

A portrait of William IV
by Sir David Wilkie.

London in an open carriage, grinning all over his face, frequently removing his hat to reveal his bullet-head and bowing low to any of his new subjects who appeared interested. He allowed himself to be kissed by street-walkers and was liable to stop his carriage and ask any-one who looked moderately respectable if they wanted a lift. It must have been a hideous experience for courtiers who had modelled themselves on the aloof and remote George IV. William's habit of spitting – frequently and copiously – when in public was considered as indicating a lack of gentility.

William's delight in his new position was summed up when he asked 'Who is Silly Billy now?' as the Privy Council lined up to kneel before their new master. The King had been practising his new signature 'William R' for several months. There was a backlog of literally thousands of documents from the previous reign. The new monarch kept on signing 'William R' far into the night – with a basin of warm water to ease the pain of chalk stones in his hands. But William soon showed himself to be more than an amiable old fool. To the horror of his court, he insisted on the simplest of coronations. He would not hear of the new robes and vast banquets indulged in by George IV. William was adamant that his coronation would cost only a tenth of the expense incurred in 1821. When some old-fashioned peers threatened a boycott, the King replied 'I anticipate from that greater convenience of room and less heat'. Royal economy was popular with hard-pressed tax-payers and even the King's detractors had to admit that he was received with great acclamation.

Queen Adelaide was in constant dread of revolution and prayed that she would behave as well as Marie Antoinette when taken to the guillotine. William, on the other hand, looked at the future with greater confidence. A Whig government committed to sweeping changes came to power in November 1830. Wellington warned the King that Lord Grey was an 'ill-tempered violent man' but William got on well with his new premier. He assured Grey that he had 'complete confidence in your integrity, judgement, decision and experience'. In April 1831 Grey asked the King to dissolve Parliament so that the Whigs could secure a larger majority to carry their proposals for parliamentary reform. As there had been an election less than a year earlier, William could have refused and the Reform Bill of 1832 would have been postponed – perhaps very dangerously.

But William accepted Grey's request. Court officials told the King that he could not go to Westminster at short notice. There would be no time for the guards to line the streets or for the royal grooms to plait the manes of the horses for the state coach. William turned to Grey and said, 'My Lord, I'll go if I go in a hackney coach'. The King walked into the

House of Lords, his crown on crooked, and read the speech of dissolution. He returned to the Palace through cheering crowds. 'Well done, old boy', they cried, 'Served 'em right.'

William did not long remain the hero of progressives and was soon to be accused of tricking Grey and going back on his promise to create peers to get the Reform Bill through the Lords. After his initial enthusiasm, William was finding the pace of reform rather too hot. In November 1834 he abruptly dismissed the Whigs from office and persuaded Peel to become prime minister. The experiment failed and by the following spring he had to submit to the humiliation of asking the Whigs to return. The two politicians William most loathed were Brougham and Lord John Russell. He said of Russell, 'If you will answer for his death, I will answer for his damnation'.

The pleasures of kingship which William had so eagerly embraced were further embittered by quarrels within the royal family. The heir to the throne was the King's niece Victoria, daughter of Edward Duke of Kent. The Duke had died in 1820 and between the Duchess and the King there was much bad feeling. Victoria was not allowed to come to court because her mother said it was a hot-bed of vice. Although the King was not a man to mince his words, even in the presence of young girls, the charge was absurd. The King responded by circulating crude stories about the Duchess of Kent's relationship with Sir John Conroy, the Controller of her household. In 1836 the Duchess of Kent took over a large suite of rooms in Kensington Palace without the King's permission. William was furious. If he died now, Victoria would not be old enough to rule without her mother as Regent. At a public dinner, attended by more than a hundred guests, William said that he hoped his life would be spared long enough to prevent such a calamity. His wish was granted; he lived for one month after Victoria's eighteenth birthday. William IV died on 20 June 1837, muttering 'The Church, the Church' – a remark completely out of keeping with the rest of his life.

VICTORIA

r. 1837–1901

QUEEN VICTORIA WAS BORN at Kensington Palace in London on 24 May 1819, the daughter of Edward, Duke of Kent, and Princess Victoire, the widow of the Prince of Leiningen. The Duke of Kent was the fourth son of the reigning monarch, George III. Princess Victoire was the daughter of the Duke of Saxe-Coburg, and the sister of Leopold of Saxe-Coburg, who afterwards became King Leopold I of Belgium – Queen Victoria's uncle, to whom she turned so frequently for advice on political and other matters until his death in 1865. The Duke and Duchess of Kent wished to name their baby Victoria, but the Prince Regent – the future George IV – insisted that she be named Alexandrina after her godfather, Tsar Alexander I of Russia, and she was therefore christened Alexandrina Victoria. Her father died when she was eight months old. His three elder brothers had no surviving children, and when, on the death of George IV in 1830, the Duke of Clarence succeeded him as King William IV, Princess Victoria, at the age of eleven, became heir presumptive to the throne.

After her father's death, her mother the Duchess of Kent had fallen under the influence of the Controller of her household, Sir John Conroy, an ambitious Irish officer. Conroy was generally thought to be the Duchess's lover, and as he took complete control of her household and of Princess Victoria, it was rumoured that he was planning to become the power behind the throne in the event of William IV dying before Princess Victoria was eighteen and the Duchess of Kent becoming Regent. Conroy organised a number of 'journeys' on which the Duchess of Kent took Princess Victoria travelling in semi-regal pomp through the west Midlands and the north of England. William IV was annoyed at these tours, and took steps to curtail the honours which were to be paid to the Duchess and to Princess Victoria.

But Conroy's hopes of exercising power during a regency were disappointed. Princess Victoria reached the age of eighteen in May 1837, twenty-seven days before William IV died on 20 June; and as she disliked Conroy, and resented his control, her first act as Queen was to free herself from his influence and from her mother's. Conroy was excluded from Court, to the great distress of the Duchess.

During her first years on the throne, Queen Victoria's closest confidants were her governess, the German Baroness von Lehzen, and the prime minister, Lord Melbourne. Melbourne, who was aged fifty-eight in 1837, was a Whig of the old school, whose attitude to the great campaigns for the reform of the political and social systems was summed up in the phrase that he used whenever any reform was suggested: 'Why not leave it alone?' He showed no concern over the sufferings of the poor in the mines, factories and workhouses which were causing great social unrest. A symptom of this unrest was the attempt to assassinate, or at least to assault, the Queen when she was driving in her carriage in London in 1840. Two similar attempts were made in 1842, and other attempts in 1849, 1850, 1872 and 1882.

Melbourne's charm, his perfect manners and his gallantry to the ladies had made him the centre of London society, and he developed a respectful and avuncular intimacy with the Queen. He delighted in the company and friendship of his young female sovereign; and her attitude to him is shown by such entries in her diary as 'Lord Melbourne rode near me the whole time', 'Lord Melbourne sat near me the

Victoria and Albert in the early 1840s, a detail from Landseer's painting entitled 'Windsor Castle in modern times'. Victoria looks admiringly at her husband who sits with his dogs and the game he has shot. The Queen described the painting as 'very cheerful and pleasing'.

The young Queen Victoria riding out from Windsor with Lord Melbourne, her first prime minister. Victoria had a great affection for Melbourne and was very dependent on his advice until her marriage to Prince Albert.

whole evening', 'I am so fond of Lord Melbourne'. She accepted Melbourne's opinion on all matters from politics to the comparative merits of Shakespeare's plays.

This led to a political crisis in 1839, when Melbourne resigned after a defeat in Parliament, and Queen Victoria invited Sir Robert Peel, the Conservative leader, to form a government. Peel insisted that the Queen's Whig ladies of the bedchamber should be replaced, in accordance with the usual practice, by Tory ladies; and when the Queen refused to agree, Peel refused to form a government, and Melbourne and the Whigs returned to office for another two years. Queen Victoria's victory was only temporary, because never again did she challenge the principle that the officers of the royal household should change with the government.

In the same year, the Queen became very unpopular as a result of the case of Lady Flora Hastings. Lady Flora, one of the Queen's ladies-in-waiting, suffered from a cancerous growth on the liver which made her appear to be pregnant, and as she was unmarried this gave rise to scandal. The Queen was very ready to believe the worst, because on one occasion Lady Flora had been seen alone in a carriage with Sir John Conroy. Lady Flora was virtually compelled, against her protests, to submit to a medical examination, which proved that she was a virgin, and a few months later she died of the cancer. Public opinion strongly condemned the conduct of the Queen and court in the affair, and Queen Victoria was hissed on the racecourse at Ascot, and greeted with shouts of 'Mrs Melbourne'.

As soon as the festivities of the coronation of June 1838 were over, the Queen's advisers considered the question of her marriage. When one of the candidates, her cousin Prince Albert of Saxe-Coburg, visited London in 1839, the Queen fell in love with him. Prince Albert was three months younger than Queen Victoria.

His father was duke of a German state which was about the size of Worcestershire. When Prince Albert was seven years old, his father divorced his mother on a charge of adultery with an officer at his court, and she was sent to live in Switzerland on a pension and forbidden to see her children. This subsequent accusation of adultery against his mother appears to be the only real ground for the rumour which arose many years later, that Prince Albert's father was not the duke, but another officer – a Jew – with whom his mother was alleged to have had an affair. Prince Albert always remembered his mother with great affection. He did not immediately reciprocate Queen Victoria's feelings for him – perhaps he was never as deeply in love with her as she was with him – but a strong affection for her, as well as a sense of mission, made him willingly agree to marry her. The wedding took place in London in February 1840, when both bride and bridegroom were aged twenty. It was very unpopular in certain quarters. To Queen Victoria's great indignation, Parliament made difficulties about voting a suitable allowance for Prince Albert and about granting him precedence over the Queen's surviving uncles; and Radical journalists and ballad-writers jeered at the 'pauper Prince' who had come begging to England, and instead of being sent to the workhouse, like other beggars, had been given the hand of England's Queen.

The marriage was very happy. Now that the royal archives are open to inspection it is known – which no one suspected at the time – that Queen Victoria and Prince Albert sometimes quarrelled about such matters as the upbringing of the children and the influence which Baroness Lehzen still held over the Queen. But these were unimportant incidents in a very happy relationship. They had nine children – in 1840, Victoria, the Princess Royal, who married the future Emperor of Germany Frederick III; in 1841, Edward, Prince of Wales, the future King Edward VII; and three boys and four girls followed.

Prince Albert was considered to be very handsome, and his arrival had caused considerable excitement among the ladies of the court; but he showed no interest in them. His attitude had repercussions far beyond the family circle. At the beginning of the nineteenth century a great moral revival had been launched by Wilberforce and his Society for the Suppression of Vice, as part of the campaign to inculcate religion and discipline among the working classes as an antidote to the Radical and free-thinking propaganda which followed the French Revolution. At first the gambling, heavy drinking, and sexual licence, which were common in aristocratic society, continued unabated; and although the aristocracy made every attempt to present a moral face in public while they sinned in private, their vices, and those of the royal dukes, were well known, and featured prominently in Radical propaganda. Under Queen Victoria and Prince Albert the royal family became moral, and set an example which was followed, at least to some extent, in society as well as among the middle classes. Both Queen Victoria and Prince Albert strongly disapproved of any sexual misconduct, especially if practised by their sons or ministers, though they reacted differently. Queen Victoria sadly resigned herself to the fact that men have love affairs; but Prince Albert reacted with an almost hysterical indignation when he heard that his son, the Prince of Wales, had had an affair with an actress, or that the Foreign Secretary, Lord Palmerston, had attempted to enter the bedroom of one of the ladies-in-waiting in the middle of the night at Windsor Castle.

Prince Albert also influenced Queen Victoria's attitude towards social problems. Her first mentor, the Whig Lord Melbourne, had advised her not to read Charles Dickens's *Oliver Twist*, because it dealt with paupers, criminals and other unpleasant subjects with which she should not be troubled; but Prince Albert invited Lord Ashley – later Lord

Shaftesbury – to the palace and told him how moved he and the Queen had been at Ashley's revelations in Parliament about the sufferings of the children who worked in the mines. Ashley invited Prince Albert to preside at meetings of the committee of the Labourer's Friend Society; and when, despite all the apprehensions of the government and court, Prince Albert attended the meeting and delighted the other members of the committee by his interest, Ashley noted that this was the way to defeat the Chartists and the Socialists. As well as showing interest in plans for model workers' houses and the relief of poverty, Prince Albert interested himself in projects for the encouragement of trade and industry. His most ambitious venture in this field was the Great International Exhibition of 1851, for which he was chiefly responsible. It encountered considerable opposition, both from those who objected to the felling of the trees in Hyde Park and the interference with the riding in Rotten Row, and from patriots who resented the influx of foreigners into Britain; but it was a great success.

The fall of Melbourne's government in 1841 brought the Tories to power. The Queen was very distressed to lose Melbourne, and said so frankly to her new prime minister, Peel; but she soon abandoned her practice of writing to Melbourne about state affairs, and partly thanks to Prince Albert's influence she came to have a high regard for Peel. She supported the policy of Peel's Foreign Secretary, Lord Aberdeen, of a diplomatic *rapprochement* with France, and played her part in it when she visited the French King, Louis Philippe, at the Château d'Eu at Tréport in 1843, this being the first time that a reigning English sovereign had met a foreign sovereign since the reign of Henry VIII. In the following year King Louis Philippe paid a return visit to England. In the next decade Queen Victoria similarly exchanged state visits with the French Emperor Napoleon III.

When the Whigs returned to power in 1846, with Lord John Russell as prime minister and Palmerston as Foreign Secretary, the Queen and Prince Albert soon came into conflict with Palmerston. The first clash came in connexion with the civil war in Portugal in 1846-7, and more serious disagreements arose during and after the revolutions which broke out in so many countries of Europe in 1848. Palmerston, who had begun his political career as a junior minister in a Tory government, had not basically changed his political opinions at the age of sixty; he was still profoundly conservative, anti-revolutionary and anti-democratic. But he was convinced of the superiority of the British system of constitutional monarchy over the absolutist monarchies of the continent; he was eager to embarrass and weaken foreign governments in order to improve the relative position of Britain; and he was playing for Radical support in British home politics. He therefore gave moral support to revolutionary Liberal, and even Radical, movements throughout Europe. Queen Victoria and Prince Albert, on the other hand, believed in solidarity with the sovereigns of Europe, many of whom were their friends and relations, and favoured a policy of preserving peace and avoiding revolution by international co-operation between rulers. They were too logical, broad-minded and cosmopolitan to share the attitude of Whigs like Russell and Palmerston, who, on hearing that the Austrian military authorities had flogged rebellious patriots in Italy and Hungary, could exclaim in all sincerity 'The Austrians are really the greatest brutes that ever called themselves by the undeserved name of civilised men', almost on the same day on which they themselves authorised the wholesale flogging of peasants who had risen in revolt against British rule in the Ionian Isles. Queen Victoria and Prince Albert could not see what right the British government had to protest against the suppression of revolution in the territories of foreign Kings who had never protested to Britain against the suppression of revolution in Ireland or the sentences passed on Chartist rioters. They

The opening of the Great Exhibition by Queen Victoria on 1 May 1851. The Princess Royal and Prince Albert Edward stand beside the Queen whose figure can be distinguished by the blue Garter ribbon.

TO THE
QUEEN'S PRIVATE APARTMENTS

THE QUEEN AND PRINCE ALBERT AT HOME.

The happy family life of Victoria and Albert was a popular theme with sentimental cartoonists.

did not share the enthusiasm of nearly the whole of the British people for Garibaldi; and when Garibaldi visited England in 1864, Queen Victoria was indignant that aristocrats and society hostesses should acclaim and fall in love with a revolutionary Radical. 'Brave and honest though he is', she logically commented, 'he has ever been a revolutionist leader.'

The Queen, with Prince Albert acting as her private secretary, insisted on her constitutional right to have all Palmerston's despatches to foreign governments submitted to her before they were sent off. She and Prince Albert often altered Palmerston's text, in order to delete or soften the most provocative passages. Palmerston therefore sometimes sent off despatches without submitting them to the Queen. In the summer of 1850 Queen Victoria and Prince Albert asked Lord John Russell to dismiss Palmerston from the Foreign Office. Russell told them that this was impossible because of Palmerston's great popularity in the House of Commons and in the country; but the Queen and Prince bided their time. In December 1851 Palmerston for once made a move which was unpopular with the majority of Englishmen, especially his Radical supporters, by congratulating Louis Napoleon Bonaparte – the future Emperor Napoleon III – on his coup d'état in France. Queen Victoria and Prince Albert seized their chance, and persuaded Russell to dismiss Palmerston from the Foreign Office. Within six weeks Palmerston had brought down Russell's government in the House of Commons, and a year after he left the Foreign Office he returned to office as Home Secretary in Lord Aberdeen's coalition government.

In 1854 the Crimean War broke out – the first major European war for forty years – when Britain and France declared war on Russia in support of Turkey. For nearly a year before the declaration of war, the prime minister, Lord Aberdeen, tried to avoid war by pursuing a conciliatory policy; Palmerston, in the Cabinet, urged a tougher policy which he believed was the only way of deterring the Russians from attacking Turkey. Prince Albert supported Aberdeen's policy, and drafted a memorandum containing a plan which he believed would prevent war. Although the memorandum was secret, Prince Albert's pacific policy and his opposition to Palmerston became generally known, and made him very unpopular at a time when there was a great clamour for war with Russia and for Palmerston to lead it. The rumour spread that Prince Albert was a Russian spy and had been arrested and sent to

the Tower of London after the authorities had intercepted his communications with the Russians. Pamphlets were published attacking him, and pointing out that the husband of a reigning Queen could be put on trial for high treason against her; and a ballad, 'Lovely Albert', circulated in the streets of London:

> It is rumoured over Britain's isle
> That A … is in the Tower;
> The Postmen some suspicion had,
> And opened the two letters;
> 'Twas a pity sad the German lad
> Should not have known much better.

As the news reached England of the set-backs and incompetence in the Crimea, public opinion maintained insistently that only Palmerston could win the war, and the Queen was compelled, very reluctantly, to accept him as prime minister in February 1855. Although the efficiency of the army in the Crimea did not noticeably improve after Palmerston came to power, the war was won and, thanks chiefly to Palmerston's firm attitude at the Peace Congress, Russia was compelled to cede territory to Turkey and to relinquish the right to maintain a fleet in the Black Sea. Once war had been declared, Queen Victoria had supported it enthusiastically; she showed great concern over the sufferings of the soldiers in the Crimea, and wrote: 'I feel so *proud* of my dear noble troops.' She approved of Palmerston's conduct of the peace negotiations, and formed a more favourable view of him as prime minister than she had done when he was Foreign Secretary, not least because he succeeded in 1857 in persuading Parliament to agree at last to her wish that the title of Prince Consort should be bestowed on Prince Albert. There were signs of the old tensions in 1864, when Palmerston and his Foreign Secretary, Lord Russell, supported Denmark in the German-Danish war, while Queen Victoria sympathised with Prussia; but when Palmerston died in office in 1865, the Queen commented: 'We had, God knows! terrible trouble with him about Foreign Affairs. Still, as Prime Minister he managed affairs at home well, and behaved to me well. But I *never* liked him.'

In December 1861 Queen Victoria suffered a great personal tragedy when Prince Albert died of typhoid fever at the age of forty-two. A few days before his death he had made an important diplomatic intervention. On the outbreak of the American Civil War, the British government's sympathies were with the South, because although British public opinion had previously supported the campaign for the abolition of slavery in the United States, Palmerston and Russell could not resist taking advantage of the situation to weaken the United States, which they regarded as a growing menace to British international power, and to assist a process which might lead to the United States being permanently divided into two nations. A few months after the outbreak of the Civil War, a US warship stopped and boarded a British merchant ship, *The Trent*, in the Caribbean Sea and removed two envoys of the Southern Confederacy who were travelling on diplomatic business to Europe. The British government demanded that the two envoys be released, and when President Lincoln's government refused, public indignation in both Britain and the United States reached such a pitch that war seemed probable. The US minister in London afterwards stated that he believed that if the Atlantic cable, which was laid a few years later, had been in existence in 1861, war would have been inevitable, but that as despatches took a month to travel between London and Washington, there was time for passions to cool. At the height of the crisis the Prince Consort, though seriously ill, rose from his bed to alter the wording of a draft despatch from the British government to the United States so as to make it less provocative, and to make it easier for the US government to accept the British demands. The US gave way and released the two envoys, and thus avoided a war

Queen Victoria and Princess Alice mourn for the death of Prince Albert beside his bust. 'The World is gone for me', wrote Victoria, but she was to reign another forty years without Albert's support.

between Britain and the United States which might have altered the future course of history.

Queen Victoria was prostrated by Prince Albert's death. It was an accepted convention at the time that widows should display their grief and show signs of mourning in a way that would seem morbid today; but the Queen's reaction seemed excessive even by the standards of 1861. She withdrew into complete seclusion, and refused all her ministers' requests that she should open Parliament in person and show herself at least occasionally to her subjects, though throughout this period, from the very first days after Prince Albert's death, she insisted on reading all the diplomatic despatches and on carrying out her constitutional duties in the privacy of her closet. She spent much time in the Scottish Highlands at her house at Balmoral, which she and Prince Albert had acquired in 1847 and where they had spent happy times together.

It was during the decade after Prince Albert's death that Queen Victoria came under the influence of John Brown, a Scottish servant. Brown's blunt manner and kindly concern pleased the Queen, who did not resent it when he addressed her as 'woman' as he put a scarf around her shoulders to keep her warm or bullied her into taking care of her health. Queen Victoria believed, as Prince Albert had done, that the working class, who showed their loyalty to the throne without observing the accepted conventions of court etiquette, were far more worthy than the arrogant and often immoral aristocracy with whom, to her regret, her son the Prince of Wales associated. Her ideal of government was a benevolent sovereign ruling constitutionally over a contented and loyal people; and she thought that this ideal was thwarted both by a selfish, pleasure-loving aristocracy and by Radical agitators with their belief in democracy.

The Queen's friendship with Brown caused resentment among her family and courtiers, and stories spread in society, and were published in foreign newspapers, that the Queen had secretly married Brown. References to 'Mrs Brown', meaning the Queen, were common at society dinner tables in London. The Queen's isolation was resented. Radical spokesmen publicly stated that she was not earning the money that the State paid her, and some of them, especially the prominent Liberal politician, Sir Charles Dilke, spoke in favour of abolishing the monarchy and replacing it with a republic. The campaign for a republic caused some stir in 1871, but rapidly died out.

The last thirty-five years of Queen Victoria's reign were a period of struggle between the new Liberal Party and the Conservatives. The forces of Liberalism were led by William Ewart Gladstone, who had begun his political life as a Tory, but at the age of fifty, when he was Chancellor of the Exchequer in Palmerston's government, had developed Liberal and almost Radical ideas which aroused his prime minister's opposition and alarm. Queen Victoria's relations with Gladstone were worse than with any of her other prime ministers. His sincere devotion to the throne and to the Queen as a woman was expressed in a pompous and impersonal way, and although he was very eager to win her approval, he failed completely to do so. As in the case of her hostility to Palmerston in earlier years, her personal dislike of Gladstone was not as important a factor as her political opposition to the cause which he represented. On the great issues which dominated British politics in the last quarter of the nineteenth century – the extension of the Parliamentary franchise, the limitation of the power of the House of Lords, social reform, home rule for Ireland, and the new, aggressive Conservative imperialist policy abroad – Queen Victoria strongly sympathised with the Conservatives and disapproved of Gladstone and the Liberals.

In 1868 Benjamin Disraeli became prime minister, and though he held office for only nine months, he established a very close relationship with the Queen which became more intimate after he returned to office in 1874 for his second term as premier, which lasted for six years. He told a friend: 'Everyone likes flattery, and when you come to royalty, you should lay it on with a trowel.' He spoke and wrote to the Queen in the most exaggerated and fulsome language; but it was not too exaggerated or fulsome for Queen Victoria's liking. She became genuinely attached to Disraeli, paid him the signal honour of visiting him in his private house in the country, and was deeply unhappy when he fell from power in 1880. When he died in the next year, she wrote to his private

Disraeli, Victoria's favourite prime minister in her later years, had the inspiration to make her Empress of India by the Titles Bill of 1876. In this cartoon he offers her the imperial diadem in place of the British crown.

relished the title, and showed great interest in her Indian Empire. At the time of the Indian Mutiny in 1857 she had been one of the very few people in Britain who did not join in the clamour for indiscriminate slaughter of Indians in revenge for the murder of British women and children at Cawnpore and elsewhere; and she and Prince Albert supported the Governor-General of India, Lord Canning, when he aroused a storm of indignation in Britain and among the British residents in India by his proclamation in which he urged the commanders in the field to show some restraint in the number of executions. The Queen was very conscious of her duties to her Indian subjects, and here, as in Britain, she believed in her ideal of paternalistic government. She always expressed her indignation when she encountered signs of racial prejudice by British officials in India. In the last years of her life she angered her courtiers by her intimate friendship with an Indian servant; and her disapproval of the attitude of the Boers towards the blacks in South Africa was an additional reason for her patriotic and belligerent attitude during the Boer War.

It was during Disraeli's second term of office that the Queen developed her deep dislike of Gladstone, with whom she had been on reasonably good terms during Gladstone's first premiership in 1868-74. She strongly approved of Disraeli's imperialist foreign policy and his support of Turkey against Russia during the Russo-Turkish war of 1876-7, and she applauded his success at the Congress of Berlin in 1878, when he thwarted Russia's plans to liberate the

secretary: 'Dear Lord Rowton, I cannot write in the third person at this terrible moment when I can scarcely see for my fast falling tears.'

Disraeli gratified the Queen in 1876 by persuading Parliament to agree to grant her the title of Empress of India. Queen Victoria

RIGHT By the year of the Jubilee, 1887, Victoria had become known as 'the grandmother of Europe' through the intermarriage of her children with the royal houses of the Continent. This Jubilee Tree shows all the descendants of Victoria and Albert by 1887. On the top right are Edward and Alexandra, Prince and Princess of Wales with their five children; their second son was to become King George V. Below them, from top to bottom are: Alfred, Duke of Edinburgh with Marie of Russia and their children; Princess Louise and the Duke of Argyll; Leopold, Duke of Albany with Helena of Waldeck-Pyrmont; and Princess Beatrice with Henry of Battenberg.

On the top left is Victoria, Princess Royal and Empress of Germany, with her husband Emperor Frederick III and their children and grandchildren. Their eldest son became Kaiser Wilhelm II, enemy of his cousin George V in the First World War. Below the German royal family, from top to bottom are the families of: Princess Alice and Louis of Hesse-Darmstadt (from whom the present Duke of Edinburgh is descended); Princess Helena and Christian of Schleswig-Holstein; Arthur, Duke of Connaught, with Louise of Prussia.

the ROYAL OAK

VICTORIA   REGINA 1837-1887

A Jubilee Genealogical Tree, showing the Descendants of Her Majesty Queen Victoria.

Balkan provinces of Turkey. This policy, which involved supporting the Sultan's oppressive régime in the Balkans against the Christians in Bulgaria and Herzegovina who were fighting for their freedom, outraged the feelings of Gladstone and the 'Nonconformist conscience' of his Liberal supporters. Gladstone and the Liberals proclaimed that England, in her foreign policy, must never support a cause that was morally wrong; Disraeli proudly claimed that his foreign policy was 'as selfish as patriotism'. The Queen thought that Gladstone and his followers were not merely misguided, but traitors to their country.

During Gladstone's last three terms as premier – in 1880-85, 1886 and 1892-4 – his relations with the Queen, to his great regret, were very strained. On most occasions her conduct was correct and courteous, but there were occasions when she administered personal slights and incivilities, and she privately passed on confidential documents of Gladstone's government to the Conservative Leader of the Opposition, Lord Salisbury. In 1885 she administered a public rebuke to Gladstone when she sent him an uncoded telegram – which was delivered to him by a local railway station-master, and became public knowledge – in which she condemned his government for not acting sufficiently promptly and energetically to relieve General Gordon at Khartoum, after she and the great majority of her subjects had been shocked by the news of Gordon's death at the hands of the Mahdi's nationalist rebels in the Sudan.

The Queen's Conservative and imperialist views coincided with those of a substantial proportion – at most times a majority – of the British people, and a Conservative government under Lord Salisbury was in power during twelve of the last fifteen years of her reign.

Her former unpopularity disappeared, and she was revered and almost worshipped by the public. Her Jubilee on the fiftieth anniversary of her accession in 1887 was the occasion for great national celebrations. On 23 September 1896 she noted in her diary that she had reigned one day longer than George III or any previous English sovereign; and on 20 June 1897 her Diamond Jubilee was celebrated amid scenes of enthusiasm which completely eclipsed those of ten years earlier, and which culminated in the Queen's visit to St Paul's Cathedral in London on 22 June, when she was cheered by a vast crowd. 'I was much moved and gratified', wrote the Queen.

During her remaining years, Britain engaged in the last of the many wars of the Victorian era. General Kitchener's success in destroying the Mahdi's successor and avenging Gordon in the Sudan in 1898, and his diplomatic triumph over the French at Fashoda, had delighted the Queen; and she enthusiastically supported the Boer War in 1899. Although distressed by the British defeats in South Africa in the opening stages of the war, she refused to permit any defeatist talk at court. 'In this house', she declared, 'we are not interested in the possibilities of defeat; they do not exist.' Before her death, the tide had definitely turned in favour of Britain in South Africa, after the relief of Mafeking and Ladysmith in the summer of 1900.

Queen Victoria died at her house at Osborne in the Isle of Wight, after a short illness, on 22 January 1901, at the age of eighty-one. None of the court officials had any personal experience of the measures which were to be taken at the death of a sovereign and the accession of a new King, and her death caused consternation among nearly all her subjects, as no-one under the age of seventy could remember living under another monarch.

George v on his favourite horse, Kildare, painted by Georges Scott.

9 THE HOUSE OF SAXE-COBURG-GOTHA

1901-10

Edward VII riding out from his favourite home, Sandringham

9 The Royal Arms

GEORGE IV AND WILLIAM IV succeeded to both the British and German possessions and so bore the post–1816 version of the arms unaltered.

On the death of William IV in 1837 the crowns were divided. That of Great Britain devolved upon his niece Victoria but that of Hanover, as it could not pass to a woman, went to the next male heir, William's brother Ernest Augustus, Duke of Cumberland.

Queen Victoria removed the shield and crown from the centre of the arms and was left with the royal arms as borne today by the present Queen. In the illustration are included three representations of the royal crown. That on the left was often used by Victoria although it is strictly speaking incorrect; that in the centre was also used by Victoria later in her reign whilst that on the right was used by George V and George VI.

The point to remember is that the shape of the crown is not significant, other than it reflects the artistic taste of the sovereign. What is important is that the crown in the arms is the royal crown, symbolising St Edward's crown, which is used at a coronation, itself symbolising the temporal authority and dominion of the sovereign under God.

It is sometimes remarked that now that the Queen is Queen of Canada, Australia and various other Commonwealth countries the royal arms should symbolise this fact. Against doing this it must be argued that the constant comings and goings within the Commonwealth would necessitate endless alteration of the royal arms, which would be impracticable. The problem has been solved by there being separate arms for each of the Commonwealth kingdoms, in which the crown is the unifying factor.

The other question which is often raised is the apparent neglect of Wales, which has never featured in the royal arms. This is because Wales was never a separate kingdom, ruled by an English king. In 1302 it was absorbed into England but became a Principality. Today Wales is represented armorially in the arms of the Prince of Wales. Over the royal arms he bears the old arms of the princes of North Wales, now used to represent the whole principality, ensigned by the coronet of the heir apparent.

EDWARD VII

r. 1901–10

PRINCE ALBERT EDWARD, the future King Edward VII, was born at St James's Palace in London on 9 November 1841, the second child and eldest son of Queen Victoria and Prince Albert. The title of Prince of Wales was conferred on him when he was twenty-five days old. His father had clear ideas as to the education and training which were necessary for a future King; above all, he wished to prevent him from reverting to the pleasure-loving and immoral life of George IV and Queen Victoria's other uncles. He provided him with a number of suitable tutors, and gave them precise instructions as to how they should perform their duties. The tutors themselves considered that the regimen was too strict, and that the child was likely to go to the bad under the pressure to which he was subjected; and the constant moral exhortation was combined with a lack of parental affection, because the Queen and Prince Albert were convinced that their eldest son 'Bertie' had no intelligence or gifts of application.

It was perhaps because of this pressure and this lack of affection that the Prince of Wales, as a child, often indulged in outbursts of rage which alarmed his tutors as well as his parents. As a boy he showed a lack of consideration, and even signs of cruelty, which gave some cause for alarm. Prince Albert, although he impressed upon him that a gentleman should show consideration for the feelings of his inferiors and servants, was distressed to find that at the age of seventeen he tormented his valet by pouring wax over his new livery, water on his clean linen, and by rapping him on the nose. The Prince of Wales soon abandoned behaviour of this kind, and in later life showed a warm-hearted loyalty to his friends and consideration for his servants. His natural assertiveness mani-fested itself in such harmless ways as blaming his partner when he lost at bridge or ordering the replanning of a golf course when he did badly at the game, and sometimes in making caustic remarks about his friends' style of dress.

The Prince of Wales performed his first important public duty at the age of eighteen, when the Queen and her government agreed, with some misgivings, to send him on a state visit to Canada and the United States in 1860. The idea of sending a member of the British royal family to the United States was indeed a novelty, because the United States was generally regarded in Britain as a land of dangerous republicans and democrats. But the Prince's visit was a great success. He endeared himself to the American people by visiting George Washington's grave in Virginia, and by his charm at the balls and receptions in Washington, where it was noticed that he showed a great interest in pretty girls.

This interest involved him in an unfortunate incident soon after his return to Britain. When he was nineteen, in 1861, he was sent on manoeuvres with the army at the Curragh in Ireland. Some of his brother-officers arranged for an actress to be smuggled into his tent one night. In due course the news of the incident reached his mother and father. Prince Albert reacted violently, though he respected the Prince of Wales for his refusal to name the officers responsible. Prince Albert died a few weeks later. Queen Victoria believed that his grief at 'Bertie's' misconduct at the Curragh had shortened his life, and she declared that she would never be able to look at 'that boy' without a shudder.

In 1863 the Prince of Wales married Princess Alexandra of Denmark. Queen Victoria was charmed by Princess Alexandra's beauty and

Edward as a child with his mother Queen Victoria and his elder sister, the Princess Royal, at Loch Laggan in 1847. The Queen commissioned this painting as a gift for the Prince Consort, who shared her deep love for Scotland.

her respectful affection; but the marriage led to political differences between the Queen and the Prince of Wales. When Prussia and Austria went to war with Denmark in 1864 over Schleswig-Holstein, Queen Victoria's sympathies were with the German states; but the Prince of Wales supported his wife's nation, as did Palmerston and Russell, the prime minister and Foreign Secretary, and most of the British people. The Prince of Wales gave further offence to his mother in the same year by visiting Garibaldi when the Italian revolutionary general came to England, and, to the Queen's indignation, was enthusiastically welcomed in London by the people and by society alike. Queen Victoria sternly reprimanded the Prince of Wales, who defended his conduct and insisted on taking the responsibility on himself when Queen Victoria blamed his Controller, General Knollys, for having arranged the interview with Garibaldi.

For the remaining thirty-seven years of Queen Victoria's reign, the Prince of Wales played his part in public life. The Queen refused to agree to the suggestion made by several of her ministers that he should be permitted to see the state papers; nor would she accept the offers which he made from time to time to visit some foreign sovereign or statesman in an attempt to help reach a settlement of an international crisis. But he increasingly performed the duties of opening bridges and public buildings, which now for the first time in history became one of the functions of members of the royal family. He also paid many state visits to European countries, including Russia; and in 1875-6 he spent four months in India. His chief interest, however, was the pursuit of pleasure. His life was a round of visits to large country-houses, with shooting, gambling, and attendance at race-meetings, followed by weeks in London with parties and banquets, and frequent visits abroad to Paris, the French Riviera, and Marienbad in Bohemia. He did not indulge in heavy drinking, but ate five large meals every day, eating ten or more courses at some of them;

and he smoked twelve large cigars and twenty cigarettes a day. By the time he was middle-aged he was fat, being forty-eight inches round the waist.

His way of life did not please the Queen. She tried unsuccessfully to convince him that a pleasure-loving and immoral aristocracy provoked the loyal working-classes into adopting Radical and democratic ideas. The Prince of Wales replied that the landed aristocracy was an essential bulwark of society, and that as long as they performed their public duties – for example, by acting as Lords Lieutenants of the counties – they should not be denied their pleasures. But the Prince's friends were not all members of the landed aristocracy; they included Jewish bankers and other business men – in fact, almost anyone who was rich enough to entertain on the scale which the Prince demanded at the house-parties which he attended and to provide the large quantity of game which was needed for a big shoot. His interest in people and his charm of manner led him to seek and obtain the friendship of outstanding individuals of all types and classes. He met the Labour leader, Joseph Arch, the founder of the National Agricultural Labourers' Union, and invited the working-class MP, Henry Broadhurst, to stay at his country house at Sandringham in Norfolk, though as Broadhurst did not possess evening dress, dinner was served to him in his private room in order to save him embarrassment. In Paris, the Prince of Wales became very friendly with General the Marquis de Gallifet, who had aroused the hatred of the French left wing by his wholesale executions during the suppression of the Paris Commune of 1871, as well as with the Radical politician, Gambetta; and he accomplished the seemingly impossible task of persuading Gallifet and Gambetta to meet each other when they lunched with him at the Café Anglais. He loved company, and could not bear to be alone. It was said of him that he liked men better than books, and women better than either.

His love of the company of beautiful women was a great contrast to the attitude of his father, and caused both his mother and many of her subjects to fear that the future sovereign was reverting to the habits of the Regency. He was on terms of intimate friendship with a number of beautiful British and Continental women – actresses like Lillie Langtry in London and Hortense Schneider in Paris, and French and English society beauties like the Princesse de Sagan, the Duchesse de Mouchy, Lady Brooke (the future Countess of Warwick), and the Hon. Mrs Keppel. He remained, however, on excellent terms with his wife, who was always faithful to him and adopted a tolerant and understanding attitude to his love affairs. He was an affectionate father. He was deeply distressed when his eldest son, Prince Albert Victor, Duke of Clarence, who was somewhat backward and had led a dissipated life, died at the age of twenty-eight. His second son was the future King George V.

On more than one occasion the Prince of Wales's friendships involved him in matrimonial disputes and other scandals, and the members of his household and of the government were sometimes obliged to take steps to prevent the scandal from becoming public and discrediting the royal family. On two occasions their efforts failed, and the Prince was obliged to give evidence in a court of law. In 1870 Sir Charles Mordaunt MP brought a divorce petition against his wife on the ground of her adultery with two friends of the Prince of Wales. Lady Mordaunt signed a confession admitting her adultery, not only with the two co-respondents, but also with the Prince of Wales. The Prince was subpoenaed as a witness, but his denial of Lady Mordaunt's allegation was generally accepted, and the court held that Lady Mordaunt was insane. The evidence, however, proved that the Prince had on several occasions visited Lady Mordaunt in the afternoons when her husband was in the House of Commons and had been alone with her, which

RIGHT Edward as Prince of Wales above a picture of Sandringham House. The emblem of three feathers and the motto 'Ich dien' (I serve) above him are held by every Prince of Wales.

Edward leads through a cheering crowd his winning horse, Persimmon, at the Derby of 1896. Edward revelled in public occasions and restored several traditional royal occasions which had fallen into abeyance in Victoria's reign.

was enough to show, in the language of the time, that his conduct had been indiscreet if not improper.

Greater scandal was caused by the baccarat case twenty years later. In September 1890 the Prince of Wales stayed with a house-party at Tranby Croft in Yorkshire when he was visiting the races at Doncaster during the St Leger week. In the evenings the guests played the illegal card-game of baccarat, and one of them, Colonel Sir William Gordon-Cumming, was accused of cheating. It was agreed that the matter should be kept secret if Colonel Gordon-Cumming promised never to play cards again; but the secret leaked out, and though the Prince of Wales exerted great pressure to prevent the case from coming to court, Gordon-Cumming sued some of the other players for slander, and at the trial in July 1891 the Prince was subpoenaed as a witness. Public opinion was shocked that the Prince of Wales had played an illegal card-game, and that, although he held the rank of Field-Marshal in the Army, he had committed an offence under the Queen's Regulations by agreeing to suppress the fact that Gordon-Cumming had cheated, instead of reporting it to Gordon-Cumming's Commanding Officer. The Prince was strongly censured in the press, the *Daily Chronicle* commenting that 'his taste for the lowest type of gambling ... has profoundly shocked, we may even say disgusted, the people who may one day be asked to submit to his rule'.

The Prince was fifty-nine when Queen Victoria died in January 1901, and he ascended the throne as King Edward VII. His reign, which has given its name to a historical era, lasted only nine years. It was an age of social change and of great intellectual brilliance; but the King had little sympathy with either development, though he enjoyed the more serious theatre as well as musical comedies. The great Liberal triumph in the general election of 1906 led to the introduction of old age pensions, national insurance, and the first steps in the creation of

Edward with his nephew Kaiser Wilhelm II during a State visit to Berlin in 1909. Beneath the outward affability lay mutual distrust.

the modern welfare state, while the Trades Disputes Act changed trade unions from persecuted into privileged bodies. Politically, the King's sympathies were with the Conservatives; he opposed the demand for votes for women as strongly as the proposal to appoint 'natives' to the Viceroy's Council in India. But as always personalities meant more to him than politics. He was on friendly terms with his first Conservative prime minister, Lord Salisbury, but did not like Salisbury's Conservative successor, Arthur Balfour; and after the Liberals came to power he liked Campbell-Bannerman, though he had strongly condemned Campbell-Bannerman's pro-Boer attitude during the Boer War, and was less friendly with his last Liberal prime minister, the Liberal Imperialist, Asquith.

He took a more active interest in defence matters, supporting the vigorous and modern-minded naval policy of the First Sea Lord, Admiral Sir John Fisher, against the more orthodox views of the other admirals.

It was in connexion with foreign affairs that the King's influence was most marked. As he pursued the same round of pleasure in which he had engaged as Prince of Wales, he closely followed international developments, and used the occasion of his visits abroad to strengthen Britain's ties of friendship with her allies and to prevent the outbreak of a European war. His state visit to Paris in 1903 marked the beginning of the *Entente Cordiale* between Britain and France, though it would be wrong to attribute this fundamental reversal of British foreign policy either to King Edward's personal dislike of his nephew, the German Kaiser William II, or to his popularity in Paris. He followed up the visit to Paris with state visits to Athens, Oslo, Berlin and Stockholm, and a meeting with Tsar Nicholas II on their yachts at the Russian Baltic port of Reval (Tallin) in 1908. This last meeting caused some controversy in Britain, owing to the hatred felt by Socialists and Radicals for the oppressive Tsarist regime in Russia, with its pogroms of Jews and its banishment of political opponents to Siberia. King Edward's action in visiting the Tsar was criticised by three Liberal and Labour MPs in the House of Commons. The King retaliated by refusing to invite the three members to his garden-party for MPs at Buckingham Palace.

King Edward's efforts to preserve peace in Europe by personal affability won him the nickname of 'Edward the Peacemaker' in Britain, and inspired a popular music-hall song: 'There'll be no war, as long as there's a King like good King Edward.' They were viewed differently in Germany. The German Kaiser considered him to be a Machiavellian enemy who was building up anti-German coalitions. He was attacked in the German press, and after the outbreak of war in 1914 German propagan-

The sentimentality and the affection of the Edwardians is revealed in this popular print of the King's last illness: a still-youthful Queen Alexandra hands a rose to her dying husband.

dists placed the blame for it on the scheming and nefarious Edward VII.

In the last year of his life, Britain faced the greatest constitutional crisis since the Reform Bill of 1832 when the Conservative majority in the House of Lords threw out the budget of the Liberal Chancellor of the Exchequer, Lloyd George, and the Liberal government thereupon set out to abolish the veto of the House of Lords on legislation. The government hoped to force the House of Lords to pass the bill abolishing their veto by threatening to ask the King to create a sufficient number of new Liberal peers to give the government a majority in the House of Lords. The King was very unwilling to take this step, and worked hard to reach a compromise; he deplored both the provocative attacks on the Lords by Lloyd George and Winston Churchill and the uncompromising attitude of the 'die-hard' Tories. After another Liberal victory in the general election of January 1910, Asquith asked the King for a promise that he would create new peers if necessary; but King Edward insisted that the issue should first be put to the electorate in another general election, and meanwhile tried again to find a compromise by arranging private talks between the party leaders. At the height of the crisis the King died, after a short illness, on 6 May 1910, at the age of sixty-eight, leaving the constitutional crisis to be solved in the reign of his son, King George V.

THE HOUSES OF SAXE-COBURG-GOTHA AND WINDSOR

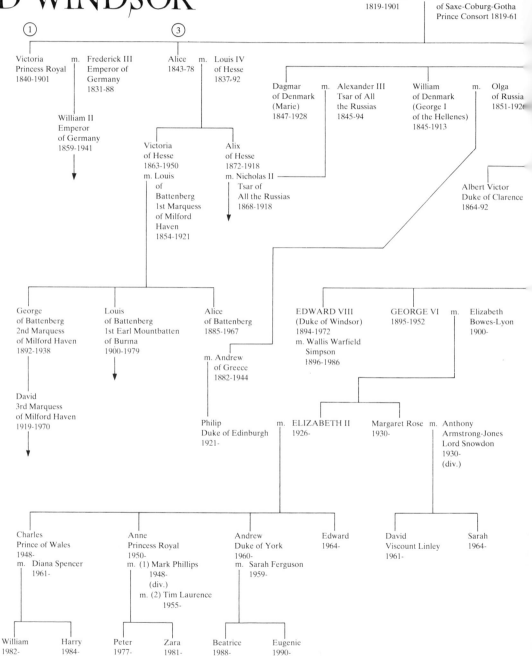

VICTORIA 1819-1901 m. Albert of Saxe-Coburg-Gotha Prince Consort 1819-61

①

Victoria Princess Royal 1840-1901 m. Frederick III Emperor of Germany 1831-88

William II Emperor of Germany 1859-1941

③

Alice 1843-78 m. Louis IV of Hesse 1837-92

Dagmar of Denmark (Marie) 1847-1928 m. Alexander III Tsar of All the Russias 1845-94

William of Denmark (George I of the Hellenes) 1845-1913 m. Olga of Russia 1851-1926

Victoria of Hesse 1863-1950 m. Louis of Battenberg 1st Marquess of Milford Haven 1854-1921

Alix of Hesse 1872-1918 m. Nicholas II Tsar of All the Russias 1868-1918

Albert Victor Duke of Clarence 1864-92

George of Battenberg 2nd Marquess of Milford Haven 1892-1938

Louis of Battenberg 1st Earl Mountbatten of Burma 1900-1979

Alice of Battenberg 1885-1967

m. Andrew of Greece 1882-1944

EDWARD VIII (Duke of Windsor) 1894-1972 m. Wallis Warfield Simpson 1896-1986

GEORGE VI 1895-1952 m. Elizabeth Bowes-Lyon 1900-

David 3rd Marquess of Milford Haven 1919-1970

Philip Duke of Edinburgh 1921-

m. ELIZABETH II 1926-

Margaret Rose 1930- m. Anthony Armstrong-Jones Lord Snowdon 1930- (div.)

Charles Prince of Wales 1948- m. Diana Spencer 1961-

Anne Princess Royal 1950- m. (1) Mark Phillips 1948- (div.) m. (2) Tim Laurence 1955-

Andrew Duke of York 1960- m. Sarah Ferguson 1959-

Edward 1964-

David Viscount Linley 1961-

Sarah 1964-

William 1982-

Harry 1984-

Peter 1977-

Zara 1981-

Beatrice 1988-

Eugenie 1990-

②　　　　　④　　　　⑤　　　　　⑥　　　　⑦　　　　⑧　　　　⑨

Alexandra　m.　EDWARD VII
of Denmark　　　1841-1910
1844-1925

Alfred
Duke of
Edinburgh
1844-1900

Helena
Princess
Christian
of Schleswig-
Holstein
1846 1923

Louise
Duchess
of Argyll
1848-1939

Arthur
Duke of
Connaught
1850-1942

Leopold
Duke of
Albany
1853-84

Beatrice
Princess
Henry
of Battenberg
1858-96

GEORGE V　m.　Mary
1865-1936　　　of Teck
　　　　　　　　1867-1953

Louise
Princess Royal
1867-1931
m. Alexander Duff
　　Duke of Fife
　　1849-1912

Victoria
1868-1935

Maud
1869-1938
m.　Haakon VII
　　of Norway
　　1872-1957

Mary
Princess Royal
1897-1965

m.　Henry
　　Viscount Lascelles
　　6th Earl of Harewood
　　1882-1947

Henry
Duke of
Gloucester
1900-74
m. Alice Montagu-
　　Douglas-Scott
　　1901-

George
Duke of Kent
1902-42
m. Marina
　　Princess of
　　Greece
　　1906-68

John
1905-19

George
7th Earl
of Harewood
1923-
m. (1) Marion
　　Stein
　　(div.)
m. (2) Patricia
　　Tuckwell

Gerald
Lascelles
1924-

m. (1) Angela
　　Dowding
　　1919- (div.)
m. (2) Elizabeth
　　Collingwood

William
1941-73

Richard
Duke of
Gloucester
1944-
m. Birgitte
　　van Deurs
　　1946-

Edward
Duke of
Kent
1935-
m. Katherine
　　Worsley
　　1933-

Alexandra
1936-
m. Angus
　　Ogilvy
　　1928-

Michael
1942-
m.　Marie-Christine
　　von Reibnitz
　　1945-

David
Viscount
Lascelles
1950-

James
1953-

Robert
1955-

Henry
1953-

Martin
1962-

Alexander
Earl of Ulster
1974-

Davina
1977-

Rose
1980-

James
1964-

Marina
1966-

Frederick
1979-

Gabriella
1981-

Mark
1964-

George
Lord St Andrews
1962-

Helen
1964-

Nicholas
1970-

10
THE
HOUSE OF
WINDSOR

King George and Queen Mary with
their grand-daughter Princess Elizabeth
driving from Crathie Church in 1932.

GEORGE V

r. 1910–36

GEORGE FREDERICK ERNEST ALBERT of the House of Saxe-Coburg-Gotha was born in London on 3 June 1865, the second son of the Prince and Princess of Wales. Most of his very happy childhood was spent at the Sandringham estate in Norfolk, with periodic family visits to London, Osborne and Abergeldie, the Prince of Wales's establishment at Balmoral. He was educated alongside his elder brother, Prince Albert Victor (known to the family as 'Eddy'), with whom he shared, as tutor, the Rev. J. N. Dalton. In 1877 the two princes, with Dalton in attendance, were sent as naval cadets to the *Britannia* at Dartmouth. Despite the fact that Queen Victoria disapproved of what she termed a 'nautical education' the experiment was considered a success. Prince George, though the youngest cadet, and at the mercy of all those senior cadets who anticipated they would never again have royalty at their beck and call, emerged with genuine popularity and an affection for most things to do with the sea. This affection was cemented when he and his brother, together with Dalton, were sent on two cruises in the training vessel *Bacchante*, the second of which took them as far as Australia and Japan.

When George reached the age of eighteen the two princes were separated. His brother was sent into the army, and provision was made for him to continue the studies that would fit him for kingship; for Prince George the future held out the promise of a professional career as a naval officer. He was short in stature, slightly snub-nosed, but distinguished both by brilliantly blue eyes set off in a good complexion, and by a notoriously loud voice. He was conscious of possessing a somewhat volcanic temper, but this was more apparent than real. He showed little interest in intellectual pursuits.

The lack of such enthusiasms was no obstacle to success as a naval officer, and by mid-1889 he had attained command of a torpedo boat. In 1891 he was promoted commander, though the pleasure he took in this advancement was dampened by a bad attack of typhoid.

It marked the end of his active naval career. On 14 January 1892, while he was still convalescing, his brother Prince Eddy died of pneumonia. 'No two brothers,' George wrote to Queen Victoria, 'could have loved each other more than we did.' The tragedy was sharpened by the fact that only a few weeks earlier Prince Eddy had been betrothed to Princess Mary of Teck, an intelligent and serious young woman who had been chosen as a steadying influence on the dissolute and brainless heir to the throne. Prince George's circumstances were now changed completely. He was created Duke of York, introduced into the House of Lords and encouraged, at the age of twenty-seven, to embark on those same studies that his brother had earlier undertaken, notably of Walter Bagehot on the English constitution, and of German. Bagehot he found rewarding; German he described as a 'rotten language which I find very difficult'. The contrasting attitudes are illuminating, particularly when it is remembered that George's father retained a distinctly Germanic pronunciation of the letter 'r'. In a phrase popular amongst radical journalists at the turn of the century there was still, in Europe, a 'trades union of monarchs'. Queen Victoria, with her sense of family and dynastic tradition and her tendency, in widowhood, to avoid public functions, sometimes appeared as the shop steward of that union. The impression was false, but it contained a kind of truth. The Prince of Wales, when he came to the throne as Edward VII, could still use the old relationship

Prince George with his mother when she was Princess Alexandra. Her children were all devoted to her and called her 'Motherdear'.

as a counter in his ventures into what has often been called foreign policy, but would more accurately be described as international public relations. Prince George, who had no early expectations of kingship, a natural and unaffected insularity, and a serious reverence for Bagehot, was better fitted than he or any of his contemporaries knew to undertake the transformation of the House of Saxe-Coburg and Gotha into the House of Windsor.

But, however much modern conditions may alter the Royal Family's concept of their rôle, they are still duty bound to fulfil the oldest royal obligation of all, the propagation of the line. Queen Victoria was deeply concerned that George should marry, and she conceived the idea that nothing could be more suitable than a match between the new heir and the girl bereaved of her future husband by Prince Eddy's death: Princess Mary of Teck. On 3 May 1893 the pair were betrothed; they were married in July and within a year their first son, Prince Edward (later Edward VIII), was born, to be followed by Prince Albert (later George VI) in 1895, Princess Mary in 1897, Prince Henry (later Duke of Gloucester) in 1900, Prince George (later Duke of Kent) in 1902 and Prince John (who died an invalid at an early age) in 1905. Thus the succession was ensured, though George was not always able to reproduce, in the case of his own sons, the happy relationship that existed between him and his own father. This relationship was intensified in the last years of the old queen's reign, since the Prince of Wales was determined that George should not

PREVIOUS PAGES The marriage of Prince George with Princess Mary of Teck in St James's Chapel in 1893. Queen Victoria, holding a fan, sits opposite the bride's mother, the Duchess of Teck, who is in the right foreground. Prince Edward and Princess Alexandra stand to the right of the bridegroom with the King of Denmark between them. The Tsarevitch of Russia, the future Nicholas II, stands on the left in the fur-bordered jacket. The two kneeling bridesmaids are Princesses Victoria and Maud, sisters of Prince George.

suffer, as he had and did, through rigorous exclusion from state affairs.

Queen Victoria died on 22 January 1901. From that time onwards George, who was soon created Prince of Wales, worked in close harmony with his father. Their desks at Windsor were placed side by side. In practical terms his father's reign meant increased involvement in those duties that he had already begun to undertake, and as heir to the throne he made tours of Australia and New Zealand, Ireland, Canada and India. He emerged as a forceful if somewhat stiff public speaker, with an evident concern not merely for the welfare of the people of Britain but also for the inhabitants of all the territories that made up the British Empire. The glories and vulgarities of his father's reign have often, in retrospect, obscured the fact that this was a testing time both nationally and internationally. The Boer War not only exposed the weaknesses both of the imperial idea and of the unreformed British army; it also made clear that Germany was becoming increasingly belligerent. Nor could the popular rejoicing of Mafeking Night disguise those tensions, attendant on the growth of organised labour, that were entirely to alter the complexion of British society. Edward VII was the inheritor of all these things, and it was his achievement to further his government's policy of acquiring allies in Europe, as well as to demonstrate that a King of England could, without condescension, show himself gifted with the common touch. But geniality and a preference for the company of self-made men was not sufficient to heal a growing constitutional crisis; rumblings indicative of a major clash of interests could be heard in the months before his death on 6 May 1910. And though he was internationally mourned there was something in the intensity of this mourning that failed to presage well for the years ahead.

The crisis that faced King George V on his accession did not concern the position of the monarchy as such, but it did impinge directly upon the King's definition of his duties. The death of his father had left him feeling 'quite stunned'; his only consolation, as he contemplated his new situation, was that he could be certain of the support of his wife. Princess Mary had brought to the marriage a capacity for sustained rather than demonstrative love, and it was now that the full value of this became apparent. Where her husband inclined to be irritable she was mild, and where, faced by contemporary trends, he was baffled, she could be relied on to see at least a glimmer of merit, and sometimes more besides. The immediate question was whether he should accede to the request of the prime minister, Mr Asquith, and create, as fount of honour, sufficient Liberal peers to ensure that Mr Asquith could pass, in the House of Lords, a bill limiting the power of that House.

The confrontation between the House of Lords and the House of Commons had its origin in the Lords' refusal to accept the Liberal budget of 1909, which increased income tax by twopence in the pound and imposed a small supertax to raise money for old age pensions and for dreadnoughts to meet the German naval threat. The matter was referred to a committee, and ultimately, after an election fought on the issue, which brought back the Liberals with a large majority, settled by the acquiescence of the Lords, who bowed to the popular will. But in the meantime King George had given Mr Asquith the understanding that he required, though he was displeased by the way in which he had been used as a political weapon; Asquith, in his view, had displayed a lack of faith in the monarchy when he required an explicit, if hypothetical, agreement. If it was the monarch's duty to keep out of party politics it was equally the duty of politicians to avoid dragging him in. It was a relief when, at the end of 1911, he set sail with the Queen for India, there to hold, in person, a Coronation Durbar at which all the peoples of India could pay homage to their Emperor. It was the King's

own idea and, to the surprise of many of his advisors, it proved a great success.

Though the imperial sway still held in the great subcontinent it was less secure nearer home. The years 1912-14 were dominated by two issues, the condition of Ireland and the threat of European war. They existed in a crude counterpoint, and both equally concerned the King. A shrill descant was provided by the militancy of the suffragettes. Of the issues the Irish question loomed most menacingly, and it was one for which the King felt keenly. His chief concern was to avert the threat of civil war, and it was at his suggestion that, in July 1914, representatives of the Government and the opposition, and of Ulster and the Irish Nationalists, met at Buckingham Palace to try to reach agreement. The conference was not successful in this aim, but there is no doubt that it created a more fruitful atmosphere for negotiation. Its end coincided with the news of Austria's mobilisation against Serbia, the move that began the almost automatic series of precautionary mobilisations which plunged Europe into a four years' struggle. It was no fault of the King's that his cousin, the Kaiser, should have persisted in a belief that Britain was bluffing when she announced her intention to come to the aid of her Russian and French allies in the event of war; he had on several occasions tried to make British intentions explicit.

For the duration the King devoted himself exclusively to the war effort. He visited military and naval units, hospitals, factories and dockyards. He made donations to the exchequer, took the pledge at Lloyd George's suggestion, and observed the rationing regulations. On a visit to troops in France he was thrown from his horse and his pelvis badly cracked. Two of his sons served in the forces. He maintained a close interest in all appointments to the high command, supporting Kitchener but secretly disapproving of the return of the volatile Fisher as First Sea Lord. He played an unobtrusive but important part

When the great ceremonies of the Indian Durbar were over, King George relaxed tiger hunting.
He is photographed directing operations from the centre elephant.

in the removal of Lord French as commander-in-chief of the British Expeditionary Force in France. Not the least of his contributions was his willingness, when anti-German agitation turned to witch-hunting in 1917, to resign himself to the loss of his family name and to accept the suggestion of his private secretary, Lord Stamfordham, that he adopt instead that of Windsor. It was a change that caught the popular imagination, as had the King's neces-

sarily unobtrusive (because of security) but incessant labours during the years of conflict. When the Armistice was signed on 11 November 1918 Buckingham Palace was the focal point for popular rejoicing.

There was no immediate return to the conditions of peace. The Government was preoccupied with the negotiations for the Treaty of Versailles, the problem of demobilising the troops, and severe trouble in Ireland, where the repression of the Easter Rising of 1916 had proved no lasting answer to a dangerously explosive situation. Revolution in Russia and the post-Armistice uprisings in Germany had demonstrated that the monarchical principle might be overthrown even in countries where it had seemed firmly entrenched. Ironically it was at this point that King George, by his entirely constitutional but discreet intervention in the handling of the divisive Irish question, demonstrated that in Britain the monarchy continued to have a practical value of the highest order. By counselling Lloyd George to pursue a policy of moderation and conciliation, and by advocating these virtues at the opening of the newly-constituted Ulster parliament in Belfast, he smoothed the path for an agreement which, if not wholly satisfactory to any of the parties involved, nevertheless saw an end to five years of violence and bitterness.

On 22 January 1924 King George faced a new challenge. As he wrote in his diary: 'Today 23 years ago dear Grandmama died. I wonder what she would have thought of a Labour Government!' The Conservatives having been resoundingly defeated in the House of Commons he had asked Ramsay MacDonald to form a government. But the ample records of the King's reactions make it quite clear that he had no deep-seated distrust of the Labour Party. He was convinced that MacDonald wished to 'do the right thing', and the major problems were social: his private secretary was sent off to see what could be done in the way of cut-price Levee uniforms. But no amount of goodwill could save the new Government from their own intense factionalism, nor from the taint of association with Communism. These two factors were played on by their political enemies who, with the aid of the forged Zinoviev letter, brought about the Government's downfall. It is interesting, and salutary, to note that the King himself had serious doubts about the authenticity of the letter, but no adequate mechanism for expressing them.

It can be imagined, however, that he greeted the new Government formed by Mr Baldwin with considerable relief. But he was as ready to check Baldwin's cabinet when, in the General Strike of 1926, they adopted an unduly aggressive attitude to the strikers as he had been to caution Lloyd George in 1921, when he proposed to reopen hostilities in Southern Ireland. The eventual fall of the Conservative Government in 1929 came at an extraordinarily difficult moment for the King, since he was just recovering from a protracted and near-fatal streptococcal infection, which kept him an invalid for the best part of a year. A surge in the figures for unemployment had brought Labour back into power, but the fundamental problems were international, not domestic, and no one party commanded the public confidence necessary to hold the country together in the conditions of the Slump. The King had a keen sense of what he called 'the gravity of our commercial and industrial situation'; he responded by surrendering part of his civil list and by actively promoting, in 1931, the idea of a National Government, which was eventually formed through the collaboration of Baldwin, MacDonald, and Sir Herbert Samuel.

The King's final years were undisturbed by any crises comparable to those of the earlier part of his reign. After his long illness his health was never entirely satisfactory. He did not care for doctors and was refractory about taking his medicine. Those who observed him in his last years suggest that his innate conservatism became more pronounced, and there can be no doubt that he looked back to the world as it was before 1914 with a certain nostalgia. Yet he was as positive as ever that it was his duty to be a constitutional monarch, the one statesman in his country, as Bagehot had put it, with a continuous political experience, but above party conflict.

He was widely known as 'the Sailor King', and this description accurately caught an important facet of his character. He had been trained for the navy, not for kingship, and he retained to the end a jocular manner (punctuated by occasional explosions) which was in part a legacy of his wardroom days. The monarch has no choice but to be a member of the Church of England; George V was distinguished for his genuine devotion and for the seriousness with which he took his duties and rights of patronage. In general he was a supporter of the manly recreations rather than the pleasures of the mind; he followed most British sports and took a close interest in the armed services. At Sandringham he lived, so far as he was able, the life of a country squire. He had two enduring passions. The first was for philately, which must rank as the most democratic form of collecting, though his stamps were patriotically deployed insofar as he restricted his interest to the countries of the British Empire. The second was for yachting. He acquired the great cutter *Britannia* on his father's death, but it was only after the war that she emerged once more in racing trim. Even then she was always run with a close eye on economy. Despite this she continued to win races in hard weather, and her appearances around the coast thrilled thousands of onlookers. It was appropriate that, after the King's death, she should have been scuttled rather than sold.

Early in 1935 preparations began for the King and Queen's Silver Jubilee. The King himself had evinced no particular enthusiasm for the proposed celebrations, and he was astonished at the warmth of the greeting offered him by the people of London. He had never cultivated popular favour; indeed his conception of the role of the king predisposed him to maintain a distance between himself and his subjects. It has been suggested, and there is undoubtedly truth in the suggestion, that it was the institution of the King's broadcast Christmas message in 1932, together with other occasions on which the King had broadcast, that created this enthusiasm. Certainly the King's deep and firm tones had been heard in places where royalty had previously seemed immeasurably distant. But, as Sir Harold Nicolson pointed out, the explanation is hardly sufficient. It seems better to attribute this outburst of popular affection to a real sense of what George V had accomplished as a constitutional monarch, and of the part he had played as a bulwark of order and tradition throughout twenty-five years of national and international upheaval. Early in his life he had had attached to him the kind of scandal which is always attendant on royalty; it needed a libel action to scotch the ludicrous rumour that he had made a secret marriage whilst stationed at Malta. In his later years the stories told about him were of another kind, mainly consisting of accounts of the salty apophthegms with which he greeted contemporary events or commented on the accidents of day-to-day existence. Perhaps, then, he had been accorded another apotheosis: as a repository of British common sense. The grief with which the news of his death at Sandringham on 20 Jan. 1936 was received demonstrates that the Jubilee was no illusion and that the people of Britain had taken to their hearts a monarch who, in his youth, made long voyages mainly under sail, yet had as one of many unsung achievements his opposition, in the heyday of disarmament, to the proposed disbandment of the RAF.

George V, the Sailor King, at the wheel of his famous yacht *Britannia*, and below, as a naval cadet.

H.M. THE KING   AS A YACHTSMAN.

EDWARD VIII

r. 1936

'AT 10.00 A SWEET LITTLE BOY was born', wrote the Duke of York in his diary at the birth of his eldest son Edward on 23 June 1894. Unfortunately his warm affection for his children as babies was overcast by chaffing and stern discipline as they grew up. 'My father was frightened of his mother; I was frightened of my father; and I am damned well going to see to it that my children are frightened of me' observed George V when a courtier suggested that he was too hard on his offspring. But if George V was frightened of his father he also felt a great affection for him; it was quite a different matter when, in the next generation, fear cast out love, for George V had little of his father's spontaneous warmth and geniality, nor was Queen Mary as open and demonstrative as George's own mother, Alexandra, had been. In fact the basic assumption that the future King Edward would profit most by an upbringing as like his father's as possible was entirely wrong. For Edward was a very different kind of person from his father, even though he could, in his own way, seem equally reserved.

He shared his father's characteristic nose and eyes, as well as his modest height. But he was slighter in build, and endowed with strikingly yellow hair – all of which contributed to a Prince Charming effect, to which his parents alone seemed impervious. The principal events of his childhood are swiftly recounted: his father became Prince of Wales in 1901 and King in 1910; Prince Edward was sent as a naval cadet to Osborne and then to Dartmouth, and after that to France where he improved his knowledge of the language. At the age of eighteen he entered Magdalen College Oxford, where he might have been expected to be more at home than in the atmosphere of naval training establishments. But he found it a 'dreary chore'

and gave no sign of academic ability, though he excelled at tennis and golf. After two years it was decided that he might profit more from a commission in the Grenadier Guards.

He joined up in time for the holocaust, but even in the first euphoria of 1914, when a short war of movement was anticipated, he was not allowed near the front. To Lord Kitchener he objected that it did not matter if he was to be killed, since he had four brothers. Kitchener replied that he was correct in this opinion, but that capture would be a different matter. He was restricted to serving in staff appointments; even so there was an occasion on which a German shell hit his car and killed the driver when the prince had left it to inspect troops. As Prince of Wales he found the constraints on his existence intolerable; after the war he rode in steeplechases, but his father forbade further such adventures when he suffered a bad fall; he learned to fly, but his father made it clear he disapproved. His official duties consisted principally in representing the King on tours of the Empire; in 1919 he set sail on HMS *Renown* to cross the Atlantic for Canada, and on his way back he took the opportunity to visit the United States, where he received a ticker-tape welcome. Shortly after this success he was sent on another tour to the Caribbean and on to Australia and New Zealand. In Australia he and his suite were involved in a railway accident, which he bore with courage, but by the end of the tour he was exhausted, and he took no pleasure in his father's decision, announced as soon as he arrived back in England, to send him off once again on a visit to India.

Though he grew less shy and nervous he remained a solitary person, unhappy at the ceremony which kept him from unaffected contact with other people, dismayed by the

Edward VIII with his great-grandmother Queen Victoria. Never before had the succession to the throne extended directly for three generations. Edward was to witness the reigns of five monarchs besides himself: his great-grandmother, grandfather and father, then his brother and his niece Elizabeth.

almost superstitious reverence of the crowds that thronged around him on his goodwill journeys, intent on 'touching' him if they were able. Sometimes there were additional tensions; when he finally visited India in 1921-2 it was to discover that Gandhi had arranged a nation-wide boycott, and that by no means all the crowds had gathered to express enthusiasm. In the event he made the best of a difficult situation, and it was generally agreed that the ultimate outcome was worthwhile. But it was a gruelling test, and on his return to England he perceived that his father was no more inclined to repose real confidence in him than he had been in earlier years. He was excluded from serious discussion of affairs of state, and he was never shown the contents of dispatch-boxes. He was conscious of possessing skills and a great reserve of energy for which no outlet existed. Increasingly he turned to his own circle of friends, though his acquaintances were not men or women of whom his father approved; indeed the King often expressed his objections in the strongest terms.

What the King hoped was that Prince Edward, like his younger brothers, would marry and settle down. But the Prince of Wales showed no sign of interest in the kind of girl of which his parents approved. He had a number of affairs, the two most notable of which were with women who had been separated or divorced. If his relationship with Lady Furness (*née* Vanderbilt) was predominantly passionate, his long association with Mrs Dudley Ward was based on more fugitive though no less telling factors: he enjoyed her conversation, accepted her sympathy and understanding, and valued her judgement of people and events. He grew increasingly impatient with his life as 'Ambassador Extraordinary', and much of this impatience broke out when, on his second visit to the United States in 1924 he decided to enjoy himself in a country that greatly appealed to him. On his return he found the King brooding over a pile of newspaper cuttings, most of them adorned with such headlines as 'Oh! Who'll ask HRH what he wears asleep'.

The Prince's friends noted that two of his characteristics intensified as he grew older. The first was his vanity; since he had difficulty in understanding the symbolic nature of his position he tended to assume that the attention focussed on him was a direct consequence of his own particular gifts. The second characteristic, the reverse aspect of the first, was a desire to escape from the whole world of publicity and of state affairs. This he was able to do at Fort Belvedere, a castellated semi-folly near Sunningdale which he modernised and where he developed an interest in gardening. It was in these surroundings that his friendship with

Wallis Simpson, an American two years younger than himself, ripened into love.

When they first met in 1931 Mrs Simpson was merely one of a group of friends, fashionable, fast, chic and sometimes witty, whom the Prince found entertaining and undemanding, and whom he could trust to be understanding about his love affairs. She had been twice married, and her second husband, though an American by birth, had become a British citizen after service in the Coldstream Guards. She appealed to Prince Edward's affection for things American, and it seems that her resolute refusal to compromise her independent birthright, her deliberate use of her American background as instrument of emancipation that enabled her to treat the Prince in a manner unthinkable in an Englishwoman, was an additional attraction. By 1934 he had determined to marry her, and their association was the subject of much comment in the foreign press. It required of the Prince no effort of imagination to gauge the likely response of his family to the news; nevertheless he wished to tell the King, but was deterred by his rapidly failing health. Mrs Simpson's final break with her husband did not take place till 1935; then was the moment when the affair might have been brought out into the open. But the opportunity never came, and in the new year the King was dead. He expired, according to his son, attended by his physician and the Archbishop of Canterbury, 'a noiseless spectre in black gaiters'. The spectre was to haunt him.

In his first months as King he did not fulfil the expectations of those who had admired those very solid achievements that had, despite his discontent, marked his career as Prince of Wales. He grew moody, bad-tempered, and disinclined to keep appointments. In the summer of 1936 foreign papers splashed romantic photographs across their front pages when the King took Mrs Simpson on a Mediterranean cruise. A gentleman's agreement restrained the British press from publishing such pictures but the public gradually became aware of the existence of Mrs Simpson. On one occasion a photograph was published which showed King Edward meeting her off a train; it was unfortunate that on the same day he had sent his brother to perform a public duty rather than go himself, the official reason, also published, being that he was still in mourning. Later in the year he visited South Wales, where the unemployment situation was acute, and earned widespread approval for his outspoken comments about the state of the poor. But those who would present him as a radical monarch should remember that he backed the strike-breakers in 1926, and that some of his comments on German National Socialism were decidedly ill-judged. His mind may have been more lively than his father's, but it was not as well ballasted.

Edward VIII had survived the bright but fitful publicity that he had received as Prince of Wales, but, with Mrs Simpson in the background, he could not hope to escape the continuing and relentless glare that a monarch must endure. Those who disapproved of him were massing their forces; his supporters, such as Winston Churchill and Lord Beaverbrook, had brilliance rather than solidity to recommend them. Archbishop Lang feared lest he be required to consecrate such a monarch; the British public, which might have welcomed an American queen, or tolerated a morganatic marriage to a woman once divorced, showed itself unwilling to accept a woman of Wallis Simpson's antecedents as wife to their sovereign. The crisis was finally precipitated by Geoffrey Dawson, editor of *The Times* and self-appointed keeper of the nation's conscience. For King Edward the agony was prolonged, the more so as Mrs Simpson, seeing what she had brought about, stated her willingness to leave him. In the House of Commons discussion of the Coronation was interrupted by a Labour MP who wanted to know what they were talking about, since there would not be one ('cries of

The handsome and charming Edward gained adulation wherever he went;
many looked forward to his reign as an era of youth and hope.

Edward VIII with Mrs Simpson during his Mediterranean cruise: pictures like this abounded in foreign papers, but in England the figure of Mrs Simpson was cut out.

"Shame", "Yes" and "Mrs Simpson"'). The King's discussions with the Prime Minister, Mr Baldwin, found no compromise. But he did not turn for aid to the 'King's Party' that his more romantic friends endeavoured to establish. Rather, he recognised that he had to choose the course to which he had bound himself by his word – marriage to Wallis Simpson – and that this meant abdication. His incredulous brother, the Duke of York, was informed, and the Instrument of Abdication drawn up. Even those closest to King Edward found it hard to believe that he was actually going to carry his purpose through. But on 10 December 1936 he put his signature to the document, and the Prime Minister told the House of Commons how his sovereign had come to this decision. On the following evening the King, now once again 'His Royal Highness Prince Edward', broadcast to the nation a farewell message which he had written with help from Winston Churchill. He then left for France, where, a few months later, he married Mrs Simpson.

Three days after his abdication Archbishop Lang, in a singularly unctuous broadcast, had prayed for God's mercy on the exile and garnished his observations with an allusion to Shakespeare: 'The pity of it, O, the pity of it'.

The ex-King's titular position was soon regularised; he became Duke of Windsor, though his Duchess, to his fury, was denied the honorific 'Highness'. Until 1939 they lived in France, and in 1937 made an ill-advised visit to Germany. With the outbreak of war the Duke's sole aim was to serve his country, which he was eventually able to do as Governor of the Bahamas. From the end of the war until his death in 1972 he lived in France, making occasional visits to England and maintaining friendly contact with his royal relatives. He died ten days after having been visited by Queen Elizabeth, preserving to the last those slightly mid-Atlantic inflections that had originally marked his homage to the United States of America, and, despite a network of wrinkles, an appearance of extraordinary youthfulness.

GEORGE VI

r. 1936-52

WHEN, ON THE NIGHT OF 11 December 1936, the former King Edward VIII took leave of his brothers at Windsor, he made his farewell by bowing to the new King. George's reaction was to exclaim: 'It isn't possible! It isn't happening!' It was not a response that, had it been widely known, would have increased public confidence in the man whose task it was to reaffirm the dignity and usefulness of an office which, during the past year, had seemed a muddy source of scandal and rumour rather than the fount of honour.

On his accession George VI had never seen a state paper. Like his father, George V, he was a second son, but the circumstances of the Abdication meant that he lacked even the briefest period of preparation for office; he had a mere three weeks in which to compose himself. By nature he was no more inclined than his brother to relish the pomps and formalities of monarchy, and he was without the persistent thread of exhibitionism that ran through his brother's character. In fact his closest resemblance was to his father, who was equally disinclined to accept the role of monarch, and equally conscientious in filling it when duty

George VI and Queen Elizabeth, as Duke and Duchess of York,
ride with their daughters in the Silver Jubilee procession of George V in 1935.

required him to do so. It is revealing that, despite an unhappy childhood, he felt none of that antipathy to George V which Edward VIII had so freely expressed.

Albert Frederick Arthur George, known as 'Bertie' in the family, was born at Sandringham on 14 December 1895. Early in life he developed gastric trouble, a direct consequence of neglect by his nurse; he also endured the misery of an acute stammer, possibly an indirect consequence of his father's instructions to his tutors that he should be broken of his left-handedness. In 1909 he followed his brother to Osborne and Dartmouth; at Osborne he passed out at the bottom of his term, whilst at Dartmouth he evaded that distinction by six places. His reputation rested mainly on his capacity for athletics and for 'skylarking'; his fellow cadets, when in an experimental mood, would prick him with pins to see if his blood ran blue. He was happier

when, in 1913, he was able to join the Fleet as a midshipman, but his hopes of experiencing action were frustrated by repeated bouts of acute gastritis. Nevertheless in 1916 he was back on HMS *Collingwood* as a sub-lieutenant for the Battle of Jutland, which he much enjoyed, though he was disappointed that his own vessel escaped unscathed. In 1917 it was decided that the navy was too much for his state of health, and he joined the Royal Naval Air Service; in 1918 he was appointed to the new Royal Air Force, and in 1919 he qualified as a pilot.

After the war he was sent for a year to Trinity College, Cambridge, and in 1920 was created Duke of York and began to carry out public duties for his father. But his most valuable services were performed in an unofficial capacity. Through his presidency of the Industrial Welfare Society he acquired a first-hand knowledge of factory conditions and became known as the

'Industrial Duke'. At his own request no red carpet was laid out for his visits; he wanted to see things as they really were. In 1921 he expanded his activities by setting up the 'Duke of York's Camps', annual events at which public schoolboys and young workers lived side by side, took part in hikes and games, and joined round the camp-fire in singing 'Under the Spreading Chestnut Tree'. In 1923 he was married to Lady Elizabeth Bowes-Lyon, a daughter of the Earl of Strathmore.

Seldom can a royal marriage have proved so successful. The bride was at once taken into the hearts of the King and Queen, marriage to a commoner struck the right note with the public, and her romantic Scottish descent delighted the press. Her freshness, spontaneity and grace commended her to all with whom she came in contact. She upheld and encouraged her husband. Moreover – though this was not immediately apparent – she brought into the royal family a taste for music and the arts that far transcended her mother-in-law's enthusiastic but uncritical garnering of royal mementoes.

The Duke's marriage encouraged the King to send him on a number of goodwill tours abroad, notably to East Africa and the Sudan in 1924 and to New Zealand and Australia in 1927. 1926 saw the birth of Princess Elizabeth, and in 1930 Princess Margaret was born. During these years the Duke's confidence increased greatly, partly as a result of his marriage, partly as a consequence of public duties successfully undertaken and partly because an Australian therapist, Lionel Logue, went a long way towards curing his stammer. Though it was never to become imperceptible, henceforth it always seemed to be under control. In 1931 King George offered the Duke and Duchess the Royal Lodge, in Windsor Great Park, as their country home, and there, when time permitted, the Duke devoted himself to his gardens and a happy family life. It was an ordered existence that was to be rudely interrupted by the events of 1936.

Yet in the Abdication crisis the Duke of York never lost his head. His policy and outlook is best summed up in the name he took, for he came to the throne not as Albert I but as George VI, thereby emphasising the continuity that he wished to establish between his father's reign and his own. The date of the coronation was not changed; he simply stepped forward in his brother's place. The service was broadcast, an innovation to which he gave his strongest approval. It made the ceremony a public act, in the fullest sense, and it confirmed the radio as the instrument by means of which the King could, in periods of crisis, promote the unity and determination of his country. It was as well that his stammer had so largely been cured.

The ensuing years were to test him to the uttermost. In the same month that the new King was crowned Neville Chamberlain took office as prime minister and began, in the face of the provocative and belligerent imperialism of the German and Italian dictators, to adopt a policy of appeasement. He did so because he believed that a peaceable solution was possible, and because he courageously regarded national humiliation as preferable to a second world war. His calculations were vitiated by his total failure to grasp the mentality of Hitler or the mood of the predominantly National Socialist German nation. There were times when the men in Parliament opposed to this policy seemed a small and wrong-headed group, and it has to be remembered that even after the outbreak of war in 1939 Mr Chamberlain continued to command wide popular support. George VI found the Nazi regime wholly abhorrent, but he had also seen how his country had suffered in four years of conflict, and had no wish to see it undergo the same agonies again. He therefore did whatever was in his power to aid Mr Chamberlain in his chosen course of action. But when, in March 1939, it seemed even to Chamberlain that Hitler must be resisted, and that the traditional British policy of minimal pledges must be reversed and a firm commitment given to those European countries who still resisted the Fascist onslaught, the King was swift to make clear his support of this new direction in foreign affairs. One of the principal motives behind his visit to North America in May and June was to further the understanding between Britain and the United States, and in this both he and the Queen played an important part. When he returned to the United Kingdom it was to a country that now expected war.

On 3 September 1939 George VI wrote in his diary: 'Today we are at War again, & I am no longer a midshipman in the Royal Navy'. That evening he broadcast to the Empire. It was to be his task not only to maintain the morale of his people but also to encourage the countries which owed allegiance to him to play their part. Australia, New Zealand and Canada declared war almost at once, but it required all the prestige of General Smuts to bring South Africa into the war. The early months were as unreal for the King as for most of his people; a measure of that unreality is indicated by his preference (for which he has been much criticised) for Lord Halifax rather than Winston Churchill as the new prime minister after Chamberlain's resignation in May 1940. Yet his relationship with Churchill, initially cool, was soon to deepen into a friendship based on a just evaluation of each other's qualities; in the New Year the King wrote in his diary: 'I could not have a better Prime Minister'.

The Blitz did not leave Buckingham Palace unscathed, and in September 1940 the King and Queen were nearly killed in a daylight raid. The public never learned just how close a thing it had been, but pictures of the damage, together with the royal visits to the most severely bombed areas of the East End, made their popularity assured. The situation was summed up by Queen Elizabeth: 'I'm glad we've been bombed,' she said. 'It makes me feel I can look the East End in the face.' The royal family had something else in common

with their people when, in 1942, the Duke of Kent died in an air accident whilst on active service.

The King interested himself in all aspects of the prosecution of the war, and, following his father's example, paid numerous visits to military units and factories. In 1943 he flew out to North Africa, where Montgomery had completed his victorious advance from El Alamein to Tunisia; he also visited Malta, whose gallant resistance to Axis attacks he had already recognised (at Leo Amery's suggestion) by the award of the George Cross to the island. He was present at the conference at which the plans for D-Day were presented, though one of the few occasions on which he had disagreed with Churchill was when the latter had resolved on an invasion of France from the Atlantic coast. On D-Day plus 10 he himself visited the troops in Normandy. On VE day, 8 May 1945, Buckingham Palace was the focal point of popular rejoicing, just as it had been in 1918.

The post-war general election produced a Labour majority, with Clement Attlee as prime minister. At first the King's relationship with Attlee was no easier than it had been with Churchill, and long silences were the principal feature of the prime minister's audiences. But once again understanding between the King and his prime minister deepened. Attlee had paid serious attention to the King's suggestions from the time that he confirmed the prime minister's own feelings by suggesting that Ernest Bevin would make a better Foreign Secretary than Hugh Dalton. Throughout the period of Labour government the King continued to exercise his right to advise and to warn; in particular he cautioned Attlee against

The coronation of George VI in Westminster Abbey, 24 May 1937. The King sits on the throne first used for the crowning of Edward II in 1307. The Queen sits to the left, awaiting her crowning. Behind her in the gallery is Queen Mary with Princess Elizabeth and Princess Margaret beside her.

King George with Princess Elizabeth after the war. The King's close relationship with his daughters was a warm contrast to the stiff family life he had known as a child.

Africa and Rhodesia, and later in the year he had the pleasure of seeing Princess Elizabeth married to Lieutenant Philip Mountbatten. In 1948 the King and Queen celebrated their silver wedding. But a projected tour of Australia and New Zealand had to be called off when he was laid low with arterio-sclerosis in the autumn of 1948, and from this he never fully recovered. In 1951 he opened the Festival of Britain and in October, after another serious illness, he was able to receive Winston Churchill, now back in office with a small majority, and to point out that his proposed appointment of a deputy prime minister was unconstitutional. On the early morning of 6 February 1952, after a day spent shooting – with his customary skill – at hares, the King died in his sleep at Sandringham.

George VI had inherited many of his father's foibles: a temper which, rarely but memorably, could be explosive; an insistence that things should be 'done properly'; a concern for the niceties of dress and decorations. These were not characteristics calculated to endear him to everybody, and on occasion those who met him found him disconcertingly cold. He too, for preference, would have liked to have been squire of Sandringham, yet the parentage that gave him Sandringham gave him greater responsibilities. But the impression of a withdrawn and formal man was not one by which he was remembered, and for every witness who found him unresponsive there are a hundred to testify to his humanity and lively interest in who and what they were. Most remarkable of all, without gestures and without drama (for this was a part of his secret) he had demonstrated the capacity of the monarchy to survive the internal stresses of abdication and the external threat of war.

too radical a process of nationalisation and too drastic a stifling of private enterprise.

His health had never been good, and the strains of the war, combined with his own tendency to overwork and his passion for detail, reduced his resistance. In 1947 he visited South

RIGHT For King George, one of the most moving moments of the war was sailing into the battle-scarred island of Malta in 1943. He wrote afterwards: 'Every bastion and every viewpoint (were) lined with people who cheered as we entered'.

ELIZABETH II

r. 1952–

PRINCESS ELIZABETH ALEXANDRA MARY was born at 17 Bruton Street, the London home of her maternal grandparents, on 21 April 1926: 'a little darling', Queen Mary recorded in her diary, 'with a lovely complexion & pretty fair hair.' Within a decade, on the abdication of her uncle, Edward VIII, she was the heir presumptive, and her upbringing was designed to fit her to rule. But there were none of those stringencies and tensions that had marred the childhood of so many of her elder

George VI as Duke of York, holds the baby Princess Elizabeth. At her birth it seemed most unlikely that she would ever be queen.

relatives, and visitors to the schoolroom thought that they detected, in the way that she looked after her occasionally refractory sister, Princess Margaret Rose, a temperament suited to what the future held in store for her. Her education was organised by her mother, with an emphasis as much on social accomplishments as on academic achievement. In her evident liking for the country and for country pursuits such as riding she followed family tradition; she is reported to have told an enquirer that, if she had not been heir to the throne she would wish 'to be a lady living in the country, with lots of horses and dogs'.

The war years were spent at Windsor, but at the beginning of 1945 Princess Elizabeth at last persuaded her father to let her undertake her National Service 'as other girls of my age do'. She joined the Auxiliary Transport Service, and proved an able driver and a competent mechanic. Before the war attempts to allow the princesses to meet their contemporaries without the constraints imposed by formal Palace etiquette had not proved wholly successful, except in the case of the children of their parents' friends; now, as Second Lieutenant Elizabeth Windsor, she was able to meet men and women from all kinds of backgrounds. That she should meet men, particularly young men, was the concern of both her parents, though it is unlikely that they hoped she would settle her affections outside a fairly restricted social circle. The problem, as the King wrote to his mother, was that her affections were already fixed, but that he found it improbable that she could have fallen in love with the first young man she had ever met in such a way that she should commit herself for life.

The young man in question was Prince Philip of Greece, whose father, Prince Andrew,

Princess Elizabeth with Prince Philip at their engagement in July 1947.
His influence was to invigorate the monarchy and broaden its interests.

had been banished from his country as a result of a military coup in 1922. In order that his son should not become involved in the maelstrom of Balkan politics he entrusted his upbringing to his British relatives, the Mountbattens. In 1939 Prince Philip entered Dartmouth, and served with distinction in the Royal Navy throughout the war, being mentioned in dispatches after the Italian defeat at Cape Matapan. As a third cousin of Princess Elizabeth he was welcome at Windsor, and during the war became anxious to assume British nationality, without which he would not be able to pursue a career as a professional naval officer. The matter was tangled and politically delicate but his naturalisation as Lieutenant Philip Mountbatten, RN, was accomplished early in 1947.

The young couple considered the possibility of marriage as early as 1946, but the King was anxious that Princess Elizabeth should have reached her twenty-first birthday before coming to a decision. It was a few weeks after this event, on 10 July 1947, that the betrothal was finally announced. The wedding, which took place on 20 November, was broadcast and televised, and served to testify to the continued stability of the monarchy and to the country's feeling for the royal family. On 14 November 1948 the Princess gave birth to a son, Prince Charles, who was followed by a daughter, Princess Anne, in 1950, and two more sons, Prince Andrew in 1960 and Prince Edward in 1964.

Princess Elizabeth and her husband, who was

now created Duke of Edinburgh, suffered from importunate crowds of sightseers on their honeymoon, and were driven to take refuge in Scotland. In 1948 they made a triumphant visit to Paris, and in the remaining years of George VI's life they performed numerous public duties, the King's illnesses effectively increasing the burden on his daughter. The news of the King's death reached them whilst they were visiting Kenya, and they at once flew back to England. On 2 June 1953 Elizabeth was crowned: 'Elizabeth the Second, by the Grace of God, of Great Britain and Northern Ireland and of her other Realms and Territories, Queen, Head of the Commonwealth, Defender of the Faith'. If the middle part of the formula seemed a little loose, it nevertheless adequately represented a rapidly changing state of affairs.

In 1947 her father had ceased to be Emperor of India, in 1948 Ceylon achieved dominion status, in 1949 Burma became independent, and Malaya a Federation with dominion status. The next decade was to see the secession of Egypt, the independence of the Gold Coast, and the formation of the ill-starred Federation of Rhodesia and Nyasaland. With the keystone of India gone the whole imperial arch collapsed. In its place was a loose union of disparate peoples with a shared administrative history, a tendency to use English for official business, and a common allegiance to the Queen as their head. Royal visits assumed a greater though more local importance than they had in the years before the war; at the same time their consequences were by no means as obvious.

In such circumstances as these, matched by an equally dramatic shift in the attitudes and aspirations of ordinary Britons, who rapidly came to take the welfare state for granted, and to see the end of the Empire as inevitable and unregrettable, it was appropriate that aspects of the royal family should change also. The principal agent of change, the continual catalyst, was the Duke of Edinburgh. When he was at school his headmaster had commented on his capacity for leadership, but qualified this by reporting that there were times when he was inclined to 'impatience and intolerance'. As consort the Duke (whom the Queen, at Mr Macmillan's suggestion, honoured with the title of Prince in 1957) displayed all these qualities, though his alleged intolerance was perhaps least in evidence. He set himself to modernising the image of the monarchy, and 'image' is in this instance the appropriate word. Radio, the cinema and, above all, television, had made the presentation of Royalty an exercise in public relations that could no longer be left to the Earl Marshal and the College of Heralds. Philip reorganised domestic arrangements at Buckingham Palace and Windsor Castle, initiated the Duke of Edinburgh's Award Scheme, flew, made films, played polo on Sundays and introduced into his speeches asides, jokes, and colloquialisms of dubious provenance. Prince Charles followed him to Cheam preparatory school and to Gordonstoun, a progressive public school that Prince Philip had enjoyed attending. The aim was no longer to keep the royal children apart from the outside world, but to involve them in it.

The experiment (if something irrevocable can be termed an experiment) was not wholly successful. Change, however premeditated, will always strike onlookers as too fast or too slow. In 1955 it was widely rumoured in the press that Princess Margaret would marry Group-Captain Peter Townsend, who had been the innocent party in a divorce case. Speculation reached the point where it was necessary for her to make a public declaration to the effect that, having considered both the church's teaching on marriage and the constitutional position, she had decided not to marry him. This statement shocked those who could not understand why such archaic notions should still be taken seriously, just as it shocked those who felt that she should not have entertained the thought of such a union in the first place. Press reporting of the incident, and of the Princess's later en-

Queen Elizabeth and the Duke of Edinburgh on their visit to India in 1961.

gagement to Anthony Armstrong-Jones (created Lord Snowdon on their marriage), illustrated the intrinsic paradox of a monarchy that
pursues a policy of being seen to share in the
day-to-day life of the nation: in so doing it lays
itself open to a closeness of scrutiny that can be
unfairly and irrelevantly damaging.

In 1957 the Queen was the subject of criti-
cisms of a different kind, since they were direct
and did not depend on gossip. Lord Altrincham,
writing in the *National Review*, said that: 'The
Queen has a manner of public speaking that is
a pain in the neck and she has the voice of a
priggish schoolgirl. She is out of touch with
the modern world and her advisers are a tweedy
entourage who know nothing of life outside
the restricted circle of the Establishment'. The

word 'Establishment', then much in vogue,
identifies this outburst as part and parcel of the
widespread discontent with the existing order of
things that followed the débâcle of British intervention at Suez. The royal family came in for
a good deal of incidental abuse, and the Queen
was criticised (in ignorance of the facts) for her
request to Mr Macmillan to form a government
after Sir Anthony Eden's resignation. Yet here
she had acted in strict accord with constitutional precedent, and on the advice of the
cabinet. In 1963 she had to go through the form
of discussing with the elders of the Conservative party whom they wished to succeed
Harold Macmillan as Prime Minister. The
obvious candidate was R. A. Butler, but Macmillan had made it his object to prevent this at

351

all costs (not excluding defeat for his party in 1964), and the Queen was obliged to assent to the succession of Sir Alec Douglas-Home. Subsequently the Conservatives decided to elect their leader, thus relieving her of a perennially embarrassing problem. Her prerogatives remain unaltered and in the event of a tied election – as nearly happened in 1974 – the monarch's choice would prevail.

The fortunes of the monarchy since 1957 have had less to do with constitutional issues than with its reflection in the press and on television. The Queen has undertaken many arduous tours, several of which, such as her visits to Ghana in 1961, to Canada in 1964, and to Australia in 1992, were made in circumstances that at the time appeared unpropitious. Both Canada and Australia continue, in 1993, to acknowledge her as Head of State; in Canada, beset by the question of Québécois separatism, the monarchy remains valuable as a symbol, however fragile, of national unity, but in Australia the Labor party have made the creation of a republic one of their stated aims, although the timetable has been left open. The Queen's personal commitment to the Commonwealth is generally recognized, although some commentators have seen in it a distortion of political reality.

The round of public appearances has been accelerated by modern conditions; one way of easing this has been the participation of the Queen's children, and the monarchy, at least until 1992, came increasingly to mean a family rather than an individual. This emphasis was stressed by the Queen when, in her 1973 Christmas message, now televised, she singled out as the two events in the year which meant most to her the Commonwealth Conference at Ottawa and the marriage of Princess Anne (subsequently the Princess Royal) to Captain Mark Phillips, a young army officer whose father, a commoner, was the director of a firm producing sausages and meat-pies. The couple shared a passion for horses and show-jumping,

Mark Phillips riding in the Olympic team. Television put the final seal on monarchy as family when the Queen consented to the making of a film about day-to-day life, which concentrated on the ways in which this was like, rather than unlike, that of others. By the time of Princess Anne's wedding the cameras had even got behind the scenes and, for a moment, the appearance on the palace balcony was shown from Royalty's point of view, and we were allowed to overhear their remarks as they left the stage.

It was to be twenty years before the hazards of this approach became fully apparent. The nation shared the Royal Family's grief in 1979 when Earl Mountbatten of Burma, George VI's cousin and its valued, if not always infallible, mentor was murdered by the I.R.A., in his eightieth year. It rejoiced when, in July 1981, Prince Charles was married to Lady Diana Spencer, the twenty-year-old daughter of the eighth Earl Spencer by his first marriage, who after secondary education had worked as a nursery school teacher. Surprisingly little publicity was accorded to the separation in 1976 and divorce in 1978 of Princess Margaret and Lord Snowdon, or to the remarriage of the latter in the same year. It was perhaps not widely appreciated how significant a change of principle this indicated. As it was, the announcement of the divorce conveniently coincided with the surprise resignation of Harold Wilson. A few day later the Queen announced that she had given Prince Michael of Kent permission to marry a Roman Catholic divorcée.

A son, Prince William, was born to the Prince and Princess of Wales on 21 June, 1982, and a second, Henry (Harry) in 1984; the Princess Royal and Captain Phillips had a son, Peter, in 1977 and a daughter, Zara, in 1981; at their mother's request neither received titles. In 1986 Prince Andrew, created Duke of York in that year, married Sarah Ferguson, the daughter of a retired Guards officer and polo organizer; their first child, Princess

Beatrice, was born in 1988, and their second, Princess Eugenie, in 1990.

In the 1980s the Royal family received unprecedented coverage in the media. The Queen lost no popularity because of her supposed dislike of Mrs Thatcher. Prince Andrew, an officer in the Fleet Air Arm, flew helicopters in the Falklands war. Though it was apparent in the later years of the decade that all was not well with the marriage of the Princess Royal, the press was relatively reticent; her tireless work for the Save the Children fund had earned her considerable public respect, whilst reporters had learned that she did not suffer fools gladly. But the Prince and Princess of Wales could readily be made to conform to two much publicized stereotypes of the period, the 'Young Fogey' and the 'Sloane'. The Prince publicly championed the cause of traditional architecture and his advocacy had a perceptible and reactionary effect on the look of new building. The Princess had not only lived in the haunts of the Sloanes, she also wore 'the uniform', and though she rapidly grew out of this to become a leader of fashion and a mistress of the photo-call, the red-haired 'Fergie', once a chalet-girl, was at hand to take her place. The Prince was prominent in forwarding 'Green' causes. The Princess became the patroness of charities associated with AIDS sufferers and with hospices; in this role she was able to make an independent claim for seriousness. For four or five years the younger generation of the Royal family were keen to present themselves as 'the Team' and under this name entered clay-pigeon competitions at game fairs.

But the scale of this publicity was unhealthy, and the more that the Royal family was made to resemble a soap opera, the more a backlash became inevitable. The size of the Civil list made it an object of jealously; not all the foreign tours made by the younger Royals seemed strictly necessary; the construction of a ranch-style house in Windsor Great Park for the Duke and Duchess of York was widely regarded as both extravagant and environmentally undesirable. Rupert Murdoch, a publishing and television entrepreneur of America citizenship and Australian extraction, whose papers included *The Sun* and *The Sunday Times*, made no secret of his republican sympathies and was not troubled by personal scruples if revelations about the Royal family promised to improve sales. Even so, news of the collapse of the marriages of both the Prince of Wales and the Duke of York, though widely reported in the foreign press, was not published in Britain until 1992 when, amidst an orgy of press innuendo, both couples announced legal separations. The Princess of Wales was at first accorded a good deal of sympathy until the Chairman of the Press Council disclosed that she had been responsible for 'invading her own privacy'.

In the autumn a fire seriously damaged part of Windsor Castle. The Queen, speaking in the City, describing the year as having been, for the Royal family, an 'Annus Horribilis'. She subsequently restricted the scope of the Civil List and announced, through the Prime Minister, that in future she would pay income tax. The Princess of Wales stated her intention of continuing to undertake public engagements, and the Prime Minister, John Major, informed the House of Commons that there was no reason why she should not in due course be crowned as Queen of England. The Archbishop of York said that events indicated that it was time that the disestablishment of the Church of England was reconsidered. The Princess Royal, after a few months of divorce, was married to a former naval equerry by a minister of the Church of Scotland. But despite these excitements it is probable that the most important question about the monarchy for the future is its constitutional position should Britain become involved in the further stages of European integration envisaged by the Treaty of Maastricht.

INDEX

Abdication, 341, 343
Aberdeen, Lord, 301, 303
Acts of Parliament: Acts
of Attainder, 154; Civil
List Act, 249; Act of
Indulgence, 249;
Mutiny Act, 249; Penal
Acts, 249; Royal
Marriage Act, 287; Act
of Settlement, 250, 262;
Act of Six Articles, 187,
192; Act of Succesion,
202; Test Acts, 235–49;
Triennial Act, 249;
Trade Disputes Act,
320; Act of Union with
Scotland, 255, 257
Adelaide of Louvain,
Queen of Englans, 39
Adelaide of Saxe-Coburg-
Meiningen, 292, 293
Agincourt, battle of, 125,
127, 129, 130
Albert of Saxe-Coburg,
Prince Consort, 298–
306, 314
Albert Victor, Duke of
Clarence, 316, 326, 330
Albert, Duke of Austria,
119
Alamein, battle of, 344
Albemarle, George
Monck, Duke of, 235
Alençon, Charles, Duke
of, 206–8
Alexander III (Pope), 47, 54
Alexander I, Tsar, 296
Alexander III, King of
Scotland, 86
Alexandra, Queen, 314,
315, 326, 336
Alice, Queen, 55, 57
Altrincham, Lord, 351
America, 208, 278, 282,
285, 344; Civil War,
304; Rebellion, 279;
War of Independence,
279
Anabaptists, 187
Andrew, Prince Duke of
York, 349, 352, 353
Andrew, Prince of Greece,
348
Anglo-Dutch Wars, 232,
235, 242

Anglo-Dutch Treaty, 249
Anglo-Saxon Chronicle,
38
Angus, Earl of, 207
Anjou: County of, 39, 41,
46, 63, 65, 76, 127;
Counts of, 38–46;
Charles of, 76; Geoffrey
of, 26
Anne, Queen, 251–7, 262,
277
Anne, Princess, 349–53
Anne of Bohemia, 113
Anne of Cleves, 187
Anne of Denmark, 219,
221
Anselm, Archbishop of
Canterbury, 32–37
Aquitaine, 42, 46, 55, 57,
63, 96, 106, 118, 126,
127, 137
Arch, Joseph, 316
Argyll, Marquis of, 242
Armada, 210, 211
Arthur (King), 98, 99, 105
Arthur of Brittany, 63, 65
Arthur, son of Henry VIII,
170–177, 198
Arras, Peace of, 133
Arundel: Archbishop of,
124, 126, 133, 136;
Henry, Earl of, 205;
Richard, Earl of, 111–
14, 120, 126
Ascham, Roger, 203
Ashley, Catherine, 202,
203
Ashley, John, 203
Asquith, Herbert, 320, 331
Atlee, Clement, 344, 346
Atterbury, Bishop, 266
Audley, Lord, 173
Augusta of Saxe-Gotha,
272, 276
Australia, 326, 330, 336,
343, 344, 346, 352
Austria, 57, 276, 315, 331
Ayscough, William, see
Salisbury

Babington Plot, 210
Baccarat Case, 319
Bacon, Francis, 220
Bagehot, Walter, 326,
330, 333

Baldwin of Flanders, 26
Baldwin, Stanley, 333, 341
Balfour, Sir Arthur, 320
Balliol family, 102
Balliol, John, 86, 87
Balmoral, 305
Baltic, 219, 265, 266, 320
Banbury, battle of, 152
Bannockburn, battle of,
99, 93
Bari, Council of, 37
Barnet, battle of, 144, 153,
154, 159, 165, 168
Basilikon Doron, 218
Baynards Castle, 162
Beauchamp, Anne, 149
Beaufort Castle, 169
Beaufort, Edmund, 138,
139, 169
Beaufort, Henry, 126, 169
Beaufort, Joan, 149
Beaufort, John, 169
Beaufort, Margaret, 162,
168, 169, 177
Beaufort, Thomas, 126,
130
Beaverbrook, Lord, 338
Becket, Thomas, 47, 54
Bedford, John Beaufort,
Duke of, 130, 133
Bedingfield, Sir Henry,
204, 205
Belgium, 246, 296
Berengaria of Navarre, 57,
60
Berline, Congress of, 306
Berkeley Castle, 96, 120
Bernstorff, Baron von, 263
Berwick, 87, 102, 140, 161
Bevin, Ernest, 344
Bible: English, 187, 193;
Authorised Version,
217, 218
Bill of Rights, 249
Bishops' War, 226
Black Death, 106
Black Prince, 106–10
Blacman, John, 133, 135,
140
Blanche of Lancaster, 118
Blanche, Queen of France,
75
Blenheim, battle of, 255
Blois, Counts of, 39–42,
47

Blount, Bessie, 182
Boer Wars, 306, 308, 320,
330
Bohemia, 220, 315
Bohun, Mary de, 118
Boleyn, Anne, 182–9, 198,
202
Boleyn family, 205
Boleyn, Mary, 182
Boleyn, Sir Thomas, 182
Bolingbroke, Henry St
John, Viscount, 257,
262–5, 270, 272
Book of Martyrs, 201
Born, Bertrand de, 67
Boroughbridge, battle of,
93
Bosworth Field, battle of,
158, 164–171, 175, 205
Bothmar, Baron von, 262,
263
Bothwell, Earl of, 207
Bourbon, House of, 285
Bouvines, battle of, 67
Boyne, battle of, 245
Braganza, Catherine of,
235, 236
Bramham Moor, battle of,
123
Brandon, Charles, Duke
of Suffolk, 179
Brandon, Francis, 179, 194
Brakespeare, Nicholas,
181
Bray, Sir Reginald, 173,
174
Breda, Declaration of, 232
Brelume, battle of, 39
Bretigny, Treaty of, 106
Breze, Piers de, 140
Brighton Pavilion, 287,
288
Brittany: 47, 54, 63, 163,
169; Duke of, 137, 154
Broadhurst, Henry, 316
Brooke, Lady, 316
Brown, John, 305
Bruce, David, King of
Scots, 102, 106
Bruce, Robert, King of
Scots, 87–93, 102
Brummell, George
(Beau), 287, 288
Brunswick, Caroline of,
287

Brussels, Treaty of, 232
Bryan, Lady, 190, 202
Buckingham: Duchess of,
    158; Duke of, 161–5,
    169; George Villiers, 1st
    Duke of, 219–21, 226,
    229; Palace, 320, 331,
    334, 344, 348, 350
Burgh, Hubert de, 74
Burgundy: 123, 144, 152,
    153, 155, 159; Charles
    of, 152–5; John the
    Fearless, Duke of, 126–
    30; Margaret of, 171;
    Mary of, 155; Philip,
    Duke of, 129, 133
Burley, Robert, 110, 113
Burley, Simon, 118
Burley, William Cecil, 1st
    Lord, 205, 207, 210, 211
Burnell, Robert, 81
Burrough, Sir Edward,
    189
Bute, Earl of, 276–8
Butler, Lady Eleanor, 151,
    162
Butt, Robert, 287
Byrd, William, 207

Cabal, the, 235, 236
Cabinet, the, 250, 254,
    265, 303
Cade's Rebellion, 137
Calais, 105, 106, 113, 126,
    127, 131, 137, 139, 152,
    154, 201, 211
Calvinism, 205, 217, 220,
    245
Cambridge Reformers,
    189, 190
Cambridge, Richard, Earl
    of, 138, 242
Campbell-Bannerman,
    Henry, 320
Campeggio, Cardinal, 183
Canada, 276, 314, 330,
    336, 344, 352
Canning, George, 306
Carberry Hill, battle of,
    207
Caribbean, 210, 276, 304,
    336
Caroline of Anspach, 264,
    269–74
Caroline of Brunswick,
    287
Caroline, Princess, 273
Castiglioni, Battisti, 202
Castile, 112, 118, 171
Castillon, battle of, 137,
    138
Catesby, William, 155

Catherine of Aragon,
    170–1, 177, 182, 186,
    194, 195, 198
Catherine the Great, 279
Catherine of Valois, 137,
    129, 133, 169
Caxton, William, 155
Chamberlain, Neville, 343
Charles I, 73, 76, 219–32,
    238
Charles II, 232–49, 257,
    276
Charles IV of France, 102
Charles V of France, 106
Charles VI of France,
    126–9, 138
Charles VII of France,
    129–37
Charles VIII of France, 164
Charles V, Emperor,
    180–3, 187, 190
Charles, Prince of Wales,
    349–53
Charlotte of
    Mecklenburg-Strelitz,
    277, 281
Charlotte, Princess, 287,
    292
Chartists, 301
Chaucer, Geoffrey, 118
Chesterfield, Lord, 270
Church of England, 183,
    190, 205, 221, 229, 232,
    242, 245, 250, 254, 262,
    334, 353
Church of Scotland, 216,
    226
Churchill, Henrietta, 254
Churchill, Winston, 321,
    338, 341, 344, 346
Civil List, 270, 353
Civil War, 83, 229
Clarence: George, Duke
    of, 152–5, 158–61, 171;
    Thomas, Duke of,
    126–9
Clarendon: Constitutions
    of, 54; Council of, 54
Clarendon, Edward Hyde,
    Earl of, 232, 235, 242,
    243, 257
Claude, Queen of France,
    182
Clement III, Pope, 32
Clement VII, Pope, 182,
    183, 186, 198
Clifford, Lord, 235
Cobbett, William, 287,
    288
Colet, John, 179
Commons, House of, 106,
    138, 216, 218, 219, 220,

221, 226, 229, 231, 235,
    242, 247, 249, 255, 266,
    303, 316, 320, 331, 333,
    338, 341
Commonwealth, 350, 352
Commynes, Phillipe de,
    151, 154
Compton: Bishop, 252;
Compton, Spencer, 270
Conroy, Sir John, 296,
    298
Conservative Party, 298,
    305, 308, 320, 321, 333,
    351, 352
Council of Regents, 189,
    192, 202
Counter-Reformation,
    207
Covenanters, 231, 232
Cox, Richard, 190
Cranmer, Thomas, 183,
    187, 189, 192, 201
Crécy, battle of, 105, 106
Crimea War, 303
Cromwell, Oliver, 231,
    232, 238
Cropredy Bridge, battle
    of, 231
Crusades, 36, 39, 57, 76,
    78, 80
Cyprus, 57, 119

Dalton, Hugh, 344
Dalton, Rev. J.N., 326
Darnley, Lord, 207, 211,
    216
Dartmouth, 326, 336, 342,
    349
Daubeny, Lord, 173
Dawson, Geoffrey, 338
David, King of Scots, 41,
    46
Dee, John, 205
Defence of the Seven
    Sacraments, 180
Dekker, Thomas, 211
Deloraine, Lady, 273
Denmark, 303, 315
Derby: Earl of, 80; Henry
    of, 105
Dereham, Francis, 189
Derwentwater, Lord, 265
Despenser, Hugh the
    Elder and Hugh the
    Younger, 93, 96, 122
Dettingen, battle of, 273
Diana, Princess of Wales,
    352, 353
Dilke, Sir Charles, 305
Disraeli, Benjamin, Earl of
    Beaconsfield, 305, 306,
    308

Dobson, William, 231
Domesday Book, 28, 30
Dormer, Jane, 190
Douglas, Earl of, 122
Douglas-Home, Sir Alec,
    352
Dover: 81, 181, 210;
    Treaty of, 235
Drake, Francis, 207, 210,
    217
Dudley, Robert, Earl of
    Leicester, 176, 177, 194
Duke of Edinburgh's
    Award Scheme, 350
Dunbar, William, 171
Dunes, battle of the, 238
Dunster, 183
Dutch Republic, 232, 235,
    245, 251

Eadmer, monk of
    Canterbury, 35
Easter Rising, 333
East India Bill, 281
Eden, Sir Anthony, Lord
    Aden, 351
Edgar, King of Scots, 36
Edgehill, battle of, 231, 232
Edinburgh: 161, 194, 231,
    242, 265, 273, 291;
    Treaty of, 206
Edith, Queen, 36, 39
Edmund, Prince, son of
    Edward III, 138
Edmund, Prince, son of
    Henry III, 76, 121
Edward I, 73, 78–83, 86–9,
    102, 121
Edward II, 81, 86, 88–98,
    110, 114, 115
Edward III, 83, 93, 96–108,
    118, 149, 173, 187
Edward IV, 140, 144, 149,
    150–71
Edward V, 155, 161, 162,
    169
Edward VI, 187, 190, 192,
    193, 194, 198, 202
Edward VII, 299, 305, 314,
    315, 316, 319–21, 326,
    330
Edward VIII, 330, 336, 337,
    338, 341, 342, 348
Edward, the Black Prince,
    106–110
Edward the Confessor, 26,
    76, 78, 121
Edward, Prince, son of
    Henry VI, 138, 140, 144,
    154, 159, 169
Edward, Prince, son of
    Richard III, 159, 163

Edward, Prince, son of Elizabeth II, 349
Egypt, 76, 350
Eleanor of Aquitaine, 42, 46, 55, 63
Eleanor of Castile, 79
Eleanor of Provence, 75
Eleanor, Duchess of Gloucester, 136
Eleanor Crosses, 79
Elizabeth I, 171, 174, 183, 189, 190, 194, 198, 202–11, 216, 220
Elizabeth II, 343, 346, 348–53
Elizabeth, Queen (The Queen Mother), 343, 344, 348
Elizabeth of York, Queen, 163–5, 168–70, 176
Elizabeth, Queen of Bohemia, 220, 221, 262
Ely, Bishop of, 206
Empson, 176, 177
Engagers, 231
Entente Cordiale, 320
Erasmus, 177, 179, 198
Ernest Augustus, Elector of Hanover, 262
Essex: Robert, Earl of, 211; Thomas, Earl of, 183, 187, 189, 190, 198
Eustace, Prince, 42, 43, 46
Evesham, battle of, 78, 80, 91
Exclusion Bill, 236
Exeter, Duke of, 152

Fairfax, Thomas, 231
Falkirk, battle of, 87
Ferdinand of Spain, 170, 176, 180
Fidei Defensor, 180
Field of Cloth of Gold, 181, 182
Fisher, Admiral Sir John, 320, 322
Fisher, John, bishop of Rochester, 180, 186
Fitzclarence family, 292
Fitzherbert, Mrs Maria, 287, 288
Fitzpatrick, Barnaby, 190
Fitzroy, Henry, 182
Flamank, Thomas, 173
Flambard, Ranulf, Bishop of Durham, 32, 39
Flanders: 27, 36, 105, 181, 251; Count Baldwin of, 26, 30
Fleury, Cardinal, 277
Flint, battle of, 121

Flodden, battle of, 178, 195
Fox, Charles James, 279, 288
Fox-North Coalition, 281
Foxe, John, 201
France, 41, 102, 123, 124, 125, 126, 133, 140, 152, 155, 169, 171, 177, 180, 194, 206, 207, 221, 232, 246, 249, 251, 266, 278, 281, 292, 301, 303, 320, 331, 332, 336, 341, 344; Edward III's campaigns in, 102, 105, 106; Henry V in, 127–30; loss of English possessions, 137–8; Henry VIII in, 181–2; loss of Calais, 201; war of Grand Alliance against, 254–6
Francis I, King of France, 180, 181, 187
Francis II, King of France, 194, 195, 206
Frederick, Elector Palatine, 220
Frederick, Prince of Wales, 271–6, 281
Frederick the Great of Prussia, 276
Frederick III of Prussia, 299

Gallifet, General the Marquis, 316
Gandhi, 337
Gardiner, Stephen, Bishop of Winchester, 187
Garibaldi, 302, 315
Garter, Order of, 102, 175, 285
Gascony, 76, 79, 81, 102, 105, 106, 137
Gaunt, John of, Earl of Lancaster, 106, 108, 110, 112, 114, 118, 120, 126, 138, 149, 169
Gaveston, Piers, 88–93, 98, 110
General Strike, 333
Geoffrey, Prince, son of Henry II, 46, 55, 57
George I, 262, 273, 281
George II, 266–77, 281
George III, 276–91, 296, 308, 314
George IV, 281–96
George V, 316, 321, 326, 330–38, 341, 342, 344
George VI, 330, 337, 341–50

George, Prince of Denmark, 252, 255
Germany, 60, 63, 274, 276, 287, 330
Gladstone, William Ewart, 305–8
Glanvil, Ranulf, 63
Glendower, Owen, 122–6
Gloucester: Humphrey of, 133, 136–8; Isabella of, 65; Prince Henry, Duke of, 330; Robert of, 41–6; William, Duke of, 252
Godolphin, Francis, 254
Godolphin, Sidney, 254–7
Good Parliament, 106
Gordon of Khartoum, 308
Gordon riots, 277
Gordon-Cummings, Sir William, 319
Grafton, Duke of, 278
Grand Alliance, 251
Grand Remonstrance, 229
Great Contract, 218
Great Exhibition, 301
Greenwich, 177, 178, 183, 194, 195, 262, 272
Gregory VII, 35
Gregorian reform, 35, 37
Grenville, Charles, 292
Grenville, George, 278, 285
Grey, Lady Jane, 179, 194, 198, 203
Grey, Lord, 291–4
Griffiths, 175
Guiana, 220
Guise, House of, 206
Guisnes, 181
Gunpowder Plot, 218
Gwynne, Nell, 236

Habsburg Monarchy, 181, 189, 205–8, 217
Hainault: 96, Count of, 96; William of, 120
Halford, Sir Henry, 292
Halidon Hill, battle of, 102, 105
Halifax, Lord, 263, 344
Hampton Court, 179, 187, 189, 201, 217, 231
Handel, George Frederick, 265, 272
Hanover, House of, 266
Harfleur, Siege of, 127
Harley, Robert, 255, 257
Harold II, 26–28
Harold, Hardrada, 27, 28
Harlech Castle, 123, 140
Hastings, battle of, 28

Hastings, Lady Flora, 298
Hastings, Lord, 153, 161–5
Hatfield, 198, 202, 205
Hatton, Christopher, 206, 208, 211
Henrietta Maria, Queen, 221, 229, 232
Henrietta, Princess, 235
Henry I, 35–46
Henry II, 42–7
Henry III, 72–80, 102, 118
Henry IV, 113–29, 138, 149, 162, 165
Henry V, 115, 118, 121–35, 169
Henry VI, 129–40, 144, 149–53, 159, 165, 168, 169, 174
Henry VII, 158, 161–77, 194, 198, 216
Henry VIII, 155, 168, 171–98, 202, 207, 301
Henry, King of France, 26, 30
Henry V of Germany, 39
Henry, the Young King, 46, 47, 54–7
Henry, Prince, son of Henry VIII, 182
Henry, Prince, son of James I, 219, 221
Herbert, William, 168
Hereward the Wake, 28
Herleva of Falaise, 26
Hervey, Lord, 271, 272
Hexham, battle of, 140, 150
Holbein, Hans, 183, 187
Holland, 211, 232, 236, 238, 262, 266
Holy League, 177
Holy Roman Empire, 181, 262
Holy Roman Emporor, 154, 220, 251
Hooper, Bishop of Gloucester, 201
Hotspur, Henry Percy, 122, 125
Howard, Catherine, 187, 189
Howard, Elizabeth, 182
Howard, Frances, 219
Howard, Henrietta, 270
Howard, Thomas, 190
Huguenots, 207, 263
Hundred Years' War, 105, 138, 178, 201
Hunsdon, 190, 198, 202, 207
Hunt, Leigh, 286
Huntingdon, Earl of, 122, 127

Hyde, Anne, Duchess of York, 236, 238, 252
Hyde, Edward, *see* Clarendon, Earl of

India: 315, 320, 330, 331, 336, 337, 350; Emperor of, 306, 331, 350; Governor General of, 306; Mutiny, 306
Indulgence, Declarations of, 232, 235, 243
Industrial Welfare Society, 342
Innocent III, Pope, 65, 67
Innocent VIII, Pope, 170
Interdict of 1208, 65
Ireland: 63, 79, 114, 120, 127, 138, 139, 173, 211, 226, 245, 249, 251, 262, 291, 301, 305, 314, 330–3, 350; Home Rule, 305; Nationalists, 331
Isabella of Angoulême, 65
Isabella, Queen, wife of Edward II, 81, 90–98, 102
Isabella, Queen, wife of Richard II, 113, 126
Isabella of Spain, 170
Italy, 177, 179, 181, 287, 301

Jacobite rebellion, 265
Jacobites, 252, 266, 272, 277
Jaffa, 60, 119
James I, 123, 168, 171, 211, 216–21, 262
James II, 235–8, 242–9, 252, 257
James I of Cyprus, 119
James III, King of Scots, 161
James IV, King of Scots, 171, 173, 202
James V, King of Scots, 178
Japan, 326
Jersey, Lady, 287
Jerusalem, 60, 119
Joan of Arc, 133
John, King, 46, 55, 57, 60, 63–7, 73, 79, 127
John, King of France, 106
John, son of George V, 330
Jones, Inigo, 231
Jonson, Ben, 231
Jordan, Mrs, 292
Joseph, Michael, 173
Julius II, 177
Jutland, battle of, 342

Kelmanns, Charlotte Sophia, 264
Kendal, Duchess of, 264, 266
Kenilworth Castle, 96
Kenmure, Lord, 265
Kensington Palace, 295, 296
Kent: Earl of, 122; Edward, Duke of, 295, 296; George, Duke of, 330, 344; Joan of, 110; Victoire, Duchess of, 295, 296
Kerouaille, Louise de, *see* Portsmouth, Duchess of
Keppel, Hon. Mrs, 316
Ketts Rebellion, 194
Kew Palace, 281, 282
Kings Bench, 243
Kings College, Cambridge, 135
Kingston, treaty of, 74
Kirk o' Field, 207
Kitchener, General Lord, 308, 331, 336
Knights Hospitaller of St John, 119
Knighton, Sir William, 291
Knollys, General, 315
Knollys, Lettice, 208
Konigsmark, Philip von, 263
Labour Party, 315, 333, 338, 344
Lancaster: Blanche of, 118; Edmund of, 80; Henry of, 98; House of, 108, 118, 120, 168; Thomas of, 91, 93, 96, 108; Town of, 63
Lanfranc, Archbishop, 28, 30–32
Lang, Archbishop, 338, 341
Langtry, Lillie, 316
Latimer, Bishop, 189, 201
Latymer, Lord, 189
Laud, Archbishop of Canterbury, 226
Lehzen, Baroness von, 296, 299
Leicester: Earl of, 96; Earldom of, 118; House set, 266, 272, 273; Robert Dudley, Earl of, 206–11
Leiningen, Prince of, 296
Lennox, D'Aubigny, 216
Lennox, Lady Sarah, 276
Leo, X, Pope, 180–2

Leopold I of Belgium, 296
Leopold, Duke of Austria, 57, 60
Lewes, battle of, 78
Liberal Party, 301, 305, 308, 319, 320, 321, 331
Lightfoot, Hannah, 282
Lincoln: battle of, 41–3, 74; Earldom of, 118; John de la Pole, Earl of, 171, 173
Lionel, Prince, son of Edward III, 138
Llewelynn, Daffydd, 81, 83
Lloyd George, David, 321–3
Logue, Lionel, 343
London, Tower of, 110, 114, 121, 133, 138–40, 144, 153, 171, 173, 187, 194, 201–4, 210, 219, 253, 265, 303
Longchamp, William, 63
Long Parliament, 226, 229
Lords Appellant, 113, 118, 120
Lords of the Congregation, 206
Lords of the Covenant, 207
Lords, House of, 226, 236, 272, 281, 292, 294, 305, 321, 326, 331
Lords Ordainers, 91
Lostwithiel, battle of, 231
Louis VI of France, 39
Louis VII of France, 46, 47, 55
Louis VIII of France, 67, 72, 74
Louis IX (St) of France, 140, 151–5, 159, 161, 165
Louis XII of France, 178–80
Louis XIII of France, 221
Louis XIV of France, 246–51
Louis XV of France, 277
Louis XVI of France, 281
Louis Philippe, King of France, 301
Lovell, Francis, 165, 171
Lowestoft, battle of, 242
Ludlow, battle of, 139, 158; town of, 171, 175, 195
Lusignan, Hugh of, 65
Luther, Martin, 179, 180

MacDonald, Ramsay, 333

Macmillan, Harold, 250, 351
Madrid, 217, 221
Mafeking: 308; Night, 330
Magna Carta, 67, 74
Maine, County of, 26, 32, 63, 76, 127, 137
Major, John, 353
Malplaquet, battle of, 257
Malta, 334, 344
Mancini, Dominic, 151, 155, 159, 161, 165
Mar, Earl of, 265
March: Earl of, 115, 120, 122, 127; Edward of, 139
Marcher, Lords, 93
Margaret, Queen, wife of Edward I, 81
Margaret, Princess, daughter of Henry VII, 168, 171, 178, 202, 207
Margaret, Princess, daughter of George VI, 343, 348, 350, 352
Marlborough, John Churchill, Duke of, 251–7
Marlborough, Sarah Churchill, Duchess of, 252–7
Mary I, 182, 187, 189, 190, 194–206
Mary II, 235, 245–53
Mary, Queen of Scots, 194, 206–11, 216
Mary, Queen (Princess Mary of Teck), 326, 330–36, 348
Mary, Princess, daughter of Charles, I, 238
Mary of Modena, 242, 244
Mary, Princess, daughter of Henry VII, 168, 171, 179, 194
Mary, Princess Royal, daughter of George V, 330
Masham, Abigail, 255
Matapan, battle of, 349
Matilda, Empress, 39–46, 198
Matilda, wife of William I, 2, 30, 35
Matilda, wife of Stephen, 41
Maximilian, Emperor, 171, 173, 176, 181
Melbourne, Lady, 286
Melbourne, Lord, 296–301
Merchant Adventurers, 176

Merciless Parliament, 113, 118

Meulan, Robert, Count of, 36

Middleham, 150, 158, 159, 163

Middlesex, Lionel Cranfield, Earl of, 220

Milan, 119, 201

Milford Haven, 164

Monck, General George, see Albemarle, Duke of

Monmouth: Duke of 242, 249; rebellion, 242; town, 118

Montagu, Lord, 140

Montfort, Simon de, 77, 78, 80, 91

Montgomery, Treaty of, 81

Mordaunt, Lady, 316

Morduant, Sir Charles, 316

More, Sir Thomas, 155, 165, 170, 180, 186

Mortain, Robert, Count of, 26

Mortimer, Anne, 138

Mortimer, Edmund, 122

Mortimer, Robert, 96, 98

Mortimer's Cross, battle of, 149

Morton, Archbishop, 173

Mouchy, Duchess de, 316

Mountbatten family, 349, 352

Namur, battle of, 251

Napoleon Bonaparte, Emperor, 291

Napoleon III, Emperor, 301, 303

Netherlands, 158, 176, 181, 201, 210, 220, 245, 246

Neville, Anne, 144, 159, 164

Neville, Cicely, 149, 158

Neville family, 120, 139, 140, 150

Neville, George, 144, 150

Neville, Isabel, 152, 155, 159

Neville, Ralph, 149

Neville's Cross, battle of, 106

Newcastle, Duke of, 270, 273, 274, 277; Earl of, 232

Newfoundland, 176

New World, 179, 201, 207

Nicholas II, Tsar, 320

Nicolson, Sir Harold, 334

Nithsdale, Lady, 265

Norfolk: Catherine, Duchess of, 152, 195; Howard, 2nd Duke of, 163, 170; Howard, 3rd Duke of, 182, 186, 187, 189, 198; Thomas, 4th Duke of, 207

Norham Castle, siege of, 173

Normandy, 26, 28, 30, 32, 35–8, 42, 46, 47, 60, 63, 76, 105, 127, 138, 344

Normandy, Robert, Duke of, 26

Norris, Henry, 187

North, Lord Frederick, 276–9

Northampton: battle of, 139, 140; Treaty of, 102

Northumberland: 226; Earls of, 120–2, 207; Earldom of, 150' John Dudley, Duke of, 194, 198, 202–6; John Neville, Earl of, 150, 153, 165, 170

Norway, Maid of, 86, 87

Nottingham, Thomas Mowbray, Earl of, 113, 114, 120, 122

Nymegen, Peace of, 235

Oates, Titus, 242

Oath of Succession, 186

Odo of Bayeux, 26, 28, 32

Orange, House of, 245

Orleans, Duke of, 126

Osborne, 308, 326, 336, 342

Osnabruck, 266, 268

Oudenarde, battle of, 255, 269, 271

Owen, Dr, 204

Oxford: 122, 231, 326, 238, 243, 255, 336; Castle, siege of, 41; Robert de Vere, Earl of, 110–13, 118, 127

Palmerston, Lord, 299–305, 315

Paris: 80, 119, 120, 125, 127, 129, 130, 221, 323, 315, 316, 320, 250; Commune, 316; Treaty of, 76, 102

Paris, Matthew, 79

Parker, Matthew, 205

Parliament, 278, 279, 281, 285, 291, 292, 294, 298, 299, 301, 304, 305, 321, 331

Parr, Catherine, 189, 190, 194, 198, 202, 203

Parry, Thomas, 203

Paston, Sir John, 152

Peasants' Revolt, 110, 111

Peel, Robert, 291, 294, 298, 301

Pembroke, Earl of, 93

Percy family, 139, 162

Percy, Sir Henry, 188

Pergami, Bartolomo, 287

Perrers, Alice, 106

Peter the Great of Russia, 265

Petition of Right, 221

Philip II of Spain, 199–211

Philip IV of Spain, 220

Philip, Prince, Duke of Edinburgh, 346–53

Philippa of Hainault, 96

Philippa, Princess, daughter of Henry IV, 118

Phillips, Mark, 352

Pickering, Sir William, 205

Picquigny, Truce of, 154, 159, 161

Pilgrimage of Grece, 187

Pinkie, battle of, 194

Pitt, William the Elder, 274, 277, 278

Pitt, William the Younger, 281, 285, 288

Plague, Great, 235

Poitiers, battle of, 106

Poitou, 65

Pole, Cardinal Reginald, 199, 201, 204

Pole, Sir Michael de la, 111–13

Pope, Sir Thomas, 205

Popish Plot, 236, 242, 247

Portsmouth, Louise de Kerouaille, Duchess of, 236, 276

Portugal, 179, 235, 301

Presbyterians, 231, 232

Pretender, the Old, 244, 252, 262, 265, 268

Pretender, the Young, 273

Princes in the Tower, 158, 161, 162, 165, 169, 171, see also Edward V and Richard, Duke of York

Privy Council, 242, 243, 293

Protestantism, 179, 194, 205, 208, 211, 242, 243, 259, 285

Prussia, 276, 299, 303, 315

Puritanism, 205, 208, 216, 2317, 221, 231

Pym, John, 229

Radcote Bridge, battle of, 113, 118

Raleigh, Sir Walter, 206, 208, 217, 220

Ratcliffe, Sir Richard, 165

Readeption of Henry VI, 140, 144, 155

Reformation, 192; Edwardian, 199

Reform Bill, 294, 321

Regency Bill, 282

Regent, Prince, see George IV

Reims, 133

Renard, Simon, 198

Reresby, Sir John, 242

Restoration, 235

Rhodes, Cecil John, 119

Rhodesia, 346, 350

Richard I, 46, 55, 57, 60, 63, 76, 81

Richard II, 108, 110–15, 118, 120, 122, 126, 127

Richard III, 144, 150, 153, 154–65, 168, 169, 170

Richard, Prince, son of William I, 30

Richmond, Edmund Tudor, Earl of, 168, 169

Richmond Palace, 173, 174, 205, 211

Ridley, Bishop, 194

Ridolfi Conspiracy, 207

Rivers, Anthony Woodville, Lord, 155, 162

Robert, Duke of Normandy, 30–2, 35, 36, 38

Robinson, Mrs Perdita, 285, 286

Robsart, Amy, 206

Roches, Peter des, 74

Rochester, Earl of, 255

Rochford, Lord, 187

Rockignham, Lord, 278, 279

Roger of Salisbury, 38–41

Rome: 183; Church of, 199, 216; Council of, 37; Sack of, 182

Roman Catholics, 231, 242, 249

Rouen: 42, 129, 150; Archbishop of, 63; Castle, 38

Roundheads, 231

Rowton, Lord, 306

Royal Air Force, 334, 342
Royalists, 229–32, 235, 242
Rufus, *see* William II
Runnymede, 67
Russell, Lord John, 294, 301, 303, 304, 315
Russia, 265, 279, 296, 303, 306, 315, 333
Russian Revolution, 333
Russo-Turkish War, 306
Rye House Plot, 236
Ryswick, Peace of, 251

Sacheverell, Henry, 257
Sagan, Princesse de, 316
St Albans, battle of, 139, 140
St George's Chapel, Windsor, 144, 174, 187
St James's Palace, 183, 201, 238, 245, 265, 270, 273, 276, 314
St Paul's, 139, 144, 171, 282, 308
St Quentin, battle of, 201
Saladin, 57, 60
Salisbury: William Ayscough, Bishop of, 135, 139; Alice of, 149; Richard, Earl of, 139, 149; Robert Cecil, Earl of, 211, 216–19
Samuel, Sir Herbert, 333
Sandringham, 316, 326, 334, 342, 346
Sandwich, battle of, 74
Saracens, 76
Savoy, Duke of, 205
Scotland, 32, 47, 83, 86–8, 91, 106, 110, 112, 122, 124, 140, 171, 173, 194, 202, 207, 211, 216, 218, 226, 229, 232, 242, 255, 257, 262, 265, 277, 350
Scrope, Richard, Archbishop of York, 122
Seven Bishops, trial of, 243
Seven Years' War, 276
Seymour, Lady Jane, 186, 187, 189, 198
Seymour, Sir John, 187
Seymour, Sir Thomas, 194, 198, 203, 211
Shaftesbury: Anthony Ashley Cooper, 3rd Earl of, 235, 236; Anthony Ashley Cooper, 7th Earl of, 299, 301

Shaw, Dr Ralph, 162
Sheldon, Lady, 195
Ship Money, 226, 229
Shore, Jane, 155
Short Parliament, 226
Shrewsbury, battle of, 122, 125, 165
Shrewsbury, Earl of, 36, 37; Duke of, 257, 262
Sicily, 57, 63, 76, 80
Simnel, Lambert, 171, 173
Simpson, Mrs Wallis, Duchess of Windsor, 338, 341
Slave Trade, 292
Sluys, Battle of, 105
Smeaton, Mark, 186
Smithfield, 110, 201, 202
Smuts, General, 344
Snowdon, Antony Armstrong-Jones, Lord, 351
Socialists, 301, 320
Solebay, battle of, 242
Somerset: Duchess of, 257; Edward Seymour, Duke of, 189–94, 198, 202, 203; Robert Carr, Earl of, 219
Somme, 105
Sophia Dorothea of Celle, 262, 263, 266, 270
Spain, 113, 118, 177, 179, 201, 203, 205, 207, 208, 216, 220, 21, 246
Spenser, Edmund, 207
Spurs, battle of the, 178
Stamford Bridge, battle of, 28
Stamfordham, Lord, 332
Stanley, Lord, 165, 170; Sir William, 171
States General, of Holland, 247
Stephen, King, 39, 41–3, 46, 47, 198
Stirling Bridge, battle of, 87
Stoke, battle of, 171
Stone of Destiny, 87
Strafford, Earl of, 226
Strathmore, Earl of, 343
Stuart, House of, 168, 194, 202, 287
Sudan, 308, 343
Suez, 351
Suffolk: Edmund de le Pole, Earl of, 173; family, 202, 203, 219; Henry Brandon, Duke of Suffolk, 190; Henry Grey, Marquess of Suffolk, 179, 194

Suffragettes, 331
Sunderland: 2nd Earl of, 243, 245, 257; 3rd Earl of, 255, 263, 266
Sunningdale, 337
Surrey, Earl of, 173, 177, 178, 189
Sweden: 205, 246; Eric of, 205
Swein, King of Denmark, 30
Swynford, Katherine, 126, 169

Talbot, Lord, 137, 138, 151
Tancred, King of Sicily, 57
Tewkesbury, battle of, 144, 153, 154, 159, 165
Thatcher, Margaret, 353
Therouanne, siege of, 178
Thirty Years' War, 220
Thomas, Rhys ap, 175
Throckmorton, Bess, 208
Tindebrai, battle of, 36
Tories, 236, 242, 251, 254, 255, 257, 263, 272, 273, 291, 301, 305, 321
Torrigiano, Pietro, 174
Toulouse, Count of, 47
Touraine, 60, 63
Tournai, 171, 178
Townsend, Peter, 350
Towton, battle of, 140, 149, 154, 158, 165
Tranby Croft, 319
Trinity College, Cambridge, 189, 342
Troyes, Treaty of, 129
Tudor, House of, 168, 170, 194, 211, 216
Tudor, Jasper, 149, 153, 168, 169, 175
Turenne, 238
Turkey, 303, 306, 308
Tyler, Wat, 110
Tyrwhit, Sir Robert, 203

Udall, Nicholas, 198
Ulster, 331, 333
United States, 304, 314, 336, 337, 342, 344
Usk, Adam of, 121, 124
Utrecht: Adrian of, 181; Treaty of, 257

Valois, House of, 181, 189
Van Dyck, 221, 231, 232, 270
Venice, 119, 177
Vergil, Polydore, 162

Verneuil, 129
Versailles, Treaty of, 333
Vertue, Robert, 174
Vexin, the, 30, 32, 47
Victoria, Queen, 180, 295–308, 314, 315, 319, 326, 330; Golden Jubilee, 308; Diamond Jubilee, 308
Victoria, Princess Royal, 299

Wakefield, battle of, 140, 149, 158
Wales: 32, 47, 79, 81, 83, 93, 110, 113, 114, 122, 123, 125, 126, 149, 152, 159, 169, 170, 175, 198, 336; Statute of, 83
Wallace, William, 87
Walpole, Horace, 264, 277
Walpole, Horatio, 270
Walpole, Robert, 263, 266, 270—3
Walsingham chronicler, 108
Walsingham, Francis, 206, 208, 211
Walsingham, Thomas, 124
Walter, Hubert, 60
War of the Grand Alliance, 254
War of the Polish Succession, 272
Warbeck, Perkin, 171, 173
Ward, Mrs Dudley, 337
Warham, Archbishop, 177
Warkworth, Henry, 144
Warren, Dr, 282
Wars of the Roses, 138, 144, 158, 163, 165, 175
Warwick, Earl of, 113, 114, 120; Thomas Beauchamp, Earl of, 126; Richard Beauchamp, Earl of, 133; Edward, Earl of, 171, 173; Richard Neville (the King-maker), Earl of, 139, 140, 144, 149–55, 159, 161, 163, 168
Washington, George, 314
Waterloo, battle of, 291
Welfare State, 320, 350
Wellington, Duke of, 291, 293
Welsh Marches, 36, 129, 139
Wenceslas of Bohemia, 119

Westminster Abbey, 28, 76, 115, 140, 144, 170, 173, 174, 177, 183, 201, 236, 268, 287

Westminster, Council of, 54

Westminster, Treaty of, 43, 46

Westmorland, Earl of, 207

Westmorland, Neville, Earl of, 122, 126, 140

Whigs, 236, 242, 249, 251, 255, 257, 262, 263, 265, 270, 272, 273, 277, 287, 291, 292, 293, 294, 296, 298, 301

Whitehall, Palace of, 183, 202, 203, 231

Wilkes, John, 278

William I, 26–31, 35, 39, 43

William II, 30–9, 43

William III, 235, 244–54, 262, 263

William IV, 292–6

William, Prince, son of Henry I, 39

William, Prince, son of Henry II, 46

William, Prince, son of Stephen, 43

William the Marshal, 74

William the Silent, 210, 245

William II (Kaiser) of Germany, 320, 331

William II of Orange, 245

Windsor, 91, 120, 122, 135, 150, 206, 231, 282, 285, 287, 291, 299, 220, 332, 241, 343, 348, 349, 350, 353

Windsor, Duke of see Edward VIII

Witt, John de, 245, 246

Wolsey, Thomas, 178, 179, 181–3, 189, 195

Woodville, Elizabeth, Queen, 151, 155, 161–3, 170

Woodville family, 161

Woodville, John, 152, 155

Worcester: battle of, 232;

Earl of, 122; John Tipcroft, Earl of, 155

Wyatt, Sir Thomas, 182, 201–4

Yarmouth, Lady, 272–4

York: Edmund of, 114, 120; Prince Richard, Earl of, 162, 165, 171; Richard, Earl of (father of Edward IV), 136–40, 149, 158

Zinoviev Letter, 333

Zouche, William de la, 105